THE
LONDON
THEATRE WORLD,
1660–1800

Edited by
ROBERT D. HUME

SOUTHERN ILLINOIS UNIVERSITY PRESS
CARBONDALE AND EDWARDSVILLE

FEFFER & SIMONS, INC.
London and Amsterdam

Designed by Bob Nance

Library of Congress Cataloging in Publication Data

Main entry under title:

The London theatre world, 1660–1800.

  Festschrift in honor of Joe [i.e. Arthur
Hawley] Scouten.
  Includes index.
  CONTENTS: Milhous, J. Company management.—
Langhans, E. A. The theatres.—Visser, C.
Scenery and technical design. [etc.]
  1. Theater—England—London—History.
2. English drama—Restoration, 1660–1700—History
and criticism.   3. English drama—18th century—
History and criticism.   4. Scouten, Arthur
Hawley, 1910–   I. Hume, Robert D.
II. Scouten, Arthur Hawley, 1910–

PN2592.L64   792′.09421   79-20410
ISBN 0-8093-0926-2

THIS BOOK
IS AFFECTIONATELY
DEDICATED TO A. H. SCOUTEN
ON THE OCCASION OF
HIS SEVENTIETH BIRTHDAY
BY HIS COLLEAGUES IN THE
FIELD OF ENGLISH
THEATRE HISTORY.

Contents

CONTENTS

Illustrations

ILLUSTRATIONS

Preface

*S*erious interest in English drama between the Renaissance and the latter part of the nineteenth century has been a fairly recent phenomenon. Scholarship of the sort started by Montague Summers and Allardyce Nicoll in the 1920s and 1930s flagged soon thereafter. The current high estimation of even the best-known plays largely follows from the exciting critical readings which started to appear in the 1950s in books by Thomas H. Fujimura, Dale Underwood, and Norman Holland. Renewed interest in these plays led next to questions about the stage history of the plays and about the nature of the theatre that spawned them. Publication of the five parts of *The London Stage, 1660–1800,* in the course of the 1960s opened up whole new worlds of possibilities. *The London Stage* led naturally to the monumental Highfill-Burnim-Langhans *Biographical Dictionary of Actors, Actresses, Musicians, Dancers, Managers, and Other Stage Personnel in London, 1660–1800* (1973–), now in progress, and that in turn is spurring new interest in eighteenth century theatre history. Up to the present, however, the drama of the period has received a good deal more scholarly attention than the theatre world in which it flourished.

The London theatre after 1660 was indeed a new world. The restriction to two companies—so ruinously reaffirmed in 1737—became an increasingly significant fact. The introduction of actresses, changeable scenery, and increasing doses of music, dance, and spectacle quickly make a sharp differentiation from the Caroline theatre closed by the Puritans in 1642.

PREFACE

There is definitely some continuity in both plays and actors, but within a very few years after 1660 we find ourselves in a new and distinctive world.

The present book is an attempt to define (and where possible to advance) our current understanding of some of the most important parts of that theatre world. The introductions to the five parts of *The London Stage*—widely influential in paperback form—have made a great difference to our view of many of these subjects. Some (audience, politics) have already been the subject of considerable research. Others (music, play publication) remain almost uncharted territory. We do not yet have the kinds of bibliographies and background studies available to scholars of Renaissance drama and theatre. This book will, we hope, serve the dual function of summing up where scholarship now stands and inspiring new research in the eighties.

This book is a *festschrift,* but not in the usual sense of that term—a mixed bag of oddments from former students and colleagues. Rather, this book is a systematic assessment of the field, with each essay written by a leading authority, young or old. Among those included in this volume we do have one former doctoral student (Pedicord), an original *London Stage* editor (Stone), a new *London Stage* editor (Milhous), and three collaborators (Hughes, Loftis, Hume). Participation in this venture, however, has been decided solely on the basis of expertise. We designed to honor a distinguished friend and colleague—but to do so by putting together in collaboration a serious and useful book. All of us who work in English drama and theatre, 1660–1800, owe Joe Scouten and his fellow pioneers (Van Lennep, Avery, Stone, and Hogan) an immense debt for their perseverance in a project of daunting proportions and difficulty. The quality of the work that emerged is tribute to all of them. Where would we be without *The London Stage?* We simply could not do the work we now take for granted if we had to start from Genest—as everyone did less than twenty years ago—and to do serious work at all in this field would be immensely more difficult.

Some tribute to the dedicatee is customary when one is presenting a collection of essays upon the occasion of a seventieth birthday, but such exercises are seldom meaningful. To try to say why I love and admire the man would be to embarrass us both. A sketch of the life would make a picaresque tale worthy of Defoe's talents—how our protagonist, a football-playing orphan at LSU, received his nickname from Huey Long,

PREFACE

contributed to the character of Jack Burden in *All the King's Men,* and went on (most improbably) to become a formidably learned Swift bibliographer and an exuberant practitioner of the dryest kind of documentary theatre history. But this is, I think, a tale for another occasion. We honor Joe Scouten for his enthusiasm, his generosity, his friendly help to students and fellow scholars, and above all for the work he has done in a field whose present state he helped make possible.

ROBERT D. HUME

Pennsylvania State University
July 1979

Abbreviations

BD

Philip H. Highfill, Jr, Kalman A. Burnim, and Edward A. Langhans, *A Biographical Dictionary of Actors, Actresses, Musicians, Dancers, Managers, and Other Stage Personnel in London, 1660–1800*, 16 vols. in progress (Southern Illinois University Press, 1973–).

LS

The London Stage, 1660–1800. Part 1, 1660–1700, ed. William Van Lennep, Emmett L. Avery, and Arthur H. Scouten (Southern Illinois University Press, 1965). Part 2, 1700–1729, ed. Emmett L. Avery (2 vols., 1960). Part 3, 1729–1747, ed. Arthur H. Scouten (2 vols., 1961). Part 4, 1747–1776, ed. George Winchester Stone, Jr (3 vols., 1962). Part 5, 1776–1800, ed. Charles Beecher Hogan (3 vols., 1968).

Notes on Contributors

JOSEPH DONOHUE is Professor of English at the University of Massachusetts, Amherst. He is author of *Dramatic Character in the English Romantic Age* (Princeton University Press, 1970), *Theatre in the Age of Kean* (Blackwell, 1975), and articles on eighteenth- and nineteenth-century theatre history in a variety of journals. He is editor of *The Theatrical Manager in England and America* (Princeton, 1971), and with James Ellis he is cogeneral editor of *The London Stage, 1800–1900* (in progress).

PHILIP H. HIGHFILL, JR, is Professor of English at George Washington University. He is author of articles on actors in such journals as *Theatre Notebook, Theatre Survey,* and *Studies in Philology,* and coauthor of *In Search of Restoration and Eighteenth-Century Theatrical Biography* (Clark Library, 1976). With Edward A. Langhans and Kalman A. Burnim, he is coauthor of *A Biographical Dictionary of Actors, Actresses, Musicians, Dancers, Managers, and Other Stage Personnel in London, 1660–1800,* 16 vols. in progress (Southern Illinois University Press, 1973–).

LEO HUGHES is Professor of English at the University of Texas. He is author of *A Century of English Farce* (Princeton University Press, 1956), and *The Drama's Patrons* (University of Texas Press, 1971), and articles in *Philological Quarterly, Modern Philology,* and other journals. He is coeditor with A. H. Scouten of *Ten English Farces* (Texas, 1948), and editor of *The Plain-Dealer* for the Regents Restoration Drama Series (University of Nebraska Press, 1967).

NOTES ON CONTRIBUTORS

SHIRLEY STRUM KENNY is Professor of English at the University of Maryland, where she served as Chairman from 1973 to 1979. She has edited *The Conscious Lovers* for the Regents Restoration Drama Series (University of Nebraska Press, 1968) and *The Plays of Richard Steele* (Clarendon Press, 1971). She has published articles on bibliography, theatre history, and early eighteenth-century drama in such journals as *Studies in Bibliography, Modern Philology*, and *Theatre Notebook*. Her edition of *The Plays of George Farquhar* is forthcoming from the Clarendon Press.

EDWARD A. LANGHANS is Professor of Drama at the University of Hawaii, where he has served as Chairman of the Department of Drama and Theatre. He has published articles on promptbooks and theatre architecture in such journals as *Theatre Notebook, Theatre Survey*, and *Modern Philology*. With Philip H. Highfill, Jr, and Kalman A. Burnim he is coauthor of *A Biographical Dictionary of Actors, Actresses, Musicians, Dancers, Managers, and Other Stage Personnel in London, 1660–1800*, 16 vols. in progress (Southern Illinois University Press, 1973–), and author of *Restoration Promptbooks* (forthcoming from Southern Illinois University Press).

JOHN LOFTIS is Bailey Professor of English at Stanford University, where he served as Chairman of the department from 1973 to 1976. His numerous books include *Steele at Drury Lane* (University of California Press, 1952), *Comedy and Society from Congreve to Fielding* (Stanford University Press, 1959), *The Politics of Drama in Augustan England* (Clarendon Press, 1963), *The Spanish Plays of Neoclassical England* (Yale University Press, 1973), and *Sheridan and the Drama of Georgian England* (Blackwell, 1977). He is coauthor (with A. H. Scouten and others) of Volume V of *The Revels History of Drama in English* (Methuen, 1976), coeditor of Volumes IX and XI of the "California" Dryden, and editor of *The Memoirs of Anne, Lady Halkett and of Anne, Lady Fanshawe* (Clarendon Press, 1978). He has been general editor of the Regents Restoration Drama Series from its inception.

JUDITH MILHOUS is Associate Professor of Theatre History and Codirector of Theatre in the Department of Speech and Dramatic Art at the University of Iowa. A specialist in theatre management and finances, she is the author of *Thomas Betterton and the Management of Lincoln's Inn Fields, 1695–1708* (Southern Illinois University Press, 1979), coeditor of Elizabeth Polwhele's "lost" 1671 comedy, *The Frolicks* (Cornell University

Press, 1977), and author of numerous articles in such journals as *Theatre Notebook, Theatre Survey,* and *Harvard Library Bulletin.* In collaboration with Arthur H. Scouten and Robert D. Hume she is now at work on revisions of Parts 1 and 2 of *The London Stage, 1660–1800.*

HARRY WILLIAM PEDICORD is Professor Emeritus of English at Thiel College. He is author of *The Theatrical Public in the Time of Garrick* (1954; rpt. Southern Illinois University Press, 1966) and articles on theatre history in such journals as *PMLA, Philological Quarterly,* and *Theatre Survey.* With Frederick L. Bergmann he is coeditor of *The Plays of David Garrick,* forthcoming in 6 volumes from Southern Illinois University Press.

CURTIS A. PRICE is Assistant Professor of Music at Washington University, St. Louis. A specialist in music of the Restoration theatre, he has published articles in *Harvard Library Bulletin, Early Music,* and *Music & Letters.*

GEORGE WINCHESTER STONE, JR, is Professor Emeritus of English and Dean of the Library, New York University. He was Executive Secretary of the Modern Language Association of America from 1956 to 1963 and President in 1967. He is editor of Part 4, 1747–1776, of *The London Stage, 1660–1800,* 3 vols. (Southern Illinois University Press, 1962) and author of numerous articles on eighteenth-century theatre history in such journals as *PMLA, Studies in Philology,* and *Shakespeare Quarterly.* His biography of David Garrick (written in collaboration with George Kahrl) was published by Southern Illinois University Press in December 1979.

COLIN VISSER is Associate Professor of English at New College, University of Toronto. He has published articles in *Theatre Notebook* and *Theatre Survey* on Restoration staging practices and is at work on a book about the plays of Dryden.

CALHOUN WINTON is Professor of English and Director of Graduate Studies at the University of Maryland. He is author of the standard two-volume biography, *Captain Steele* and *Sir Richard Steele, M.P.* (Johns Hopkins University Press, 1964, 1970), editor of Steele's *The Tender Husband* for the Regents Restoration Drama Series (University of Nebraska Press, 1967), and author of articles on eighteenth-century drama and theatrical milieu in various journals and collections.

THE
LONDON
THEATRE WORLD,
1660–1800

1

Company Management

JUDITH MILHOUS

TO UNDERSTAND the workings of repertory theatres in the late seventeenth and eighteenth centuries requires both a solid historical grounding and some imaginative effort. To assert that the drama of the period 1660–1800 is an outgrowth of the theatre system in which it flourished is easy: To demonstrate particulars of that generalization is more difficult. Matters of theatre architecture, the repertory itself, acting styles, changeable scenery, the audience, and censorship will be dealt with elsewhere in this book. Here my concern is with the way the major theatre companies were financed and operated. A natural starting place is with legal authority—the patent or license that gave a company the right to act in public. (I am not concerned in this essay with unlicensed, "fringe" theatres.) Second comes ownership and corporate structure: Some very different schemes were tried in the course of the one hundred and forty years under consideration. Third, we must consider finances: Comparison of what managements chose to do with their money is one of the clearest ways to see changes in the London theatre in this period. Finally, we must look at the daily operation of the business—allocation of responsibility for rehearsals, advertising, recruiting, and all the other chores vital to the well-being of a theatre company. There were few abrupt changes during our period, but comparisons will show considerable differences between earlier and later companies—and will, I hope, provide a clearer picture of how the London theatre companies were structured and run.

I Legal Authority

When Charles II reconstituted the theatre after the Restoration, he set it up in an absolutely unprecedented way. To Sir William Davenant and Thomas Killigrew he granted patents giving not only them but *their heirs and assigns* the right to operate theatres in London as a monopoly.[1] This arrangement was to haunt the theatre for nearly two hundred years. The patents granted the two owners near-total control over their theatres, specifically giving them the right to hire, fire, and set salaries for men and women actors and house servants, the right to mount comedies, tragedies, operas, and any other sort of show (providing they took responsibility for the content of the scripts), the right to build new theatres in approved locations, and the right to set admission prices.[2] Enforcing the monopoly took several years, and Sir Henry Herbert, Master of the Revels, forced the patentees to pay for his licensing of scripts. But the essential conditions of the patent grants held until the Actors' Rebellion of 1694–95.

That such sweeping powers should be restricted to two men, and be assignable by them, was a new arrangement in London theatre. Until 1639 Jacobean and Caroline companies had operated strictly by license from the Lord Chamberlain, who had replaced individual noblemen as sponsor and protector toward the end of Queen Elizabeth's reign.[3] The Lord Chamberlain, acting for the monarch,

1. The first appearance of the "hereditary" patent concept is in the grant to Davenant in 1639. For Davenant's (unused) patent of 1639 see Gerald Eades Bentley, *The Jacobean and Caroline Stage,* 7 vols. (Oxford: Clarendon Press, 1941–68), VI, 304–6. The first mention of the hereditary clause after the Restoration is in the draft warrant by which Davenant attempted to gain control of theatre in Ireland. See Leslie Hotson, *The Commonwealth and Restoration Stage* (1928; rpt. New York: Russell and Russell, 1962), pp. 209–10.

2. For convenient transcriptions of the patent grants, see Percy Fitzgerald, *A New History of the English Stage,* 2 vols. (London: Tinsley, 1882), I, 73–80. The last clause in each transcription appears to be spurious. Both the Killigrew Patent (on loan to the Victoria and Albert) and the Davenant Patent as recorded in P.R.O. C 66/3009 conclude with provisions that the patents "shall be in all things good and effectual in the law" regardless of other legislation.

3. See E. K. Chambers, *The Elizabethan Stage,* 4 vols., corrected ed. (Oxford: Clarendon

granted licenses to sharing groups of actors to perform "during pleasure." Sharers' lists changed frequently, and so did noble sponsors. Despite a resolution of 1598 to limit the number of acting companies to two, as many companies performed as could draw audiences: All were able to get some form of license. No correlation existed, we should note, between the building and the acting company. A given company could rent any of several buildings for varying lengths of time. Legally speaking, the situation before the Civil War was very much freer than after the Restoration.

Both the benefits and the dangers of the more restricted post-1660 design became apparent during the lives of the original patentees.[4] Davenant, who exercised daily control over his company, set up and ran a successful business. When he died in 1668 his immediate subordinates, Thomas Betterton and Henry Harris, had the training and experience to take over, and they managed successfully on behalf of the sharing actors and Davenant's heirs. Killigrew, in contrast, took only a desultory interest in his company. He made grandiose plans, but did not carry them out, leaving daily operation to a committee of senior actors. His company quickly ran into censorship difficulties; discipline was slack, recruitment erratic, and money tight. Although the stockholders pulled together and rebuilt after fire destroyed their theatre in 1672, the King's Company never altogether recuperated from that disaster. The last ten years the company existed were spent bickering over control, first among the actors, then between Killigrew and his son Charles. Though Charles won a court suit for possession of the patent in 1677, the actors refused to work with or for him. The Union of the two companies—and the patents—in 1682 was a desperation move on the part of Charles Killigrew, who was trying to salvage some value from his patrimony.

Christopher Rich secretly bought into the United Company, providing money for Alexander Davenant, the last member of the family to run the business. Rich seized control after Alexander

Press, 1945), I, 269–388, for a discussion of the contest between the City of London and the Crown for control of the theatres.

4. See Hotson, *Commonwealth and Restoration Stage,* chaps. 5 and 6, and my *Thomas Betterton and the Management of Lincoln's Inn Fields* (Carbondale and Edwardsville: Southern Illinois Univ. Press, 1979), chaps. 1 and 2.

absconded to the Canary Islands in 1693. He represents an ugly variation on the Killigrew approach to management: He was concerned with the company solely as an investment. He set about bilking and mistreating the actors, confident that the monopoly provision, a well-established precedent by 1695, would be enforced. The actors rebelled, and to Rich's chagrin, legal opinion held that the patents did not preclude a later monarch's granting licenses for other companies.[5] Via the Lord Chamberlain, William III gave the rebels a license. It was granted to a group of actor-sharers for no fixed time period, at the pleasure of the monarch and the Lord Chamberlain.[6] The years following 1700 produced great confusion. Vanbrugh obtained a license and opened a new theatre in 1705, taking in the Lincoln's Inn Fields Company (apparently with its full consent). Between 1705 and the death of Queen Anne in 1714 no management under license remained unchanged longer than two seasons. The shifts became kaleidoscopic after June 1709, when the Lord Chamberlain exercised his authority and silenced Rich, patent or no patent.[7] During this period the vogue for Italian opera blossomed, and after some convoluted infighting everyone concerned came to realize that opera was best left unentangled with theatre companies. This realization was to lead to the long-standing custom of opera run under separate license.

After August 1714 all theatrical enterprises had to reapply for sanction under the new monarch. The stable triumvirate of Wilks, Booth, and Cibber at Drury Lane took this opportunity to oust a useless figurehead, the courtier William Collier, proposing to replace him with essayist, playwright, and stalwart Whig, Richard Steele.[8] Christopher Rich and his son John, having renovated the

5. Colley Cibber, *Apology for the Life,* ed. Robert W. Lowe, 2 vols. (1889; rpt. New York: AMS, 1966), I, 192–93. Steele cites an opinion by Sir Francis Pemberton that the patents remained in force after the death of Charles II, but that the monopoly clause did not stand; and that, acting not being *malum in se,* the Lord Chamberlain or other officials acting for the King could grant new authority to act. See Steele's *The State of the Case Between the Lord Chamberlain . . . and the Governor of the Royal Company of Comedians* (London: W. Chetwood, 1720), pp. 13–21. Steele gives no date for the opinion, but Pemberton retired in 1696.

6. For the license see P.R.O. LC 7/3 (25 March 1695).

7. For a detailed account of company reorganizations and legal complexities in these confusing years see *Vice Chamberlain Coke's Theatrical Papers, 1705–1715,* ed. Robert D. Hume and myself, forthcoming.

8. Cibber, *Apology,* II, 162–64.

old theatre in Lincoln's Inn Fields, persuaded the new king to rescind the 1709 silencing of their company under the Davenant patent. According to Cibber, George I followed precedent in this case: "He remember'd when he had been in *England* before, in King *Charles* his Time, there had been two theatres in *London;* and as the Patent seem'd to be a lawful Grant, he saw no Reason why Two Play-houses might not be continued."[9]

Thus after years of having plays under various managements intermittently at Drury Lane and the Haymarket, London audiences could expect two companies doing plays, and (when sponsors could be found) another group producing Italian operas. The two-company monopoly, though not discussed in print as an issue between 1695 and 1714, was reaffirmed by the new king: No one, least of all those who made their living in the theatre, wanted open competition. When an entrepreneur built the Little Theatre in the Haymarket in 1720, it could function only as what we call a road house, booking transient companies which took no interest in its upkeep.[10]

No challenge to the joint monopoly during the eighteenth century can be called a lasting commercial success. The fringe theatres that sprang up during the 1730s were extremely vulnerable. Much less potent a weapon than the Licensing Act of 1737 would have sufficed to silence them. Samuel Foote's Haymarket license of 1766 was granted for personal considerations, limited to his lifetime, and carefully arranged so that its season would not compete with that of the two larger patent houses.[11] Given this official protection from competition, the patent companies fully realized the wisdom of not offending the government and thereby risking loss of an increasingly lucrative business. A compelling sense of "the King's pleasure" never ceased to haunt the managers.

On one other issue the reestablishment of 1714–15 may have had a significant effect: the notion of two playhouses (plus a separate establishment for opera). No one in the eighteenth century tried

9. Ibid., pp. 165–66.
10. *LS,* Part 2, I, xxxv–xxxvi.
11. *LS,* Part 4, I, xliii. Foote's license was renewed after his death for Colman, but still not infringing on the main season.

systematically to stretch the authority of a single patent to cover simultaneous performances in two buildings. John Rich functioned that way for a brief period just after he opened Covent Garden in 1732, but soon gave up of his own accord, finding the logistics too much of a strain. Moreover as the monopoly, codified by the Licensing Act, asserted its privilege over the course of the century, place and patent became intertwined in popular thought, if not in law. No manager seems ever to have proposed dividing a company. Instead, to accommodate ever-larger crowds, they built ever-larger theatres, a development which culminated in the monster buildings of the 1790s.

II Ownership and Administration

Prior to 1660 possession of a license had relatively little to do with the administration or location of a company. Actors moved from one license to another, companies rented one building or another, as they could arrange to work.[12] A single representative of the license-holding group was often appointed manager. As a rule the actors had to rent from a landlord a playing space they did not own. In sharp contrast, the patents granted by Charles II put exclusive authority in the hands of single *owners,* both of whom chose to finance their own buildings rather than rent them from an independent landlord. (To be sure, few pre-Commonwealth theatres had been left standing, but Davenant, at least, proposed to operate a theatre with changeable scenery, and needed new quarters anyway.) Although obliged to pay ground rent and to take in some outside investors, members of the original Duke's and King's companies owned a substantial interest in the theatres they built, Dorset Garden (1671) and Drury Lane (1674) respectively.

Both patentees recognized the necessity for deputing some of their powers, but Davenant did so much more successfully than Killigrew. Davenant drew up a formal contract with his actors in 1660, outlining responsibilities and contingencies on each side.[13]

12. See Chambers, *The Elizabethan Stage,* I, 352–55, for a discussion of business arrangements in these companies.
13. For the contract, see *The Dramatic Records of Sir Henry Herbert,* ed. Joseph Quincy Adams (New Haven: Yale Univ. Press, 1917), pp. 96–100.

Killigrew apparently let the senior men in his company arrange the administration to suit themselves, and even gave them power of attorney (which he later revoked).[14] The problem was to find a balance between the source of power (the holder of the patent) and the people necessarily deputed to make the company operate. Where the chain of command was clearly defined, daily business ran much more smoothly than where an owner dropped in irregularly and asserted his prerogative haphazardly. Both companies allowed actors to buy stock, though outside investors had to be sought almost immediately to raise needed capital. In the mid-1670s, for example, the actors in the Duke's Company held approximately half of 20 shares, the balance belonging to members of the Davenant family and "adventurers." A distinction must be made, however, between shares held by "sharing actors" and those which conveyed some right in the patent. In modern terminology we would say that Davenant established two separate classes of stock.[15] Neither patentee appears to have given any thought to the dangers of subdividing his patent. Both sold and mortgaged shares quite freely. The price of a one-fifteenth share in the Duke's Company in the 1660s seems to have been about £700.

The patterns established in the 1660s are important because long after Davenant's controlling interest in his company had been dispersed to investors, the design on which he had established the company enabled it to run smoothly. The first test came with his death, when his young son inherited the patent. Neither Charles nor his mother could have run the theatre. Neither tried: They simply continued with the managers who had been chief assistants to Sir William—Henry Harris and Thomas Betterton. When Charles reached his majority the same smooth transition occurred.[16] Killigrew, in contrast, could not control his company, but neither would he willingly give it up, presumably looking on it as an investment that would someday be profitable.

14. See Herbert, *Dramatic Records*, p. 101n. Already by October 1660 Herbert was taking Mohun, not Killigrew, to court. Killigrew gave three of his chief actors a power of attorney to run the company for him at an undetermined date in the early 1660s. See Hotson, *Commonwealth and Restoration Stage*, pp. 244–45.

15. For details see my article, "The Duke's Company's Profits, 1675–1677," *Theatre Notebook*, 32 (1978), 76–88.

16. See Hotson, pp. 226–27.

7

The balance of power in a company varied with the interest and qualifications of the principal owner. Davenant could dictate a company structure in part because he had a clear idea of how a theatre operated and what he wanted to do with it. Killigrew, less knowledgeable and less concerned with innovation, left the business to people he had reason to think knew how to run it. A later contrast to Davenant's approach was that of Christopher Rich, who tried after 1693 to operate the United Company according to a literal interpretation of the powers stated in the patents. Although ignorant of theatre as a business, he was always aware of his rights. He employed a single actor-manager, partly because he needed expert assistance to get plays staged, but also to serve as a buffer between himself and the company when he lowered salaries or made other unpopular decisions.[17] This pattern of consciously removing the owner from the business he ran was one repeated by several owners in the eighteenth century.

The 1695 rebellion of senior actors against Christopher Rich produced an organizational plan which was essentially a throwback to the Elizabethan arrangement. The Lincoln's Inn Fields license was issued to a group of actors who stipulated that the limited number of shares in their enterprise be assigned only with the consent of the majority. In theory the company started out as a cooperative, though in practice Betterton, Mrs Barry, and John Verbruggen did most of the managerial work. Serious disciplinary problems developed by 1700, forcing the Lord Chamberlain to give Betterton some executive powers just to keep the company going.[18] When the cooperative was dissolved and the license was transferred to Vanbrugh and Congreve in 1704–5, the actors became strictly salaried employees, not stockholders. The great majority attained no higher status throughout the course of the eighteenth century.

The permutations of company design in the years between the issue of the Lincoln's Inn Fields license and the 1714–15 patents of George I are beyond clarification in this essay. Three important points need to be made about them, however. First, the two recog-

17. Cibber, *Apology,* I, 255–56.
18. See P.R.O. LC 5/153, fol. 23 (11 November 1700).

nized theatres had spawned a third competitive venture, the opera, which nobody could altogether classify or control, but which remained legitimate largely because it interested the king. Second, temporary licenses became a way of life in the London theatre. The distinction between a patent and a license blurred more and more as the century wore on, but initially it was plain enough. A license was not transferable; it was temporary; and it was entirely subject to the pleasure of the Lord Chamberlain, who might speak for the king but might also speak for the government. A patent (in the original, 1660 sense) was perpetual and hence transferable, but it was also subject to the pleasure of the monarch. Even a holder of one of the original patents could be "silenced," as Rich was in 1709, but such interference was temporary, not final. In 1732 this distinction was further weakened by the creation of a new class of patents, renewable after 21 years, designed to be stronger than a license but not quite so boundless as the original patents.[19] From time to time these distinctions were tested, overlooked, or ignored, occasionally with peculiar results. But for the most part they held true. (For a summary of patent and license descent, see Table 1.)

The third point follows from the broils at Drury Lane in which Wilks, Booth, and Cibber nudged Steele out of daily operations and then continued to operate for a decade on the authority both of a license and what was, technically, Steele's patent.[20] This distinction between silent and active partners is a sign that theatre had grown by the 1720s so large and potentially profitable that it was possible to divorce daily operations from ownership almost entirely and to speculate in ownership as a separate commodity. Such speculation, however, almost always had disruptive effects on the business.

For example, consider Garrick as an owner in the Davenant

19. I can find no definite documentation to support the idea that a twenty-one-year patent was associated with a particular building and was lost if the building was destroyed. (See, for example, *LS*, Part 5, II, 1179 [1789–90]: The problem in this case was rights to the site. The Lord Chamberlain was reluctant to grant a patent without some sureity of site, and the Duke of Bedford was unwilling to lease the site without more security than Sheridan could offer that he would build a better theatre there.)

20. See Cibber, *Apology*, II, 165–66. For more detailed and comprehensive accounts, see George A. Aitken, *The Life of Richard Steele*, 2 vols. (1889; rpt. New York: Greenwood, 1968) and John Loftis, *Steele at Drury Lane* (1952; rpt. Westport, Connecticut: Greenwood Press, 1973), esp. pp. 139–49 and 155–58.

1. Patents and licenses, 1660 to the present

1660	Thos. Killigrew, 1660, 1662 Chas. Killigrew, 1677	Sir Wm. Davenant, 1660, 1663 Chas. Davenant, 1668
1682	└──────── United, 1682; ────────┘ Killigrew patent dormant	
1695	Christopher Rich, 1694–1709	License to LIF Cooperative
1704–5		"Transferred" to Vanbrugh and Congreve
1707–8		Leased to Swiney; opera established
1708–9	C. Rich's theatre silenced; licenses issued almost yearly to actors at DL	as separate from theatre
1713–14	License to Wilks, Booth, Cibber, Doggett, and Collier	1714–61
1714–15	License, then patent, to Steele, Wilks, Booth, Cibber, and Doggett (Steele barred from active participation in January 1720)	Davenant patent renewed for John Rich at LIF, later at CG: in 1733 Rich
1732	After Steele's death, new patent issued to Wilks, Booth, and Cibber with 21-year time limit	bought the dormant Killigrew patent
1733–34	Sold to Highmore et al., later to Chas. Fleetwood et al., Macklin as manager	
1744–45	Sold to bankers Green and Amber; manager, John Lacy, who bought a share in the spring of 1747	
1747–48	Sold to Lacy and Garrick; patent extended another 21 years in 1753, again in 1762, and in 1774	
1761–67		Beard (Rich's son-in-law)
1767–71		Colman, Wm. Powell, Th. Harris, et al.
1771–74		Harris outlasted other active partners
1776–77	Sheridan, et al., bought in; various managers, till 1808–9, when he was forced to retire (21-year patent extension granted in 1783 to run through 1816); Killigrew patent purchased in 1793	Harris retired, 1809 The Royal Opera House, Covent Garden, still operates under the
Present	The Theatre Royal Drury Lane, still operates under the original Killigrew patent	original Davenant patent

10

tradition, one who managed with help from subordinates but retained control of theatrical decisions. (Lacy originally drew Garrick into the venture to take care of what he did not understand himself.) In the seven seasons for which figures are extant, Garrick made between £3,000 and £6,000 profit.[21] On this basis, what he led Sheridan to expect when he sold his share in Drury Lane, and what he asked as a price (£35,000) seem fair enough.[22] But Sheridan proceeded to operate rather like Killigrew, depending heavily on his staff to run the business but never hesitating to assert his position when he felt like it. He bought Drury Lane with the intention of making money out of it, though he was constitutionally unable to keep his mind on the details that made the difference between profit and loss. Expenses and receipts listed in season introductions to *The London Stage,* Part 5, between 1794 and 1800 are challenged by Professor Donohue below—and regardless of how they are tabulated, we have no guarantee of the initial accuracy of the extant accounts. Nonetheless, I will hazard some speculations. Returns for Drury Lane between 1776 and 1800 were very erratic—much more erratic than those for Covent Garden. In twenty-four seasons they range from a £16,000 or £17,000 profit to a £1,600 loss. While only two seasons appear to have ended in the red, for only eight did Drury Lane clear much more than £3,000, and in only five did it go noticeably over that sum. Nor were all the profits being made by Covent Garden patentee Thomas Harris. Except for five seasons early in their rivalry, Harris's profits *added to* Drury Lane's would not have brought the total up to Garrick's £3,000. We should note, however, that between 1790–91 and 1795–96 (three of the five seasons that came near Garrick's top profit), J. P. Kemble, Wrighten, W. Powell, Stokes, and Westley ran the theatre. This knowledgeable staff, left to its own devices, made money despite the upheaval of working in temporary quarters while a new theatre was built. In April 1796 Kemble resigned as manager, and figures over the next three years fluctuate wildly again. Sheridan's profits averaged far less than Garrick's. In

21. For the profits see *LS,* Part 4, Appendix D. We have no way of knowing whether other seasons were as profitable.
22. *Survey of London,* XXXV (London: Athlone Press, 1970), 16.

part, this is because the scale of the whole operation had gotten so out of hand, but Kemble's success as manager indicates that money could be made by a competent man who kept his mind on the business.

Sheridan had "bought on speculation," as he himself acknowledged at the outset.[23] But he was not quite the cynic about his investment, and about the buffer value of capable subordinates, that his sometime cohort William Taylor was. John Ebers reports that when he asked how Taylor could run the King's Theatre from debtors' prison Taylor replied: "How could I possibly conduct it if I were at liberty? I should be eaten up, Sir, devoured. Here comes a dancer—'Mr. Taylor, I want such a dress'; another, 'I want such and such ornaments'. . . . No, let *me* be shut up, and they go to Masterson [Taylor's secretary]; he, they are aware, cannot go beyond his line, but if they get at *me*—pshaw! no man at large can manage that theatre; and in faith . . . no man that undertakes it ought to go at large."[24] Sheridan and Taylor both viewed ownership of a patent chiefly as a speculative venture, and they are a telling index to how far apart ownership and management had drifted by the end of the eighteenth century.

At Covent Garden Thomas Harris was manager from 1767 to 1809. Though initially without practical theatre experience, he ran his business much more sensibly than his competitors. He operated on a smaller budget than Drury Lane, usually with fewer performers, though he produced more plays. Although his profits were lower, his venture was on the whole more stable, and his performers generally better satisfied with their lot.[25] Sheridan's was not the only way to run even a monster theatre.

III Finances

English theatre companies, unlike some Continental troupes, had no subsidy to rely on. Consequently their operations had to be

23. Sheridan to Thomas Linley, Sr, *The Letters of Richard Brinsley Sheridan*, ed. Cecil Price, 3 vols. (Oxford: Clarendon Press, 1966), I, 93–95.
24. *Survey of London*, XXIX (London: Athlone Press, 1960), 231.
25. On a mutiny against Harris (successfully suppressed) see *LS*, Part 5, 1799–1800 Season Introduction.

scaled to box office receipts—plus whatever capital sums could be raised from outside investors. Price scales are, therefore, extremely important, and so is the possibility of raised prices for special occasions—a favorite device of late seventeenth-century companies to help pay for new productions or expensive operas. Routine expenses—authors' benefits, scenery, advertising, and so forth—are well explained in the various introductions to the five parts of *The London Stage.* Here my concern is with comparisons in three realms: financing theatre buildings, the accumulation and disposition of routine operating income, and the changing salary structure.

To build a Restoration theatre apparently cost between £2,500 and £9,000. A century later "Sheridan's" Drury Lane of 1794 cost above £80,000 to build. Even at the outset of the period, building or altering a theatre normally required capital that had to be raised from outside investors—though this group often included actors from within the company. To whom were shares offered? What rights did purchase convey? The answers vary considerably. Building shares were usually kept separate from shares in the profits of the acting company (many of the latter belonging, before 1700, to senior actors). Early in the period, building shareholders were entitled to a flat daily "rent" for use of the building (£5 14s per acting day at Drury Lane, for example). In later years a percentage was sometimes paid on the profits of the acting company, and one or more passes entitling the shareholder to free seats were often part of the deal. The agreements were usually longterm (e.g., 99 years); in such cases they were also transferable.[26]

Most "adventurers" holding shares in the early acting companies seem to have had little if any say in the operation of the company. Christopher Rich, though he served as omnipotent dictator, was what we would call a "managing general partner"—he was not a majority stockholder. A serious disadvantage to the company inherent in "adventurers'" shares was that they diluted profits with no further advantage or return to the people who actually ran the business. Another problem—never solved—was the undefined re-

26. Sharers' terms are discussed in *Survey of London,* Vols. XXIX and XXXV, chronologically by theatre building.

lation of small stockholders to the authority embodied in the patent.

Later managements solved these problems, or minimized them, by writing clearer contracts with more limitations. The Lincoln's Inn Fields Sharers' Agreement of 1695 carefully excluded investors who were not engaged in the company's daily business, an extreme reaction to Christopher Rich which in effect deprived them of capital.[27] Vanbrugh used a device that suggests he possessed great talent for salesmanship as well as for designing Baroque palaces: For £100 the twenty-nine contributors to his new theatre in the Haymarket (1705) received lifetime passes for themselves only, and the privilege of sitting on a committee that would determine ten days' worth of special request programs each year.[28] They got no rent and no profits—and we have no evidence that the special request programs were ever instituted.

A more equitable contract between builder and capitalists is that drawn up by John Rich for his 1730–32 construction of the Covent Garden Theatre. He sold fifty shares of £300 each, for which the buyer got two shillings' rent on performance nights and a transferable complimentary ticket. These privileges appear to have been tied to the lease of the property (originally written for 61 years), so there was a terminal date built into the contract. The importance of a short term in such an agreement becomes clear when we look at the situation of the Drury Lane Theatre around mid-century. Rent to building shareholders between 1747 and 1753 cost Garrick and Lacy about £840 a year for capital long since spent. But when that lease expired, the two managers had consolidated a 21-year patent, a ground lease, and a building lease in their names alone. They were freed from the old investors, and they could raise new capital on the basis of a 21-year contract.[29] With Lacy's son, Garrick did the same thing again when that contract expired.

Naturally the short term did not always appeal to investors.

27. See Nicoll, I, 361–62. A public gift subscription helped the company get started, but we know little about it. For details see my *Thomas Betterton and the Management of Lincoln's Inn Fields*, chap. 3.

28. See my "New Light on Vanbrugh's Haymarket Theatre Project," *Theatre Survey*, 17 (1976), 143–61.

29. See the discussion in *Survey of London*, XXXV, 15–16.

Sheridan and his partners, trying to line up subscribers for a new building on the Drury Lane site in 1790, found the public dubious. In order to obtain a new ground lease the patentees needed large sums to invest in a new building—but would-be investors questioned the wisdom of putting money into a concern that had only a 21-year patent, not a "permanent authority to act." To interest subscribers, the partners had to buy the dormant Killigrew patent from the Covent Garden management as surety for the new Drury Lane building. Finances and ownership of that theatre proved so complex that after the fire of 1809, the patentees were replaced by a joint-stock company, created by Act of Parliament. The tangles that developed at Drury Lane tell us why Thomas Harris arranged to finance his 1792 Covent Garden expansion through a loan from the Duke of Bedford, who owned the site, and out of his own resources, rather than try to sell subscriptions.[30] When possible—which it seldom was—theatre companies were plainly better off obtaining capital by mortgaging future profits rather than by selling shares or agreeing to pay rent indefinitely. Even in the 1670s "house rent" seems to have constituted an item of 25 to 40 percent of fixed daily expenses—no inconsiderable proportion.

Fortunately for the theatre companies, they rarely needed large amounts of capital. They did, of course, need some cash reserves for "furnishing" themselves, and for routine operating expenses, including the costs of new productions. Throughout the eighteenth century extant account books show a small amount of cash carried over from the end of one season to the beginning of the next—but after that the company depended almost entirely on box office receipts. This is one reason why few new productions—especially fancy ones—were mounted until late fall at earliest. Bills and even regular performers' salaries were paid when there was money available; otherwise, claims were postponed. For example, as late as Garrick's last season, 1775–76, salaries were "short-paid" the week ending 30 September, and only in November did full payments become fairly predictable.[31] Treasurers' books constantly note payment of back bills.

30. Ibid., pp. 72–73, 75–77.
31. *LS,* Part 4, 7 October 1775.

15

Some managements wisely maintained a "sinking fund" on which they could draw in emergencies or when short of cash. Our records are so fragmentary that it is impossible to say much about such funds, especially since a company might keep three or more going at once (see Drury Lane, 2 June 1774 and 10 June 1776). If seventeenth-century companies used such a device we have no record of it. As another means of acquiring small amounts of capital, managers from time to time sold additional renters' shares. A buyer received the same rent and free pass as the original investors, but the term involved was shorter—usually the remainder of the current 21-year patent—and the price might be proportionately lower.[32] I must disagree with Professor Stone when he implies that such sales represented a regular part of income each season.[33] The capital was desirable, but the rent paid on such shares increased overhead, and adding to the number of passholders (40 more in the Drury Lane arrangement of 1775) meant cutting potential box-office receipts for immediate gain. In a 180-night season, if 50 "renters" were paid 2s each per night, that would drain £900 out of the treasury for up to 21 seasons—as against a £12,500 capital sum originally obtained from them. To take a particular example: In 1781 Thomas Harris made a 20-year agreement with a new renter for the usual £250 cash price. Over the term of 20 years Harris paid him £360 in dividends, and of course the renter held a free pass. This was a customary but not a very satisfactory way of raising large sums of money.

Basically, the theatres operated on what patrons paid to get in, and season customs put definite limits on the patent theatres. After 1766 a licensed summer theatre occupied time once open to young performers to gain big-city experience, and to veteran actors anxious to supplement their income. Early in the century the benefit system had already become codified to the point that the managers had to make their profits before Easter, even though the company played on through May and into June. Of course the theatre normally made its expenses on these late spring dates—but that was all. Until Michaelmas Court term brought people back to town there

32. *Survey of London*, XXXV, 14–16, 75–77.
33. See *LS*, Part 4, I, xlv–xlvi.

was little money to be made in the fall: The social season long remained linked to court terms.[34] Lent was another bad time: Early in the century the ban on Wednesday and Friday performances became absolute, and of course there could be no acting at all in Passion Week. Toward mid-century, managers tried hard to produce oratorios in Lent or to rent their quarters to musicians, but no great amounts of money can have been made this way.

Including benefit nights, managers found that about 210 nights were the maximum they could hope to play in a regular season, and some of those dates offered little hope of much profit. Naturally they tried to pack their houses with popular actors and with whatever added attractions might be made to pay—song, dance, and pantomime. The only obvious way to increase receipts was to raise admission prices. In the late seventeenth century the theatres customarily raised prices for special new productions and for expensive operas.[35] Extra expenses were directly compensated, if not covered, under this arrangement. Early in the eighteenth century, after John Rich discovered the drawing power of pantomime, he began to charge "advanced prices" more and more often. Audiences objected to paying extra for productions no longer new, regardless of how large a cast and crew they involved. A compromise was reached: Audience members who paid the full rate but left before the pantomime began could get a refund, unless the performance had been advertised as not allowing refunds.[36] Prices ran like this:

	Common				Advanced			
1660–1700	4s,	2s 6d,	1s 6d,	1s	5s,	4s,	2s 6d,	1s 6d
							(operas higher)	
1700	4s,	2s 6d,	1s 6d,	1s	5s,	4s,	2s,	1s
1744–45 at DL	5s,	3s,	2s,	1s				
(withdrawn)								
1745–46 at DL	4s,	2s 6d,	1s 6d,	1s				
at CG	5s,	3s,	2s,	1s				
1746–47 at both	5s,	3s,	2s,	1s				

34. *LS*, Part 3, I, xliii–xliv.
35. *LS*, Part 1, p. lxx.
36. *LS*, Part 2, I, lvii–lviii.

During the 1730s more and more performances were advertised at advanced prices, with or without a pantomime and regardless of whether anything new had been added to the production. When Charles Fleetwood opened Drury Lane in 1744–45, he apparently charged 5/ 3/ 2/ 1/ as *common* prices, though he did not dare list the rates in newspaper ads until 19 October. A month later, rioters forced him to back down at least to the extent of offering refunds, which he had been refusing to do. The next season, under new management, Drury Lane retreated to the old, lower rates, but Covent Garden charged the higher ones, and John Rich made the increase stick. Thereafter 5/ 3/ 2/ 1/ was the standard scale, without a refund option. At the same time they raised prices overall, managers stopped charging extra for new productions, no matter how expensive. Overall the trade-off came out to their advantage. But Garrick had to mount his *Chinese Festival* in November 1755 without any help from raised prices, and he then spent the rest of the season trying to find ways to recoup the losses. The trade-off left less room for speculation in new productions, and it enforced more careful accounting, since all additions to stock and increases in personnel had to be financed out of current and unaugmented box-office receipts.

Another price increase occurred with the rebuilding of Covent Garden and Drury Lane in the last decade of the century, but this one was prepared for by astute advertising. In 1787–88 Covent Garden stopped listing prices in its ads, though Drury Lane continued to do so. For the following three seasons neither theatre advertised prices. While the Drury Lane Company played at the King's Theatre in the Haymarket, they charged 6s, 3s 6d, and 2s, excusing the advance because they were playing in rented quarters. Covent Garden assiduously posted the same old prices that season, but when Harris opened his new theatre in the fall of 1792, he used the 6s, 3s 6d, 2s scale, adding a 1s gallery under duress.[37] The rebuilt Drury Lane naturally charged the same rates. Thus were some of the monstrous costs of the 1790s theatres passed along to the public. The wonder is that ticket prices remained as constant as they did.

37. For uproar over the lack of a 1s gallery, see *LS*, Part 5, II, 1467.

The changed scale of theatrical operations in London during our period is obvious enough from "house charges" and approximate annual budgets. At the height of the Restoration period the usual fixed daily expenses ran about £25; the total annual income in a decent year probably ran no more than about £7,000. By 1776–77 (Sheridan's first season at Drury Lane) the "house charge" was £105 and annual income for a patent theatre was running about £34,000. A quarter century later £50–60,000 was normal, and house charges were £140 at Covent Garden and £200 at Drury Lane. Where did this money go? We have enough figures available to make some interesting comparisons. The overall trend is of course toward ever larger-scale operations, but some of the particularities are surprising and significant.

The crucial item in budgets is usually salaries. Unfortunately, we have little information about salaries prior to 1700, and the situation is complicated by the practice of paying "sharing actors" a percentage of profits rather than a straight salary (plus benefit), as became customary in the eighteenth century. In the original patent companies there was a major distinction between sharers and "hirelings." Shares went to the best (or most powerful) senior actors; they were assigned, and not transferable. Sharing actors usually had some say in company policy, the amount varying considerably with owner and manager. Exact figures are scarce, but we do know that in the mid-1670s a Duke's Company share seems normally to have produced £50 or £60 per annum. Betterton held 3.25 shares (good for about £170), Henry Harris 2.75 (about £140), William Smith, Nokes, and Underhill 1.5 each (about £80). This, we should stress, is *annual* income for top actors in the London theatre before the benefit system was instituted. Of course it does not include summer earnings (if any); and the benefits that became customary for all senior actors around the end of the seventeenth century might essentially have doubled this income. The custom of actor-sharers broke down at about the same time: Neither company admitted to making any profits c. 1700, and actors naturally prefered to contract for a straight salary (not paid in full in hard times), plus a benefit for which they could energetically peddle tickets. After 1709 the few actors who owned "shares" were

19

dealing in patent power: Company ownership was involved, not status as an actor or interest in a building.[38]

We can get an instructive comparison of salary scales at the beginning and end of the eighteenth century by setting the plan for a united company (1703) in P.R.O. LC 7/3 against figures derived from account books in *The London Stage,* particularly those for Drury Lane in 1795–96.[39] Exactly how many people are involved in each case is extremely hard to determine, especially where nonperforming personnel are concerned. The number of performers more than doubled during the century. The 1703 plan calls for 31 actors and actresses, 6 singers, 7 dancers, 20 musicians, and some 40 support personnel. This is probably a larger total than for any actual company of the time, save those which briefly mounted both plays and operas. A list for such a company in 1709 specifies 31 actors, 10 singers, 28 musicians, and 1 dancer.[40] (The number of servants is not given.) Professor Stone's estimate of about 26 servants in 1740–41 seems low,[41] but a figure between 40 and 50 in the first half of the century seems excessively high for a plain acting company. The 1703 plan overlooks or retitles some important posts (prompter and call boy, for example) and does not include some positions which later eighteenth-century companies filled (e.g., chorus master, scene designer). But insofar as titles are comparable, consider these *weekly* salaries:

1703 Plan	*Drury Lane 1795–96*
2 treasurers at £2 10s each	1 treasurer (£8 in 1798–99) and 1 subtreasurer
12 doorkeepers 13s each	31 doorkeepers 9s 6d each, and 21 boxkeepers 8s 6d each
Betterton, to teach, £3 10s	John Philip Kemble, in addition to acting, £20

38. I have in mind Wilks, Booth, Cibber, Garrick, and William Powell.

39. Although the 1703 plan estimates costs for a company which was never constituted, the distribution of actors is close to that of known companies, and many of its features are confirmed by other sources. I take Drury Lane in 1795–96 in particular because it is the last season of stable management under Kemble, but it also reflects the company's circumstances in the new 1794 theatre. On the 1703 plan see my "The Date and Import of the Financial Plan for a United Theatre Company in P.R.O. LC 7/3," *Maske und Kothurn,* 21 (1975), 81–88.

40. P.R.O. LC 5/155, p. 3 (24 December 1709).

41. *LS,* Part 4, Appendix D.

8 dressers 4s 6d	23 dressers 9s
(no prompter listed as such)	1 prompter £4 and an assistant

In new buildings between 1794–95 and 1799–1800 Covent Garden averaged about 87–90 performers, Drury Lane about 85. Support staff was at least two-thirds as large as the performing company (i.e., about 60). A noticeable escalation seems to have occurred by 1766–67, and neither house had much luck reducing these proportions. If we look at the salaries, we find that most servants' jobs in 1795–96 brought them twice what they would have made (if paid in full) in 1703, except for doorkeepers and boxkeepers, who were never paid much because they were known to embezzle from the theatre and to accept bribes from the public for preferential treatment.

The contrast between the increased salaries paid to major actors and those paid to servants is more striking. It reflects the disproportionate status a leading actor could command by 1795–96, to the direct cost of his fellow employees. In the calculations that follow I have computed weekly rates from the annual pay on the 1703 list over the course of a normal thirty-week season. These figures compare straight salaries; benefit income is not included, since we have no reliable way to assess it.

1703 Plan		per week	*Drury Lane 1795–96*		per week
Betterton	£150 and		J P Kemble	£16 plus	
	£50 to teach	= £6 13s		£20 as acting	
Verbruggen	£150	= £5		mgr.	£36
G Powell	£150	= £5	Bannister, Jr		£16
Wilks	£150	= £5	J Palmer		£16
Doggett	£100 plus a		King		£16
guinea a time when he acts		= £3 6d+			
Mrs Barry	£150	= £5	Mrs Siddons		£31 10s
Mrs Bracegirdle	£150	= £5	Miss Farren		£17
Mrs Oldfield	£80	= £2 13s	Mrs Crouch		£14
Mrs Mountfort			Mrs Jordan at £10 10s		
(the younger)	£30	= £1		a night	?
Mrs Betterton, housekeeper					
and to teach to act £80		= £2 13s			

Kemble's total salary was nearly six times that projected for Bet-

21

terton on the 1703 plan; but whereas Betterton was listed for not quite three times as much as his treasurer and over six times as much as his doorkeepers, Kemble made four times what his treasurer got and about seventy-five times as much as his doorkeepers. Kemble was clearly exceptional, and so was Mrs Siddons. The next rank of actors and actresses at the end of the century made only three times as much as their predecessors, but they were paid only about twice what the treasurer made.

What are we to conclude from such comparisons? Total budgets increased by a factor of four or five during the eighteenth century. Professor Avery estimates from Lincoln's Inn Fields account books that as late as 1724–25 John Rich spent about £11,000; in 1795–96 Drury Lane spent over £44,000; Covent Garden, £52,000. Very simply, this means that the percentage of expenses represented by salaries falls substantially in the course of the century, most dramatically after the new theatres open in 1792 and 1794. (See Table 2.)

The shifts shown in these figures are particularly interesting because through Garrick's last season (1775–76) the percentage of other key expenses remained quite constant. The amount paid in "renters' shares" hovered between 6 percent and 10 percent. Scenery, costumes, and upkeep as Professor Stone calculates them stayed under very tight control, for the most part running about 10 percent. Unusual circumstances could raise that figure: When Rich was investing heavily in pantomime in 1724–25, scenery and costumes accounted for nearly 20 percent of his budget, and Garrick spent 16 percent his last year. In sharp contrast, Sheridan owed 13 percent to 17 percent of his expenses *to "renters"* in debt-service, the amount varying a bit with the number of nights the company played and the total budget. Harris likewise paid his performers a smaller and smaller percentage of his total budget after the rebuilding of Covent Garden. A telling conclusion is inescapable: Despite the huge salaries paid to a few principal performers at the end of the century, the percentage of the budget spent on performers of all kinds was roughly half at the end of the century what it had been in Garrick's day.

2. Percentage of budget spent on salaries

Company	Year	Approximate Number of Performers*				Percentage
Duke's Company	1675–76	16m	12f†			—
	1676–77	20m	14f			—
Company Plan, LC 7/3	1703	20m	11f	7d	6s	53%; + music, 62%
Lincoln's Inn Fields	1724–25	24m	13f	15d	7s	40%
Covent Garden	1740–41	28m	21f	29d	5s	44%; + music, 45%
CG	1746–47	32m	21f	20d	7s	40%; + music, 44%
CG	1760–61	40m	30f	30d	13s	62%; + music, 67%‡
CG	1766–67	36m	28f	23d	12s	41%; + music, 45%
Drury Lane		38m	23f	16d	3s	59%; + music, 62%
DL	1775–76	72m	24f	13d	13s	64%; + music, 68%
CG	1780–81	45m	28f	19d		48%§
DL		41m	32f	15d	7s	69%
CG	1787–88	40m	28f	10d		34%
DL		41m	31f	9d		58%
CG	1795–96	45m	34f	27d	12s	25%
DL		59m	33f	8d	34s	43%
CG	1798–99	58m	41f	39d	13s	21%
DL		42m	35f	25d	34s	42%
CG	1799–1800	55m	41f	37d	28s	26%
DL		44m	34f	26d	22s	27%

*In this table, m = actor, f = actress, d = dancer, s = singer, music = orchestra.

†The King's Company had similar numbers of performers at this time. We have no budget figures for either company.

‡See *LS*, Part 4, II, 869–70, for reductions in some salaries on account of the death of George II.

§*LS*, Part 5, does not list music as a separate category.

IV Daily Operations

Division of labor among managerial personnel varied a good deal from company to company: To specify responsibility too precisely is perhaps to invite the reader to think of exceptions. We can, however, make some basic statements. To keep a theatre going required a manager (who might or might not be a principal owner, but who chose and mounted plays, supervised rehearsals, and so forth); a prompter, who prepared prompt copies, saw to the copying of parts, and generally assisted the manager; and a treasurer, who had to collect and record income, pay bills (after receiving authorization to do so), calculate "shares" and salaries due and pay them. There is some variation in responsibilities, depending largely on how much part an owner took in daily business, but this pattern holds good for all of the stable managements.

Leaving aside some troubled periods we can easily lay out managerial organization across these 140 years. (I omit some minor and transient figures.)

Company	Owner	Manager	Prompter	Treasurer
Original Duke's, and successors to 1705	Davenant; Davenant family and others	Davenant, succeeded by Betterton with Harris, then Smith, then Verbruggen	Downes	Cross; later Alexander Davenant; later others

After Davenant's death in 1668 authority in the Duke's Company rested almost entirely on the managers. This company was absorbed by the Vanbrugh-Congreve enterprise at the Haymarket in 1705. The Davenant patent, held by Christopher Rich from the Union of 1682, passed down to John Rich in 1714, first as proprietor of the third company to occupy Lincoln's Inn Fields, then at Covent Garden.

Company	Owner	Manager	Prompter	Treasurer
LIF/CG 1714–61	John Rich	John Rich for pantomime; Quin, Macklin, et al., for plays	Stede; later Carmichael	Wood; later White

John Rich left the theatre to his son-in-law Beard.

Company	Owner	Manager	Prompter	Treasurer
CG 1761–67	John Beard	Ross	Stede; then Younger	Ballard; later Garton

Harris, Colman, and Powell bought Beard out in 1767, and after several acrimonious years, Harris got control in 1774.

Company	Owner	Manager	Prompter	Treasurer
CG 1774 through the end of the century	Harris	Hull; later Lewis	Wild	Garton; later Barlow.

The other original patent company and its successors can be traced as follows:

Company	Owner	Manager	Prompter	Treasurer
Original King's Company	Killigrew	Mohun, Hart, et al.	Booth	Henry Hayles(?)

This arrangement lasted from 1660 to 1677, when Charles Killigrew wrested control from his father. Unable to run the company profitably, he negotiated the Union of 1682.

Company	Owner	Manager	Prompter	Treasurer
"Rich's" Patent Company 1695–1709	Christopher Rich, Skipwith, et al.	G. Powell, et al.	Newman	Baggs
Triumvirate 1709–33 at Drury Lane	Wilks, Booth, Cibber, et al.	Wilks, Booth, and Cibber	Chetwood, c. 1715– 1741 (with interruptions)	Castleman, 1711–39

A stormy decade followed. A responsible management solidified between 1744 and 1747 and ran through 1776.

Company	Owner	Manager	Prompter	Treasurer
Drury Lane 1747–76	Garrick and Lacy (first father, then son)	Garrick	Cross; later Hopkins	Pritchard; others after 1763

In 1776 Garrick sold his interest to a shifting group in which the principal constant was R. B. Sheridan.

Company	Owner	Manager	Prompter	Treasurer
Drury Lane 1776 through the end of the century	R. B. Sheridan and others	R. B. Sheridan, T. Sheridan, Younger, Linley, Sr, J. P. Kemble, Wroughton, Aickin	Hopkins; later Harwood; later Wrighten	Evans, Westley, Peake, and others

Surveying this brief outline, we can readily see that the more successful theatre operations enjoyed a good deal of managerial continuity. Betterton and his partners before 1694, the triumvirate, Garrick, and Harris all had ups and downs, but overall they are models of success. We see also that ownership rarely shifted hands without precipitating a period of readjustment, and that when more than one or two members of a management team changed in a short time, the business was apt to fall apart.

As a rule, it was helpful to have a single clearly dominant manager. In this respect the Wilks-Cibber-Booth triumvirate was clearly exceptional, working together smoothly for some twenty years. The mess at Lincoln's Inn Fields c. 1699–1700 is more typical of group managements. Likewise the combine, Colman, Harris, and Powell who bought Covent Garden in 1767, suffered endlessly from infighting. Even after Powell had died and Harris agreed to let Colman manage, in 1769–70, one actress complained privately that the long-time prompter, Younger, was the only person holding the company together.[42] In 1774 Colman sold out to Harris, who made Covent Garden a stable operation through 1809, keeping the same staff together for long periods. Two managers, one prompter (plus assistants), and two or three principal treasurers worked for him through the turn of the century. During those same years, Sheridan and his partners at Drury Lane went through eight managers, three prompters, and at least four treasurers. The difference in stability is clear. Harris could get more people to work for less money and put on more shows, at least in part because his organization was not in constant turmoil.

An owner who was heavily involved in daily operations was hard to replace. Betterton and Harris achieved the feat in 1668, probably because Davenant had more or less trained them in management. The uproar at Drury Lane in 1732–33 is suggestive. Without its longtime actor-managers the theatre had a stormy season, with a naïve owner trying to fend off the presumptuous Theophilus Cibber, who regarded himself as heir apparent. The next year Macklin, a forceful manager, more or less restored order with the aid of an experienced staff. *Someone* had to keep a tight grip on things. If the owner did not do so, then he needed a strong manager who could and would. Sheridan's inadequacy as Garrick's successor was a matter of application, not ability. He tried initially to trim expenses and staff, but he could not be bothered to keep monitoring them as Garrick had always done. He even foresaw the results: A note on a

42. Miss Macklin in a letter to her father, cited in *LS,* Part 4, III, 1692.

1777 memorandum says, *"If with this plain Account before us we are inattentive or extravagant—shall we not deserve the Ruin which MUST follow?"*[43] The Lincoln's Inn Fields-Covent Garden Company, in which the manager was usually a strong force separate from the owner, got through the century without the extreme shake-ups which bedeviled "Sheridan's" Drury Lane.

In general, selection of repertory, and especially choice of new scripts fell to the owner himself. He might seek advice or keep his own counsel, but nobody, not even Garrick, got off unscathed from this job, and some, like Cibber, found themselves widely abused.[44] Once the owner or manager accepted a new script he and the author discussed casting, with the option of consulting the prompter and (at least in the seventeenth century) the senior actors. Garrick wrote in 1775 that "every author since my management distributed his parts as he thinks will be of most service to his interest, nor have I ever interfered, or will interfere, unless I perceive that they would propose something contrary to common sense."[45] The success of a new play was usually of greatest concern not to the company but to the author, especially after the Union of 1708. The manager could always fall back on stock plays. Indeed, managers hated to take risks with unknown scripts from authors who would have to be given expensive benefits. A. H. Scouten quotes Davies as saying that Barton Booth "often declared in public company, that he and his partners lost money by new plays; and that if he were not obliged to it, he would seldom give his consent to perform one of them."[46] Back in the height of theatrical warfare (the 1670s and 1695–1700) each company often staged ten or a dozen new plays each year, and a production could be gotten up from scratch in three to six weeks. Later managers seldom had to produce more than half that number of new scripts each year, and the schedule was not so hectic.

Actors were not given much choice about the parts they accepted. Some consultation and discussion among senior actors

43. Sheridan, *Letters,* I, 115.
44. See Dougald MacMillan, "David Garrick as Manager," *Studies in Philology,* 45 (1948), 630–46; Barker, *Mr. Cibber of Drury Lane,* pp. 112–16; and Cecil Price, "Thomas Harris and the Covent Garden Theatre," in *Essays on the Eighteenth-Century English Stage,* ed. Kenneth Richards and Peter Thomson (London: Methuen, 1972), pp. 105–22.
45. *LS,* Part 4, III, 1933.
46. *LS,* Part 3, I, cxxxviii.

probably took place in the seventeenth-century companies, but as early as 1675 the King's Company fine schedule specified the forfeit of a week's wages for refusing a part.[47] Few actors could afford such a fine, and eighteenth-century penalties became even heavier. In 1792–93 the forfeit was £5 at Drury Lane and a staggering £30 at Covent Garden.[48] For at least 80 percent of the Drury Lane actors £5 was more than a week's wages. As for Covent Garden, we may safely conclude that Thomas Harris disliked having actors refuse parts. The fines applied to parts in old plays as well as new ones. Actors often looked with dubiety on parts in a new play, since there was a considerable chance that the piece would die in its first week, thus wasting a lot of trouble. Revivals, however, were likelier to provoke demonstrations of temperament, since the relative value and difficulty of each part was much clearer than in a new play, and was a direct index to status.

We possess no direct evidence, but Professor Stone makes the reasonable suggestion that a conference was held early each fall to discuss repertory choices and casting.[49] At such a meeting owner, manager (if different), prompter, and treasurer would have tried to settle details and anticipate contingencies. On a day-to-day basis the prompter seems to have wielded a good deal of authority, even in companies that had a strong manager. As early as the King's Company forfeit schedule, mentioned above, the prompter is identified as the official agent of the manager, authorized to speak in his name: To refuse a request from him was to refuse the manager's request. The term "prompter" conveys a misleading impression to the modern reader. In the late seventeenth- and eighteenth-century theatre he seems to have had many of the responsibilities we associate with the stage manager.

I would suggest that the treasurer's presence at a policy conference might be as important as the prompter's. Together they could tell the owner or manager a lot about costs and possible profits. Prompter Richard Cross kept a record of estimated attendance, which, Stone suggests, would have enabled him to comment on the

47. Nicoll, I, 324n.
48. See Thomas Gilliland, *The Dramatic Mirror,* 2 vols. (London: C. Chapple, 1808), I, 138–40.
49. See *LS,* Part 4, I, clxix, clxxvii, clxxxiv, and xlv.

28

drawing power of plays already in the repertory. The treasurer should have had past receipt figures, and a record of actual expenses for each show—a factor not to be ignored in choosing revivals. As John Powel says in *Tit for Tat* (his unpublished recriminations against Garrick), costs for "all nights will not amount to the same, as for example the play of *Macbeth* requires more incidents [i.e., incidental expenses] than a common play. . . . Whereas in another play, such as the *Orphan,* perhaps there are few or no incidents, and consequently the charges must be less."[50] Authorizations for payment signed by Wilks, Cibber, and Booth document differences after 1715. Earlier than that we must rely largely on inference, but clearly the "English operas" mounted by Betterton at Dorset Garden cost far more to perform (even after the disproportionate initial investments were paid off) than plays without choruses, crowds, and elaborate scene shifting. One of the treasurer's jobs was to know what things cost; another was to relay the manager's decisions to the company. Notes from the triumvirate to their treasurer Castleman show that he was to explain what the theatre would and would not pay for.[51]

The terms on which the actors worked were largely governed by a set of rules and fines. Parts could not be refused or costumes removed from the theatre. Prompt attendance at rehearsals was required. Prior notice of intention to leave the company was demanded. But except for the highest-paid performers (and eventually designers), few people seem to have had written contracts.[52] As Cibber says, "we neither ask'd any Actor, nor were desired by them, to sign any written Agreement (to the best of my Memory) whatsoever: The Rate of their respective Sallaries were only enter'd in our Daily Pay-Roll."[53] Thus at the start of each season someone recorded the terms agreed upon, and the treasurer's pay list was the official record of employment.

A few popular performers might negotiate contracts with a vari-

50. Ibid., p. 121.
51. E.g., 2 June 1716, quoted in *LS,* Part 2, I, cviii.
52. Avery suggests that the handful of contracts from the first decade of the new century in LC 7/2 and 7/3 may represent an attempt to regulate the informal practice of the past (*LS,* Part 2, I, xlii–xliii). If so, the experiment was not continued.
53. *Apology,* II, 113.

ety of special provisions.[54] Below those who rated individual treatment came four groups paid on differing scales.[55] A comparable hierarchy existed among the "servants," of whom few besides the prompter, treasurer, and what we would call box office staff got benefit privileges—and then only after they had proven themselves competent. One of the treasurer's trickier tasks must have been the complex bookkeeping involved in calculating the profit or debit of each performer's benefit (or worse, shared benefit). A very few performers rated a "clear benefit"—one for which they received all proceeds, without deduction—but most were charged at least part of the fixed expenses of the house. The actual amount charged could vary from person to person, and was sometimes the subject of negotiation or recrimination.

Some comment on the meaning and nature of "house charges" may be in order here as a kind of capsule view of changing operations in the eighteenth-century theatre. Between 1660 and 1695, before benefits were customary, "charges, certain and incident" per performance were deducted from the gross receipts to cover ground rent, house rent, taxes, and costs of particular performances, including the salaries for those members of the company who were not "sharers."[56] These expenses determined whether or not actor-sharers made any money and whether or not the theatre was breaking even. A few losing days were tolerable, but no company could afford to play to houses bringing less than this figure for long. These basic expenses seem to have run about £25 a day in the 1670s, which is why the King's Company preferred to cancel performances in the spring of 1681 when houses totaled £4 and £5.[57] As the structure of companies changed and the number of salaried employees increased, the financial balance between management

54. As early as 1695 John Verbruggen had a special three-year contract with Rich. It contains no terms for a benefit play, probably because benefits were not yet common. For details see Nicoll, I, 382–83. Several of the 1709 contracts in LC 7/3 have special clauses; see Nicoll, II, 286–87 for summaries.

55. See LS, Part 4, I, lxxxi–lxxxii. A specific example of a scale of weekly pay rates c. 1792–93 is given by Gilliland in The Dramatic Mirror, I, 138–40: 30s or less; 30s to £3: £3 to £6; £6 to £9; and over £9.

56. I take this phrase from lawsuits that flourished after the rebellion of 1695 over rights to the profits of acting, "certain and incident charges having been paid."

57. LS, Part 1, p. lvi; Hotson, p. 267.

and employees underwent two major adjustments. First, benefits very quickly became a major part in an actor's annual income. Consequently how many benefits, when they would be scheduled, what plays might be used, and how much the house would charge became significant issues at contract time. The second adjustment, partly a result of the benefit system, is the unnoticed redefinition of "house charges." Since many more people were paid salaries than previously, the total daily expenses were higher (if we disregard for the moment managements which notoriously did not pay their employees). In 1694 Christopher Rich declared that the Patent Company cost £30 a day to run, though we cannot tell how much of that was theoretically allotted to salaries. In the 1696 contract for *Woman's Wit* he claimed £40 a day from Cibber. By 1702 he was rumored to be charging an actor £34 for a benefit, and three years later we have a documented case at slightly over £38. By 1707 the "house charges" for benefits had risen to £40, which remained a normal figure into the 1720s.[58] But at some time between 1694 and 1707 the rates charged for benefits became negotiable and consequently no longer a means by which the theatre historian can calculate the real minimum daily cost of running a theatre. At least in theory, the actor-sharers of the United Company had paid their hired staff and been content with whatever profits were left, "taking the bad with the good."[59] Once the benefit system became entrenched, the patentees absorbed part or even all of the cost of staffing benefit performances.

Let us look at a mid-century example of benefit costs and charges fully documented, and then note some variations. In the fall of 1761 the itemized "Expenses" at Covent Garden included renters, barber, music, candles, coals, lamps, bill stickers and bills, ads, a wardrobe allowance, a properties allowance, extras, sums paid to

58. The *Woman's Wit* contract is summarized by Nicoll, I, 381–82. See also *LS,* Part 1, p. lvi (citing Nicoll and *A Comparison Between the Two Stages,* 1702), and Part 2, I, lxviii (1724–25). The expenses projected in the 1703 company plan work out to approximately £49 per day over 180 days, including all the set salaries but no extra allowance for the men paid a guinea a time when they act. The 1709 contracts vary between £40 and £50 in house charges.

59. This phrase is from the Petition of the Players (1694) in LC 7/3. Hotson suggests that accounting was not always accurate.

John and Christopher Moser Rich, and to guards.[60] The standard total came to £36 6s 5d. On 23 October the company gave a benefit performance for the victim of a fire, and although expenses are listed that day at £33 5s 6d, the beneficiary was charged £85. The next day happened to be payday, and the total for the six-night week 16–24 October was £341 17s 7d, which works out to about £56 per night in salaries. So the actual cost of the benefit 23 October was about £89, or £4 more than the beneficiary was charged. How does this figure compare with charges to members of the company? In the preceding season oratorios had run lowest at £35; most actors and the prompter and treasurer paid £63; box office staff between £70 and £80. Two other cases of beneficiaries without special influence show that company members were favored: When Tindal appeared 25 April 1761 "for the first time on any stage," it cost him £84, and a "Gentleman under misfortune" also paid £84 on 12 May.

The variations worked on this plan have to do with what items a given owner figured in his "Expenses" and what part of the actual cost of benefit performances he was willing to absorb for various people and groups. John Rich had, in fact, followed a policy of scaled charges as early as 1724–25.[61] When John Beard inherited Covent Garden from Rich he did not put a salary for himself in the "Expenses," but he did raise the rates charged to box office staff and charities.[62] Drury Lane used a similar scale of charges. Over the next decade the lower end of this scale rose, though the upper end remained stable. However, one of Sheridan's first decisions when he took over Drury Lane was that the charge for benefits the next season would be £105.[63] If the average salary list in 1777–78 was £530 at Drury Lane, £360 at Covent Garden, their companies were

60. *LS*, Part 4, 20 September 1760 and 24 September 1761.

61. Compare figures in *LS*, Part 2, with those published by Frederick T. Wood, "The Account-Books of Lincoln's Inn Fields Theatre, 1724–1727," *Notes and Queries*, 164 (1933), 220–24, 256–60, 272–74, and 294–98. Rich charged himself, his actors, treasurer, and prompter £40 for a benefit (or whatever cash came in, if less). But while he charged his dancing master, Mr Griffith, £50, most of his box-office staff paid only £30, perhaps in an attempt to encourage them to be honest. He charged authors of new plays £45 or more (depending on costs?). No doubt he could be more lenient when he had fewer obligations than after he built Covent Garden and had to pay off investors.

62. See *LS*, Part 4, 1 January, 18 February, 25 May 1767, and 20 and 23 December 1766.

63. *Letters*, I, 113.

costing £88 and £60 a night without making any allowance for other routine expenses, rents, taxes, or payment to owners.[64]

Toward the end of the century the managers put their money into theatre buildings and fancy staging, not into performers. A few exceptional individuals did manage to come out better than ever. For example, when John Philip Kemble resigned as manager at Drury Lane Sheridan had to pay him £24 a week to keep him as a performer, £8 higher than his last salary for acting. Sheridan had also to pay a new manager, who, feeling shortchanged, demanded a raise of £140 in 1797–98. That was too much; the first replacement for Kemble was replaced. But in 1798–99 *Pizarro* opened and played thirty-one times. The next season both Kemble and Mrs Siddons were holding Sheridan up for £30 10s per week just to act. We must note, however, that since the average salary figure at Drury Lane dropped in 1799–1800 (though the number of performers remained constant), their raises came not out of Sheridan's pocket, but out of their colleagues'.

Reflecting on changes in theatre management during the eighteenth century one must grant that most of them were probably an inevitable result of the changed scale of operations that followed from the restriction to two patent theatres. Back in the Restoration, actors were heavily influential in the way theatre companies operated, and when a hard-nosed businessman like Christopher Rich intruded he was violently resented. By the end of the eighteenth century ordinary actors could not hope to have any real say in the operation. A concommitant change can be seen in attitudes toward teaching and recuitment. The Restoration companies expected to train apprentices, and at times to subsidize a "Nursery." As late as the 1703 company plan Betterton was penciled in for a whopping £50 per annum salary "to teach." But as theatres flourished in Dublin and the provinces, the London theatres abandoned their teaching avocation and simply employed what talent developed elsewhere. When the scale of the operation escalated it tended to get taken over by big-business management no longer willing to take risks, or very interested in plays except as vehicles for stars or spectacle. Garrick's management was the last to preserve the *actors'*

64. These figures are from *LS*, Part 5, I, 105 and 108.

interest paramount (though always within the limits of fiscal responsibility). Ultimately, the history of the eighteenth-century theatre shows us an actors' theatre gradually submerged by big-time, big-city show business.

2
The
Theatres

EDWARD A. LANGHANS

WHEN THOMAS KILLIGREW and Sir William Davenant were granted patents by Charles II to establish two acting companies and erect playhouses for them, those courtier-playwrights must surely have considered their options. By the fall of 1660 there was already a fair amount of theatrical activity in London, carried on by a mixture of old and new male players at three playhouses that had been built before the wars: the Red Bull, Salisbury Court, and the Cockpit (or Phoenix) in Drury Lane. The first served as a temporary home for many of the actors who eventually joined with Killigrew and became the King's Company, while Salisbury Court was a sometime house for a number of the young players who became affiliated with the Duke's Company under Davenant. The Cockpit was used by various people, including Davenant himself. We have crude pictures of the first two and can guess that they were something like the old Elizabethan public and so-called private playhouses—that is, theatres without the proscenium arches and the wing-border-shutter scenery that were part of the English and Italian Renaissance court theatre tradition. The Cockpit, on the other hand, had some scenic capabilities, for Samuel Pepys saw a French production using scenery there on 30 August 1661.[1]

---

1. Perhaps the production was the one in *The Description of the Great Machines, of the Descent of Orpheus Into Hell. Presented by the French Commedians at the Cock-pit in Drury-lane* (London: Robert Crofts, 1661).

35

The Red Bull in 1660 may have been the only surviving example of a prewar public theatre, which was typically open-air, roughly circular, octagonal, or square in outside shape, and probably had tiers of galleries wrapping around a standee's pit, into which thrust a platform stage. Doors from backstage opened onto the acting area, and some arrangement—curtained inner stages, or a pavilion—made it possible to present "discovered" scenes.[2] Salisbury Court may have resembled what scholars think the private theatres of earlier years looked like: Physical features very like those in public playhouses, but rectangular in shape, fitted with benches in the pit, and artificially illuminated.[3] The Cockpit was converted from its sporting use to a theatre about 1617 by Inigo Jones; plans for it at Worcester College, Oxford, show an interesting cross between a private and court theatre.

Both Davenant and Killigrew must have seen that the least expensive way to get their companies into operation was to settle into existing playhouses and pick up London's theatrical activity virtually where it left off in 1642, when the Puritans silenced the actors. To try to provide the public with the elaborate features of the earlier court theatres—scenes, machines, fancy costumes, music, singing, dancing—would have been a very costly undertaking indeed, and who could say whether or not the general public would take to such presentations? Either the Red Bull or Salisbury Court could have been operated with a small company of players, a few stagehands, the actors' own clothes (plus a few special costumes), and a supply of standard properties. Davenant and Killigrew, despite their court connections, were not wealthy men, and

2. The pavilion theory is presented in A. M. Nagler's *Shakespeare's Stage* (New Haven: Yale Univ. Press, 1958).

3. See Irwin Smith, *Shakespeare's Blackfriars Playhouse* (New York: New York Univ. Press, 1964). Glynne Wickham in *Early English Stages 1300 to 1660*, Vol. II, Part 2 (London: Routledge and Kegan Paul, 1972), pp. 144–47, suggests that Inigo Jones's drawings 7B and 7C at Worcester College Library, Oxford, may be for Salisbury Court, but Iain Mackintosh in "Inigo Jones—Theatre Architect," *Tabs,* 31 (September 1973), 99–105, and John Orrell in "Inigo Jones at the Cockpit," *Shakespeare Survey,* 30 (1977), 157–68, prove that the plans are for the Cockpit in Drury Lane. See also D. F. Rowan, "A Neglected Jones/Webb Theatre Project," in *The Elizabethan Theatre II,* ed. David Galloway (Toronto: Macmillan, 1970); Edward A. Langhans, "A Picture of the Salisbury Court Theatre," *Theatre Notebook,* 19 (1965), 100–101; and William Van Lennep, "The Death of the Red Bull," *Theatre Notebook,* 16 (1962), 126–34.

the theatrical ventures on which they were embarking had unpredictable futures. London had been without regular theatrical activity for eighteen years, and many citizens had grown up without a theatregoing tradition. Any theatre manager in his right mind would have decided to begin modestly with some old plays in an old sceneryless playhouse. The one innovation planned—the use of women in female roles—should have been quite enough to attract audiences.

The manager least likely to have been interested in a sceneryless theatre was Killigrew. He had spent part of the interregnum in Venice, which by the middle of the seventeenth century had some of the most advanced theatres of the time. Killigrew also had a thirst for court life and would surely have wished to attract the king's favor by presenting the kind of scenic spectacles Continental monarchs enjoyed. But, remarkably, he chose not to use any existing playhouse but to convert a tiny tennis court in Vere Street, Clare Market, into something like an Elizabethan private theatre, with no scenery (see Figure 1). Was he simply trying to begin

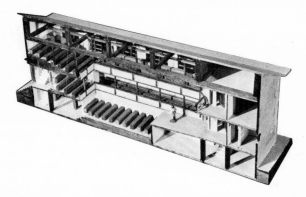

1. Vere Street Theatre 1660. Model reconstruction by Edward A. Langhans

performing as soon as possible after his troupe was organized? Perhaps, for the records in *The London Stage* show that the King's Company was operating almost eight months before the rival

Duke's players could open their new playhouse. Pepys on 20 November 1660 said Vere Street was "the finest play-house, I believe, that ever was in England." Spoken like an expert.

Davenant also spurned the old playhouses and converted a tennis court into a theatre, but from the beginning he chose to perform with scenic wings, borders, and shutters (Figure 2). Fitting up his

2. Lincoln's Inn Fields Theatre, 1661. Model reconstruction by Edward A. Langhans

Lincoln's Inn Fields house took several months, during which time his troupe acted sporadically at Salisbury Court. Davenant must have realized how risky it was to let his rivals establish themselves so quickly. He probably hoped to attract the upper class of London playgoers, many of whom had been in exile on the Continent and had seen the kind of elaborate shows Giacomo Torelli designed for Venice and Paris in the 1640s. Davenant's choice was the right one. As soon as he opened his new theatre, Killigrew's troupe had to begin laying plans for a new playhouse where they, too, could present scenic productions. Pepys noted on 4 July 1661 that Vere Street, "that used to be so thronged," was playing to small houses because of Davenant's success. Scenes and machines won the day, and wittingly or unwittingly Davenant and Killigrew set the pattern for the English-speaking theatre of today by departing from the practice of the sceneryless Elizabethan public theatre.

The two earliest Restoration playhouses, Vere Street and Lincoln's Inn Fields, despite differences in the layout of the stage area, were similar in size. We have no pictures of their interiors (unless the familiar *Wits* frontispiece of 1673 shows the Vere Street stage), nor have any plans survived, but I estimate the exterior dimensions of Vere Street at about 25′ x 70′, and Leslie Hotson suggests that Lincoln's Inn Fields may have measured about 30′ x 75′.[4] If each had benches in the pit, a U-shaped level of boxes wrapping around the pit, and one U-shaped gallery, and if each had an auditorium area taking up about half the length of the building, neither could have had a capacity of much over 400. Since the 25–30′ heights of seventeenth-century tennis courts would have allowed for a second gallery at each house, perhaps the theatres could have accommodated 500 to 600. But even if there was an upper gallery at Lincoln's Inn Fields—the larger of the two buildings—a playgoer sitting on the bench furthest from the stage would have been only about 45′ from an actor standing at the footlights. Theatres with that kind of intimacy encouraged dramatists to write plays in which the spoken word was of primary importance; we might not today have Restoration comedies of wit had the playhouses been larger.

A sizeable capacity in a small space was achieved, as plans of other Restoration and eighteenth-century theatres prove, by using two-foot-high backless benches about a foot deep, with sometimes no more than a foot between benches. In the eighteenth century, and doubtless earlier, flaps (hinged sections of the benches) were used instead of aisles in many playhouses to utilize the precious auditorium space as efficiently as possible. In a full house spectators would have had little elbow room.

By 1663 both patent companies had theatres capable of handling scenic shows, but not until the mid-1670s, when the troupes were at their playhouses in Dorset Garden and Drury Lane, did London begin to see what could be described as truly spectacular productions (Figures 3 and 4). These were new theatres, built in 1671 and

4. *The Commonwealth and Restoration Stage* (Cambridge, Mass.: Harvard Univ. Press, 1928), pp. 114–27.

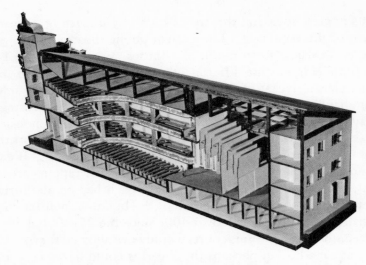

3. Dorset Garden Theatre, 1671. Model reconstruction by Edward A. Langhans

1674 respectively, and there is the possibility that one or both of them may have been equipped with the sophisticated Continental pole and carriage system of mechanical sceneshifting.[5] Despite the trend toward larger buildings—Dorset Garden was almost twice the size of Lincoln's Inn Fields—a typical intimate feature of English theatres remained: the forestage, or, more correctly, the pro-scenium or "theatre," an acting area forward of the curtain line, flanked by entrance doors. Some plays, especially farces, written for Restoration theatres contain stage directions indicating that the stage action was often within the scenic area upstage of the curtain line, but most of the playing in heroic tragedies and comedies of manners seems to have taken place on the forestage. It was an acting area admirably suited to scenes that emphasized the spoken word and the expert delivery of it. Shakespeare's platform stage had survived. Richard Southern raises the possibility that the forestage was important chiefly for dramatic as opposed to operatic produc-tions. For some operas in the eighteenth-century temporary fron-

5. A proclamation issued by Charles II in 1673, preserved at the Public Record Office (LC 7/3), speaks of "those vast Engines (which move the Scenes and Machines)."

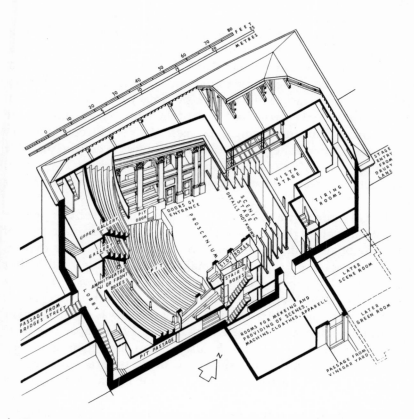

4. Drury Lane Theatre, 1674. Reconstruction by Richard Leacroft from his *Development of the English Playhouse.* Courtesy of Mr Leacroft and Eyre Methuen Ltd.

tispieces seem to have been built forward of the proscenium wall, concealing the entrance doors and bringing the scenic area closer to the front edge of the stage, Continental style.[6]

Of the five main public theatres in use between 1660 and 1700 even the largest, Dorset Garden, was small in comparison with

6. *Changeable Scenery* (London: Faber and Faber, 1952), pp. 182–87. See also Graham Barlow, "Sir James Thornhill and the Theatre Royal, Drury Lane, 1705," in *The Eighteenth-Century English Stage,* ed. Kenneth Richards and Peter Thomson (London: Methuen, 1972), pp. 179–93 and pls. 3–12.

some of the houses of later years. But when the King's and Duke's troupes merged in 1682 the United Company chose to use Drury Lane for most productions and reserve Dorset Garden chiefly for spectacles. That would suggest that Dorset Garden, perhaps from its opening, may have been found too cavernous for legitimate drama. A good measure of a theatre's intimacy is the distance from the front of the stage to the back wall of the front boxes (those at the back of the auditorium, facing the stage).[7] At Vere Street, Lincoln's Inn Fields, Drury Lane, and probably Bridges Street the distance was about 30'–35'; at Dorset Garden it was perhaps twice that. Architects of modern theatres try to keep that measurement 75' or less.

When London playhouses were altered or rebuilt in the eighteenth century the crucial distance from the stage to the back of the front boxes did not increase as much as one might expect. Architects increased capacity by making houses wider and higher but not much deeper except in the upper galleries. In Henry Holland's Covent Garden Theatre of 1792, which seated about 3,000, a spectator at the back of the front boxes was only a bit over 50' from the stage; at the huge Drury Lane of 1794 (capacity 3,611) the distance was only 74' (see Figure 5). But the remarkable intimacy of the Restoration houses of a century before was gone.

Not only was the actor-audience relationship close in the early playhouses, the sight lines must have been good from the majority of seats. Richard Leacroft in *The Development of the English Playhouse* has demonstrated that until late in the eighteenth century most London theatres had fan-shaped auditoriums.[8] That meant poor sight lines only for the relatively few people sitting in the side-boxes, and it is likely that they chose to sit there because they wanted to be seen, not because they came to pay attention to the play.[9] There were other poor seats, of course. The few times Pepys

7. The center front box was, for many years, the royal box; it was in time moved to the side of the auditorium, next to the stage, where the royal view of the backstage area must have been splendid.

8. (London: Eyre Methuen, 1973), pp. 89–117. I must express my special gratitude to Mr Leacroft, not only for his fine book with its marvelous drawings but for a very helpful correspondence over the years.

9. Restoration audience behavior is well documented in A. M. Nagler, *Sources of Theatrical History* (New York: Theatre Annual, 1952), pp. 208–13. Information about eighteenth-century audiences may be found in Harry William Pedicord, *The Theatrical Public in the Time*

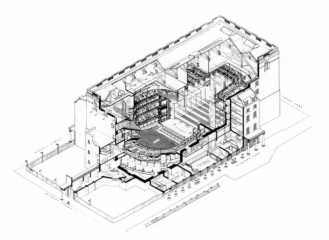

5. Drury Lane Theatre, 1794. Reconstruction by Richard Leacroft from his *Development of the English Playhouse.* Courtesy of Mr Leacroft and Eyre Methuen Ltd.

complained, he was usually at the court theatre or at Lincoln's Inn Fields. On 8 January 1663 he was "forced to sit almost out of sight at one end of the lower forms" in the pit, apparently, at Lincoln's Inn Fields. There on 6 February 1668 in the 18d gallery he "sat mightily behind, and could see but little, and hear not all." But these were exceptions.

The intimacy of the early theatres may have been enhanced by the primitive lighting. Flickering wax candles in sconces or chandeliers, and footlights, illuminated the auditorium and the stage throughout a performance. Dimming was not unknown in the seventeenth century, and stage directions in some Restoration plays—*Love in the Dark* and *Thyestes* are two examples—call for the darkening of the stage area. But English auditoriums were not

of Garrick (New York: King's Crown Press, 1954); Leo Hughes, *The Drama's Patrons* (Austin: Univ. of Texas Press, 1971); and the volumes of *The London Stage*. The *Theatrical Monitor* of 19 March 1768 gave a typical description of box loungers in the eighteenth century: "During the time of the representation of a play, the quality in the boxes are totally employed in finding out and beckening to their acquaintances, male and female; they criticize on fashions, whisper cross the benches, make significant nods, and give hints of this and that, and t'other body." I have seen exactly such behavior in the boxes at the Metropolitan Opera House. Fashionable audiences have not changed much.

dimmed, and that made for a very different kind of theatrical experience than we are familiar with today.

Between 1695 and 1715 drama and theatre in London changed in a number of ways and for a variety of reasons. Attacks on the imitations of immorality on the Restoration stage reached a peak; there was an influx of Dublin players who had been schooled more in Shakespeare than in Restoration comedy and heroic plays; foreign singers and dancers began appearing in entr'acte entertainments as managers fought for audiences; more people from the middle class began coming to the theatre; and a number of new playwrights began their careers at the very time several older ones ended theirs.[10] It was surely not mere coincidence that during that same transitional period one London theatre underwent alterations, two new ones were built, and another was reconverted from tennis court use.

By 1695 Drury Lane was London's main playhouse, the theatre in Dorset Garden being then infrequently used. That year Thomas Betterton and some of the older players broke with the Drury Lane management of Christopher Rich and turned Lincoln's Inn Fields back into a theatre. In 1696 or thereabouts Rich made a significant alteration at Drury Lane: To increase capacity he cut back the theatre's forestage and replaced the downstage proscenium doors with stage boxes.[11] That had the effect, as the actor-playwright-manager Colley Cibber later complained, of forcing the performers ten feet upstage: "But when the Actors were in Possession of that forwarder Space to advance upon, the Voice was then more in the Centre of the House, so that the most distant Ear had scarce the least Doubt or Difficulty in hearing what fell from the weakest Utterance: All Objects were thus drawn nearer to the Sense; every painted Scene was stronger [how so? we must ask]; every grand Scene and Dance more extended; every rich or fine-coloured Habit had a more lively Lustre: Nor was the minutest Motion of a Feature

10. This transitional period was discussed in three related papers by Shirley Strum Kenny, Calhoun Winton, and Edward A. Langhans at the 1972 convention of the Modern Language Association; abstracts may be found in *Seventeenth Century News*, Spring 1973, p. 25. My paper, which covered the playhouses and actors, is in *Theatre Annual*, 29 (1973), 28–39.

11. Most authorities date the alteration 1696, but I have found historians using 1692, 1698, and 1699. Take your choice; the work was certainly done in the 1690s.

. . . ever lost, as they frequently must be in the Obscurity of too great a Distance."[12] That was the beginning of the withdrawal of the actor into the scenic area.[13]

In 1705 a new theatre opened, the first playhouse built in London since 1674 (see Figure 6). It was the Queen's (later King's) Theatre in the Haymarket, designed by Sir John Vanbrugh along rather unusual lines, as the *Diverting Post* of 7–14 April 1705 noted:

> WHen *I their Boxes, Pit, and Stage, did see,*
> *Their Musick Room, and middle Gallery,*
> *In* Semi-circles *all of them to be;*
> *I well perceiv'd they took peculiar Care*
> *Nothing to make, or do, upon the* Square.

Though the statistics we have suggest a playhouse about the size of Dorset Garden, estimates of the original capacity go no higher than 950. Yet it was an opera house, as the players soon discovered, and even after alterations made about 1708 the theatre did not prove satisfactory for plays. From 1710 to the end of the century the buildings on that site were used chiefly for opera productions.

In 1714 yet another theatre opened, John Rich's new Lincoln's Inn Fields, which was a proper theatre and not a converted tennis court. We have been in the dark about the building's size, but at the Guildhall in 1977 I discovered a plan (MS 11,936D; item 52) of the building as it existed in 1806, and it measured 56' x 100'—smaller than the first Drury Lane. It may, however, have seated as many as 1,400 , or nearly three times the capacity of the earliest Restoration

---

12. *An Apology for the Life of Mr. Colley Cibber,* ed. Robert W. Lowe, 2 vols. (London: John C. Nimmo, 1889), II, 85–86.

13. The players did not readily relinquish the forestage. In *An Essay on the Opera* (London: Printed for L. Davis and C. Reymers, 1767), p. 97, Count Algarotti ridiculed the continued use of it: "The actors, instead of being so brought forwards, ought to be thrown back at a certain distance from the spectator's eye, and stand within the scenery of the stage, in order to make a part of that pleasing illusion for which all dramatic exhibitions are calculated. But by such a preposterous inversion of things, the very intent of theatric representation is destroyed; and the proposed effect defeated, by thus detaching actors from the precincts of the decoration, and dragging them forth from the scenes into the midst of the parterre; which cannot be done by them without shewing their sides, or turning their shoulders to a great part of the audience." His view prevailed. The forestage remained—it was about 15 feet at Drury Lane in 1794—but by then it was little used except by entr'acte performers.

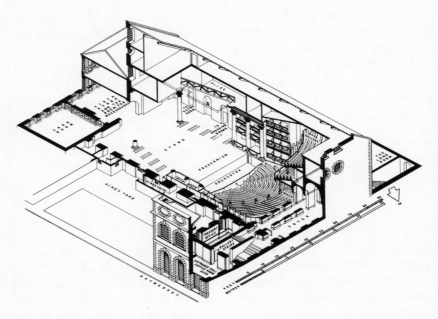

6. Queen's Theatre, 1708. Reconstruction by Richard Leacroft from his *Development of the English Playhouse.* Courtesy of Mr Leacroft and Eyre Methuen Ltd.

playhouses, as Emmett L. Avery shows in his volumes of *The London Stage.*[14]

The history of the major London houses during the rest of the eighteenth century is one of constant alterations, redecorations, reconstructions, and building from scratch, the trend being toward larger and larger theatres. Rich built himself a new playhouse in Covent Garden in 1732, and Lincoln's Inn Fields gradually fell into disuse; Covent Garden was altered several times before it burned in 1808 (Figure 7). Wren's Drury Lane went through similar growing pains, including an extensive redesigning by Robert Adam in 1775 (Figure 8), and was replaced by a mammoth new building in 1794; that theatre, designed by Henry Holland, burned in 1809 (see

14. *LS,* Part 2, I, xxxiii–xxxiv.

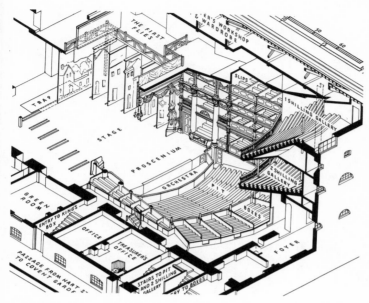

7. Covent Garden Theatre, 1732. Reconstruction by Richard Leacroft from his *Development of the English Playhouse.* Courtesy of Mr Leacroft and Eyre Methuen Ltd.

Figure 5). The King's was also altered several times over the years, burned in 1789, was rebuilt in 1791, and burned in 1867. Is there any significance in the fact that in more primitive Restoration days there was only one theatre fire (Bridges Street, in 1672)?

Architects found ingenious ways to increase the capacity of a theatre without tearing down the basic shell. In the case of Drury Lane, property was acquired that permitted the depth of the building to be increased, but even in 1775, when that dimension had almost doubled, the width was what it had been a century before. One way architects were able to use valuable building width for seating rather than stairways and passages was to build the former into the thickness of the theatre walls and place the latter outside the walls in buildings adjacent to the playhouse. Michael Novosielski's 1782 plan of the King's Theatre clearly shows how

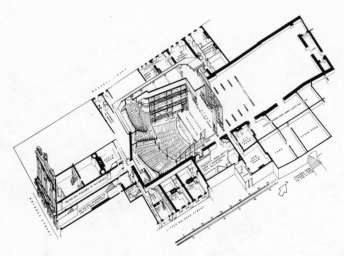

8. Drury Lane Theatre, 1775. Reconstruction by Richard Leacroft from his *Development of the English Playhouse*. Courtesy of Mr Leacroft and Eyre Methuen Ltd.

the walls of the original shell were perforated to provide access to the passageways. One way or another, designers contrived to make London's main theatres larger. Before Wren's Drury Lane was demolished in 1791 its capacity had been increased from about 700 to perhaps as much as 2,300, and its stage depth (from the front of the stage to the farthest reaches of the scenic area) had doubled. Remarkably, the acoustics of the theatres up to the last decade of the century were not seriously damaged by the changes in size. Much wood and fabric was used in playhouses then, and the very fussiness of some of the interior decorations helped rather than hindered the sound.

Though building sizes increased, playgoers were not given more legroom. The architect George Saunders wrote in 1790 that people "should not submit to be crowded into such narrow seats: 1 foot 9 inches is the whole space [at Covent Garden] allowed for seat and void; though a moderate-sized person cannot conveniently sit in a less space than that of 1 foot 10 inches from back to front, nor comfortably in less than that of 2 feet."[15] That kind of squeezing in small Restoration playhouses was understandable; one wonders why theatregoers a century later in more spacious auditoriums submitted to it. They seem not to have complained, perhaps because the crowding helped keep them warm in the ill-heated houses.

The growing number of playgoers, attracted by the increasingly varied theatrical fare, encouraged managers to expand their seating capacities and offer more spectacular shows, which attracted more theatre patrons—and so on.

The size of the playhouses, especially toward the end of the century, did not inspire playwrights to attempt works that needed intimate theatrical surroundings. One would therefore expect plays written for the small theatres of Restoration times to be dropped from the repertoire of eighteenth-century companies, but many were revived with some regularity. Emmett Avery's study of Congreve's plays on the eighteenth-century stage shows that the works held their own remarkably well until the 1790s.[16] But, like the theatres, Restoration plays were altered. They were cleaned up, to be sure, but John Brownsmith's *Dramatic Time-Piece* of 1767 makes it clear that the most severe changes had to do with length.[17] *Love for Love* had a shortened running time of 2:16, *The Way of the World*, 2:21; *The Country Wife*, 2:01; *All for Love*, 2:31; and *Venice Preserv'd*, 2:09. We know, too, that plays were sometimes presented with important characters omitted. Clearly one of the reasons plays were severely cut was to provide time for the other entertainments on an evening's bill—the entr'acte songs and dances, a pantomime, an afterpiece. The size of the theatres worked against uncut performances of straight plays and in favor of varied lighter, shorter fare. The longest work listed by Brownsmith was *The Beggar's Opera* (3:05), a variety show in itself.

Technically, the late eighteenth-century London theatres were highly sophisticated, as Richard Leacroft's splendid reconstructions

15. *A Treatise on Theatres* (London: Printed for the Author, 1790), pp. 83–84.
16. *Congreve's Plays on the Eighteenth-Century Stage* (New York: Modern Language Association, 1951).
17. (London: For J. Almon, T. Davies, and J. Hingeston, 1767).

show. The backstage areas were vast. Wings, borders, shutters, drops, and ground rows were the chief scenic units, but scenery could be thrust up through openings at almost any plane of the stage, and elaborate machines could be lowered from above. Stage floors had traps of various sizes, and lighting equipment was very advanced. Garrick's scene designer Philippe Jacques De Loutherbourg introduced to Londoners a realism in staging effects that must have been dazzling. Henry Angelo said De Loutherbourg "astonished the audience, not merely by beautiful colouring and designs, far superior to what they had been accustomed to, but by a sudden transition in a forest scene, where the foliage varies from green to blood colour. This contrivance was entirely new, and the effect was produced by placing different coloured silks in the flies [above the stage], or side-scenes, which turned on a pivot, and with lights behind, which so illuminated the stage, as to give the effect of enchantment."[18]

Garrick's Drury Lane of 1775, as altered by Robert Adam, may have been the best of the theatres of our period (Figure 8). It was a considerable improvement over earlier playhouses, and it was not as elephantine as the later ones. An anonymous writer in the *Public Advertiser* of 30 September 1775 gave it high praise:

At first View I was a good deal surprised to find that by some means or other the ingenious Artists had contrived to give an Appearance of greater Magnitude to the House. I knew it was *not* rebuilt, but only repaired; and consequently that there could be no additional Space within the old walls and Roof. Upon Reflection I perceived that one Way by which this was effected, was from having removed the old heavy square Pillars on each Side of the Stage, and by that Means I suppose they have procured more Width from one Side-box to the other.

I also observed, that the Sounding Board was much raised on the Part next the Stage and that the Height given to it increased greatly the Appearance of Magnitude in the House. This having brought the Ceiling or Sounding Board nearly on a Level, has a wonderful good Effect to the Eye; and what astonished me greatly was to find that the Sound of the

18. *Reminiscences,* with notes and a memoir by H. Lavers Smith, 2 vols. (Philadelphia: J. B. Lippincott, 1904), II, 248.

Music and Actors Voices both improved by this additional Height. . . .

Small Pilasters, the Height of which is confined to the different Tiers of Boxes, support and adorn them: They are made more light and more gay by inserting in Front of each a Pannel of Plate Glass, which in the lower Order is placed over a Foil or Varnish of spangled Crimson, which looks both rich and brilliant. The Capitals are gilt, and are what our Artists call the Grecian Ionick. . . .

The upper tier of Boxes is adorned with Therms, of which the Busts are gilt, and the Pannels underneath are filled with painted Ornaments. . . .

All the ornaments in the Friezes and on the Dados, or Fronts of the Boxes, are elegant and splendid. Nothing can, in my Opinion, answer better than the Festoon Drapery upon the Front of the first Tier. The gilt Ornaments on the Faces of the . . . Pilasters (from whence the Branches for the Candles spring) ought not to be omitted in the Catalogue of elegant Ornaments, neither must I omit the Decoration of the Ceiling, or Sounding Board, which . . . give[s] the Ceiling the Appearance of a Dome, which has a light and airy Effect.

. . . I heard some Criticks alledge, that they thought the Decorations of the House *too* elegant, and too splendid, and that it obscured the Lustres of the Scenery and the Dresses. My Answer to these Observations was, that I thought the Decorations of a Theatre could *not* be too brilliant, and that I did not doubt but, by the Assistance of a Loutherbourg, the Managers could and would soon remove these objections, and bring the whole into perfect Harmony.

He was not so sure he liked the dark crimson drapery over the stage, nor was its gold fringe brilliant enough. But Drury Lane had clearly been given both spaciousness and a dazzling new look.

Between 1775 and 1795 London saw another period of change in the theatres and in literary taste as the Romantic movement gained momentum. The old playhouses were drastically altered or, as in the case of Drury Lane, demolished and built anew on a grander scale. One needs only look at Edward Dayes's marvelous 1795 watercolor of Drury Lane to understand the excitement of theatregoing then (Figure 9). But the new house was clearly too big for straight plays; it was the size of an opera house, and the two figures on the stage seem like Lilliputians. Garrick's "natural" style would

9. Drury Lane Theatre, 1795. Watercolor by Edward Dayes. Courtesy of the Henry E. Huntington Library and Art Gallery

have been lost in such a space, and one can understand why actors of the last decade of the eighteenth century used, as Mrs Siddons evidently did, a larger, more "classical" style. Dayes's picture shows some members of the audience paying attention to the performance and as many more paying attention to themselves. It is an image of the drama and theatre of the eighteenth century: The play and the audience, the stage and the auditorium are all part of a theatrical event, a performance by all concerned, a social occasion at which the play was not necessarily the thing.

John Byng, later Viscount Torrington, saw Mrs Siddons act on 14 May 1794 and longed for the earlier playhouse:

I adjourned to Drury Lane Playhouse where I enjoy'd the highly wrought exhibition of Mrs S's performance in Catherine in Henry 8th, altho' lost and sent to waste in this wild wide theatre, where close observation cannot be maintain'd,—nor quick applause received!

Restore me, ye overuling powers to the drama, to the warm close, observant, seats of Old Drury where I may comfortably criticise and enjoy the delights of scenic fancy: These now are past! The nice discriminations, of the actors face, and of the actors feeling, are now all lost in the vast void of the new theatre of Drury Lane.

Garrick—thou didst retire at the proper time—for wer't thou restor'd to the stage,—in vain, would now thy finesse,—thy bye play, thy whisper,— thy aside,—and even thine eye, assist thee.—

Thus do I crawl about in London!—Where are my old friends? All gone before me—!!! Where are thy new ones? Why, they understand me not; they speak a new language,—they prescribe fashions,—I think they do not understand comforts. "Why here is a fine theatre," say they? "Aye, it may be fine, it may be magnificent; but I neither hear, nor see in it!!" "Thats your misfortune"—"So it is I allow, but not yet my failing."

"Does it proceed from the narrowness of my faculties; or the width of your new stage? Answer me that? Is my decrease equal to your increase?" No; No; fill your stage with monsters—gigantic cars, and long train'd processions—whilst the air vibrates with the sound of trumpets, and kettle drums: These will beat all your actors, and actresses out of the field. Who will listen to, or who can hear the soliloquies of Shakespeare, the inward terrors of the mind—perturbed imaginations and the strugglings of a guilty conscience—?

To see a *fellow* hunting a dagger about the stage—; or an old *princess* wasting in a great chair?

Who will go hereafter to see their tiresome attitudes? To hear them none will attempt,—so let us have the battlements,—the combat, the sulphur, the torches,—the town in flames,—and the chorus.[19]

Richard Cumberland also lamented the new supremacy of scenes and machines over "the labours of the poet," just as Ben Jonson had expostulated in the early seventeenth century that the scenic em-

19. *The Torrington Diaries*, ed. C. Bruyn Andrews (London: Eyre and Spottiswoode, 1938), IV, 18–19.

bellishments of Inigo Jones had become the soul of the masque. Like Torrington, Cumberland preferred the earlier house:

Since the stages of Drury Lane and Covent Garden have been so enlarged in their dimensions as to be henceforward theatres for spectators rather than playhouses for hearers, it is hardly to be wondered at if their managers and directors encourage those representations, to which their structure is best adapted. The splendor of the scenes, and the ingenuity of the machinist and the rich display of dresses aided by the captivating clamours of music now in a great degree supercede the labours of the poet. There can be nothing very gratifying in watching the movements of an actor's lips, when we cannot hear the words that proceed from them; but when the animating march strikes up, and the stage lays open its recesses to the depth of a hundred feet for the procession to advance, even the most distant spectator can enjoy his shilling's-worth of show. What then is the poet's chance? . . .

On the stage of the Old Drury in the days of Garrick the moving brow and penetrating eye of that marvellous actor came home to the spectator. As the passions shifted, and were by turns reflected from the mirror of his expressive countenance, nothing was lost; upon the scale of modern Drury many of the finest touches of his art would necessarily fall short. The distant audience might chance to catch the text, but would not see the comment, that was wont so exquisitely to elucidate the poet's meaning and impress it on the hearer's heart.[20]

The huge London playhouses of the late eighteenth century are no longer standing, but Covent Garden and Drury Lane today are not so unlike their predecessors of 175 years ago. The Covent Garden auditorium especially, with its tiers of seating, has something of what I think may have been the feel of the theatres of Mrs Siddons's time (Figure *10*). And if you scale down the present Covent Garden—reduce the tiers to two and the capacity to less than a thousand, replace the individual seats with backless benches and the electric lighting with candles, and build a forestage and flanking doors where the orchestra pit now is—you might have something like the theatre as Pepys knew it (Figures *1* and *2*). The legacy of Davenant and Killigrew is still very much with us.

20. *Memoirs* (London: Lackington, Allen, 1807), II, 384–85.

10. Covent Garden Theatre, 1965

There were many more places of entertainment in Restoration and eighteenth-century London than have been cited so far. Indeed, they are numberless, for if we include the temporary theatre "booths" at the summer fairs, some of which were fitted up like the permanent houses, we cannot say how many different theatrical establishments there were between 1660 and 1800. *The London Stage,* which does not attempt to include performance data on many minor places of the last half of the eighteenth century, still lists over two hundred different theatres, fair booths, music rooms, taverns, pleasure gardens, and the like. There were probably hundreds more, legal and illegal, during those 140 years. Some were fairly substantial and important, like the Haymarket, Giffard's theatre in Goodman's Fields, the Pantheon, and the Royalty; some were small, like the fair booths, the converted tennis courts, and the "nurseries" where young players were trained; some were part of such pleasure gardens as Sadler's Wells, Vauxhall, and Ranelagh; some were designed for equestrian shows—like Astley's and the Royal Circus; some were concert rooms at which occasional play performances were given, such as Hickford's and York Buildings. About most of those we have some performance information but very little data on the structures themselves, but even the music rooms seem to have been laid out in something like the pattern established in the early Restoration public playhouses and continued with variations to the end of the eighteenth century and beyond.

If I have made the history of the Restoration and eighteenth-century playhouses seem relatively clear-cut, let me correct the impression by citing two examples of how tangled is the web of information we have.

One theatre mentioned above is architecturally interesting, historically important, and a frustration to theatre historians. It is the second of two theatres in Ayliffe Street, Goodman's Fields, designed by Edward Shepherd in 1732 for the actor-manager Henry Giffard. The scene painter William Capon drew a plan of it, with notes, after visiting what remained of the theatre in 1786 and again after the building burned in 1802 (Figure *11*). The small playhouse had a fan-shaped pit, a tier of boxes, and one gallery; the capacity was probably no more than 750. The forestage was wide and shallow, just deep enough to accommodate one proscenium door on each side. Much of the acting may therefore have taken place within the scenic area or with the scenery close behind the players, serving as an environment rather than as a decorative background. The theatre would have been ideal for an actor who wished to use a more natural style than his predecessors. Indeed, this was the

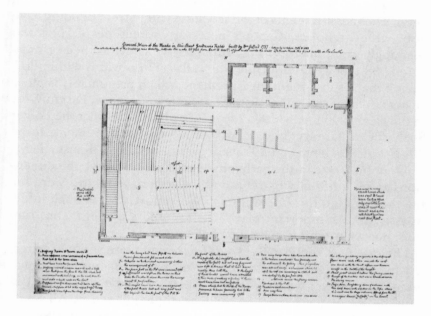

11. Goodman's Fields Theatre, 1732. Copy by James Winston of William Capon's plan of 1786 and 1802. By permission of the Folger Shakespeare Library

theatre in which David Garrick made his first London appearance.

The information we have about the playhouse has confused historians.[21] For a number of years they mistook this theatre for an

21. For clarifying matters we are indebted to Sybil Rosenfeld, "Theatres in Goodman's Fields," *Theatre Notebook,* 1 (1946), 48–50; Charles Beecher Hogan, "The New Wells, Goodman's Fields, 1739–1752," *Theatre Notebook,* 3 (1949), 67–72; Robert Eddison, "Capon and Goodman's Fields," *Theatre Notebook,* 14 (1960), 127–32—from which the following Capon quotations are taken; and Laetitia Kennedy-Skipton, "Notes on a Copy of William Capon's Plan of Goodman's Fields Theatre," *Theatre Notebook,* 17 (1963), 86–89.

earlier Ayliffe Street playhouse, which stood on the same site and was, we now know, demolished to make way for the Shepherd-Giffard theatre. It was also confused with a third theatre in the Goodman's Fields area, one now identified as the New Wells, Leman Street. When reference is made to the Goodman's Fields Theatre, one cannot always be certain which playhouse is being cited. The measurements of the second Ayliffe Street building have also baffled scholars. Capon's notes are sometimes cryptic and seemingly contradictory. For example, he said the theatre measured "88 feet exactly outside the walls / 47 do width within do," calling that a subsequent measurement, which presumably is more correct than his statement that "The whole house from East to West in the clear is 90 feet width 52 feet." The ground plan at the Folger Shakespeare Library (one of two) shows the measurements to be 90'-6" outside depth and 49' inside width. Robert Wilkinson in his *Londina Illustrata* in the early nineteenth century gave the dimensions as 88' x 48'-6" and did not say whether the figures were for the theatre's interior or exterior.[22] We almost have enough information on this important playhouse to build a model reconstruction, but what figures are we to believe?

The case of Wren Plan 81 is a different and more serious matter, for it involves larger discrepancies in measurements and much disagreement over what theatre, if any, the plan depicts. Plan 81 in Volume IV of the papers of Sir Christopher Wren at All Souls College, Oxford, has intrigued scholars for years. It shows a playhouse with a semicircular seating arrangement that anticipates that of Vanbrugh's theatre of 1705, and a sketch of a proscenium arch reminiscent of the scenic façade Inigo Jones provided for the Cockpit in Court in 1629–30 (Figure *12*).[23] The drawing does not contain a scale; the *Survey of London* thinks the plan measures 90' x 40', but Donald Mullin in his reconstruction of the Bridges Street

22. (London: R. Wilkinson, 1819–25), II, following p. 166.

23. The classical semicircular plan can also be seen in a Jones/Webb design that was clearly influenced by the work of Sebastiano Serlio and by the Teatro Olimpico of Andrea Palladio and Vincenzo Scamozzi; it is also at Worcester College and shows a semicircular amphitheatre facing a stage with a scenic façade pierced by two side doorways and a large central arch through which can be viewed a built-perspective avenue. Donald Mullin (see n. 24 below) sees this as a possible basis for the Bridges Street playhouse design of 1663.

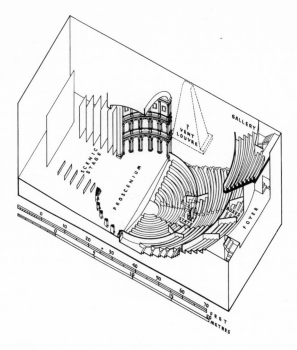

12. The Hall Theatre at court(?). Reconstructed from Wren Collection, IV, Plan 81, by Richard Leacroft in his *Development of the English Playhouse.* Courtesy of Mr Leacroft and Eyre Methuen Ltd.

Theatre says it is 135' x 58'.[24] The plan has been conjecturally identified as for the Bridges Street Theatre of 1663, or for the Bridges Street alterations of 1666, or for the Drury Lane of 1674, or for the Hall Theatre at court.[25] Scholars approach such materials

24. *Survey of London,* Vol. XXXV: *The Theatre Royal Drury Lane and the Royal Opera House Covent Garden,* ed. F. H. W. Sheppard (London: Athlone Press, 1970), p. 40; Donald Mullin, "The Theatre Royal, Bridges Street: A Conjectural Restoration," *Educational Theatre Journal,* 19 (1967), 26. The *Survey of London* volumes are a mine of valuable and reliable information on old theatres.

25. If the *Survey of London* dimensions are close to correct, and I believe they are, the plan fits best with the measurements of the Hall Theatre. I once thought Plan 81 might have been for the Bridges Street Theatre of 1663; see my "Pictorial Material on the Bridges Street and Drury Lane Theatres," *Theatre Survey,* 8 (May 1966), 81–84. I am not so sure now. Donald Mullin (in the article cited in n. 24 above) suggests that Plan 81 may have been Wren's suggestion for the alteration of Bridges Street in 1666. Graham Barlow (cited in n. 6 above) suggests that the plan may have been for the 1674 Drury Lane.

at their peril, but since the public theatre of the English-speaking world of today was born in the late seventeenth century in London, trying to find the truth about our roots is a matter of considerable importance. We certainly know far more now than we did at the beginning of this century; with diligence and good fortune, perhaps by the end of it we will find the missing pieces of the puzzle.

Statistical Comparisons

No one seems to have tried to gather some of the vital statistics about the playhouses of the Restoration and eighteenth century, and for a few of them, at least, we have some actual or conjectural figures. Since I did not want to clutter the text, I have put such information into tabular form (see tables 3–6). Included are those playhouses about which we have sufficient information or educated guesses to make citation worth while, but for sake of comparison I have added a few about which we know very little. I wish I could vouch for the accuracy of the figures, but for many I cannot; too often my sources were vague about whether a measurement was for the interior or exterior of a building, or about what was meant by stage or auditorium depth. Information about theatre capacities is especially confusing, for such data can be arrived at by many routes, none of them entirely trustworthy. Since playgoers sat on benches, the capacity of a house could vary according to how closely people were willing to sit.[26] Sometimes I have had to give approximate figures based on averages of estimates from several sources. Sources are indicated with asterisks in the "Bibliography for 'The Theatres'" (at the back of the book); footnoting each individual figure would have made the charts incomprehensible. Stage depth is measured from stage front to the rear of the stage area. Auditorium depth is measured from stage front to the rear of front boxes. Figures in brackets are pure conjecture; an asterisk in these tables indicates the likeliest figure.

26. Harry William Pedicord provides many conjectures about theatre capacities in *The Theatrical Public in the Time of Garrick;* his system of computing them is questioned by Leo Hughes in *The Drama's Patrons,* p. 182. See n. 9 above.

3. Statistical comparisons

	Cockpit in Court	Cockpit in Drury Lane	Covent Garden		
	Turned into theatre by Inigo Jones in 1629–30; used 19 Nov. 1660 to end of 1664	Designed by Inigo Jones c. 1617; used Feb. 1660 to Oct. 1662	1. Designed by Edward Shepherd; cost £6,000; used 7 Dec. 1732 to 29 May 1782 (see Fig. 7)	2. Altered by John Inigo Richards; used 23 Sept. 1782 to 1 June 1792	3. Altered by Henry Holland; cost £25,000; used 17 Sept. 1792 to 20 Sept. 1808; burned
Exterior width	61'	42'	62'	62'	62'
Exterior depth	61'	c. 73'	117'	c. 180'	c. 180'
Interior width	58'	37'	56'	56'	56'
Interior depth	58'	c. 53' excluding stairs	112'	c. 172'	c. 172'
Stage depth	c. 26'	25'	c. 55'	c. 93'	90'
Auditorium depth	c. 25'	25'	40'	c. 55'	54'-6"
Forestage depth	16'	c. 15'	12'	c. 16'	15'-6"
Proscenium width	25'-35' forestage width	23' forestage width	c. 25'	c. 30'	29'
Proscenium height	22' forestage height	21'-6" forestage height	c. 23'	20'	19'-7"
Capacity		c. 496	c. 1400	c. 1,500–2,200	c. 3,000
Notes	See reconstructions by Leacroft and Wickham	Jones's drawings 7B and 7C, Worcester College, identified by Mackintosh as for this theatre; confirmed by Orrell	Measurements from c. 1774 plans See *Survey of London,* Vol. **XXXV**, and reconstructions by Leacroft		Altered in 1793 1794, and 1803

4. Statistical Comparisons

	Dorset Garden	Drury Lane			
	Designed by Robert Hooke(?); cost £9,000; used 9 Nov. 1671 to June 1709; demolished (see Fig. 3)	1. (Bridges Street) Designed by John Webb(?) or Richard Rider (?); cost £2,400(?); used 7 May 1663 to 25 Jan. 1672; burned	2. Designed by Christopher Wren; cost c. £4,000; used 26 Mar. 1674 to 27 May 1775 (see Fig. 4)	3. Altered by Robert Adam; cost c. £4,100; used 23 Sept. 1775 to 4 June 1791; demolished (see Fig. 8)	4. Designed by Henry Holland; cost c. £151,000; used 12 Mar. 1794 to 24 Feb. 1809; burned (see Figs. 5, 9)
Exterior width	57'		[58'-59']	58'-59'	86'
Exterior depth	c. 148'	100-102'(?)	114' Wren section	194'	204'
Interior width	[53']		[52'-6"]	53'-6"	80'
Interior depth	[143'-6"]		108'-6" Wren section	c. 189'	198'
Stage depth	[51']		66'-6" Wren section	c. 130'	92'
Auditorium depth	[61'-6"]		32'-6" Wren section	c. 51'	74'
Forestage depth	[19'-6"]		21' Wren section	11'	c. 15'
Proscenium width	[30'-6"]		[31'-6"]	c. 28'	43'
Proscenium height	[18'-6"]		16'-9" Wren section	21'-6"	38'
Capacity	c. 1200	c. 700	c. 500*-1,000; c. 1,800*-2,300+ by 1762	c. 1,300-2,300	3,611
Notes	Inside figures are from reconstruction by Langhans; see also reconstruction by Spring	Altered in 1666; see conjectures by Mullin	Altered in 1696, 1747, and 1762; see conjectures by Langhans, Barlow, and Mullin-Koenig	Altered in 1783 and 1787	Altered in 1797 and 1806
			See *Survey of London,* Vol. XXXV, and reconstructions by Leacroft		

5. Statistical Comparisons

	Goodman's Fields		Hall Theatre at Court	Haymarket	James Street Tennis Court
	1. Converted from throwster's shop by Thomas Odell; used 31 Oct. 1729 to 23 May 1732; demolished	2. Designed by Edward Shepherd for Henry Giffard; cost £2,300+; used 2 Oct. 1732 to 27 May 1742 (see Fig. *11*)	Designed by John Webb(?); cost £737+; used Spring 1665 to Jan. 1698; burned (see Fig. *12*)	Built by John Potter; cost £1,500(?); used 29 Dec. 1720 to 1820 demolished	Used 26 Nov. 1713 to 1770
Exterior width		c. 52'	45'	48'(?)	40'
Exterior depth		c. 90' (or 88'?)	100' with passageway	136'(?)	60'
Interior width		c. 47'	c. 39'-6"		
Interior depth		c. 87' (or 83'?)	c. 87'		
Stage depth		50'	32-33'		
Auditorium depth		c. 32'	43'		
Forestage depth		4'-6" (9' to 1st wings)	0'(?)		
Proscenium width		23'	25'		
Proscenium height			23'		
Capacity	c. 700 (?)	c. 750(?)		c. 800; c. 1,500 about 1790	
Notes	These theatres were on the same site in Ayliffe Street	One gallery	See *Survey of London,* Vol. XXXV, Boswell, and Leacroft; Wren Plan 81 may be for Hall Theatre not Bridges Street or Drury Lane	Altered in 1744, 1766, 1777, and 1782	Variously called Fawkes', Punch's, Lilliputian, Old Theatrical Showshop

6. Statistical Comparisons

	Lincoln's Inn Fields			Queen's/King's			Vere Street
	1. Originally Lisle's Tennis Court; converted by John Webb(?); used June 1661 to Mar. 1674 (see Fig. 2)	2. Used 30 Apr. 1695 to 20 Oct. 1705	3. Designed by Edward(?) Shepherd; used 18 Dec. 1714 to 11 Dec. 1744	1. Designed by John Vanbrugh; cost £3,000+; used 9 Apr. 1705 to 29 July 1782 (see Fig. 6)	2. Altered by Michael Novosielski; used 2 Nov. 1782 to 17 June 1789; burned	3. Designed by Michael Novosielski; cost £73,000(?); used 21 Feb. 1791 to 1867; burned	Originally Gibbons's Tennis Court; used 8 Nov. 1660 to May 1663; used as Nursery Apr. 1669 to May 1671 (see Fig. 1)
Exterior width	c. 30'		56'	60'	62'	c. 91'(?)	[c. 25'?]
Exterior depth	75'		100'	130'	135'	c. 169'(?)	[c. 70'?]
Interior width	[c. 29']			56'	53'	c. 85'(?)	[24'?]
Interior depth	[c. 74']			106'	130'	c. 163'(?)	[69'?]
Stage depth	[34' (or 31'?)]			60' later 90'	80'	45' later 60'	[22']
Auditorium depth	[c. 37']			46'	60'	66'	[33'-6"]
Forestage depth	[7'-6" (or 9'?)]			13'	c. 12'	15'	[15']
Proscenium width	[20']			38'	c. 25' (or 34'?)	45'-5" (or 37'?)	[14'] forestage width

64

Proscenium height	[13'-6"]			c. 27'		34'	[17'] forestage height
Capacity	[352 (or c. 570?)]		c. 1400 maximum	c. 700–950; 2,000 by 1735		over 3,000	c. 418 (or 500–600?)
Notes	Returned to tennis court use between 1674 and 1695; see reconstructions by Scanlan, Langhans	Probably very similar to 1; had one gallery	Redecorated in 1723 and 1725; possibly altered in 1733; measurements from 1806 plan	Altered c. 1708, 1719, 1766, and 1778; figures above date 1764; see reconstructions by Leacroft, Mullin		Altered in 1794, 1796 1799, and later	Figures are for un-published reconstruction by Langhans

See *Survey of London*, Vol. XXIX, and Macomber

3
Scenery and Technical Design

COLIN VISSER

PLAYWRIGHTS in the Restoration and eighteenth century promoted their plays by finding literary and critical precedents for decisions that were more often inspired by practical considerations. Plays were intended for the stage, not the closet; they were composed not in retirement but in the intimate and self-absorbed world of the theatre.

Plays might ostensibly conform to some critical precept, but in fact they more often imitated the latest success at the rival playhouse. The descent of Amariel in Dryden's *Tyrannick Love,* for instance, followed immediately upon the descent of Nell Gwynn, piquantly cast as an angel, in *The Virgin Martyr.* Dramatists wrote for specific actors and actresses: When Betterton and his associates left the United Company in 1695, Congreve sent *Love for Love* with them because the parts could not be so well taken by others. Plays were written to exploit the technical resources of the theatre for which they were designed; they might even contain scenes written to take advantage of a particular setting or stage machine.

The physical disposition of the stage, in turn, fostered theatrical conventions. The proscenium walls with their doors and balconies dictated a range of dramatic possibilities; wings and shutters generated their own conventions; certain kinds of discovery became habitual; precedents were established for the use of traps and machines. Often these conventions were passed down from pre-

Restoration theatres, which the Restoration playhouses in many ways resembled. The most accomplished playwrights were those who best exploited these conventions.

Information on the physical features of the stage is difficult to come by. Contemporary engravings falsify for the sake of the visual impression; descriptions are usually of the auditorium, not of the stage or its resources. Promptbooks are helpful, although often difficult to assign to specific productions. The main body of evidence is to be found in the plays themselves.

The plays are often thought to be a questionable source of information, and it is true that playwrights did not always get what they asked for. But it is also true that they rarely asked for what they could not get. Stage directions, used cautiously, can tell us a good deal about the physical characteristics of the stage.

The theatre is a conservative institution. Actors and playwrights cling to conventions, and innovations are recognized as such only in relation to tradition. Garrick was original only in comparison with Quin; Mrs Siddons achieved greatness as Lady Macbeth in opposition to Mrs Pritchard. In describing the evolution of scenery and technical design in the theatre we may speak of innovations, but not of complete breaks with the past; the process is one of continuous development.

The most influential theatre of the entire period is the one that Davenant created in 1661, in the converted tennis court at Lincoln's Inn Fields. It combined features of the public and private playhouses of the years just before the war with elements of the masquing stage of Inigo Jones; to the platform stage, doors, and upper acting levels of the one it added the scenic arrangements of the other. The continuity of forms entailed a continuity of conventions.

Over the next 150 years the main lines of development are clear. The action moved from the forestage to the scenic area behind the proscenium. Lighting was increased in the scenic area, the proscenium doors that led onto the forestage were reduced in number, and eventually the doors and the forestage itself were eliminated. The withdrawal behind the proscenium coincided with a greater interest in the stage picture and a demand for more elaborate set scenes. These required in turn to be set up or struck behind a curtain. The scene painter or designer ceased to be a nameless craftsman, his name on the bills assuring him personal recognition. What follows is a systematic survey of the technical resources— both physical and scenic—of the Restoration theatre as they evolved in this period.

I The Forestage, and the Walls, Doors, and Balconies of the Proscenium

Sir William Davenant's playhouse at Lincoln's Inn Fields combined a stage designed to show perspective scenery with a forestage that projected beyond the proscenium opening into the pit. It joined the picture stage that Inigo Jones had developed for the masques of the Jacobean and Caroline court with the platform stage of the public and private playhouses. In bringing about this union, Davenant set the form of the English theatre for the next hundred and fifty years.

At first most of the acting took place on the forestage, which at the 1674 Theatre Royal, Drury Lane, projected about twenty feet into the pit. The need was not yet felt to set the actor within the scene. The scenery behind the proscenium opening was merely a decorative background; it might not even pretend to show the place in which the action was supposed to occur.

From his position on the forestage the actor projected his voice without difficulty into the auditorium, and his least gesture made its effect. Colley Cibber spoke with nostalgia of the forestage at Drury Lane before Rich's alterations of 1696 had reduced it in size: "But when the Actors were in Possession of that forwarder Space to advance upon, the Voice was then more in the Centre of the House, so that the most distant Ear had scarce the least Doubt or Difficulty in hearing what fell from the weakest Utterance. . . . Nor was the minutest Motion of a Feature (properly changing with the Passion or Humour it suited) ever lost, as they frequently must be in the Obscurity of too great a Distance."[1]

1. *An Apology for the Life of Mr. Colley Cibber,* 2 vols., ed. Robert W. Lowe (London, John C. Nimmo, 1889), II, 85–86.

In the second part of *The Siege of Rhodes,* which was first acted at Lincoln's Inn Fields in June 1661, there is in the first scene, *"A Shout within, and a Noise of forcing of Doors."* Shortly after Ianthe and her two women enter "at the other Door" (1663; I. i. 6, 8).[2] There are no references to doors in the first part of Davenant's opera, acted at Rutland House in 1656, and transferred two years later to the Cockpit or Phoenix in Drury Lane. When he built the new stage for his converted tennis court, Davenant incorporated into it the doors that had characterized the earlier public and private playhouses. These doors were now set in the walls that flanked the proscenium opening. There were at least four of them, two in each opposing wall.[3] In Etherege's comedy, *She wou'd if she cou'd* (LIF 1668), *"The Women go out, and go about behind the Scenes to the other Door,"* they reenter, *"and after 'em* Courtal *at the Lower Door, and* Free[man] *at the upper on the contrary side"* (II.i.17). The doors were surmounted by balconies that could be used by actors or spectators.

Two plays by Dryden show how the doors and balconies in the proscenium wall were exploited. In *The Conquest of Granada,* Part II (Bridges St., 1671) Almanzor hesitates between two doors in the proscenium wall. One of them leads to Almahide's apartment. "I grow impatient," he says, "this, or that's the room." Later he *"goes to the door* [where] *the Ghost of his Mother meets him, he starts back: the Ghost stands in the door."* He then *"Goes to the other door, and is met again by the Ghost."* Zulema and Hamet now assault the Queen, who runs *"schrieking"* across the stage to the opposing doors. Abdelmelech tries unsuccessfully to help her; *"he goes off at one door, while the Queen escapes at the other"* (1672; IV. 129–36). The scene supposes four proscenium doors, two in each opposing proscenium wall.

2. The title of the play is followed by the name of the theatre in which it was first acted, and the date of the first performance. Quotations are followed by the date of the edition (when the date differs from that of the first performance), act, scene, and page, or act and page.

3. At the theatre which John Rich opened in 1714 on the site of Davenant's old theatre in Lincoln's Inn Fields, there were, apparently, three pairs of proscenium doors. Manuscript promptbooks prepared for Rich's theatre refer to three doors on each side. See Edward A. Langhans, "Three Early Eighteenth-Century Manuscript Promptbooks," *Modern Philology,* 65 (1967), 114–29. Not all the doors were necessarily set in the proscenium walls, however. One pair of doors might have consisted of opposing wings or set pieces placed behind the proscenium opening.

The doors and their surmounting balconies figure again in the Dryden-Newcastle collaboration, *Sir Martin Mar-all* (LIF, 1667). Warner, the ingenious servant, devises a way in which Sir Martin can impress Millisent. He tells him to "get up into your Window . . . in the mean time, I'll play in the next Room in the dark, and consequently your Mistress, who will come to her Balcone over against you, will think it be you." Millisent and Rose enter *"with a Candle by 'em above,"* while Sir Martin *"appears at the adverse Window"* (1668; V. 53–54).

The proscenium walls were no mere appendages, nor did doors and balconies serve only as entrances onto or exits from the stage; they had a scenic function as well. The walls, in conjunction with the wings and back shutters or a drop scene, could represent the exterior of a house or houses. The proscenium walls could also represent an interior. They could even represent an interior while an exterior was simultaneously shown on the wings and back shutters.

Characters might pass through the proscenium doors as from the outside to the inside of a house and vice versa. They might pretend to enter a house by leaving the stage through a proscenium door and immediately reenter through the same or the adjacent door or from the wings: The proscenium wall and/or stage would now represent an interior. In Centlivre's *The Platonic Lady* (Haymarket, 1706), III.i shows "the outside of *Lucinda's* House." Isabella is told to enter by the footman, and the next direction reads, *"Re-enter* Isabella *and* Shread *as into the House"* (1707; pp. 37–38).

These conventions had evolved in the earlier public and private playhouses. There, too, the tiring-house wall could represent the interior or the exterior of a house. Characters could exit by going into the house through one door and immediately reemerge through the same or another door; they would now be inside the house they had just entered. The area above had served the same purpose as the balconies above the doors on the Restoration stage. Killigrew's *The Princess* is a link between the earlier and the later theatres. It was first acted by the King's Company at the Blackfriar's, revived at Vere Street in 1661, and first published in the Folio of 1664. Here in IV.v Facertes appears outside Paulina's house. He remarks, "hereabout should be the door," and leaves the stage. Immediately Paulina and Cicilia enter and we are now in Paulina's house. Shortly after *"One knocks"* and Facertes enters the house (pp. 37–38). The continuity of these conventions was assured by the incorporation into the Restoration stage of the walls (equivalent to the tiring-house wall) and the doors of the earlier playhouses.[4]

A complex use of the opposing proscenium doors and balconies was devised at Lincoln's Inn Fields in Davenant's production there in January 1663 of Tuke's "Spanish" comedy, *The Adventures of Five Hours*. Here the opposing proscenium walls represent the exteriors or the interiors of opposing houses. When the wall represents an exterior, the lower door is the front street entrance into the house, and the upper door leads from the street into the garden. When the wall is an interior, the lower door opens from the house into the street, and the upper door leads into an inner room or apartment, which, in turn, has an entrance into the garden. The balconies look onto the street or, when the garden is shown behind the proscenium, onto the garden, in which case the proscenium wall is now the garden façade of the house.[5]

By the mid-eighteenth century the conventional use of proscenium walls to represent the exterior or interior of houses had declined. Houses were now shown behind the proscenium opening on a side scene, or on a pair of back shutters, or as a practicable set piece.

The proscenium doors and balconies and the forestage itself became obsolete as the actors retreated behind the curtain line. The doors were suppressed or converted into stage boxes. Entrance doors were moved behind the proscenium. Cibber gives precise details of one phase in this change. He says of the Drury Lane stage that before 1696, "It must be observ'd, then, that the Area or Platform of the old Stage projected about four Foot forwarder, in a

4. The importance of the plays of Thomas Killigrew as a link between the pre-Restoration and the Restoration stage is discussed in Colin Visser, "The Killigrew Folio: Private Playhouses and the Restoration Stage," *Theatre Survey*, 19 (1978), 119–38.
5. For a detailed account of the staging of this play see Colin Visser, "The Anatomy of the Early Restoration Stage: *The Adventures of Five Hours* and John Dryden's 'Spanish' Comedies," *Theatre Notebook*, 29 (1975), 56–69, 114–19.

Semi-oval Figure, parallel to the Benches of the Pit; and that the former lower Doors of Entrance for the Actors were brought down between the two foremost (and then only) Pilasters; in the Place of which Doors now the two Stage-Boxes are fixt. That where the Doors of Entrance now are, there formerly stood two additional Side-Wings, in front to a full Set of Scenes, which then had almost a double Effect in their Loftiness and Magnificence."[6] When Cibber wrote, the downstage doors at Drury Lane had been converted into stage boxes and doors had been set behind the proscenium.

By 1826 stage doors had almost entirely disappeared from the London theatres. In that year Charles Dibdin wrote that "Stage doors are wholly dispensed with."[7] The disappearance of the doors entailed the disappearance of the forestage. Even before the eighteenth century had concluded, George Saunders had remarked on the increasing reluctance of actors to turn the forestage to account. "Most performers," he observed, "will not be at the trouble of advancing even when the best of opportunities offer." He recommended, therefore, that in the future "the stage front . . . should be straight, and project no more before the scene than does the frontispiece." The actor, he concluded, "will appear (as he certainly should do) among the scenery."[8]

II Wings, Shutters, and Borders

Behind the proscenium opening at Lincoln's Inn Fields Davenant placed his perspective scenes in an arrangement that may be inferred from Webb's designs for *The Siege of Rhodes* at Rutland House. These show a frontispiece and six wings: three on each side of the stage, fixed one behind the other, parallel to the curtain line, and converging on a group of shutters that close off the stage midway between the frontispiece and the back wall of the theatre. The wings, to enhance the perspective effect, decrease in height as they approach the back shutters. The stage is raked, rising from the

6. Lowe, II, 84–85.
7. *History and Illustrations of the London Theatres* (London: Proprietors of the "Illustrations of London Buildings," 1826), p. 29.
8. *A Treastise of Theatres* (London: n.p., 1790), pp. 37, 86.

forestage to the back shutters, and then leveling off. Possibly the number of wings was increased at Lincoln's Inn Fields where Davenant had more space than had been available to him earlier. It seems likely that whereas at Rutland House the wings were fixed to posts set into the floor, at Lincoln's Inn Fields they could be changed to match the back shutters and ran in grooves on the stage, supported in matching grooves suspended from the flies. The fly space was masked by borders suspended from wing to wing.

The stage picture in *The Siege of Rhodes* could be terminated by the shutters, pushed on from the sides to meet in the middle and close off the stage. Several shutters were grouped together, and the scene could be changed by drawing off one pair of shutters to reveal another in position behind them or by pushing a pair of shutters together in front of a pair already in place. These shutters could be cut to reveal scenes placed in the area behind them, constituting a scene on several planes or a scene in relieve.

Behind the shutters lay the discovery area, closely related to the discovery area in the earlier private and public playhouses. Here scenes and characters could be revealed. In *The Siege of Rhodes,* Part II, *"The Scene is Chang'd.* Being wholly fill'd with *Roxalana*'s Rich Pavilion, Wherein is discern'd at distance, *Ianthe* sleeping on a Couch" (1663; IV.37). The shutters and the area behind them constitute on the Restoration stage the "scene," to be distinguished from the "stage," which extended from the shutters to the outer edge of the platform. This distinction dates to the pre-Restoration period, for in the 1652 edition of Brome's *A Jovial Crew* (1641), Springlove *"opens the Scene; the* Beggars *are discovered in their postures; then they issue forth"* (I.c₃ᵛ).

The frequent demand for two successive discoveries implies that possibly at Lincoln's Inn Fields, and certainly in later theatres, the shutters were grouped in at least two sets, the one sufficiently downstage from the other to allow a discovery to be effected, not only behind the upstage shutters, but also between them and the shutters placed further downstage.

In plays written between 1660 and 1700 when characters are discovered they are consistently instructed to come forward. The scene might then close behind them as it does in *The Female Prelate*

(DL, 1680). In I.ii of Settle's play the scene is the Vatican. Guards are instructed to thrust Saxony out "and shut our Gates against him." The scene *"shuts upon him* [i.e., behind him], *and the Consistory closes."* Saxony is left onstage and only later exits (p. 19). Or a character might exit by having the shutters close on him. In Dryden's *The Rival Ladies* (Bridges St., 1664) Act V is set on board ship. After a short conversation with a pirate the Captain remarks, *"Don Rod'ricks* Door opens, I'll speak to him." *"The Scene draws, and discovers the* Captains *Cabin:* Rodorick *on a Bed, and two* Servants *by him."* Rodorick is carried onto the stage in his bed, for he says at the end of the scene, "Draw in the Bed, I feel the cold." The direction follows "*[Bed drawn in,* Exeunt" (pp. 55–57). He is taken into the scene and the shutters are drawn in on him. These directions suggest that in the earlier theatres at least the shutters were placed well upstage.

By the middle of the eighteenth century, however, shutters could be run on behind any wing position. The sets of wings and shutters were numbered from the footlights up, as were the positions or cuts occupied by the wings or shutters in the set. In Garrick's promptbook of Vanbrugh's *The Provoked Wife* (originally at LIF, 1697), for instance, the sequence of scenes runs: "I. Ch Ch/2d gr; Pic + Chr/Toilet/3gr; II. Old Pal/4 Gr; P Cher/Table [3rd gr?]; III. Pal 4/ 2gr; . . . Act IV/Ch Ch 1gr; Wood/4gr," etc.,[9] which indicates that shutters are run on, or perhaps scenes dropped, at the first four wing positions.

The back scene could be composed not only of a single pair of shutters standing in grooves on the stage or running in tracks under it but also of a second pair suspended above the first. These composite "great" shutters, used in conjunction with arched borders, almost doubled the height of the scenes.[10] The upper shutters could open independently of the lower to reveal a scene in the "heavens." In Dryden's *Albion and Albanius* (DG, 1685) for instance, *"The farther part of the Heaven opens and discovers a Machine; as it moves*

9. (Dublin, 1743), Folger Prompt P 42.

10. It is perhaps to an arrangement of this kind that the *Post Boy* of 12–15 June 1697 refers when it says of a performance of Settle's *The World in the Moon* at Dorset Garden that the scenes include "several new Sets and of a moddel different from all that have been used in any Theatre whatever, being twice as high as any of their former Scenes."

forwards the Clouds which are before it divide, and shew the Person of Apollo" (II.18), an effect perhaps achieved by making the discovery behind the upper shutters.

The wings and shutters on the English stage are usually thought always to have run in grooves placed on the stage parallel to the front edge of the platform. It seems, however, that by the mid-eighteenth century oblique wings were commonplace. Aaron Hill speaks of them in a letter written to Garrick in 1749, about the staging of the last act of *Merope*,[11] and in Bate's forepiece, *The Dramatic Puffers* (CG, 1782), the puffer, Zephyr, says to the author whose work he is promoting, "I have sketch'd something in the oblique way, which I conceive however will have a fine effect." The author replies, "I understand you; in the *side wing* way . . . well gentlemen, I'm indifferent whether the scene be a *flat,* or an *oblique* one, provided its effect be strikingly convey'd to the galleries" (pp. 13–14).

The use of oblique wings suggests that in some theatres at least the Continental system obtained of running carriages under the stage to which were fixed wings, which were carried through slots in the stage floor. This allowed a variety of wings to be used and set at various angles. Figure *13* shows possible wings, borders, and wing positions. Downstage is a carriage and simple wing and behind it is a profiled wing. The third is an oblique wing, and the fourth and fifth are booked wings.

When the wings ran in grooves on the stage they were pushed on and off by sceneshifters. In those theatres in which the Continental system obtained they were moved by a machine under the stage, which simultaneously drew off one set of wings and brought on another. The mechanical principle is illustrated by Jacopo Fabris's drawings for the Danish theatre executed in 1760, which provide the basis for Figures *14* and *15*. Figure *14* shows four carriages, each with two wheels running on a track under the stage. A rope is

11. "The chief *difficulty* will be found your *painter's;* For, considering, how crowded a confusion, has, before, been represented to the *audience,* in the speech of *Euricles,* 'twill call for all the *pencil's* art, to fill the temple (through side openings, seen twixt columns, standing separate from the slanted scenes, which are to be set back as far as possible with such significantly busied groupes of interested people, as were spoken of in the description." *Works of the Late Aaron Hill,* 4 vols. (London: n.p., 1753), II, 376–77.

13. Wings, borders, and wing positions. Drawing by Ken Forsyth

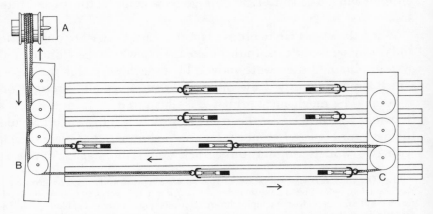

14. The operation of wing carriages. Drawing adapted from Jacopo Fabris, *Instruction in der Teatralischen Architectur* (1760), by Ken Forsyth

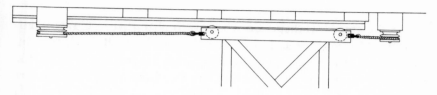

15. Sectional view of a wing carriage. Drawing by Ken Forsyth

wound around a windlass (A), and one end passing over a pulley (B) is attached to the first carriage. A second rope is attached to the opposite end of the first carriage, and passing around a pulley (C) is attached to the second carriage. The second carriage in turn is attached to the other end of the rope wound around the windlass. When the windlass is revolved in a clockwise direction the first carriage is pulled on while the second carriage is simultaneously drawn off. When the revolution is anticlockwise the movement is reversed. The second carriage can be disconnected and the first carriage attached to the third, and the third to the windlass; or the first can be disconnected and the second attached to the third or the fourth and so on. Figure *15* gives a sectional view of the second carriage. It shows the carriage running on a track, drawn by ropes running over pulleys and attached to each end of the carriage.

Evidence exists that as early as 1673 scenes on the English stage were moved by machines: A proclamation of that year refers to "those vast Engines (which move the Scenes and Machines),"[12] an innovation possibly first introduced at Dorset Garden. Evidence for a similar arrangement at Drury Lane in 1714 is contained in an account for February 1713/4, which records the following purchases:

For 6 pounds of new Rope for the Scen[e]/frames in the celer att 8 p pound - -	£ s d
	0 4 - 0[13]

Some of the confusion that exists about the rival systems of scene-changing—scenes moved in grooves on the stage or by machines

12. Public Record Office LC 7/3.
13. Folger MS Wb 110.

under the stage—is dispelled when we realize that in Covent Garden in 1744, and possibly in other theatres as well, both systems were used. Both grooves and machines are referred to in the inventory of scenes and properties in the Covent Garden theatre drawn up in 1744 for John Rich.[14] The carriages were used only for wings, while the grooves accommodated the shutters. This interpretation is supported by the essay on dramatic machinery in Rees's *Cyclopedia* published in London in 1819. The shutters or "flats" at "the Late Theatre Royal, Covent Garden" (i.e., the pre-1808 theatre) were, we are told, "moved in grooves, composed of parallel pieces of wood fixed upon the stage, and so constructed that they may be removed with facility from one place to another. The upper part of the framing is also confined by a groove, to retain the perpendicular position of the flat scene."[15] The grooves were simply pegged down where they were needed. When they were no longer necessary they could be moved out of the way of the players or dancers.

While the shutters run in grooves on the stage, the wings are moved by a machine under the stage that works on the principles illustrated by Fabris. An engraving of the wing machinery (Figure *16*) at the pre-1808 Covent Garden Theatre, shows four frames (BB, CC). Each frame, we are told by Rees, "runs upon two small wheels, to diminish the friction, and all passing through longitudinal apertures in the stage, which serve as guides, rise to a sufficient height above the stage to support the wings which are attached to them in front, so as to be quickly removed, and others substi-

14. The inventory has been transcribed and printed by Philip H. Highfill, Jr, in *Restoration and Eighteenth Century Theatre Research*, 5 (May 1966), 7–17; 5 (November 1966), 12–26; 6 (May 1967), 28–35. All references are to the May 1967 issue. The inventory lists in the "first flies," "12 top grooves with 6 iron braces and ropes" (p. 29). These are, presumably, six pairs of grooves or sets of grooves suspended from the flies to support six pairs of wings or shutters. In addition there are listed as "on the stage," "30 bottom grooves of different sizes" (p. 31). In the cellar under the stage we find "the scene barrel fixt with cog wheels etc. 12 pr. of scene ladders fixed with ropes" (p. 31), while on the stage are listed "24 blinds to scene ladders 192 tinn candlesticks to do" (p. 31). These last one assumes are the frames to attach to the twelve pairs of scene ladders. Each "blind" is backed by a strip of eight candles to throw light on the scene behind it.

15. "Dramatic Machinery," *The Cyclopedia; or, Universal Dictionary of Arts, Sciences, and Literature*, 39 vols., ed. A. Rees (London: Longman, Hurst, Rees, Orme, and Brown, 1819), XII, n.p.

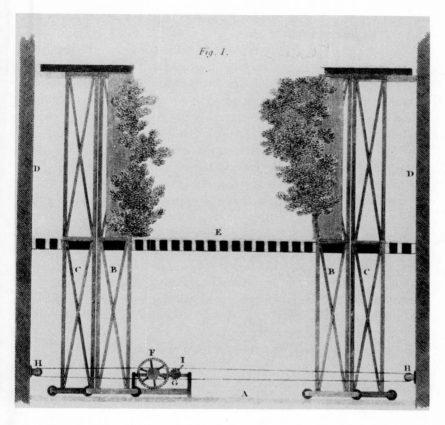

16. Wing machinery. Engraved by Wilson Lowry for *The Cyclopedia* (London, 1819)

tuted. . . . At F is a long cylinder, or barrel of wood, revolving upon iron axles, and extending from the front to nearly the back of the stage, so as to move all the wings at once. It will appear, by inspecting the plate, that the cords, or endless lines, passing from pulley H back to the same frame, are so disposed that when the upper part of the barrel is moved towards the right, the front frames B,B will move forward upon the stage, and the back frames C,C will be withdrawn. . . . When the motion of the barrel is reversed, that

79

of the frames will also be inverted; the back frames will advance, and the front ones will recede."

The *Siege of Rhodes* designs show that the scenes in the discovery area did not at first run in grooves, but had to be placed in position behind closed shutters which drew to reveal them. As the discovery area in later theatres was extended downstage, and as discoveries could finally be effected behind any wing position, the discovered scene could be composed, like any other, of wings, borders, and shutters. It remained, of course, a discovered scene, and therefore more amenable to set pieces and large properties than the scene that changed in the sight of the audience.

The possibility of making discoveries both determines and articulates various theatrical conventions, and these can often be traced back to similar conventional discoveries on the pre-Restoration stage. The shutters opened to reveal scenes of horror, death, and torture: Victims were shown being broken on the wheel, roasted over fires, or thrown down on the gaunches. Prisons were revealed in which the captives were allowed sufficient length of chain to wander beyond the restricted discovery space. Hells or Heavens were shown, and tombs and vaults.

Tombs made a striking appearance in revivals of *Romeo and Juliet* and in Otway's *Caius Marius* (DG, 1679). In V.ii of Otway's play the shutters show a churchyard; then the *"Scene draws off, and shews the Temple and Monument"* (1680; p. 61). Marius discovers Lavinia when he *"Pulls down the side of the Tomb"* (p. 62). In *Romeo and Juliet* published "As it is Performed at the Theatre Royal in Drury Lane" in 1763, V.iv is similarly *"A Church yard: In it, a Monument belonging to the Capulets"* (p. 65). Romeo enters and *"breaking open the monument . . . Brings her* [Juliet] *from the tomb"* (p. 68).

James Boaden in his *Memoirs of Mrs Siddons* remarks caustically how in this scene "our stage Romeo batters a couple of doors fiercely with the crow in his grasp, which very naturally fly open outwards."[16] The moment is parodied in an engraving by Cruikshank and Woodward published in 1797 (Figure *17*). A provincial Romeo grasping his crowbar discovers Juliet in a compromising

---

16. (London: Henry Colburn, 1827), 2 vols., II, 283.

17. *An Itinerant Theatrical Sketch.* Woodward del., Cruikshank sculp. Published Allen and Co., 1797. Courtesy of the Harvard Theatre Collection

situation. Above her is the sign "Tihs [*sic*] is the Monument of the Capulets."[17]

Often a temple exterior was shown, which opened to reveal an altar around which was staged an elaborate ceremonial. Dryden and Howard started the fashion with *The Indian Queen* (Bridges St., 1664), and it was still effective in Sheridan's *Pizarro* (DL, 1799), well over a hundred years later. The altar was likely spontaneously to ignite or extinguish itself, to be struck by lightning, or sink into the ground. The back shutters could open onto or discover a cave or

17. Michael Edkins, painting for the theatre in Bristol in the eighteenth century, records in his ledger this entry for 29 July 1768, "To Painting and Writ[ing]/Large Roman Capitals on /Juliets Monument: 0-2-6." See Kathleen Barker, "Michael Edkins, Painter," *Theatre Notebook,* 16 (1961–62), 43.

18. Mrs Siddons in *The Grecian Daughter.* Engraved for the *Lady's Magazine.* Published G. Robinson, 1783. Courtesy of the Harvard Theatre Collection

grotto: Mrs Siddons stands before one with a neatly fitted door in an engraving from Murphy's *The Grecian Daughter* (DL, 1772), executed for *The Lady's Magazine* in 1783 (Figure 18). Seas were revealed, and so were arbours and bed chambers. Low shutters represented a garden wall, which opened to reveal a garden, or represented the wall of a city, which was subsequently exposed to view. Once created, these discoveries became part of the vocabulary of the theatre.

The space behind the back shutters could be extended to the back wall of the theatre beyond the scenic area itself, and even on occasion into the street beyond. This facilitated the creation of especially deep or "long," as opposed to shallow or "short," scenes. In "long" scenes it seems that wings or groundrows were placed in a converging perspective to the back wall of the theatre. This may first have been used at Dorset Garden where it appears in Shadwell's version of the Davenant-Dryden adaptation of *The Tempest* (DG, 1674). Act I, Scene ii, describes *"the habitation of* Prospero," which is *"Compos'd of three Walks of Cypress-trees, each Side-walk leads to a Cave . . . The Middle-Walk is of a great depth, and leads to an open part of the Island"* (1676; p. 5). Later the "long" scene was a speciality of the Opera in the Haymarket where it was used, for instance, in Granville's *The British Enchanters* (1706), in which in I.i "Urganda *retires down the Scene . . . 'till out of sight"* (p. 5). In II.i characters are again instructed to *"walk down the Scene into the Forest, following the Musick, which seems to play at more and more Distance 'till out of hearing"* (p. 14).[18] At Drury Lane in September 1761, during a performance of *Henry VIII,* "The stage was . . . opened into Drury Lane; and a new and unexpected sight surprised the audience, of a real bonfire, and the populace huzzaing and drinking porter to the health of Queen Anne Bullen." The result, however, was disastrous, for, "During this idle piece of mockery, the actors, being exposed to the suffocations of smoke, and the raw air from the open

18. Not all "long" scenes, however, were composed of wings or groundrows extending to the back wall of the theatre. They might simply consist of a pair of shutters or a cloth with a scene in deep perspective painted on it. The inventory of scenes at the Theatre Royal, Crow Street, Dublin in 1776 lists a damaged item: "Long wood, a *hole* in it" (James Boaden, *Memoirs of the Life of John Philip Kemble,* 2 vols. [London: Longman, 1825], I, 472), which suggests that on this occasion at least the long scene was merely a drop.

street, were seized with colds, rheumatisms, and swelled faces."[19]

On the wings and shutters were painted not only scenes but also people; the early theatre did not object to the mingling of real and painted figures.[20] In I.i of Lee's *Theodosius* (DG, 1680), the wings or *"side Scenes shew the horrid Tortures with which the* Roman *Tyrants persecuted the Church; and the flat scene, which is the limit of the prospect, discovers an Altar richly adorn'd, before it* Constantine, *suppos'd kneels"* (p. 1). Even Constantine is here only in effigy. When in the second part of *The Conquest of Granada* (Bridges St., 1671) the Vivarambla place *"appears fil'd with Spectators"* (1672; V.141), they too were no doubt painted on the back shutters. "A little Skill in Criticism," Addison later objected in *The Spectator,* "would inform us, that Shadows and Realities ought not to be mix'd together in the same Piece" (No. 5, 6 March 1711).

A third element, the borders, masked the fly-space and completed the stage picture. The borders changed to match the wings and shutters but were restricted to basic types: sky, tree, and architectural borders, and arched borders used in conjunction with a tall or "great" back shutter. Examples of these borders are shown in Figure *13* above their matching wings. The borders could be worked by a machine which simultaneously raised one set of borders and lowered another. The Covent Garden inventory lists "6 borders and 6 pair of cloudings fixt to battins with barrels wts, and ropes" (p. 31). The "cloudings" were, it would seem, extensions to the sky borders, perhaps to disguise the unsightly junction of border and wing. The inventory also lists "a hook to draw off the cloudings" (p. 30), which suggests that the cloudings, unlike the borders, were drawn off to the sides.

III   Set Scenes and Pieces

So effective was the wing and shutter system that it dominated the English stage for a hundred years and more, a span that inevitably revealed its limitations. The convergence of wings on back shutter or drop, the predilection for a central vanishing point,

19. Thomas Davies, *Memoirs of the Life of David Garrick,* 2 vols., rev. ed. (London: Longman, et al., 1808), I, 365 ff.
20. We have already seen an example of this in Hill's letter to Garrick. See n. 11 above.

resulted in a fixity of design. The part of the stage behind the proscenium was ultimately inhospitable to the actor, who could not move up or down it without threatening the perspective effect.

The scene could be varied, however, by shifting the vanishing point to one side or the other of the stage, resulting in the *scena per angolo,* invented, perhaps, by Juvarra, and popularized by the Bibiena family. In England, John Devoto began experimenting with such scenes in the first decades of the eighteenth century.[21] A contemporary promptbook of Ayscough's *Semiramis* (DL, 1776) in the Folger Library refers to "Bibianis [Bibiena's?] Drop" (III.i.30) and "Bibianies Palace" (III.vi.38)—evidence, perhaps, of the use of the *scena per angolo.*[22]

The movement away from a central vanishing point encouraged the use of set scenes. These were composed of "pieces" as well as of wings, drops, or shutters. Pieces are defined in Rees's *Cyclopedia* as those scenes "which may be occasionally placed and displaced, such as the fronts of cottages, cascades, rocks, bridges, and other appendages." One might add to this rostrums or platforms, steps, ramps or inclined planes used instead of steps to lead to a rostrum, raking pieces or triangular pieces used to mask-in the sides of ramps, and a variety of groundrows. The last served to mask a row of lights placed on the stage or to mask a rise or a drop in the stage level. Scenes were set up in advance behind a shutter or drop and then revealed to the audience: For the charm of visible scene change was substituted the charm of discovery.

Pieces were used in relieve scenes and discovered scenes as early as *The Siege of Rhodes.* In the mid-eighteenth century the Covent Garden inventory lists as "Painted peices in the scene room": "Shakespeare's monument. Macbeth's cave. Oedipus tower." Pedestals appear in the inventory as well as boards for scaffolding, trestles, and steps. Groundrows include "6 ground peices to the trees in Orpheus . . . hedge stile and fence 4 peices . . . a ground peice in two parts . . . the water piece to bridge . . . a peice ground landskip" (p. 28).

21. See Sybil Rosenfeld, *A Short History of Scene Design in Great Britain* (Oxford: Blackwell, 1973), p. 70.
22. (London, 1776), Folger Prompt S 27.

De Loutherbourg elaborated the set scene at Drury Lane in the 1770s, and it became increasingly popular. As with the discovery scene, conventions were soon established, and certain set scenes recur in play after play. The practicable town wall or ramparts with gates is one of these. Besieging armies storm the gates, while the besieged appear on the walls; the town is taken, and the gates open to admit the conquering army. In Dryden and Lee's *Oedipus* (DG, 1678) the king appears *"above"* at the close of the play. To the noise of thunder he flings himself from a window and the Thebans gather about his body (1679; V.i.77–78). The anonymous commentator on Muralt's *Letters* (1726) adds some details that explain the nature of "Oedipus Tower," as it is called in the Covent Garden inventory: "The *Swiss* [Muralt] says nothing of that extraordinary Incident in this *English* Tragedy; where *Oedipus* appears at the Window, as having his Eyes put out, and then, as from a Tribunal, he makes a beautiful Harangue, which he concludes comically, by throwing himself out of the Window, and killing himself by that extravagant Fall: Nevertheless it is not the Actor that represents *Oedipus,* who throws himself out of the Window; but a Man of Pasteboard, made like him, which is thrown down: For had it been the Actor, he would really have killed himself. The People usually laugh very heartily, at so bold and heedless a Leap; Thus ends that fine Tragedy, whose catastrophe evidently shews, what kind of Brain the Author had."[23] Perhaps the same technique was used in Cibber's *Papal Tyranny* (CG, 1745) in which Arthur appears *"on the Walls of a Castle* (V.i.54). Later he *"leaps from the Walls, and is cover'd by a Parapet between his Body and the Audience"* (p. 55). When Salisbury passes he *"sees the Body of* Arthur *in the Ditch"* (p. 55). Here, clearly, a groundrow conceals the body.

Setting the scene behind a drop or shutters allows the stage to be built up in several levels. An example of this occurs in Starke's *The Widow of Malabar* (CG, 1791). Act III, Scene i, is described as *"A spacious Quadrangle, surrounded with Rocks—At the farther end, the Pagod of* Eswara*—a Funeral-Pile in the middle of the Quadrangle, with a Platform, leading from the steps of the Pagod to the top of the Pile"*

23. Béat Louis de Muralt, *Letters describing the character and customs of the English and French Nations,* 2nd ed. (London: T. Edlin, 1726), p. 20.

(p. 33). Later *"a grand Funeral Procession advances from the Pagod . . . and crossing the Platform, descends upon the Stage"* (III.ii.35). The platform could be mounted by stairs or a ramp. A common effect was to have a ramp or series of ramps concealed behind groundrows to represent the descent from a mountain. In Brooke's *The Siege of Sinope* (CG, 1781) V.i shows *"on the right Hand a Road over a Mountain, from whence* Pharnaces *descends with his Army"* (p. 55). So, too, in Colman's *Bluebeard* (DL, 1798) "ABOMELIQUE, *and a magnificent train, appear, at the top of the Mountain—They descend through a winding path:—sometimes they are lost to sight, to mark the irregularities of the road"* (I.i.6).

The setting by Thomas Greenwood the elder of the second act of Burgoyne's adaptation of Sedaine's *Richard Coeur de Lion* (DL, 1786) illustrates the complexities of the set scene, composed on several levels with practicable pieces. A contemporary engraving of the setting reveals the direction taken by scene design in the closing decades of the century (Figure 19). *"The Theatre,"* we are told, *"represents the inner Works of an old Fortification. Towards the Front is a Terrace inclosed by Rails and a Fosse; and so situated, that when* Richard *appears upon it, he cannot see* MATILDA, *who is upon the outer Parapet"* (II.i.23). This is the moment that is represented in the engraving. Later Richard *"walks to the farther end of the Terrace,"* Matilda and Antonio enter *"on the other side the Fosse and Parapet"* (II.i.24–25). Richard retires into the Castle while *"another party sieze* MATILDA, *and passing over a draw-bridge, bring her into the front of the works"* (II.i.28).

In a three-volume collection of stage designs in the Folger Library, Thomas Greenwood the younger has written opposite one of the drawings (Figure 20): "a Relic of the Old School/this Scene 2d act [of] Lodoiska/all practicable—very heavy/Set and always took (including striking/the 1st scene) 20 minutes. It was/very effective—painting by T. Malton/Luppino and Demaria."[24] *Lodoiska* was written by Kemble for the 1794 Theatre Royal, Drury Lane, and was designed to show its capabilities. The scene, we are told, *"represents Lodoiska's Tower, upon a high Terrace, within the castle"* (II.i.26). The movements of the characters on the various

24. *Drawings of Theatrical Scenery for J. Kemble* (1789), Folger Art, Vol. d 19–21.

19. Mr Kemble and Mrs Jordan in the characters of Richard and Matilda in *Richard Coeur de Lion*. Richardson sculp. Published A. Hogg, 1787. Courtesy of the Harvard Theatre Collection

levels of the set are complex. Lodoiska exits *"into the Tower,"* Floreski enters *"from an inner Court"* and exits *"through a vaulted Passage"* (p. 27). Varbel enters *"from a distant Casemate"* (p. 28), and Gustavus *"passes along the Terrace into Lodoiska's Tower"* while *"The Count and Varbel retire into a Recess under the Terrace"* (p. 29). Lodoiska enters from the tower, *"The Baron, hearing voices in the recess, sends Sebastian to take Lodoiska away, then leads his guard round through the vaulted passage, and, while Sebastian hurries the Princess into the Tower, surprises the Count and Varbel"* (p. 34). Finally *"Lodoiska and Sebastian come down from the Tower"* (p. 36).

These set scenes demonstrate a new attitude to the stage picture. Formerly the scene had been composed of wings and shutters and had served as a decorative background to the action. The scene was changed in sight of the audience, and this visible and magical transformation was part of the charm of the theatre. But the set scene was arranged behind a curtain or shutters and then discov-

20. The setting for Act II of Kemble's *Lodoiska*. Originally designed by Malton, Lupino, and Demaria. From a sketchbook by Thomas Greenwood the Younger. From the Art Collection of the Folger Shakespeare Library

ered. It invited the presence of the actor and required that he retreat behind the proscenium and define himself in relation to the scenery.

In the closing decades of the eighteenth century the stage picture increasingly drew attention to itself. This coincided with the rise to prominence of the scene painter. Whereas before the 1770s the scene painter was one of an anonymous team of craftsmen, now for the first time the scene painter's name begins to appear on the playbills and even in play texts. The logical final step would be for the scenes to supplant the play, and with the invention of de Loutherbourg's "Eidophysikon" this is precisely what happened. De Loutherbourg created a model theatre that presented to the public scenes unencumbered by actors or dialogue. This was one solution to the conflict between text and image, which has so often bedeviled the stage.

IV Curtains, Hangings, and Drops

Within the proscenium opening hung a curtain, traditionally green, which after the prologue drew up in shallow festoons.[25] Usually it was not lowered until the end of the play. There are instances, however, when it was lowered between the acts to prepare for a particularly spectacular change of scene.[26]

By the latter half of the eighteenth century it had become customary to drop a second curtain or act drop immediately behind the front curtain at the end of each act of the play. Richard Southern suggests that the act drop was first introduced by de Loutherbourg at Garrick's Drury Lane.[27] It might, however, have been used at Lincoln's Inn Fields as early as 1714. The *Public Advertiser* for 16 April 1789 records that at Covent Garden a few days before, "the drop curtain with the King's arms in it shown when the front curtain first rose was the original curtain exhibited at the opening of Lincoln's Inn Fields theatre [in 1714]. . . . It has lain by in the scene-room of Covent Garden theatre nearly seventy years, but was rescued from oblivion, retouched, and the appropriate ornaments added for the occasion."

Drops between scenes were introduced at the Haymarket in 1799 but were rejected by the public. The *Morning Chronicle* for 4 September 1799 observed that "this method of preparing for a new scene disjoints the business, and of course tends greatly to injure the effect." Not until the end of the nineteenth century did it become customary to lower a curtain or drop to hide every change of scene.

Many theatres employed a traverse, that is, a curtain that drew apart rather than up, directly in front of or immediately behind the

25. On occasion the prologue might be revealed. In Dryden and Howard's heroic play *The Indian Queen* (Bridges St., 1664), for instance, "As the Musick plays a soft Air, the Curtain rises softly, and discovers an *Indian* Boy and Girl sleeping under two Plantain-Trees . . ." ("Prologue," *The Indian Queen, Five New Plays,* 1692). They then wake and speak the prologue.

26. In IV.viii of Caryll's *The English Princess* (LIF, 1667), for instance, the direction reads, *"The Curtain is let down."* Catesby enters *"and* Ratclife *at one of the Doors before the Curtain."* Lovel then enters *"at the other Door before the Curtain"* (p. 47). At the beginning of the next scene, *"The Curtain is opened. The King appears in a distracted posture"* (p. 48), and at the end of the scene, *"The Curtain falls"* (p. 49).

27. *Changeable Scenery* (London: Faber and Faber, 1952), p. 168.

shutters that closed off the upstage discovery area. It derived from the hangings that had concealed the discovery area in the tiring-house wall of the Jacobean and early Caroline theatres. These curtains are employed in Lee's *Caesar Borgia* (DG, 1679) where in V.i the scene draws and shows Bellamira strangled. Her body is removed, Borgia and Machiavel are left, and the direction reads, "Draw here the Curtains on 'em" (1680; p. 59).

Two instances of the use of this back curtain can be found in plays by Dryden. In the final act of the Dryden-Lee collaboration *The Duke of Guise* (DL, 1682), the Duke is called for by the King and leaves the stage. The back shutters are drawn open and behind them is a traverse. In an ingenious double discovery, the Duke is murdered in front of the traverse, which is then drawn to reveal the King and his Council.

The second reference to a traverse occurs in a promptbook of Dryden's *Tyrannick Love* (Bridges St., 1669) prepared, it has been suggested, for the King's Company at Lincoln's Inn Fields, after the destruction by fire of the Bridges Street Theatre in 1672.[28] Here in IV.i the scene is "[An] *Indian Cave*" (1672; p. 29).[29] This has beside it the notation, "The bl[ack] Curten." The curtain might be a drop, in which case, unless the promptbook is much later than 1672, this is the earliest reference to a drop scene that I have been able to discover. It is far more likely that it is a traverse. In V.i the prompter notes "Drawe [i.e., close] *the* Curten *and* sett up *the* Wheele" (p. 48). A subsequent direction reads, *"The Scene opens, and shews the Wheel"* (p. 55). Here—and on many similar occasions—it seems that when a scene is described as opening or closing, a traverse is drawn. Perhaps it is a traverse of this kind that appears in Rich's Covent Garden inventory as "a red curtain fixt to battin lines *and* pulleys" (p. 29).

Curtains or hangings could be set up in the discovery area behind the traverse, drop curtain, or back shutters. In the second act of Behn's *The Emperor of the Moon* (DG, 1687) the scene changes to the

28. See Henry H. Adams, "A Prompt Copy of Dryden's *Tyrannic Love*," *Studies in Bibliography*, 4 (1951–52), 170–74. The copy is in the Folger Library: Folger Prompt, T 40.
29. The scene of the play is Aquileia in Italy. The reference to an Indian cave is startling until one realizes that the request is for the cave that had been used in the earlier production at Bridges Street of Dryden and Howard's *The Indian Queen* (1664).

inside of a house. *"The Front of the Scene"* (that is, immediately in front of the discovery area), we are told, *"is only a Curtain or Hangings to be drawn up at Pleasure"* (p. 25). Scaramouche then *"goes with all the Company behind the Front Curtain."* He places them all *"in the Hanging, in which they make the Figures, where they stand without Motion in Postures"* (p. 27). The curtain *"is drawn up, and discovers the Hangings where all of them stand"* (p. 28). The device was so successful that it appeared again in Betterton's adaptation of Fletcher and Massinger's *The Prophetess* (DG, 1690). Here III.i is *"a Room, Chairs in it, the Hangings and Figures Grotesk"* (p. 27). Later *"The Figures come out of the Hangings and Dance: And Figures exactly the same appear in their Places"* (p. 36).

The curtain that constitutes the front of the scene in Act II of *The Emperor of the Moon* might be a drop curtain or drop scene. These seem to have been introduced at Dorset Garden in the closing decades of the seventeenth century. Drop scenes are certainly employed in *The Prophetess* acted at Dorset Garden in 1690. Here in III.i *"A Curtain falls representing the entrance into the inner part of a Magnificent Palace"* (p. 31). In IV.i we find *"The Great Curtain"* (p. 43), which later *"rises and shews a stately Tomb"* (p. 46).[30]

Drop scenes could be dropped from the flies in any wing or shutter position. No English theatre built between 1660 and 1800 had sufficient height for the scenes to be flown; they had to be folded up on themselves, or more commonly run down from rollers. Figure 21 shows a typical drop mechanism: Two ropes pass over pulleys and are attached to opposite ends of the drop which can be rolled up or down. When a drop was run down in a downstage or forward position, scenes could be prepared behind it to be revealed later. The prompt in Sheridan's *The Critic* (DL, 1779) remarks that "the carpenters say, that unless there is some business put in here before the drop, they shan't have time to clear away the fort" (1781; II.i.78).

30. In 1716 *The Prophetess, or the History of Dioclesian* was in the repertory of John Rich's company at Lincoln's Inn Fields. In March 1718, Settle's opera *The Lady's Triumph* was performed at the same theatre. A contemporary MS of the play survives with numerous promptnotes which have been transcribed by Edward A. Langhans in "Three Early Eighteenth-Century Manuscript Promptbooks" (see n. 3 above). Langhans speculates about the references to a "Dior" or "Dioc" curtain. These are references, it seems to the "Diocle-

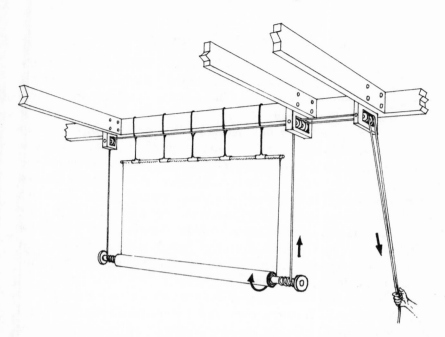

21. The operation of a drop curtain. Drawing by Ken Forsyth

Back scenes composed of shutters were never entirely superceded by drops during our period: Practicable scenes could be more
easily contrived using shutters. Nevertheless from the mid-1700s
drop scenes were increasingly popular. When Kemble opened
Sheridan's new Drury Lane Theatre in 1794 he used no shutters in
his production of *Macbeth*. A contemporary reviewer grumbled
that, "the scenes were made to drop as at the Opera House, and we
do not think the effect so good as when they were made to close."[31]
The *Morning Herald* for 22 April commented on the same production that, "All the scenes were new. They were probably about
fourteen, and all, except the parts at the sides, were lowered from
the ceiling."

---

sian" curtain, perhaps the original Dorset Garden curtain, or possibly a new one made for
Lincoln's Inn Fields, and now pressed into the service of another play.
  31. News cutting preserved in J. P. Kemble's Scrapbook in the Folger Library.

V Traps and Trapwork

In Settle's *Cambyses,* given at Lincoln's Inn Fields in January 1671, the curtain falls at the end of the third act in preparation for a spectacular opening to Act IV. The scene is *"drawn,"* and "Cambyses *is discover'd seated in a Chair sleeping. The Scene representing a steep Rock, from the top of which descends a large Cloud, which opening, appear various Shapes of Spirits seated in form of a Councel, to whom a more glorious Spirit descends half way, seated on a Throne; at which, the former Spirits rise and Dance: in the midst of the Dance arises a Woman with a Dagger in her hand; at which the Scene shuts"* (p. 49). Here, in a simple form, are demonstrated two resources of the stage: People, properties, machines, and scenes could be raised onto it from below and lowered onto it from above. These possibilities had been exploited in earlier theatres; the Restoration stage simply continued the existing tradition.

Rees's *Cyclopedia* shows the ground plan of a stage in which six traps are indicated: four side or corner traps (E), a grave trap (F), and a cauldron trap (G) (Figure 22). The basic principle on which these traps worked was, as Rees illustrates it, a simple one (Figures 23, 24). The trap consists of a platform (S) that slides along two upright grooves (V, V). In front of these posts are two others (U, U), which carry a cylinder (T), turned by a winch to raise and sink the trap. The trap could be counterpoised but this, according to the *Cyclopedia,* "is seldom, if ever, done." However, in its account of machines to be found in the cellar at Covent Garden, the inventory of 1744 consistently lists traps with barrels, weights, and cordage, which suggests that traps were more often counterpoised than Rees allows.

It is likely that traps were included in the earliest Restoration stages. Beaumont and Fletcher's *The Maid's Tragedy,* revived at Vere Street in November 1660 and reprinted in 1661, contains a masque in which *"Night rises in mists"* (B^r) and Neptune rises (B2^r) and subsequently sinks (B3^r). Lincoln's Inn Fields does not seem to have been particularly well provided with traps. A trap downstage is implied by the prologue to Edward Howard's *The Womens Conquest* (LIF, 1670), which is spoken by the ghost of Ben Jonson rising from

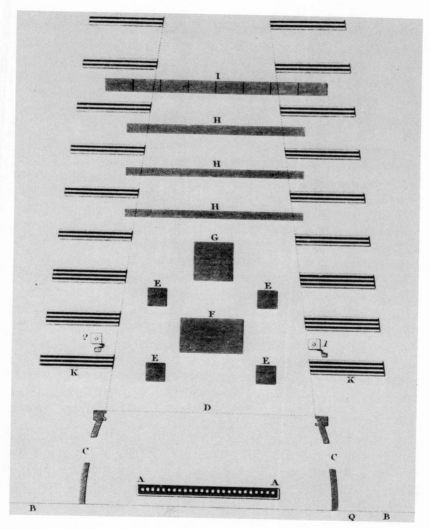

22. Ground plan of a stage. Dramatic machinery, engraved by Wilson Lowry for *The Cyclopedia* (London, 1819)

23. Trap mechanism, front view. Dramatic machinery, *The Cyclopedia* (London, 1819)

the ground. The appearance of the woman in Settle's *Cambyses* and the direction in Boyle's *Guzman* (LIF, 1669), which states that Francisco "knocks with his Foot, and four Boys appear within the Scene" (1693; II.13), both suggest the existence of a further trap "within the Scene," that is behind the back shutters.

Traditionally the appearance from below is of ghosts, demons, allegorical figures, or gods. The spirit, as in *Guzman,* is frequently summoned by someone stamping his foot on the stage. The conven-

24. Trap mechanism, side view. Dramatic machinery, *The Cyclopedia* (London, 1819)

tion is parodied in *Cupid and Psyche* at Drury Lane in 1734, in which Harlequin "stamps with his Foot, and a formidable Figure arises." Pierrot then "takes up his Wand, and strikes the Stage as Harlequin did before . . . *Pistolet* arises" (p. 13). The noise of the trap rising and of the trap doors opening was covered by thunder and lightning. In Fielding's satire on the theatre, *Pasquin* (Little Haymarket, 1736), three ghosts are sent up in succession. "Pray Mr. *Fustian,*" Sneerwell cuttingly enquires, "why must a Ghost always rise in a Storm of Thunder and Light'ning?" (IV.9).

The grave trap derived its name from the function it fulfilled in *Hamlet,* the cauldron trap from its use in *Macbeth.* The Covent Garden inventory lists as "in the Cellar," "the grave trap . . . Banquo's trap with barrel *and* cordage . . . the cauldron in Macbeth" (p. 31). Sir Walter Scott recalled the mishap that attended the appearance of the armed head in the fourth act of Kemble's *Macbeth* at Drury Lane in 1794. The armed head, he says, "ought to have arisen, but . . . though the trap-door gaped, no apparition arose. The galleries began to hiss; whereupon the scene-shifters in the cellarage, redoubling their exertions, and overcoming, perforce, the obstinancy of the screw which was to raise the trap, fairly, out of too great and urgent zeal, overdid their business, and produced before the audience, at full length, the apparition of a stout man, his head and shoulders arrayed in antique helmet and plate, while the rest of his person was humbly attired after the manner of a fifth-rate performer of these degenerate days."[32] A contemporary engraving of the scene suggests that the armed head appeared in the cauldron itself (Figure *25*).

A trap could serve as a woodhole,[33] a cellar,[34] a vault,[35] or a well.[36] Ravenscroft in *The London Cuckolds* (DG, 1681) uses a corner trap as an entrance to a cellar. Here Ramble stands beneath Arabella's window and asks her maid, Engine, if he can insinuate himself into the house. "Is there no hole or window to creep in at?" he pleads.

Eng. Just there below, is a cellar window with a bar out, the shutter in the inside is unpin'd, and will give way, try if you can get in there, if you can, I will go down and show you up.

Ram. I have found it there—even with the ground.

(1682; III.i.31)

32. *Quarterly Review,* 34 (1826), 228. Cited by Joseph W. Donohue Jr, "Kemble's Production of *Macbeth* (1794)," *Theatre Notebook,* 21 (1966–67), 63–74, esp. p. 70.
33. Etherege, *She wou'd if she cou'd* (LIF, 1668; I.i.3), Shadwell, *The Virtuoso* (DG, 1676; III.i.146).
34. Shadwell, *The Humorists* (LIF, 1670, IV.i.57), Crowne, *The Country Wit* (DG, 1676; V.i.77).
35. Howard, *All Mistaken* (Bridges St., 1665 or 1667; 1672, IV.i.46).
36. Behn, *The Feigned Curtezans* (DG, 1679; V.i.53); Doggett, *Hob* (DL, 1711; 1715, p. 15).

25. "An Apparition of an armed head rises" *(Macbeth IV.i).* From the Art Collection of the Folger Shakespeare Library

Ramble climbs down and sticks fast in the opening, perfectly placed for a chamber pot, which is emptied on his head.

The persistence of theatrical conventions is demonstrated by the use of a trap situated behind the back shutters to represent an entrance to a subterranean passage out of a room. In Marston's *The Wisest of Women; or, Sophonisba,* given at Blackfriars in 1605, a rear stage-trap leads from the interior of a castle to a distant forest (III.i). Fifty years later, during the interregnum, Killigrew included in *2 Bellamira* a scene in which a trap leads from a prison to a distant seashore (1664; V.iii.568). At the very end of the period, when Franklin wrote *The Egyptian Festival* (DL, 1800), we again have a dungeon in which there is a trap which opens onto a subterranean passage leading to the sea (II.35).

Large traps were used upstage to raise properties and pieces. In Dryden's *Tyrannick Love* (Bridges St., 1669), for instance, Damilcar stamps on the ground and a bed rises.[37] In other plays tables and chairs rise and sink.[38] Dryden's spectacular *Albion and Albanius* (DG, 1685), provides an instance of a machine rising on a trap. In the third act, *"A Machine rises out of the Sea: It opens and discovers* Venus *and* Albanius *sitting in a great Scallop shell, richly adorn'd . . . The Shell is drawn by Dolphins: It moves forward, while a Simphony of Fluts Doux, etc. is playing till it Lands 'em on the Stage, and then it closes and sinks"* (p. 27).

Behind the trap (G) in the *Cyclopedia* (Figure 22) are a series of longitudinal apertures or flaps (H) across the stage, which, we are told, "are covered by planks moveable upon hinges, so that by throwing them back, the stage may be opened in a moment. The use of these is to allow the flat scenes to sink through the stage, when required." Behind these is an aperture or slider (I), through which scenes stored below stage could be raised.

The earliest references to scenes being raised up through flaps seem to be to Dorset Garden where, for instance, in Betterton's *The Prophetess* (1690), "there rises from under the Stage, a pleasant Prospect of a Noble Garden" (V.i.67). The practice was standard too at Drury Lane in the mid-eighteenth century, for Garrick requires in his *Cymon* (DL, 1767) magical effects that depend on scenes rising and sinking. In V.i Urganda *"Waves her wand, and the scene changes to the black rocks."* She waves her wand again, and *"the Black Tower appears"* (p. 80). To the accompaniment of thunder, *"the tower and rocks give way to a magnificent amphitheatre, and* Merlin *appears in the place where the tower sunk"* (p. 81).

According to the *Cyclopedia* no permanent machinery was attached to the flaps or sliders, "for as these apertures served generally for the passage of the flat scenes through the stage, the machinery must depend upon the particular effects which it is necessary to produce."[39]

37. (1670; IV.i.32). Beds rise and sink in Behn, *1 Rover* (DG, 1677; III.ii.40), Cibber, *Xerxes* (LIF, 1699; II.i.13).

38. Shadwell, *The Tempest* (DG, 1674; 1676, IV. ii. 59), Duffett, *The Mock-Tempest* (DL, 1674; 1675, IV.iii.42), Duffett, *Psyche Debauch'd* (DL, 1675; 1678, I.24).

39. This is confirmed by the Covent Garden inventory in which are listed, for instance, "a

VI Machines for Descents, Water Effects, Sea Machines, and Ships

Both Lincoln's Inn Fields and Bridges Street possessed machines for descents onto the stage. At Dorset Garden the machines were of a complexity unsurpassed during the following century. There, individuals or groups could descend onto or ascend from the stage in chairs, thrones, chariots, or on lines and platforms. The movement could be a simple vertical descent and ascent, or the vertical could be combined with a horizontal movement from stage right to left, or from up- to downstage. The *Encyclopédie* of Diderot and d'Alembert illustrates a machine for a simultaneous vertical and horizontal movement (Figure 26), which is very like that subsequently illustrated in Rees (Figure 27).

In Figure 26 the chariot or car (C) is drawn across from stage right to left, while it is simultaneously lowered. Rees shows a box or frame (B) running on a track (A, A). The box is drawn across horizontally by the cord (F), while the car (C) is lowered.

The machine was masked with a "blind" of board or canvas. When appropriate, the blinds took the form of clouds. Clouds could descend and break to reveal one or several platforms of seated figures. In the anonymous *Cupid and Psyche,* for instance, given at Drury Lane in 1734, *"the Curtain rises, and the Stage appears cover'd over with Clouds; which, breaking up by degrees,* Jupiter *and* Juno *are discover'd on a magnificent Throne; and* Neptune [etc.] *. . . rang'd as in Council, on each side"* (I.i.1). At Covent Garden in 1744 painted pieces in the shop included "twelve peices of breaking clouds in Apollo and Daphne" (p. 29). A machine that would allow clouds to decend at differing speeds is illustrated in Figure 28. The clouds are suspended from barrels of different circumferences, turning on a single axis. The revolution of the barrels lowers the clouds at differing speeds. The figures on the middle cloud are revealed by the opening out effect.

Flying, like elaborate trapwork, was associated with supernatural manifestations of various kinds and was employed in masques

---

barrel groove and wt to tree in Orpheus. 6 trees to do. the post and barrel to pidgeon house . . . the Pallisadoes barrel cordage etc." (p. 31).

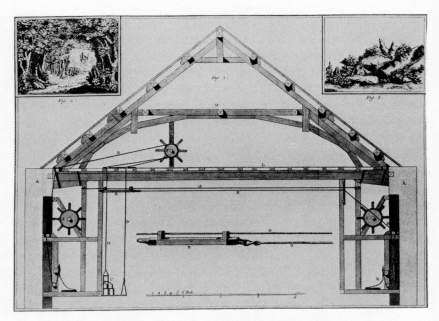

26. Machine for horizontal and vertical movement. Radel del., Benard fecit. *Encylopédie Méthodique* (Paris, 1787–1832)

presented in the context of "straight" plays, and in operas, pantomimes, and afterpieces. The most spectacular machines for descents were those used at Dorset Garden in the extravaganzas staged there under Betterton's direction. In his adaptation of *The Prophetess* (1690), for instance, a machine descends "so large, it fills all the Space, from the Frontispiece of the Stage, to the farther end of the House; and fixes it self by two Ladders of Clouds to the Floor. In it are Four several Stages, representing the Pallaces of the Gods" (V.i.67).

The descents were not without danger. In 1736, after a particularly serious accident during a performance of *The Fall of Phaeton*—an ill-omened title—the *Daily Advertiser* for 2 November noted that "The Director [of Drury Lane] has resolv'd, for the future, to suffer no living Persons to be concern'd in any Flights, or

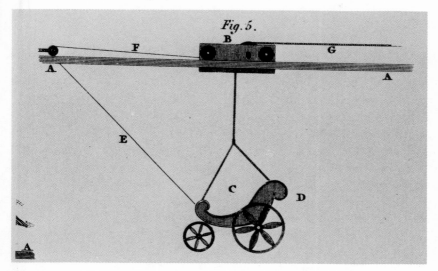

27. Machine for oblique ascent or descent. Dramatic machinery, *The Cyclopedia* (London, 1819)

hazardous Machinery, but to have Figures made for that Purpose." This resolution is illustrated in a short piece that George Colman, Jr, wrote for the Little Theatre in the Haymarket in 1795. Two charwomen are sweeping the stage, and one refuses to go upstairs to sweep the dressing rooms. "Why," she explains, "at the top of the—the Flys be the name on't I fancy—where all the clouds be—just at the landing place, there be a huge man—A Polly, I do think the carpenters call him—stuff'd out wi' Straw." "Simpleton," the first Char replies, "it's the stuff'd Apollo, in Midas" (*New Hay at the Old Market,* p. 18).

Model figures were used not only in machines but also, as we have seen in Dryden and Lee's *Oedipus,* for other purposes. Small scale models, some of which were working models, of figures and various contrivances were used in upstage areas to create scenic effects. When *The Touchstone* was revived at Covent Garden in 1789, for instance, it included a Jubilee procession in Rome, "which," the *Morning Post* for 1 December 1789 remarked, "consisted of artificial figures, horse and foot, cars etc; it was very well managed."

103

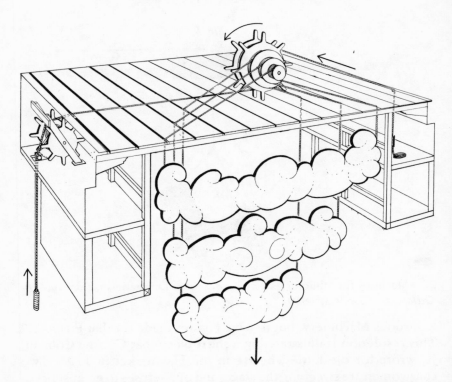

28. Machine to lower clouds at different speeds. Drawing adapted from *Encyclopédie Méthodique* (Paris, 1787–1832) by Ken Forsyth

The machines that could be used on the stage were restricted in number only by the imagination of the machinist. One group of effects will serve as an illustration: the water, sea, and ship effects, which became particularly popular on the stage in the last quarter of the eighteenth century.

Painted or perhaps practicable fountains have their apotheosis in the final act of Settle's *The Fairy Queen,* given at Dorset Garden in 1692. Here "The Scene changes to a Garden of Fountains," which terminates in walks rising to "the top of the House," while, "Near the top, vast Quantities of Water break out of the Hills, and fall in mighty cascades to the bottom of the Scene. . . . In the middle of the Stage is a very large Fountain, where the Water rises about

104

Twelve Foot" (IV.i.40). The fountains might on this occasion have been mere paint, but later water effects were often indisputably real. The Haymarket Opera House advertised a working waterfall in May 1711. At the opening of the 1794 Theatre Royal, Drury Lane, the first presentations concluded with part of the stage being flooded from the cisterns, which would later prove to be so disastrously inadequate. How this might have been done is suggested by an engraving of 1803 in which a contemporary melodrama is satirized (Figure 29). A dog leaps into an expanse of water to rescue a child, here transformed into Sheridan, who is saved from financial ruin by his animal performer. Water is pumped into a container from two sides of the stage.

Sea effects could more conveniently be represented by the simple device of revolving cylinders illustrated by Sabbatini in his *Pratica di fabricar scene e machine ne' teatri* (1637), and illustrated as still current in Rees's *Cyclopedia* almost two hundred years later

29. *The Manager and his Dog.* Published Humphrey, 1803. Courtesy of the Harvard Theatre Collection

(Figure 30). The existence of a similar device at Covent Garden in 1744 is confirmed by the inventory, which lists "6 handles *and* 12 bracketts for the sea" (p. 29).

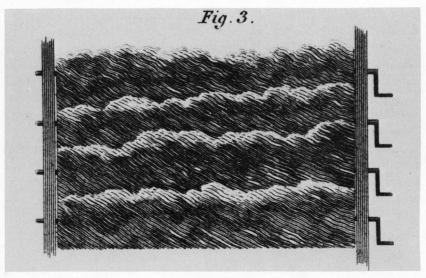

Fig. 3.

30. A common method of executing a sea scene. Dramatic machinery, *The Cyclopedia* (London, 1819)

After 1775 plays showing ships at sea were in vogue. At Covent Garden, for instance, they appeared in Thompson's *The Syrens* (1776), Dibdin's *The Seraglio* (1776), Pilon's *The Siege of Gibraltar* (1780), and Brooke's *Rosina* (1782). In Pilon's play the last scene shows "Rodneys *Fleet in the Bay . . . a Boat is seen to come from one of the Ships; a Lieutenant and several Sailors come on shore afterwards*" (p. 30). Here, no doubt, a model was used, but the ship could be practicable. Rees illustrates a practicable ship (Figure 31). The ship is fixed to a moving platform (A, A) and can be moved up and down on its axis (B) by the cord (C) attached to its stern. The front of the ship is weighted to return it to its original position. Figure 32 conflates the ship and wave machines to show how the effect of a ship at sea might have been achieved.

31. Plan of a small boat. Dramatic machinery, *The Cyclopedia* (London, 1819)

Hogarth's engraving of *Strolling Actresses Dressing in a Barn,* is a compendium of common stage machines (Figure 33). Two of Sabbatini's waves rest against a wooden partition, affording a perch for a hen and her chickens. A pair of stockings dries on the clouds, which form a blind for a chariot drawn by dragons. The chariot itself half obscures a cloud on which can just be made out two heads and the inscription "Oedipus, Jocasta." In Dryden and Lee's *Oedipus* (DG, 1678) the cloud draws *"that veil'd the heads of the Figures in the Skie, and shews 'em Crown'd, with the names of* Oedipus *and* Jocasta *written above in great Characters of Gold"* (1679; II.i.19). This *coup de théâtre* lingers with the other machines in Hogarth's decrepit barn.

VII Sound Effects

The sounds that were traditionally represented on the Restoration and eighteenth-century stage were heard in earlier theatres: Here, too, the conservatism of the stage is clear. Birds sang, as they had done on Shakespeare's stage, thunder rolled, cannons roared, and muskets rattled.

107

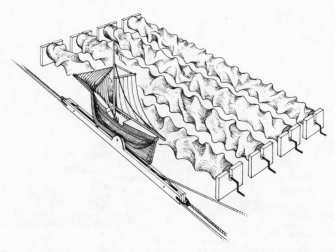

32. A ship and wave machines. Drawing adapted from Rees, *The Cyclopedia* (London, 1819), by Ken Forsyth

A late seventeenth-century prompt note in Genest's copy of Otway's *Caius Marius* (DG, 1679) demands that in the garden scene in Act IV, "Bird calls play before they [Caius and Lavinia] come on" (1680; p. 38).[40] The bird calls could be various: D'Urfey's *Cinthia and Endimion* (DL, 1696) specifies that *"Variety of Birds are heard Singing"* (1697; I.i), or they could be particular: In Stapylton's *The Stepmother* (LIF, 1663) "The Nightingale sings in a Hawthorn Bush" (1664; IV.i.60). Bird song is frequent in the following century. In Mallet's *Alfred* (DL, 1751), for instance, *"The warbling of birds is heard"* (III.ix.68). No doubt the traditional pipes or pipes blown into a bowl of water were used to imitate birdcalls on the Restoration as on the earlier stages.

Thunder could be produced by the same method that produced mustard: by rolling a ball in a thunder as opposed to a mustard bowl. A more effective method was the thunder run, in which balls ran down a wooden trough or "trunk." The thunder run was sometimes situated over the auditorium so that the house not only sounded but shook to the roar of thunder. To thunder might be added wind and rain. Rich's Covent Garden inventory lists "2 rain trunks *and*

40. Folger Prompt, C 8.

33. W. Hogarth, *Strolling Actresses Dressing in a Barn.* Published 1738.
From the Art Collection of the Folger Shakespeare Library

frame" (p. 30), which worked perhaps on the principle, cited by
Davies in his *Dramatic Miscellanies,* of "rattling a vast quantity of
peas in rollers."[41]

The paraphernalia for creating storm effects appears, too, in
Hogarth's engraving of actresses in a barn (Figure 33). In the
right-hand corner Juno cons her lines from a book supported on a
trunk and leaning on a saltbox. She rests her foot on a wheelbarrow
while her stocking is being mended. Lichtenberg comments on this
part of the engraving: "How if the wheelbarrow were simultaneously push- and thunder-cart? Loaded with stones and trundled
over loose boards on *that* wheel of decidedly unequal radii, it would
certainly have a splendid effect. . . . Where the thunderbolt hovers,
thunder is surely not far off, never mind where it comes from. If, in
addition, the trunk proves to be just the one in which the downpour

41. (London: Printed for the Author, 1784), 3 vols., II, 58.

and the hailstorm have made their journey here, then that group would acquire a dignity and a magnitude whose description would scorn mere prose."[42] Perhaps the saltbox, which Lichtenberg confines to its role as musical instrument, housed the saltpeter for the lightning.

The means of creating wind effects is suggested in Holcroft's satirical prelude *The Rival Queens* (1794), preserved in the Larpent collection. Here the rival Queens are the Covent Garden and Drury Lane theatres. "Why now," asks the first Drury Lane man, or assistant, in a passage that deserves to be given at length,

what have you to compare to our last burning Mountain?

1st. C.G. Man. A burning mountain made of the smoke of the flame of a twopenny Link! Was that to be nam'd with our Earthquake!

1st. D.L. Man. An Earthquake forsooth! so you call a Calf's hide belaboured by a rope's end, an Earthquake!

1st. C.G. Man. As good at least as your storm, when you scrape the sharp edges of two or three bits of deal, against a yard and a half of Silk, and pretend it is the roaring of the wind.

(n.p.)

Ironic as this might be, the wind machine illustrated in Contant's engravings of English theatrical machinery,[43] and reproduced here (Figure 34,) works on exactly the same principles as those castigated by the Drury Lane man. A piece of silk (A), held taut by a weight (B), is stretched over a revolving drum with wooden teeth which scrape against the silk to produce the wind effect.

To tradition it was possible sometimes to add inspired improvisation; but one wonders how successful was the expedient noticed at Covent Garden in October 1775: "The discharge of cannon [was] imitated by the unnatural slamming of one of the Green Room doors."[44]

42. Georg Christoph Lichtenberg, *The World of Hogarth: Lichtenberg's Commentaries on Hogarth's Engravings,* trans. Innes and Gustav Herdan (Boston: Houghton Mifflin, 1966), pp. 158–59.

43. Clément Contant and Joseph de Filippi, *Parallèle des principaux théâtres modernes,* 2 pts. (Paris: n. p., 1859–61).

44. Theatrical intelligence, *Covent Garden,* Folger News Clipping. Cited in *LS,* Part 4, III, 1918.

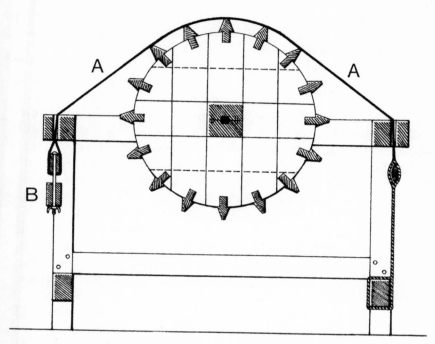

34. Wind machine. Drawing adapted from Contant and de Filippi, *Parallèle des principaux théâtres modernes* (Paris, 1860), by Ken Forsyth

VIII Lighting

In the early Restoration, plays began in the afternoon, and the light, which fell through the theatre windows, was supplemented by candles placed within the auditorium. In some theatres a cupola admitted light and air, but also inclement weather. It was not possible, nor was it thought desirable, to extinguish houselights when the play began. Until the introduction of gaslight in the nineteenth century, houselights were up for the entire performance.

At first, chandeliers or hoops of candles were suspended above the forestage, and further hoops hung from the flies behind the proscenium to light the scene. In the cellar at Covent Garden in 1744 survived "6 old iron rings and chains for branches brought from Lincoln's Inn" (*Inventory*, p. 31). John Green [i.e., J. Townsend] in his undated compilation *Odds and Ends About Covent Garden* records that there were six hoops on stage there as well: "Above, over the stage, were placed six chandeliers, consisting of hoops of brass, with brass or iron chains. There were 12 candles to each chandelier. These were let down from the cloud scenes, to a sufficient height, so as not to touch the heads of the actors."[45]

The hoops or rings obscured the view of the stage, particularly from the galleries. For this reason Garrick, following the French precedent, in the season of 1765–66, abolished the hoops at Drury Lane. Covent Garden and the Haymarket followed suit. In 1767 the *Public Advertiser* reported of the Opera House that, "by their following Mr. Garrick's example, in removing the pendent lustres, and lighting after the foreign manner, you have a full view of the whole stage." With the removal of the lights over the forestage, lighting was necessarily increased in the area behind the proscenium.

The scenic area behind the proscenium was lit in the Italian and French manner. Candles and subsequently lamps were attached to the back of the wings. The Covent Garden list of 1744 records the existence on the stage of "24 blinds to scene ladders 192 tinn candlesticks to do" (p. 31), which allows eight candles to each wing. Additional fixed lighting poles could be added as sidelights between the wings. At Covent Garden in 1744 we find "12 do [i.e., tin candlesticks] fixt to a post with five canopys" (p. 31). Machines were furnished with their own additional light sources. Battens, or overhead lighting units, were little used; perhaps, as on the Continent, fear of fire in the inaccessible upper reaches of the stage prevented it. This lighting scheme had necessarily to be boosted when the lights above the forestage were abolished. The increasing use of set pieces and ground rows allowed for concealed lights to be placed on the stage. Lamps had also to be placed to light the backscene or drop adequately.

The frontispiece to Kirkman's *The Wits* (1672) shows a stage lit

45. Issued by Evan's Music and Supper-Rooms, Covent Garden (London, 1866?), p. 14.

by chandeliers and also by a row of footlights. It seems likely that from the reopening of the theatres in 1660 footlights were regularly employed. Lamps eventually supplanted candles or were perhaps used as footlights from the start. Oil lamps had taken the place of candles for all stage lighting by the middle of the eighteenth century.

Sudden contrasts of bright and dark scenes characterized the Baroque theatre. Darkness onstage could be suggested simply by characters appearing with candles or torches, but it seems that at Dorset Garden in the last quarter of the seventeenth century an effective means must have been devised for darkening the stage. In Shadwell's operatic revision of Davenant and Dryden's version of *The Tempest* (DG, 1674) the play opens with a ship at sea. *"And when the Ship is sinking,"* we are told, *"the whole House is darken'd, and a shower of Fire falls upon 'em. . . . In the midst of the Shower of Fire the Scene changes . . . and when the Lights return, discover that Beautiful part of the Island, which was the habitation of* Prospero" (1676; I.ii.1, 5). Here it seems likely that the footlights were dropped below the level of the stage.

Rees shows a device for lowering the footlights similar, according to the *Cyclopedia,* to that used at Covent Garden before 1808 (Figure 35). The frame (MM) is raised by cords passing over two pulleys (OO) fixed to a wheel (N). The device can be set in motion by the prompter or his assistants working the small barrel or cylinder (Q). The existence of a footlight trap at Covent Garden is confirmed by the inventory of 1744, which lists in the cellar "the lamps in front fixt with barrel cordage wts. etc." (p. 31), and in the list of weights the "counterpoize to front lamps 170 lb." (p. 32).

The area behind the proscenium could be darkened by drawing up the rings into the flies. The author of an open letter to Garrick suggests that in *The Coronation* (DL, 1761) Garrick should have ordered "the Lamps to sink under the Stage, and the Chandeliers to rise till they are lost among the Clouds."[46] Green in *Odds and Ends* remarks that "the beauty of the scenes must have been greatly diminished when the chandeliers hung over every part of the

46. Cited by Kalman A. Burnim, *David Garrick, Director* (Pittsburgh: Univ. of Pittsburgh Press, 1961), p. 79.

35. Mechanism for raising and lowering the footlights. Dramatic machinery, *The Cyclopedia* (London, 1819)

stage. . . . It is true when they wanted to darken a scene, they were drawn up to the ceiling" (p. 14).

The sidelights, too, could be darkened. Rees describes the method, and the sidelights appear as 1 and 2 in Figure 22. "To give a sufficient light to the stage," he explains, "side lights are used, as well as foot lights: these are generally placed between the wings, to turn upon a hinge, for the purpose of darkening the stage when necessary . . . the apparatus consists merely of an upright post, to which is attached a piece of tinned iron, forming two sides of a square, and moveable upon joints or hinges, and furnished with shelves to receive the lamps or candles." The lights could thus be directed toward or away from the stage. Alternatively metal shields or blinds could be drawn across the lamps. In a Folger Promptbook (c. 1780) of *The Merchant of Venice,* for instance, the garden at Belmont in V.i is specified as follows: "Garden Moon Light/4 gr/ ⓦ Bank on OP/Blinds turnd."[47]

Lighting effects, like so much else on the stage, were determined by earlier conventions. The sun or moon rising or setting had been

47. Folger Prompt *Merchant* 16, p. 222.

commonplaces on the masquing stage of Inigo Jones, where the effect was probably achieved by the traditional use of backlit glass vessels filled with colored water. A later means of achieving sun and moon effects is the lamp illustrated by Rees (Figure 36), which is not greatly different from the one lampooned in Colman's *New Hay*

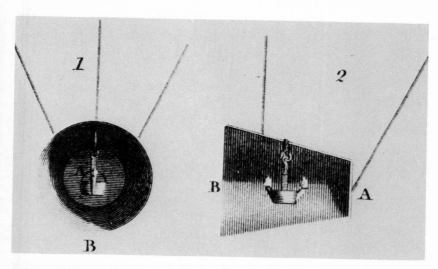

36. Apparatus designed to give the effect of a full moon. Used at Drury Lane. Dramatic machinery, *The Cyclopedia* (London, 1819)

at the Old Market (Little Haymarket, 1795) of which the carpenter complains that "the man that work'd it, run his hand through it, last year, when he was snuffing the candle" (p. 21).

Granville's *The British Enchanters* (Haymarket, 1706) furnishes a comprehensive example of the taste for conflagrations. In the fifth act, *"The Grove appears in an instant all in a Flame. Fountains from below cast up Fire as in Spouts; a rain of Fire from above"* (V.i.33). This was achieved, no doubt, through lighting and smoke effects. That more hazardous means were sometimes used is suggested in a description of the scene requirements for the final act of Quinault and Lully's *Armide,* which was sent to Garrick from France, and which was translated for him into English. The scene formed the basis for one of de Loutherbourg's most sensational settings for *The Christmas Tale,* given at Drury Lane in 1773. "When the Change or shifting of the firing of the Palace happens," the translation reads, "the Cielings are changed at the same time and from above are thrown down pieces of Timber, made of wicker *and* coverd with Cloth painted, these pieces are sett on fire by Strings of Tow tyed to them, there is also fire made betwen the side scenes by tying Tow to long Perches." The rain of fire that accompanies this "is made of Chinese fire work Composition, fixed to the Cielings of No. 3, 4 *and* 5. Mr. Gaetan Rudgiery Italian Fireworker will do this well he lodges at M. Wallé or Waller, distiller, or seller of fine liquors in the Haymarket."[48] With such dangerous procedures, it is surprising that stage, scenes, and players were not burnt in earnest. In the *Spectator* for 6 March 1711, Addison remarks that "in the mean time, to find out a more agreeable Entertainment for the Winter-Season, the Opera of *Rinaldo* is filled with Thunder and Lightning, Illuminations and Fireworks; which the Audience may look upon without catching Cold, and indeed without much Danger of being burnt; for there are several Engines filled with Water, and ready to play at a Minute's warning, in case any Accident should happen."

Transparencies were used during our period with increasing subtlety. These consisted of a drop of linen or calico painted with transparent dyes. The drop could be lit from the front to produce an opaque effect or from behind to give a transparency or vary the image. A transparent piece could be set into a wing, shutter, or drop. In a letter of 14 November 1762, "T. H." suggested to Garrick that "two large windows be made in the scene, cover'd with gauze to give a transparancy and the effect of glass."[49] Lediard had shown transparencies in his *Britannia* at the Haymarket in 1732 and a transparency appears in the Covent Garden inventory as "2 peices transparent Hell" (p. 28).

Even before de Loutherbourg began working for Garrick in 1771 the transition from festive "Baroque" to more subtle atmospheric or "Romantic" lighting was apparent. In Hawkesworth's *Edgar and Emmeline* (DL, 1761), for instance, *"one side of the horizon is tinged*

48. Folger MS Y.d. 145–46.
49. Cited in *LS,* Part 4, II, 960.

with the rays of the setting sun; the moon rising on the other" (I.i.1);
Dow's *Zingis* (DL, 1769) reverses this and shows us "The Moon
setting behind a Hill, and the Dawn of Morning" (I.1). The romantic feeling for nature had always been characteristic of English stage
lighting. Dow's direction recalls Jones's setting for Shirley's masque,
The Triumph of Peace (1634), where we are shown "a darkish sky,
with dusky clouds, through which appeared the new moon but with
a faint light by the approach of the morning."[50] In the last quarter of
the century improvements in lighting technique, stimulated by the
achievements of the *Spectacles d'optique* such as de Louterbourg's
Eidophysikon, made fine gradations of light possible and times of
day could be very precisely defined. In *Rosina* (CG, 1782) Brooke
specifies that *"in the first act the sky clears by degrees, the morning
vapour disperses, the sun rises, and at the end of the act it is above the
horizon: at the beginning of the second he [sic] is past the height, and
declines till the end of the day. This progressive motion should be made
imperceptibly, but its effect should be visible through the two acts"* (1763;
p. 5).[51]

These effects were achieved not only by varying the intensity of
the light but also through an increasingly sophisticated use of
colored screens and glasses. In his *Reminiscences* Henry Angelo
records how de Louterbourg had managed to achieve his effects.
He placed, he said, "different coloured silks in the flies, or side
scenes, which turned on a pivot, and, with lights behind, which so
illuminated the stage, as to give the effect of enchantment."[52]

After he had eliminated the overhead proscenium lights, Garrick
investigated the possibility of improved lamps, particularly for the
footlights.[53] In 1790 the assistant manager at the Royal Theatre in
Stockholm could report to King Gustavus III that the London

50. "The Triumph of Peace," *The Dramatic Works and Poems of James Shirley,* ed. Alexander Dyce (London, 1883; rpt. New York: Russell and Russell, 1966), VI, 282.
51. Mrs. Brooke's direction is a translation of Favart's corresponding scene description in
Les Moissonneurs, on which *Rosina* is based. It implies the possibility and the desirability of
reproducing such an effect on the English stage.
52. *Reminiscences,* 2 vols. (London: H. Colburn, 1821–30), II, 326.
53. See Garrick's correspondence with the theatre manager, Jean Monnet, in *The Private
Correspondence of David Garrick,* ed. James Boaden, 2 vols. (London: H. Colburn and R.
Bentley, 1831–32), II, 411 ff.

theatres had now installed Argand lamps.[54] The introduction of these lamps, which produced a vastly superior light without variations in intensity or irritating smoke, both encouraged and confirmed the retreat behind the proscenium. The entire scenic area, not merely the wings and the forestage, could now be adequately lit. Scenery could be dispersed over the stage as set pieces and the actor could place himself within the scene without sacrificing expression or gesture. A theatre that had held its players captive within the circle of the footlights and had set them against, rather than within, the scene was now superceded by one in which the actor or actress could appear within a three-dimensional and practicable setting.

54. Cited by Gösta Bergman, *Lighting in the Theatre* (Totowa, N.J.: Rowman and Littlefield, 1977), p. 219.

4
The Evidence From Promptbooks

LEO HUGHES

SOME FORTY YEARS ago the Oxford scholar F. W. Bateson came to the "disconcerting conclusion," after careful examination of several variant states of *The Critic,* "that Sheridan was capable of drawing a distinction between the acting and the reading versions of his plays."[1] The fact that many students of the drama today would fail to see anything really disconcerting in this distinction perhaps tells us something about a shift in attitudes.

A good part of Bateson's disconcertion doubtless stemmed from an attitude long fixed in the academic mind: the notion that the reading version somehow constituted a "sacred text," especially where the text of Shakespeare was concerned. Even a sensible scholar like John Genest, whose monumental work appeared in 1832 at the height of the long reign of bardolatry, lost the objectivity he usually maintained when dealing with less ethereal figures. He reports the appearance of Bickerstaffe's version of Wycherley with a rueful aside: "notwithstanding the excellence of the Plain Dealer, it could not have been performed before a modern audience without alteration."[2] He can even label Kemble's alterations of *All's Well* "very judicious" (VII, 183). He shows a strange am-

1. "Notes on the Texts of Two Sheridan Plays," *Review of English Studies,* 16 (1940), 312–17, esp. 316–17.
2. *Some Account of the English Stage,* 10 vols. (1832; rpt. New York: Burt Franklin, 1965), V, 90.

bivalence in noting the appearance in 1773–74 of *Bell's Shakespeare:* "This has been censured as the worst edition of Shakspeare ever published, which strictly speaking is true, as it presents the plays in a mutilated state—but in another point of view, this edition is very useful, as it is copied from the prompter's book" (V, 439). Too often, however, he is less objective. He falls upon the alterations appearing in *Julius Caesar* at Covent Garden in 1766, quoting some lines from the Bell edition of 1776 as "ridiculous rant" that had not appeared in "that sink of corruption—the Prompt-Book—(for such it is with regard to Shakspeare)—till after 1682" (V, 107–8). He gives us a little dialogue of the dead involving Kemble and Shakespeare that ends with the Bard's complaint, "St. Lawrence never suffered more on his Gridiron, than I have suffered from the Prompt-Book" (VIII, 133–34). He even allows his feelings to show in his index: "King Lear, by Shakspeare . . . King Lear as altered by Colman . . . King Lear mangled by Tate" (I, 1xvii).

The abuse of Tate as principal whipping boy was highly popular for generations, on down to the appearance, fifty years ago, of Hazelton Spencer's heavy-handed *Shakespeare Improved,* which finds it "impossible to exaggerate the harm these versions have done."[3] Evidently some variant of Gresham's law was applicable to the theatre. As a matter of plain fact no lasting harm has been done to the greatest of our dramatists. The very reverse of Gresham's law has operated: The versions of Tate and Davenant and Otway and all the rest have long since disappeared from the stage, not necessarily replaced by a sacred text but by some version appropriate to our own needs. "His characters are not modified by the customs of particular places, impractised by the rest of the world . . . : they are the genuine progeny of common humanity, such as the world will always supply, and observation will always find."

If Dr. Johnson's observation be sound—and who challenges it?—then it is the task of every age in producing these marvels to offer them in a fashion readily available to us lesser souls who are attached to the customs of particular places. In more practical and apposite terms there is a need for the reading version, always

3. (1927; rpt. New York: Ungar, 1963), p. 371.

improving as historians, linguists, bibliographers, paleographers work closer to the playwright's original intention, *and* the acting version, always in a state of flux, of modification. Genest need not have agonized over choosing between the sacred text and the prompter's book. No such choice is necessary. Establishing the best possible text has always been, quite properly, an important part of the scholar's task. And the "playhouse copy" as Genest called it—we would say acting version—is indeed useful and precisely for the reason he gives: It is copied from the prompter's book, which complements rather than competes with the established text.

When Genest speaks of Bell's copying "from the prompter's book" he is not of course implying that the resulting version presents the entire matter, marginalia as well as text. The acting version presents, along with conventional act and scene numbers, exits and entrances, and the like, the dialogue as it has been cut or expanded (chiefly cut); the acts and scenes in their original or changed order; the assignment of speeches, not infrequently the reassignment where the stage manager decides to reduce the number of characters. The prompter's book contains a great deal more, and it is this great deal more which I propose to examine.

I concentrate almost exclusively on promptbooks prepared in the eighteenth century proper. A principal reason is that the number of details involving staging increases sharply beyond the Restoration period, assuring a fuller picture of what went on onstage, above and below stage, and offstage. For another thing, the promptbooks that happen to be most accessible, in my own university library, the Folger, and elsewhere, represent much more fully the later decades. Finally, a very full and scholarly study of Restoration prompt copies by Professor Langhans is about to appear.

I

It might be well to begin by dividing into two parts the wealth of evidence available: 1) the notations, often cryptic, that show a company in the process of staging a play (directions for handling the scenery, the lights, the music, the effects, the stage business, and so on); 2) the numerous deletions, additions, restorations, and redeletions that involve some of the same problems of staging (the speed, the length, the order, the space added to or subtracted from a given character's role), which may have nothing to do with staging but concern social problems often unrelated to the theatre—moral judgment, taste, sensibilities, even politics. It must be obvious from these two lists that somehow the term *prompter* is being misused here, certainly being used differently from the way it is today. Thomas Dibdin, early nineteenth-century playwright, pantomimist, theatrical manager, and biographer, served for a good part of his career as prompter at Drury Lane. His graphic picture of a presumably typical day suggests that far more was involved than holding the book ready to assist the faulty memory of some performer: "I have, on a severe winter's day, been on Drury Lane stage, with one play-book after another in my benumbed fingers, from ten in the morning until near five in the afternoon"[4]—all this before his official day's work had begun. For, he goes on, after a "hasty" dinner he had to be back, this time at his table in the wings, ready to supervise the multiplicity of items involving scenery, property, cues, and so on, which were involved in the complex business of production. Since presiding over the performance might well keep him occupied until ten or eleven, one wonders when he found time for his other duties, such as making fair copies of plays to submit to the licenser, acting as secretary to the manager, and copying partbooks for individual performers.[5] *Factotum* would have been a better term. In any event the book from which he worked can tell us a great deal about what went on season after season on both sides of the curtain.

Turning then to the promptbook itself we might begin with that part of the production that strikes the eye immediately, the scenery. W. S. Clark claimed for the group of seventeenth-century promptbooks of Shakespearean plays from Smock Alley "a unique view of that theatre's scenic resources."[6] I doubt if one could make a

4. T. J. Dibdin, *The Reminiscences of Thomas Dibdin*, 2 vols. (London: H. Colburn, 1827), II, 11.

5. As we learn from still-extant theatre accounts and prompters' records, copying was a part of the prompter's regular chores, but he received extra compensation for doing it. The records in the Larpent Collection, especially the letters, usually signed by the manager though often written by the prompter, are especially valuable in identifying hands.

6. *The Early Irish Stage* (Oxford: Clarendon Press, 1955), p. 73.

similar claim for promptbooks from eighteenth-century English theatres, even though they survive in far greater numbers and tell an increasingly detailed story in their margins.

A principal limitation comes from the fact that the marginal notations are intended only as reminders to the prompter so that he may in turn remind the scenemen to go into action. Time after time we get a succession such as this one: *Chamber—Town— Chamber—Town—Chamber—New Chamber,* and so on. The only variations in this succession, which I copy from a Folger promptbook of the 1754 revival of *The Chances* at Drury Lane, are the tantalizing *New Chamber*—quite likely not painted for this particular production in spite of "new"—and the *Bagnio/Town/Sign & Bush* farther on, almost certainly a composite of Cross's *Town* with Hopkins's more specific additions for the 1773 revival. If we are looking for useful details about sets these vague signals may seem more tantalizing than helpful; yet they do speak clearly of the circumstances of production. As Miss Rosenfeld reminds us more than once, this is a repertory theatre.[7] To say nothing of the expense that would be required to provide fresh sets for every production, the very bulk of wings, shutters, drops, and borders would create insoluble problems of handling and storage. Especially in an Italian-ate comedy like *The Chances,* where *action* is paramount, the familiar, vaguely continental street plus chamber would assure greater speed—and less distraction—than some dazzling new piece calling attention to itself by sheer novelty.

By no means all scene designations in eighteenth-century promptbooks are as vague and general as those in *The Chances.* At times a suggestion of actual appearance is given: *Glass Chamber, Screen Chamber, Silver Chamber, Wainscot Chamber, Picture Chamber*—even a *Statute Chamber,* by which a careless prompter doubtless meant a *Statue Chamber*—i.e., a room in which statues figure prominently. Sometimes a function is suggested: *Chocolate Room* is admittedly vague, *Saloon* even more so.[8] *Stocks Market* is specific enough, especially when the title of the play, *The London*

---

7. *A Short History of Scene Design in Great Britain* (Oxford: Blackwell, 1973), passim.
8. *Saloon* would not of course have had its modern American signification. It was commonly a large room to which such terms as *grand* or *elegant* were attached.

Cuckolds, supplies the locale. Other London scenes appear: *Temple* (the building in Fleet Street long associated with the Inns of Court), *Covent Garden, Charing Cross*—all in a Drury Lane promptbook of Shadwell's *Squire of Alsatia* almost certainly prepared for performances in 1748. More foreign and exotic are sets labeled *Segovia* and *Tunis.* Yet here too we get an interesting puzzle. The *Segovia* appears in a promptbook of the Fletcher-Vanbrugh *Pilgrim* marked by three prompters for three different revivals, Chetwood in 1738, Cross in 1750, Wrighten in 1787.[9] The locales that were eventually designated by the name of the Spanish town are marked by Chetwood in 1738 with a mere ⊙ , the signal reminding the prompter to blow his whistle and bring the scenemen into action. Cross was to add the designation *Wood,* obviously calling for a stock set, and the groove number, *1st,* calling for a location downstage. Wrighten added *Segovia*—actually he marked the first such scene *Rural Scene near Segovia* and the second *Near Segovia.* What indications of locale appeared in the 1700 quarto on which the promptbook is based? Curiously enough, there were almost no indications. Neither on the page listing the *dramatis personae* nor at any numbered break in act or scene is there a hint of locale. At two points we get *Scene Segovia* (p. 21) for a mere twenty lines of dialogue—all of which were evidently stricken some time during the 1738 revival—and *Scene, an Altar* (p. 39) as we move into the dramatic finale. Wrighten's indications of scene, which suggest he had readers rather than his technicians in mind, are understandably used, with some revision, by the editor of the 1787 acting version.

The *Tunis,* which appears in two Penzance promptbooks, a *Royal Merchant* marked by Chetwood and a *Don Sebastian* marked by Cross, proves interesting in a different way. Since neither play is actually set in North Africa, what we have here is actually a set from the Drury Lane scene room that must have been designed for a play for which Tunis was the setting but which had now become a stock scene.

9. Leo Hughes and A. H. Scouten, "The Penzance Promptbook of *The Pilgrim,*" *Modern Philology,* 73 (1975), 33–53. The "Penzance promptbooks" (now located at the University of Texas and the University of Edinburgh) were first publicized by A. H. Scouten in 1962 at a circulating library in Penzance.

A variant on this practice would seem to appear in the use of sets named from the plays they were originally prepared for: A *Perseus Town* in a *Measure for Measure* Shattuck ascribes to Covent Garden c. 1780; a *Bon Ton:* T[transparency?] in a Folger *Florizel and Perdita;* another scene from a Garrick play, *Lethe's Open Flat,* in the same promptbook; a *Miser's Chamb^r* in an *Old Bachelor* marked by Chetwood, with emendations by his successor.

Still another variant, intriguing but not as informative as one might wish, comes in the designation of sets by the names of the designer or painter. There is a fair sprinkling throughout some of the promptbooks already mentioned here and in Shattuck's account of Shakespearean promptbooks of the period of names like Tillemans, Dall, Carver, Harvey, Hayman, even a Bibianie in a Folger promptbook of *Semiramis* (1776)—though this last name would hardly provide irrefutable evidence that a member of the famous Italian family was working for Drury Lane. All these names, and I have given only a sampling, are often little more than tantalizing. *Harvey's Palace* appears in two of the Penzance promptbooks and in the 1743 Covent Garden inventory:[10] That it may well have been elaborate and consequently expensive we judge from the accounts of Lincolns' Inn Fields Avery refers to.[11] We know from Southern that Rich invested considerable sums in Harvey's work before the opening of the new theatre in 1732.[12] But without maquettes or sketches, or even trustworthy engravings, we must depend mostly on our imaginations.

One perhaps slight but useful application can be found for such names as those above. With other evidence enabling us to pin a given designer-painter to a single company we can come closer to A. C. Sprague's demand for precise identification.[13] Two illustrations come to mind. It was the realization that Harvey had worked, so far as I can discover, only for Rich that brought me to ascribe the Penzance *Oedipus* to Rich's theatres.[14] An even more striking

10. H. Saxe Wyndham, *The Annals of Covent Garden Theatre,* 2 vols. (London: Chatto & Windus, 1906), II, Appendix.
11. *LS,* Part 2, I, lxv, cviii.
12. Richard Southern, *Changeable Scenery* (London: Faber and Faber, 1952), p. 206.
13. See discussion below and n. 24.
14. See "The Penzance Promptbook of *The Pilgrim*" (n. 9 above).

instance—and an instance of serendipity as well—brought the realization that the Folger *Julius Caesar* long misascribed to Drury Lane and Garrick was really a Covent Garden promptbook. *Dalls Palace* in the margin, obviously referring to a scene painted by Nicholas Dahl,[15] who evidently worked only for Garrick's rivals, did the trick. The name of Laguerre, also employed only at Covent Garden, appears in connection with another scene in this promptbook. Again caution is the watchword. Hayman, Carver, one or another of the several Frenches, all worked for both major companies.

Promptbooks are far more useful in illustrating how the scenes were worked and so bring us just that much closer to the actual eighteenth-century theatrical experience. Here our best help would come from scholars whose professional work has insured a familiarity with the stage: Shattuck, Burnim, Langhans, Allen, and Donohue are some of the more important names that come to mind. Here also the aid supplied by newspaper and other accounts by theatregoers, amateur or professional, graphic representations of scenes, even the proverbial laundry list, can be helpful. For once more the concession must be made: Only the occasional eighteenth-century promptbook supplies us with adequate detail.

To take a perhaps misleadingly helpful example, I move just over the border into the nineteenth century. Charles Shattuck gives us an excellent exposition of the system of grooves in his introduction to the Wister-Kemble *Merry Wives*. The edition in which Kemble's marks are recorded is from 1804, but Shattuck seems to be saying that it differs in no substantial way from the 1797 one or the 1815 one. More significant here, this particular promptbook is "unique among Kemble's books in that it gives a complete schedule of the sets. Before he marked the book in ink, Kemble penciled at the head of each scene the name of the wing-and-shutter set to be used, and the groove or grooves in which it was to stand. The sets were all taken from stock, and Kemble designated each one not according to its significance in *Merry Wives* but by the name by which the stage

15. R. G. Allen, "The Stage Spectacles of Philip James de Loutherbourg," Diss. Yale 1960 (University Microfilms, 1973), pp. 36–37. Allen gives the more accurate form of his name and the few facts which are recorded about his career at Covent Garden.

carpenter would recognize it in the scene dock."[16] There follow two and a half pages of Kemble's notations, along with the printed act and scene numbers and stage directions ("I, i before Page's House. 'Canterbury Street.' 1-2 Grooves.") plus Shattuck's full and informative commentary.

A similar though not quite so rewarding promptbook of an earlier date in the Penzance group was marked by Chetwood in a 1696 quarto of *Oroonoko* sometime during the 1730s. There are the usual calls, indications of properties to be carried on, signals for effects, but no indication of scenes except for the conventional sign ⊙ for the whistle. After Chetwood's tenure Cross added some marks, especially indications of scenes and grooves, admittedly fuller and more systematic than usual for him. With these before us we can *almost* match what Shattuck does.

Like the sets for *Merry Wives* these are stock pieces. Act I, Scene i, begins with a set labeled by Cross *N:C:/1ˢᵗG*, which I interpret to mean New Chamber in the foremost groove position just behind the proscenium—in any event an interior to be associated throughout the play with the Welldons and therefore the cynical and sophisticated Old World. Scene ii, labeled in the printed stage directions merely *An Open Place*, was first marked by Cross *L:W:* [Long Wood?] *3ᵈG*, but subsequently the 3 was marked over by a 4. That much of the stage would be used is clear enough, for most of the cast including extras, *Slaves in Chains* according to Chetwood's Call 6, appear at one time or another. "This," as Charlot Welldon says to the vicious Capt. Driver, "is your Market for Slaves."

Act II begins with more low comedy at *Widow Lackitt's House* according to the printed stage direction. Cross notes *C:Hall/1st G*, a frequently used stock set. This scene is withdrawn to reveal one undesignated in the printed text but marked by Cross *N:Town/*

16. *John Philip Kemble Promptbooks,* ed. Charles H. Shattuck, 12 vols. (Charlottesville: Univ. Press of Virginia for the Folger Shakespeare Library, [1975]), VI, ii. This is my first mention of an invaluable model for the student interested in promptbooks. These are not promptbooks in the usual sense of a book used in the wings during actual performances but a cumulative record in effect of all of Kemble's revisions of Shakespeare with the prompter's directions on the pages and on interleaves. Both the editor's informative introductions and the marks themselves are worth careful study.

2dG., possibly incongruous for the highly emotional encounter between Oroonoko and the generous Blandford. At any rate it is in the open air. This in turn is covered at Scene iii by closing a *Wood 1st G* over it—the text reads *A Plantation,* the Lieutenant Governor's establishment where he holds Imoinda, Oroonoko's lost wife, soon to be rescued from the villain's clutches by the Angolan prince and his English friends. The second act closes with a crowded and busy scene acted out before Cross's *Wood/4G,* doubtless the *L:W 4G* of I.ii. The succession of scenes suggests a "discovery," and the printed stage direction confirms this: *The Scene drawn shews the Slaves, Men, Women, and children upon the ground, some rise and dance, others sing the following Songs.* In the second-last speech of the preceding scene, Stanmore prepares us for a pastoral mood by saying, "Hark! The Slaves have done their work;/ And now begins their evening merriment." Chetwood had marked Stanmore's cue in the margin, *Slaves/Laugh,* and just before the scene withdraws he had indicated *A Dance,* most likely his own cue to alert the musicians.

In the following acts Cross provides rather fewer signs of specific scenery, but by now we know what to expect. Act III begins with no indications of sets by the prompter or help from the printed text, but the number of persons involved would appear to demand continued use of the deep set with its *long wood* backscene. The third scene of Act IV, also undesignated, clearly repeats the discovery of II.iii, for the printed stage direction indicates that another strong theatrical effect awaits the audience: *The Scene drawn shews Oroonoko upon his Back, his legs and Arms stretcht out and chain'd to the ground.* The play closes with a simple *Scene the last,* but this time Cross makes clear the use of the by now familiar deep scene: *Wood:4G.* The promptbook of *Oroonoko* adds considerable support to the text in that it makes far clearer the manager's artistic intentions: to reduce the audience to tears over the plight of the unfortunate blacks and to raise them to a fervor of admiration for the superior courage, loyalty, and sensibility of the African prince.

Other items involving technicalities of production appear in increasing detail in eighteenth-century promptbooks. Take lighting as an example. We know from various engravings, from the complex list of equipment in the Covent Garden inventory of 1743, from the accounts of theatregoers, that the possibilities of more flexible and sophisticated lighting had increased since the Restoration period when, as Richard Southern plausibly argues, "darkness was suggested by the groping action of the players, not by the lowering of the lights."[17] During the first half of the eighteenth century there were evidently some improvements though nothing drastic could be done as long as the notorious "rings" of candles hung over the stage. These could of course be raised and lowered with some effect, but anything notable had to await Garrick's return from the Continent in 1765 and his substitution of wing lights for the overhead rings. These wing lights could be both turned away from the stage and shielded, and the footlights similarly raised, lowered, and shielded. The London theatres were beginning to move toward the subtleties in lighting that De Loutherbourg was to add in the next couple of decades.[18] It would be impossible, however, to derive any clear picture of this increase in capabilities from the promptbook alone. True, there are few indications of how the lights were controlled in promptbooks before the mid-century, but a good many more appeared beyond that point. When Cross, in preparing a promptbook for Garrick's disastrous attempt to add *The London Cuckolds* to the Drury Lane repertory in 1748, entered a *Lamps down* for a street scene involving Ramble's nocturnal adventures, he was most likely calling for a conventional maneuver, not recording an innovation. The same signal, and its countersign, appears in at least two other promptbooks marked by Cross in the 1750s, a *Don Sebastian* in the Penzance group and the Folger *Chances.* Garrick's innovations are not reflected in any of the later promptbooks I have examined, but it is altogether possible that practices recorded in at least three of the Wister-Kemble books carry over from earlier ones. Kemble's *Two Gentlemen of Verona,* which according to Shattuck's account provided little more than frustration for the manager in his attempts to revive it in 1790 and 1808, calls at IV.i for *Lamps a little down,* suggesting increasing flexibility. The *Merry Wives* promptbook employs the same signal;

17. *Changeable Scenery,* p. 127.
18. R. G. Allen's richly detailed account shows how gifted the Alsatian designer was (see n. 15 above).

129

the *Macbeth* one adds other steps: On p. 23 we get *Raise Lamps a little* and *Raise Lamps a little more;* on p. 26 we get *Lamps quite up.*[19]

Sounds as well as lights required the busy prompter's attention and help from his backstage auxiliaries. Act I, Scene iii, of *The Chances* is a brief scene in which Don John responds to the call of *Woman within,* is handed a bundle he finds promising from its weight, and goes off to examine the "fortune" he is sure has dropped into his hands. Just at the point the fortune is given him the prompter enters Call 7, which is a double or triple one, calling for *John/child/one to cry.* After a brief scene of some fifteen lines— Garrick cut still another one—John returns in a fit of anger, frustration, and self-reproach over his new fortune, a crying infant. Though the "one to cry" hardly required a cue for his activities, Cross made doubly sure by repeated marginal entries of *Cries* at every few lines.

Many of the marginal notations—as playbooks shrink and signals increase, interleaves begin to appear—tell us little beyond the fact that our misnamed stage manager is indeed busy. The numbered calls are the most obvious evidence of this. The vast majority of these have to do with alerting members of the cast to be ready for entrance cues. Infrequently the numbers stand alone without names, indicating the existence of an assistant with a companion list on which matching numbers and the missing names appear.[20] The prompter himself could hardly leave his post to pursue errant actors. On occasion a numbered call has a different purpose: to provide a special alert for an offstage noise or to assure that some indispensable piece of property is ready at hand.

Perhaps most curious to the reader today, accustomed to electronic devices for remote control, are the numerous signals involving bells and whistles. The whistle, like the bell and the book always ready at hand on the prompter's table, was used to signal scene changes. Whenever the conventional ☉ (later often Ⓦ) appeared in the margin, the prompter blew his whistle and the scenemen

19. *John Philip Kemble Promptbooks,* V, VI, IX.

20. J. Brownsmith, prompter at the Haymarket as well as at several provincial theatres, defines *Call-boy,* also referred to often as prompter's boy, as "a person (in all regular theatres) appointed to call the Performers from the Green-Room, when they are to go upon the stage." *The Contrast* (Salisbury: J. Hodson, 1776), p. 17.

immediately removed a downstage set of wings and shutters or drop to disclose a new set ready in grooves further upstage, or slid on a downstage pair, which masked the deeper set of the preceding scene. More was involved here than a shift of basic wings and shutters. Simultaneously the borders, above the wings and shutters, were changed. An occasional accident or case of negligence on the part of the scenemen, allowing the clouds of an exterior scene to serve as a ceiling for an interior one, for example, emphasizes the importance of a swift, smooth, coordinated shift.[21]

The bell also became involved as a signal in these changes, further complicating our interpretation.[22] The multiplicity of bells is in fact almost bewildering at times. There were *Border Bells, Cloud Bells, Wing Bells, Drop Cloth Bells, Curtain Bells, Trap Bells, Thunder Bells,* even a *Sconce Bell.* Evidence that these were actually different bells rather than differentiated signals on one bell is supplied by the 1743 inventory of Covent Garden paraphernalia in which the last four appear, the "curtain bell and line" in the "first flies," the "thunder bell and line" in the "painting room," and the "trap bell and sconce bell" in the "cellar."

The audience, and the actors as well, became accustomed to hearing or not hearing certain sounds, just as the audience attending a highly stylized oriental play must learn to see or not see certain persons on stage. The bells I have been referring to were assumed to be inaudible to the audience. Yet the margins of the promptbook carry almost as many signals for bells that were to be heard, often with great dramatic effect. One of the lower-keyed variety appears just before the end of Act II of Thomas Baker's *Tunbridge Walks* (1703), in fact provides the occasion for the act close. The entire act is devoted to social chitchat among various London members of high society and cruder provincial types, all lounging about in a scene labeled in the printed copy as *The Walks.* In the Penzance promptbook Chetwood devotes Call 7 to a reminder: *One at the Bell.* A page later, after the only flurry of action in the whole scene, a

21. See Southern's *Changeable Scenery,* chap. 12 and elsewhere, for a fully detailed exposition of the handling of scenery in the eighteenth century. See also chap. 3 above.

22. Younger, who as Covent Garden prompter in 1766 marked the Folger *Julius Caesar,* uses ℞ for scene changes for the first four acts but unaccountably changes to the more traditional Ⓦ at the beginning of Act V.

noisy but inconsequential sword fight, he notes *Bell Rings for Prayers,* Hillaria's cue to say, "Come, Ladies, the Bell rings to Chapel." All troop off, still talking, and the act closes. Clearly the bell involved here is not the signal bell within the prompter's reach—earlier in the act Chetwood had entered an unnumbered reminder to ring it: *Ring for /Music to/ be Ready,* ready to accompany a singer introduced by Mr Maiden. For the chapel bell we might turn to Boaden, who in his *Memoirs of . . . Kemble* gives a list of properties at Crow Street in 1776, among which are "Thunder Bell, alarm bell, large bell, curtain bell."[23] There appears to be a mixture of categories here. The thunder bell and the curtain bell are without much question signal bells to send the soundmen and scenemen into action, the "unheard" type. The other two may belong to the heard variety. I am not fully confident of this classification for the former but I am of the latter, for it is the large bell that is commonly used to sound the time or to imitate a church bell. In a Folger *Merry Wives* for which Shattuck tentatively suggests a date of 1797 the prompter has written at the top of p. 59 (the first two scenes in Windsor Park begin here) *Clock ready to strike 12.* Just before Falstaff enters, mid-page, in his buck's-head disguise we get a printed stage direction, *A clock strikes twelve,* and just opposite the prompter's note, *Large/Bell.*

At this juncture reading version and acting version virtually coalesce. To take but one example, the ultimate in theatrical effects, we might look at a single act, Act II of *Macbeth*—in any edition—where sounds combine with dialogue and dramatic occasion to produce an almost unbearable tension. Two speeches, prompted by and combined with two different sounds, are all reader or audience require. "I go, and it is done; the bell invites," comes before the awful deed, followed only brief minutes later by "Whence is that knocking?/How is't with me, when every noise appalls me?" The prompter's responsibility of seeing that both bells and knocks are on cue is no light one.

The prompt markings cited so far have given us some sense of what Bateson's "acting version" was like. Actually they have given

23. James Boaden, *Memoirs of the Life of John Philip Kemble, Esq.,* 2 vols. (1825; rpt. New York: Blom, 1969), I, 471.

us more, for added to the actual text, often pruned and rearranged to speed the action, they provide some glimpse of the mechanics of production, of the activities backstage as well as onstage. They have not told us a great deal about specific solutions to specific problems. The absence of such detail is largely owing to the circumstances of repertory production, to the fact that we are observing a company presenting stock plays, most commonly using stock scenery, offering in short what must be essentially replicable material. If an actor dies or deserts, another steps into his shoes—often on the shortest notice. Time permitting, the prompter writes out a new part book for him, even coaches him through a rehearsal or two, but the main concern is that the play go on with the slightest hitch possible.

In *Shakespeare and the Actors* (1944) A. C. Sprague gives promptbooks high marks for their usefulness, "when they can be precisely identified,"[24] in telling us how this or that scene, especially how a particular piece of business, was carried out. True, he does discount this praise rather sharply for books prepared before 1800, and it must be conceded that the early eighteenth-century promptbook is often disappointingly meager. A manuscript promptbook of *The Force of Friendship* in the Folger shows the conventional marking as of 1710, the date of the play's brief run at Drury Lane. The prompter's marks—the hand is that of John Newman, then Drury Lane prompter—are quite exiguous compared with those of a century later. The names of the actors, not the more usual names of the characters, appear, unnumbered, in the margins at the point they are alerted for an upcoming entrance. There is no marginal repetition of the actor's name at the actual point of entry, though the side and the specific entrance is given: MDOP (middle door opposite prompter), LDPS (lower door prompter's side). Properties are indicated at the beginning of an act: V.i, *A Chest/on/A Chaire/A Toylet/and Book*. Scenes are indicated in general terms: *Hall, Chamber, Long Wood,* with the already conventional ⊙ for the prompter's whistle. A scene at the beginning of Act IV is labeled *Anselmo's House* as if Newman had the reader rather than the scenemen in mind, but I take this to be less than

24. A. C. Sprague, *Shakespeare and the Actors* (Cambridge: Harvard Univ. Press, 1944), p. xvii.

reliable evidence that a new scene had been painted for the play or that the actual backscene and wings were destined to bear the label of a character in Charles Johnson's failed play.

On infrequent occasions we do find markings that suggest a prompter was unwilling to leave a complex piece of business to chance or to his or the actors' fallible memory. Take, for example, the problem of the disposition of actors on the stage, especially in court scenes or banquet scenes, where traditionally in real life such matters could not be haphazard. Two such scenes, both in Folger promptbooks, would seem to contradict my point that the later the book the greater the likelihood of increased detail. Kalman A. Burnim calls attention to the fact that "there is no reference in the [1773 *Macbeth*] promptbook to the seating arrangement [at the banquet], or to the number and positions of the attendants."[25] Yet in a transcript of a promptbook of *Richard II,* dated by J. G. McManaway as having been prepared for a performance at Covent Garden on 6 February 1738, we get detailed sketches of the Combat Scene in Act I and of the Parliament Scene in Act IV with the chair of state at the center of the back stage and everyone placed in what we are assured is the historically accurate order.[26]

The far more common story is illustrated in the Penzance *Pilgrim,* where care in placement increases at each successive revival. Wrighten's very first marks in 1787 reveal his concern. Having stricken Chetwood's only mark in 1738, a *PS* for the first entrance, and Cross's explicit note of the scene, *Hay[man's] C: 1 G* (the last item is just barely discernible still), in 1750, he substitutes *A Chamber 1 Groove* and then indicates the order of entrance by placing numbers over the printed names, adding to the 3 above Seberto's name, *who goes OP.* He had initially indicated that the trio would enter *PS* but changed to *OP,* adding that they were to come on by *1 En.* He fails to be so explicit throughout the play but is at almost every point more so than his predecessors.

When earlier promptbooks do on occasion give an indication of how some particular business is handled it is usually under a particu-

25. *David Garrick, Director* (Pittsburgh: Univ. of Pittsburgh Press, 1961), p. 116.

26. *"Richard II* at Covent Garden," *Studies in Shakespeare, Bibliography, and Theater* (New York: The Shakespeare Association of America, 1969), pp. 241–63.

lar circumstance: Some member of the prompter's auxiliary force was to be involved. Take the age-old problem of the contrasted portraits in *Hamlet*. In an article now reprinted in the same collection as his study of the *Richard II* promptbook, McManaway makes some highly interesting observations on John Ward's Call *(18)* in the *Hamlet* now at Johns Hopkins. The call reads, *Hamlet/2 pictures,* a signal which provides "no alternative to believing that Hamlet brought the pictures on with him."[27]

Another piece of traditional business, the use of the "stage cloth" in death scenes, is richly documented in our promptbooks, especially in the latter half of the century. That the tradition was well established before mid-century is certified by a listing of "the Stage cloth" in the Covent Garden inventory of 1743. The earliest reference I have encountered in eighteenth-century promptbooks, after only a casual survey, is in a Folger *Julius Caesar* almost certainly prepared for the January 1766 revival at Covent Garden. Here we have *Carpet on* at the first designated scene break in Act III before Caesar's assassination, and the same notation twice in Act V in anticipation of the deaths of the assassins. The Folger *Macbeth* marked in a 1773 Bell edition calls for *Stage Cloth* in Act V. Passing over later indications of its use I call attention to a striking instance in one of the Wister-Kemble promptbooks, demonstrating conclusively that an item introduced for practical reasons—to protect the costume (and body) of an actor who would otherwise have to fall on the hard, dusty floor—became in time a symbol. Kemble seems regularly to have labeled his tragedies in the Wister collection with a *Green-Cloth* on the very first page. The striking instance occurs in *Measure for Measure,* prompting Shattuck's observation, "In spite of the play's happy ending, its overall terrible earnestness earned for it in those days the tragic designation."[28]

An even more fully documented piece of business where an alert crew of auxiliaries had to be relied on involves the stage trap, and, less often, the wire. Here the same group of promptbooks will serve to illustrate. McManaway devotes some three pages, supporting his exposition with a couple of pages reproduced from the

27. "The Two Earliest Promptbooks of *Hamlet*," *Studies in Shakespeare*, pp. 93–120.
28. *John Philip Kemble Promptbooks*, VI, ii–iii.

earlier Ward *Hamlet,* to showing how the Ghost rose and sank through the stage in all three appearances. The Folger *Julius Caesar* provides similar evidence at two points, once in Act IV during the night scene at Sardis, again in Act V at Philippi after the death of Cassius. Evidence in each case is provided by the prompter's ⓡ *Trap Bell to sink Ghost.* No other play could match the opportunities provided for supernatural apparitions offered by *Macbeth* as the several promptbooks of that play bear witness. Burnim gives ample detail on how the various apparitions were discovered, came and went at stage level, rose and sank by means of traps, or in the case of Hecate flew off "in the machine."[29] The last item was a legacy from the Restoration, Garrick having retained the "operatic" features of both music and flying. As Shattuck's edition of Kemble's promptbook, with its accumulation of practices, demonstrates, *Macbeth* became even more theatrical with the greatly expanded and mechanically more versatile theatres at the end of the century and the beginning of the next.[30]

II

The promptbook is even more useful in the sort of literary-social documentation it can provide for the student of the manners and morals, the tastes and tempers of the day. Here as nowhere else we catch the theatrical entrepreneur in repeated and often frustrated attempts to keep up with the shifting moral and esthetic sensibilities of that exacting but often whimsical monster, the audience. Here we look not so much in the margins as at the text itself to examine the cuts, the changes, the substitutions.

There is, unfortunately, an attendant difficulty: While the type of marking I refer to is in many ways more easily understandable, the demand for preciseness is far harder to satisfy, for the marks are chiefly strikeovers or other indications of cuts far more difficult to identify and therefore to fix in time and place than actual handwriting. Mere numbers or ampersands are far easier to trace to a

29. *David Garrick, Director,* p. 120.
30. See also Joseph W. Donohue, Jr., "Kemble's Production of *Macbeth* (1794)," *Theatre Notebook,* 21 (1966–67), 63–74.

particular hand than boxes or circles around material to be eliminated.

To begin with a relatively simple illustration I take a *Don Sebastian* in the Penzance group. It is common knowledge that relatively few plays are actually produced precisely as they come from the playwright's hand. With Dryden's play such full production would have been unthinkable, as the rueful author admits in his preface. Dryden had largely abandoned the theatre after *The Spanish Friar* (1680), returning to it with reluctance almost a decade later largely because of financial need. Reluctant as he may have been, he was almost uncontrollably luxuriant on his return, as his audience was quick to point out: "I forgot the usual compass of a play . . . but the first day's Audience sufficiently convinc'd me of my error. . . . Above twelve hunder'd lines have been cut off from this Tragedy, since it was first delivered to the Actors." Yet he concedes Betterton's judiciousness in the "lopping" process.

Whether he would have similarly approved of Garrick's cuts of some seventeen hundred lines for the revival of 7 December 1752, "not acted in 20 years," we can only surmise. That Garrick is responsible for the cuts seems a safe conjecture: The play had not been acted at Drury Lane in forty years, though Covent Garden gave it on occasion; the hand is that of Richard Cross. That Dryden might have used "lopping" to describe Garrick's cuts also is predictable; after all, a play running to 124 pages in the first edition was unactable as it stood.[31] That Garrick would cut more heavily in the harem scenes involving the cynically comic Antonio is also predictable. The manager of Drury Lane had had a recent lesson—the wonder is that he needed one—in his unhappy attempts with *The London Cuckolds:* The moral sensibilities of 1750 were not those of 1680. Somewhat more puzzling is the evidence of successive shifts and changes—even though the attempt at revival was also a failure, the play running only four nights. Just to take a few samples: Page 47 lost fourteen lines in what appears to be at least two stages of marking, but there are afterthoughts even beyond that and some six

31. The last page is numbered 132, but there is a gap of eight pages between 87 and 96 brought about, my colleague William Todd plausibly suggests, by a pair of compositors working independently.

or seven lines were steted, only to be restricken; one group of four lines in Sebastian's first speech after entering came and went at least four times.

Two other promptbooks marked under Garrick's supervision add telling evidence. First is an *Oroonoko* in the Penzance group, a copy which had seen long service at Drury Lane, for *Oroonoko* had been a stock play since Restoration times. The basic markings are in the hand of Chetwood, who had doubtless inherited a marked book from his predecessor Newman but who had marked a fresh copy sometime during his quarter century at Drury Lane. Many, probably most, of the cuts had been made before the book came into Cross's hands; the total reduction of some seven hundred lines bringing the play down to just over two thousand, approximately the length of *Don Sebastian* after Garrick's cuts. No single objective, except shortening, seems discernible. Some of the sexual suggestiveness in the comic subplot is eliminated, but almost as many lines of extravagant rhetoric among the slaves and their sympathizers disappear also. Cross's marks, made for the October 1751 revival, the first under Garrick's management—the playbill indicated no performances in five years—seem surprisingly few and perfunctory. The manager had no share in the performance itself and perhaps not much heart in the revival.[32] The response was not one to increase the play in his favor. There were one or two performances during the next half-dozen seasons, no great acclaim certainly but no disaster either—in the *theatre*. The critical response, well represented by a review in *Gentleman's Magazine* the first season of the revival, was distinctly unfavorable. The highly emotional presentation of the noble Angolan prince's fate caused no problem. The intrusion of the strikingly contrasting comic scenes was a far different matter. The mixing of low comedy and pathetic tragedy was bad enough; the kind of comedy that went into the mixture—suggestive, even ribald, and uniformly cynical toward love—was far worse. Garrick, whose skin was not the thickest, was

32. *Oroonoko* may well have been revived to accommodate a new actor, Dexter, who was making his "first appearance on any stage," and who earned the plaudits of the *Inspector*—see *The London Stage* for 23 October 1751—but faded from sight before his second season expired.

bound to heed these attacks on the Lackitt-Welldon-Stanmore scenes. At the same time his sense of theatre told him that there was something enormously appealing in the royal captive's story. Eventually he arrived at a solution: he would have the play rewritten, by Dr Hawkesworth, without the offending comic characters, and he would play the role of Oroonoko himself. This he did on 1 December 1759, with considerable success, the new version being played eight times within the month. But I must return to the main business at hand.[33]

A more complex and equally interesting story of revival and revision, much of it recorded in the pages of another promptbook, also involves Garrick. The Folger promptbook of *The Chances,* a mass of signals, cues, deletions, restorations, paste-ons, and tip-ins in at least three hands, represents two attempts on the part of the Drury Lane manager to revive a popular comedy written by Fletcher in the first half of the seventeenth century and greatly revised by Buckingham in the second.

The story of Garrick's adventures with *The Chances* begins in the early 1750s when word came to him that George II had expressed a desire to see again the play in which Wilks had performed so memorably as Don John. This amounted to a challenge to the actor-manager who strove mightily to please his sovereign and who loved to play Archer, Plume, Ranger, Don Felix—this last the role in which he was to bid farewell to the public in 1776. He secured copies of the play, among them a 1705 quarto that Cross was soon readying for the revival on 7 November 1754. It seems fair to assume that Garrick made no very extensive alterations for this first performance. The king had after all wished to see the play Wilks had triumphed in a generation earlier, and this would be precisely what the king, not noted for his exalted taste, would get. Garrick did expend a great deal of energy readying the performance. In a letter written shortly before the opening he speaks of his "care" in "new dressing" the play—a point he emphasizes in the bills—and in

33. This was far from being the final version of *Oroonoko.* Two others in which the comic scenes were eliminated appeared within a decade of Hawkesworth's. Yet the tragicomic mixture would not remain dead. Hogan accounts for performances of both tragic and tragicomic versions in the last decade of the century, and versions of the full-length play continued to appear after 1800.

casting, even borrowing Mrs Macklin from Covent Garden, but neither here nor in the playbills does he say a word about revisions.[34] Though George II may well have enjoyed the performance, the public, at least those who spoke out in public print, did not. There was widespread disapproval of what seemed shocking immorality in the play. And though the first month saw a satisfying ten performances, the success proved brief. When Garrick offered the play again the next fall, his bills began to emphasize "alterations." When even these brought only limited approval, there were "further alterations." But all would not do and after a few more attempts, in April 1758 Garrick put the play back on the shelf for some fifteen years.

In April 1773 he again revived the play, this time "with great alterations," for his sovereign again had spoken. This time *The Chances* was revived "by particular desire of the Queen." That Queen Charlotte, wife of quite another George, would have shared the tastes and the moral standards of her husband's predecessor is unthinkable; hence the great alterations. Actually, much of what she might have found objectionable had already been removed from the play, if I have been at all successful in distinguishing the hand of Richard Cross, dead in 1759, from that of William Hopkins, prompter in 1773.[35] In any event the hands of both prompters appear on many of the pages—Cross's on virtually every page—and the manager's on a few, chiefly in the form of tip-ins. Two items, which are irresistibly quotable, are all that time and space allow. One is a possibly last-minute addition in Garrick's hand, which serves to stretch out the clever exchange between John and 2 Constantia, now played by the incomparable Frances Abington, in the closing scene of the play.

John. What, what? I'll tell thee any thing, every thing.

2 Con. I wou'd fain know whether you can be kind to me.

John. Look in your glass, my charmer, and answer for me.

34. *The Letters of David Garrick,* ed. David M. Little and George M. Kahrl, 3 vols. (Cambridge: Harvard Univ. Press, 1963), No. 144.

35. Becket published the new acting version within the week of the revival. It is a reasonably close copy of the promptbook marked by Cross. When, in 1777, Bell published

2 Con. You think me very vain.

John. I think you devilish handsome.

2 Con. I shall find you a rogue at last.

John. Then you shall hang me for a fool; take your garters, and do it now if you will.

(*sighing.*

2 Con. You are no fool.

John. O yes, a loving fool.

2 Con. Will you love me for ever?

John. I'll be bound to you for ever—you can't desire better security.

2 Con. I *have* better security.

John. What's that, my angel?

2 Con. The tenderest affection for you now, and the kindest behaviour to you, for evermore.

John. And I, upon my knees, will swear, that, that—what shall I swear?

The other, quite possibly originating as an ad lib and missing from the promptbook, was published in Becket's acting version at the time of the 1773 revival.

Fred. That indeed is strange, but you are much altered, *John;* it was but this morning that women were such hypocrites, that you would not trust a single mother's daughter of 'em.

John. Ay, but when things are at the worst, they'll mend—example does every thing, *Frederick,* and the fair sex will certainly grow better, whenever the greatest is the best woman in the kingdom—that's what I trust too [*sic*].

This interpolation, a bit of flattery addressed to the queen, provided the occasion a few days later for a lively debate reported by Boswell. At a dinner at Oglethorpe's on 29 April Goldsmith called the addition "mean and gross flattery," but Johnson, who would allow no one but himself to attack his former pupil, rose to the actor's defense, which took a form Garrick might have found less than flattering: "And as to meanness, (rising into warmth,) how is it

---

his version he too claimed to be following Hopkins's promptbook, but in this single instance, so far as I have followed John Bell, he is unreliable. What he actually does is to reprint one of the earlier editions, which had appeared before Bell himself had started the vogue of publishing inexpensive acting versions.

mean in a player,—a showman,—a fellow who exhibits himself for a shilling, to flatter his Queen?"

Almost if not quite the last word on Garrick's efforts was spoken much later by Mrs Inchbald. Her remark sums up very well what the actor-manager-reviser was striving for and is to some degree applicable to the kind of document I have been studying here: "Don John is the character, which, most of any in the piece, must be assisted with the actor's skill, or the whole drama sinks into insipidity. . . . The continual bustle, the contrivances, the hurry of intrigue, and the mistakes, in this comedy, are its best claims to the attention of an audience—in these occurrences a reader cannot so well partake; and, as humour is more its quality than wit, of that, again, the reader is denied his equal share with an auditor. Wit is sterling coin, that passes for its genuine value in a book, as well as in a theatre; whilst humour depends upon a hundred accidents to make it current. Garrick was perfectly humorous in Don John, and made the play a favourite, when he performed the part."[36]

Here is the distinction with which we began, "between the acting and the reading versions" of a play. Granted that what Mrs Inchbald is contrasting is *acting* and *reading,* rather than printed versions, it is possible, as I have tried to show, to get a clearer conception of how a piece appeared to an audience by examining the document that kept the busy prompter, and through him the whole company, alert to all the needs of production, to all the devices, conventional and novel, by which they might "body forth the form of things unknown."

36. Elizabeth Inchbald, ed., *The British Theatre,* 25 vols. (London: Longman, et al., 1808), VI (No. 2), 3–4.

5
Performers and Performing

PHILIP H. HIGHFILL, JR

THE GROWTH of the London stage from the modest playhouses of the early Restoration to the gigantic theatres and hippodromes of the Regency was the accomplishment of many thousands of people, most of whom have been forgotten. They were of a variety of national and professional types. There were German instrumentalists, French dancers, Italian singers, Dutch jugglers, Hungarian horsemen, but the majority were people of the British Isles. Most were English, some were Welsh. Ireland contributed large numbers, Scotland few. There were actors, singers, dancers, musicians, managers, prompters, scene painters, machinists, acrobats, equestrians, sibilists, ventriloquists, monologists, pyrotechnists, magicians. They performed in (or logistically sustained) not only the patent theatres and opera houses, but the amphitheatres, pleasure gardens, fair booths, music rooms, and theatrical taverns. Their cultural influence and economic impact affected not only London but nearly every city and town in the king's dominions. The remarks that follow concentrate on people and events between 1700 and 1800: We do not have evidence in quantity sufficient to make confident generalizations about the lives or careers of the generality of common players before 1700.

I Status

It is not yet possible to write a complete "sociology" of the people of the theatre. But perhaps we know enough now about great numbers of them—their working conditions, professional abilities, and domestic arrangements—to take some counteraction against the anecdotists who have left sensational and stereotypical impressions that the males were a profligate amusing lot who, when not negligently onstage, were in gaol, bordello, or barroom, and that the women were attractively worse. In fact, most notions about "show people" held in the nineteenth and twentieth centuries are derived from the published derogation of the eighteenth. From the beginning of the Georgian period, 1714, through 1801, there were about fifty attacks in pamphlets of length—not counting newspaper squibs—provoking about twenty-five defensive pamphlets. Some would seem to have been vitiated by their comic vituperation, like *The Players Scourge* (1757): "Play-actors are the most profligate wretches, and the vilest vermine, that hell ever vomited out; . . . they are the filth and garbage of the earth, the scum and stain of human nature, the excrements and refuse of all mankind, the pests and plagues of human society, the debauchers of mens minds and morals."[1] When in 1743 a contention between players and management precipitated a publication of Drury Lane salary scales, a pamphleteer huffed to the Duke of Grafton, then Lord Chamberlain: "Is it your Pleasure that Players dress like Lords, . . . eat like Priests, keep their Mistresses, have their town and country Houses, and give Law to every Tavern and Coffee-House where they come? This many of them do already. What would you, nay, that they have more?"[2] The Lord Chamberlain, agreeing, dismissed the performers' petition to be allowed to set up their own company. He was indignant to discover that David Garrick drew £500 a year, remarking that his own son had less in the king's naval service.[3]

In mid-century Arthur Murphy, well born and highly educated, was refused admission to the Middle Temple on the ground that he was an actor.[4] The actor Thomas Jefferson was required by his

1. P. 2.
2. [James Ralph], *The Case of Our Present Theatrical Disputes* (London: J. Robinson, 1743), p. 59.
3. Thomas Davies, *Memoirs of the Life of David Garrick, Esq.,* ed. Stephen Jones, 6th ed. (London: Longman, Hurst, et al., 1808), I, 74–75.
4. Howard Hunter Dunbar, *The Dramatic Career of Arthur Murphy* (New York: Modern Language Association, 1946), p. 36.

aristocratic fiancée's father to post a bond of £500 to assure that she would never appear on the stage.[5] At the end of the century James Fennell was handed a letter from his father when about to perform for the first time. It read: "James,/ The last rash step you have taken is a disgrace to yourself and family; and if persisted in, must forever cancel the connexion between you and your late affectionate father/ John Fennell."[6] Such examples, occurring from one end of the eighteenth century to the other, could be cited by the dozens. But the matter is considerably more complicated than such citations make it seem.

Though there was some substance to parental fears and clerical condemnations, at no time during the century were significant numbers of the corps of performers deserving of the castigation of moralists. With many people, inconsistency persisted between what might be called their *public* stance—a *pro forma* distrustful attitude toward the profession—and the treatment they accorded its members. The ambivalence was exhibited most notoriously by Samuel Johnson, Garrick's mentor and friend, who excluded him for a long time from "the Club" by way of disciplining a presumptuous actor—but who refused to allow anyone to nominate Garrick's successor, decreeing a year of "widowhood."[7] Johnson was the patron of Tom Davies, thought Kitty Clive "a good thing to sit by,"[8] boasted of having had "much kiss" of Fanny Abington,[9] wheedled his dreary tragedy *Irene* onto Drury Lane's board's, and edited

5. [James Winston], *The Theatric Tourist* (London: T. Woodfall, 1805), p. 39.
6. *An Apology for the Life of James Fennell, Written by Himself* (Philadelphia: Moses Thomas, 1814), p. 196. None were as extreme as the barrister Thomas Ford, Clerk of the Arraigns, whose daughter Ann attracted noted professional musicians like Dr T. A. Arne to her Sunday musicales, where she performed as singer, viola da gamba player, and guitarist. Her father objected to her playing in public even as an amateur and obtained a magistrate's order to confine her to his house. She escaped to give subscription concerts at the Haymarket Theatre. Her father blocked the streets around the theatre with Bow Street runners, who were dispersed by Lord Tankerville's threat to call out the guards. Ann went on to a career of singing and playing on the musical glasses before becoming the third wife of the aristocratic adventurer Philip Thicknesse. See *DNB*, XIX, 610–11 and "Armonica," *Grove's Dictionary of Music and Musicians*, 5th ed. (1966).
7. *Boswell's Life of Johnson*, ed. George Birkbeck Hill, rev. by L. F. Powell (Oxford: Clarendon Press, 1934–50), I, 481n.
8. Boswell, IV, 7.
9. *The Letters of Samuel Johnson with Mrs. Thrale's Genuine Letters to Him*, ed. R. W. Chapman (Oxford: Clarendon Press, 1952), II, 389.

Shakespeare—but professed *publicly* to think that an actor was "a fellow who exhibits himself for a shilling," and Garrick "a fellow who claps a hump on his back and a lump on his leg and cries *'I am Richard the third'?* Nay, sir, a ballad-singer is a higher man."[10]

Much recent pecksniffian bridling at the people of the stage has been either hypocritical or ignorant. Sexual scandals involving actors occurred; they were scandalous because they became known; they became known because they involved prominent persons. Cohabitation, common-law marriage, bigamous relationships were as common then as they are today. In any case, no reader of the letters of Lady Mary Wortley Montagu or of Horace Walpole's letters or of William Hickey's memoirs can suppose that performers were more dissolute or produced more bastards than the nonperforming upper and middle classes did.[11] Indeed, some of the episodes that have received the most attention involved both performers and members of the upper classes. In each of them the theatrical partner seemed intent on rendering more respectable the aristocrat with whom the liaison was formed. In most of them marriage was the dénouement. The most celebrated case was that of Lavinia Fenton, who stepped from her success as the first Polly in *The Beggar's Opera* into the waiting arms of Charles Powlett, Duke of Bolton. She lived with him for twenty-three years, until the duchess died in 1751, whereupon the duke married Lavinia.

The talented Mrs Maria Susanna Cooper Hunter, actress and authoress, became the mistress of Gen. John Hayes St Leger.[12] She openly accompanied the general to the West Indies where he had been posted as commandant.[13] The exquisite Elizabeth Farren, actress and singer, had a brief affair with Charles James Fox before meeting Edward, twelfth Earl of Derby, who took her into society

10. Boswell, III, 184.

11. The reader is referred to the story of Elizabeth Chudleigh, indicted for bigamy and tried in the House of Lords after marrying the Duke of Kingston while secretly married to the Earl of Bristol. In a reversal of the usual scenario, Garrick took his proper friend Hannah More to the trial, which Walpole pronounced the best show of the season. Samuel Foote wrote a satire about the affair, *A Trip to Calais,* which the Lord Chamberlain suppressed because the countess-duchess didn't like her portrayal as Lady Kitty Crocodile. See Garrick's entry in *BD,* VI, 1–112.

12. See Tate Wilkinson, *The Wandering Patentee* (York: Printed for the Author, 1795), I, 276.

13. *Public Advertiser,* 28 July 1781.

in 1785. When the countess of Derby died in 1797, Miss Farren succeeded her. There were three children by the marriage, one of whom married the Earl of Wilton.[14]

At least two actresses might have become morganatic wives of royalty had it been permitted by law. "Perdita," Mary Robinson, attracted the passionate addresses of her "Florizel," George, Prince of Wales. But marriage was out of the question. After a few months he reneged on his bond of £20,000.[15] (The witty comedienne Dorothy Jordan kept that in mind when she captivated the Duke of Clarence. She was eventually to bear him ten children, all ennobled as FitzClarence.[16] The duke allowed her £1,000 per year, but his frugal father George III sent an equerry with a letter proposing a reduction to £500. The intrepid Dorothy tore off and returned to the king the bottom of a playbill bearing the message "NO MONEY RETURNED AFTER THE RISING OF THE CUR-TAIN.")[17]

Great competency, and even genius, occasionally sprang from the humblest beginnings, as did Frances Barton Abington, the daughter of a poor cobbler. As "Nosegay Fan" she sold flowers and sang in the streets around Covent Garden when she was fourteen. She worked her way as ballad singer, cookmaid, and minor player up to the top of her profession as comedienne and to easy association with the great.[18] But, leaving aside the billstickers and sceneshifters—the theatrical navvies—the theatres were populated very heavily by folk belonging to the middle and upper-middle layers of the socioeconomic strata. A good many were scions of the gentry. Some married sons and daughters of gentility without exciting scandal—though seldom without complaint.

The roster of legitimate and honorable familial relationships with nobility and knighthood comprises only a few people. But a list of those performers with certifiable pretensions to gentility and edu-

14. *DNB*, VI, 1094–95.
15. See *Memoirs of the Late Mrs. Robinson Written by Herself* ([London?]: R. Phillips, 1801), passim.
16. See A. Aspinall's introduction to his edition of her correspondence, *Mrs. Jordan and Her Family* (London: Arthur Barker, Ltd., 1951), pp. ix–xvii.
17. *DNB*, X, 1083; this agreeable anecdote is derided by Brian Fothergill in *Mrs Jordan: Portrait of an Actress* (London: Faber and Faber, 1965), p. 147.
18. *Theatrical Biography* (London: S. Bladon, 1772), I, 12.

cation would be very great indeed, as an hour's thumbing through their lives in the ongoing *Biographical Dictionary* will demonstrate. With actors there is, of course, a presumption of literacy. But a great many were also well educated, "literary," and many were even learned. A sizeable number had attended good public schools, a university, or the Inns of Court, and many—e.g., Garrick,[19] Henderson, T. A. Cooper, Arthur Murphy—were good classicists. When Samuel Foote was managing in Edinburgh in 1770 the audience one night demanded his popular satire against the Methodist Whitefield, *The Minor.* "Mr. Foote himself made his appearance, and in Latin intimated to the house, that the principal subject of ridicule having paid nature's great debt, he humbly submitted to their reflection whether such an exhibition would be seemly."[20] John Walker, who was on the London and Dublin stages for several years, in 1791 published his *Critical Pronouncing Dictionary and Expositor of the English Language,* the authority on its subject for half a century. At least 130 actors and actresses wrote many hundreds of plays for production, and many published novels, volumes of poems, or essays. Numbers collected fine libraries of rare books, including Shakespeare and Jonson folios.[21]

Most important to the performers—and for our understanding of their social status—were their connections with other professions, guilds, and trades before, after, and in a good many cases during, their careers in the theatre. Again, a random survey will suggest the variety of fields from which they were recruited. There were military men, like Capt. George Wathen (who had served actively and who retired after his stage career as one of His Majesty's Knights of Windsor);[22] Francis Gentleman, who was an ensign in his father's regiment during the '45;[23] Robert Palmer, who served under the

19. But Johnson told Boswell: "He has not Latin enough. He finds out the Latin by the meaning, rather than the meaning by the Latin," an opinion perhaps rather like Ben Jonson's on Shakespeare's learning. See Boswell, II, 377.

20. Press clipping in the Burney Collection, British Library. His was probably a university audience.

21. See, for example, the entries for Garrick, Edward Jones, William Havard, Thomas King, Ludwig von Holberg, and James William Dodd in the *Biographical Dictionary.*

22. Wathen's will, Prerogative Court of Canterbury, Principal Probate Register, Public Record Office; *United Service Magazine* (May 1849), p. 160.

23. Francis Gentleman, Preface to *The Modish Wife* (London: T. Evans and John Bell, 1775), p. 4.

Marquis of Granby;[24] Friedrich Hartmann Graf the flutist and composer, who served as kettle drummer in the Netherlandish campaign and was wounded;[25] Robert Bensley, who was on active duty against the French in America.[26] There were lawyers—like Daniel Egerton[27] and the Colmans[28] and Thomas Crawford,[29] and seafarers, like C. B. Incledon,[30] and apothecaries, like Richard Estcourt.[31] William Wyatt Dimond was a silver "chaser,"[32] C. C. Dubellamy a shoemaker,[33] John Cornelys a staymaker,[34] Peter Duffey a Dublin hatter,[35] Thomas Haymes a Devon coachmaker.[36] Alexander Pope (the actor) was a portrait painter, who forsook painting because he was "passionately fond of drama, and was the hero of a private theatre."[37] Thomas Death was the son of a London surgeon and apothecary;[38] John Edwin's father was a watchmaker in Clare Market;[39] Jane Pope was the daughter of a wigmaker who kept a shop in little Russell Street "adjoining the Ben Jonson's Head" and was also "barber in ordinary to Drury Lane Theatre."[40] Charles Holland, a baker's son, was apprenticed to a turpentine merchant.[41]

24. *The Thespian Dictionary* (London: J. Cundee, 1805), n.p.

25. Grove, III, 743.

26. See *The Secret History of the Green Rooms* (London: J. Owen, 1795), I, 165.

27. *DNB*, VI, 569.

28. See Richard Brinsley Peake, *Memoirs of the Colman Family*, 2 vols. (London: Richard Bentley, 1841) and Jeremy Felix Bagster-Collins, *George Colman, the Younger, 1762–1836* (New York: King's Crown Press, 1946).

29. Thomas Gilliland, *The Dramatic Mirror*, 2 vols. (London: C. Chapple, 1808), II, 712.

30. [James Winston], *The Manager's Notebook* (a collection of biographies extracted from the *New Monthly Magazine* in 14 numbers between November 1837 and December 1838, according to R. W. Lowe, James Fullerton Arnott and John William Robinson in *English Theatrical Literature 1559–1900* [London: Society for Theatre Research, 1970], p. 402, No. 4169), pp. 216–17.

31. Thomas Whincop, *Scanderbeg: or, Love and Liberty. A Tragedy . . . To which are added, A list of all the dramatic authors . . . to the year 1747* (the list probably by John Mottley, ed. Martha Whincop) (London: J. Reeve, 1747), p. 227.

32. I.e., engraver. Gilliland, I, 171.

33. Peake, II, 4.

34. *Gentleman's Magazine*, October 1818.

35. *Thespian Dictionary*, n.p.

36. Ibid.

37. [James Winston], *Manager's Notebook*, pp. 216–17.

38. *General Magazine*, November 1788, p. 564.

39. [Winston] *Manager's Notebook*, p. 400.

40. *DNB*, XVI, 132.

41. *DNB*, IX, 1031–32.

149

Virtually every trade and profession fed recruits to the acting companies—even the Church. For despite the "official" attitude of the clergy toward performers, many had family connections with organized religion. Brownlowe Ford took orders, left the Church for the Irish stage, had a lengthy career in Ireland and in London, managed a company, and then resumed his clerical duties.[42] Benjamin Griffin was a son of the rector of Buxton and Oxnead, chaplain to the Earl of Yarmouth.[43] Thomas Griffith's second wife was Ursula, daughter of the Reverend Richard Foxcroft of Portarlington, Ireland.[44] John Jackson was the son of a Berkshire clergyman,[45] Charles Dibdin the elder son of a parish clerk.[46] James De Castro's father was a rabbi.[47] The widowed actress Mrs Harris James capped a twenty-year acting career by announcing that she was "going to leave the stage, and retire . . . to a Nunnery."[48] (She did not, however, ever act Ophelia—only Gertrude.)

There is no way now to measure the comparative piety of those many hundreds of performers christened, married, or buried in Inigo Jones's little "actors' church," St Paul, Covent Garden,[49] but outward regularity was obviously to their social and (at benefit time) even pecuniary advantage, and many were bywords for rectitude and religion. Kitty Clive and Jane Pope, Mrs John Jackson, Elizabeth Inchbald, and Mrs Thomas Jefferson were all strict moralists and churchgoers, and the great comedian Ned Shuter, a

---

42. *Hibernian Journal* (4 February 1784). One of the subscribers to the *Dramatic Works of John O'Keeffe* (London: T. Woodfall, 1798) was "The Rev. Brownlow Ford, L.L.D.". William Upcott [John Watkins and William Shoberl], *A Biographical Dictionary of Living Authors of Great Britain and Ireland* (London: Henry Colborn, 1816), p. 431, said that he had been Ordinary of Newgate.

43. Notice in newsclipping, Burney Collection, British Library.

44. William Rufus Chetwood, *A General History of the Stage* (London: W. Owen, 1749), p. 53.

45. Ms. 353, fol. 65, National Library of Scotland; *Biographia Dramatica,* ed. Stephen Jones (London: Longman, Hurst, Rees, et al., 1812), I, Part 2, 394.

46. *DNB,* V, 907.

47. *The Memoirs of J. De Castro, Comedian* (London: Sherwood, Jones and Co., 1824), p. 3.

48. Richard Cross, "Diary," Folger Ms. W.a.104, entry of 22 November 1754, cited in *LS,* Part 4, II, 453.

49. See the *Registers,* ed. Rev. William H. Hunt, 5 vols. (London: Harleian Society, 1906–9). This was the performers' principal church by a wide margin, but many others were buried, baptized, or married in nearby parishes—St Anne's, Soho, St Giles in the Fields, St Martin-in-the-Fields, and so on, in widening circles around the centers of performance. Many minor players rest in the churchyard of St George's, Southwark, near the site of the Fair. Garrick and a few other major players are in Westminster Abbey.

Methodist, was said to have gone to church four times each Sunday.[50]

The fascinated focus of the journalists' telescopes on their activities revealed little record of crime. Thomas Davies notes that in "the records of Newgate and the Old Bailey, . . . you will scarcely find the name of a comedian among the many unhappy wretches who have suffered condign punishment for breaking the laws of their country."[51] The actors' most notorious tragedy in the eighteenth century involved an accident rather than a crime. A quarrel over a property wig between Thomas Hallam and Charles Macklin in the green room of Drury Lane Theatre in 1735 led to the death of Hallam when Macklin angrily thrust at him with a stick that penetrated his eye. Macklin, convicted of manslaughter, was marked in the hand with a cold iron.[52] The talented actor and portraitist Robert Dighton was disgraced (but never punished) for stealing etchings from the British Museum.[53] The only known capital execution was on Robert Carpenter, minor actor and singer. Repeatedly accused of forgery and rape, he was discharged from the Drury Lane Fund for defrauding it, and hanged at Winchester for forging seamen's wills.[54] (Few suicides are known, either: Lawrence Kennedy,[55] John Coles,[56] Robert Benson[57]—all the result of mental derangement.)

Surprisingly few duels were fatal, considering that players were specially trained in the use of the sword. From 1725, when Henry Norris killed Henry Goddard in a rencounter and was burned in the hand for manslaughter,[58] until the bloody but not fatal duels R. B. Sheridan fought over Miss Linley in 1772,[59] most appeals to the

50. Mrs Clement Parsons, *Garrick and His Circle* (London: Methuen, 1906), pp. 248–49.
51. Davies, II, 328.
52. William W. Appleton, *Charles Macklin: An Actor's Life* (Cambridge: Harvard Univ. Press, 1960), pp. 29–33.
53. Cecil Brooking, "Stage Folk in Dighton Prints," *Notes and Queries*, 179 (December 1940), 403; *DNB*, V, 979–80.
54. *Salisbury and Winchester Journal*, 4 April 1785.
55. *Hibernian Journal*, 28 June 1786.
56. *Gentleman's Magazine*, November 1800.
57. *Monthly Mirror*, May 1796.
58. *The Historical Register, Containing Impartial Relations of All Transactions, Foreign and Domestic*, X (1725), 40.
59. The story has many lurid versions. R. Crompton Rhodes attempted to pick out the correct one in *Harlequin Sheridan: The Man and the Legends* (Oxford: Blackwell, 1933), pp. 31–49.

code duello had farcical dénouements, like that between George Garrick and Robert Baddeley (whose second was his wife's lover, Mendez), when both principals fired and missed.[60]

Ties of the theatrical to the general middle-class population grew in many ways. We observe, for instance, the practice of following a secondary occupation while still employed at the theatre, apparently widespread among auxiliaries to the house and also among musicians. Dramatic actors were often too busy, and sometimes too prosperous. There were exceptions, such as the great comedian John Emery, who exhibited as an honorary member of the Royal Academy and is said to have sold paintings for a good price.[61] Susannah Yarrow and her actress mother after the death of the father presided over Dick's Coffee House, perhaps while acting, though maybe only between country and town engagements.[62] Susannah's husband (after 1749), Tom Davies, of course kept a bookshop in the interval of his lapsed acting career, where the momentous meeting of Boswell with Johnson occurred.[63] William Pritchard evidently kept a warehouse in Tavistock Street, but that was after he became treasurer of Drury Lane and ceased to perform.[64] Several of the Grimaldis were both clowns and dentists. In the summer of 1760 Giuseppe Grimaldi was at Liverpool, where he advertised his readiness "to draw teeth or stumps without giving the least uneasiness in the operation," at his lodgings.[65] In fact, the elder John Baptist Grimaldi had advertised in London as early as 1737 "Signor Grimaldi's Dentifrice" as having been in use "for years past."[66] Often house servants extended their theatrical jobs,

60. See the satirical print reproduced in *BD*, VI, 114.

61. Winston, *Manager's Notebook*, p. 53; *Theatrical Inquisitor* April 1814, p. 196.

62. They inspired James Miller to write his comedy *The Coffee House* featuring characters resembling them. See *Biographica Dramatica*, I, Part 2, 513.

63. Boswell, I, 390–92.

64. Drury Lane playbill of 18 April 1757.

65. Richard Findlater, *Grimaldi, King of Clowns* (London: MacGibbon and Kee, 1956), p. 33; Giuseppe Grimaldi, during an engagement in Bristol, advertised his services as surgeon-dentist in *Felix Farley's Bristol Journal* on 11 June 1774. On 26 August 1775 in the same journal, G. Grimaldi, "who has had the Honor of attending her MAJESTY, the Prince of Wales, and the Prince and Princess of Brunswic [*sic*], and the Happiness of having his Applications crown'd with Success," renewed his solicitation. (Information furnished by Kathleen Barker.)

66. Charles Bew, who tried and failed both as London and provincial actor in the eighteenth century, settled into dentistry early in the nineteenth and was able at last to

as did Lucy Gwinn, wife of the pit doorkeeper William Gwinn. Employed in the wardrobe at Lincoln's Inn Fields, she also dyed silk commercially.[67] Musicians also made extra money from their specialties by operating music-publishing businesses, music shops, or instrument-making concerns.

Numbers of performers joined the Ancient Free and Accepted Masons, that epitome of upper-middle-class ideals and values. Harry W. Pedicord reports that there were at least four theatrical or musical lodges of Masons: the Shakespeare, No 131, meeting at Covent Garden Theatre; the Lodge of the Nine Muses, No 330, at the Thatched House Tavern, St James's Street; the Apollo Lodge of Harmony, at the Argyle Arms, Argyle Street,[68] and the Bear and Harrow Lodge in Butcher Row.[69] Pedicord identifies performers and managers Colley and Theophilus Cibber, William Mills, Thomas Shepard, John Boman, James Quin, Dennis Delane, and Henry Giffard as known Masons. But there were others too—for instance Thomas Finch, William Neeves, Thomas Towe, Thomas Smart, Excell, Montgomery, William Havard, Jacobs, and John ("Plausible Jack") Palmer. Thomas Griffith was Deputy Master of the Dublin Lodge when he managed Smock Alley Theatre.

II Recruitment

There were only a few ways for aspirants to gain the boards of the London patent theatres. A youth of talent could be born into a family connected to a London theatre and obtain preferential treatment and early training. Only in the last quarter of the eighteenth century, however, did the great theatrical families achieve their full growth. If an aspirant was not so favored with family, other methods had to be sought: sponsorship by an estab-

---

advertise as "Surgeon Dentist to His Majesty, Their Royal Highnesses, the Duke and Duchess of Clarence and the Royal Household." Newsclipping from Brighton, Winston clippings, Folger Library.

67. Covent Garden playbill of 9 April 1739; Lalauze's benefit on that date is confirmed by *The London Stage*, which does not, however, carry the rest of the information.

68. "White Gloves at Five: Fraternal Patronage of London Theatres in the Eighteenth Century," *Philological Quarterly*, 45 (1966), 270–88.

69. "George Lillo and 'Speculative Masonry,'" *Philological Quarterly*, 53 (1974), 408.

lished manager or actor, perhaps after being introduced by an influential person; or being "discovered" during a provincial success by an agent of a metropolitan manager; or—almost a forlorn hope—hiring the Haymarket or some minor theatre or tavern for a debut which might attract journalistic and managerial attention.

Despite David Garrick's oft-expressed contempt for the affectations bred in youngsters by country companies,[70] he was careful to employ informal scouts and agents to seek them out. Sarah Siddons remembered that in June 1775 "M[r] Garrick who had heard some account of me . . . came to Cheltenham to see me act the Fair Penitent and approved of what he saw."[71] On 31 July 1775 Garrick wrote to his friend the theatrical connoisseur and editor, the Reverend Henry Bate: "If You pass by Cheltenham in Your Way to Worcester, I wish you would see an Actress there, a *M[rs] Siddon's*, She has a desire I hear to try her Fortune with Us; if she seems in Your Eyes worthy of being transplanted, pray desire to know upon what conditions She would make y[e] Tryal."[72]

Though the function of professional theatrical agent probably did not develop until the nineteenth century, Ann Catherine Holbrook in her *Memoirs* speaks of a system very like an agency flourishing toward the end of the eighteenth: "I formed a determination, as I had no engagement, of going to London and making an application for one at the Crown and Thistle, Russel-court, which has long been a kind of theatrical register-office . . . I . . . went to Mr. Baynes, who kept [that public house] . . . ; from him I learnt there were three vacancies of which I might take my choice; having fixed on my destination, he wrote to the Manager, who immediately engaged me . . . I joined the company at Lewes, in Sussex, during the races."[73] Matthew Mackintosh in his *Stage Reminiscences* says that, apparently about 1790, "A frequent resort was the 'Harp,' in Little Russell-street, nearly opposite the stage-door of Drury-lane

70. See, for instance, *Letters,* No. 297, II, 367; No. 924, III, 1019.

71. *The Reminiscences of Sarah Kemble Siddons 1773–1785,* ed. William Van Lennep (Cambridge: Harvard Univ. Press, 1942), cited in *Letters,* III, 1021n.

72. *The Letters of David Garrick,* ed. David M. Little and George Kahrl (Cambridge: Harvard Univ. Press, 1963), No. 926, III, 1021. Several such instances can be given. See also No. 357, II, 427, and No. 924, III, 1019.

73. *The Dramatist; or, Memoirs of the Stage* (Birmingham: Martin and Hunter, 1809), pp. 12–13.

Theatre, then a well-known house of call for country actors visiting London in search of engagements."[74] It was also a place where country managers could find young London aspirants.

Very naturally the idea of schools of dramatic action recurred throughout the period. So did movements toward an apprenticeship system. Neither notion was formally developed. In the late seventeenth century there had been the "Nurseries."[75] Thomas Richardson, actor and manager, in 1729 set up a "Lilliputian Theatre" in "Mr. Hewetson's Great Room" where a "Set of Lilliputian Comedians" were to play.[76] At the end of the eighteenth century there was the "Private Theatre," in Tottenham-Court-Road, "a place of great consequence in dramatic estimation," from which James Winston moved a number of students to the theatre at Richmond Surrey.[77] Isaac Reed in his manuscript "Notitia Dramatica" noted that the comic genius Ned Shuter appeared for the first time at Thomas Chapman's Covent Garden benefit, 15 April 1745, adding "Chapman was his Master kept a Coffee House Corner of Bow Street."[78] The Richmond, Surrey, playbills tell us that Chapman, manager there, brought his coffeehouse 'prentice boy Shuter onto the Richmond stage. So in this instance we appear to have a sort of double apprenticeship. Perhaps that arrangement was common among theatrical people.

Charles Macklin at different times offered instruction both in "schools" and in a sort of apprentice system.[79] Macklin, in an angry memorandum to his erring student Henrietta Leeson, wrote of "a breach of your contract as an apprentice."[80] The actor Thomas Dibble Davis advertised in the *Morning Chronicle* of 8 September 1781, offering "his assistance to ladies & Gentlemen, whose genius

74. (Glasgow: J. Hedderwick and Son, 1866), pp. 121–22.
75. "Near these a Nursery erects its head,/ Where Queens are form'd, and future heroes bred;/ Where unfledg'd actors learn to laugh and cry,/ Where infant punks their tender voices try,/ And little Maximins the gods defy." [John Dryden], *MacFlecknoe, or A Satyr upon the true-blew Protestant poet, T. S. By the Author of Absalom & Achitophel* (London: D. Green, 1682), lines 74–78.
76. Playbill of 21 January 1729.
77. Winston, *Theatric Tourist*, p. 26.
78. British Library Add. Mss. 25, 391–92.
79. See Appleton, chaps. 6 and 9.
80. Appleton, p. 167.

and inclination are ripe for an attempt in the Sock or Buskin." There were probably plenty of respondents to such advertisements from among the youths who practiced reading plays in the "spouting clubs" which convened in London taverns. Elizabeth Hartley advertised on 29 September 1772 that she was a gentlewoman "who has played Capital Characters . . . in the three Kingdoms" and would teach ladies acting at her lodgings, No 2 Queen Street, Haymarket.[81]

III Acting in the Provinces

Probably the provincial route was taken by more performers than any other path to the London theatre. If was, in fact, advantageous for performers to experience provincial conditions early, inasmuch as most would spend time on the circuits or in provincial cities later. The peripatetic Tony Aston, in his testimony against Sir John Barnard's playhouse bill before the House of Commons in 1735, is supposed to have said that if "all Country Actors must promiscuously suffer by this Act, I question if there is Wood enough in *England* to hang them all."[82] The act, which passed in 1737, was never able to stem the tide of country theatricals, and at the end of the century James Winston was able to mention over 280 theatres in circuits in England, Scotland, Ireland, and Wales.[83] In addition, the number of provincial "legitimate" theatres, in England alone, increased by the granting of nine royal patents: to Bath and Norwich in 1768, to York and Hull in 1769, to Liverpool in 1771, to Manchester in 1775, to Chester in 1777, and to Bristol and Newcastle in 1778.

It is therefore necessary to say something of theatrical life in the

81. *LS,* Part 4, III, 1660.

82. *Tony Aston's petition and speech (with his deportment before the Honble H——se of C——ns, in behalf of himself and the actors in town and country. To which is prefix'd, His visionary introduction* (London: Printed for the Author, 1735), pp. 9–11.

83. In *The Theatric Tourist* and in his correspondence with provincial managers, now in the Shakespeare Collection of the Birmingham Public Library, and in his notebooks, miscellaneous letters, and multifarious manuscript jottings in the Harvard Theatre Collection, the Folger Shakespeare Library, and elsewhere. See Alfred L. Nelson, "James Winston's *Theatric Tourist,* a Critical Edition, with a Biography and a Census of Winston Material," Diss. George Washington 1968.

provinces if we are to understand the conditions under which many actors began their professional life and to which many from time to time returned. Just as we have discovered that it is impossible to write intelligently about conditions at the London winter patent theatres without considering the whole mix of London entertainment from mountebanks to opera, so are we now discovering that no proper assessment of performers and performances in London can be made without considering country conditions.[84]

But "country conditions" covers as many varieties of performances and playhouses, accidents and incidents, as "London stage." The barn in which Hogarth satirized the dressing actresses was a far cry from Dublin's Smock Alley or Bristol's Theatre Royal, and audiences at Bath were, if anything, more discriminating than those of Covent Garden. The country actors whom Aston defended were for the most part "strollers," many of whom literally walked hundreds of miles in a season, from town to town. Among peripatetic country actors there was a wide spectrum, ranging from the early, hand-to-mouth troupes wandering with no set itinerary and depending for their existence on bribed or cajoled magistrates, to late, well-conducted enterprises like that of Tate Wilkinson in Yorkshire, playing in real theatres on an established circuit.[85]

In 1731 James Ralph said of strollers, "I am inclined to think that most of them were got under Hedges, born in Barns, and brought up in Houses of Correction,"[86] and his contemporary, Colley Cibber's daughter Charlotte Charke likened touring to "engaging in a little dirty Kind of War," thinking it "would be more reputable to earn a Groat a Day in Cinder-sifting at Tottenham-Court."[87] But if one had youthful health and belonged to a well-conducted company, strolling could be stimulating.

84. Excellent work has been done on individual theatres, towns, and circuits by Sybil Rosenfeld, Cecil Price, Kathleen Barker, Norma Armstrong, Esther Sheldon, Arnold Hare, and others. But some of this information is still in manuscript, and some work—like that of the late William Smith Clark on the Irish theatre—remains unfinished.

85. For a lively sketch, see Charles Beecher Hogan, "One of God Almighty's Unaccountables Tate Wilkinson of York," *The Theatrical Manager in England and America*, ed. Joseph W. Donohue, Jr. (Princeton: Princeton Univ. Press, 1971), pp. 63–86.

86. Ralph, p. 59.

87. Charlotte Charke, *A Narrative of the Life of Mrs. Charlotte Charke*, 2nd ed. (London: W. Reeve, A. Dodd and E. Cook, 1755), p. 187.

There were two kinds of companies operating in circuits or strolling—those ostensibly and sometimes actually run by the players themselves, called sharing companies, and those in which an organizing entrepreneur managed affairs and paid contracted salaries to his players. During the century the first gradually gave way to the second. In sharing companies players divided profits after expenses. But the system invited abuse. As Thomas Snagge observed: "The Manager's allotment is always two shares for clothes, two for scenes, one for himself, one for his wife and one for each child that performs, so he is the principal receiver as well as Manager and becomes the Leviathan for a Great Swallow."[88] Thomas Holcroft later gave the same breakdown, adding "Our manager ([Samuel] Stanton), has five sons and daughters all ranked as performers; so that he sweeps eleven shares, that is near half the profits of the theatre, into his pocket every night."[89]

In sharing companies pickings were slim for all but the manager's brood, but at least the rest, "Macbeth and the Murderer, Hamlet and the Sentinel, Lear and one of his Knights, all take an equal division of the spoil."[90] In some large salaried static or circuiting companies pay had a wide range, from the London players who were brought in for a few nights, often commanding munificent fees, and even travel expenses,[91] down to young beginners. In sharing companies choice of benefit nights was settled by rolling dice,[92] but in most good salaried companies, as at Norwich, benefits fell "in Course of Salaries."[93]

Discomforts and dangers of provincial theatrical life begot a hardihood and flexibility, which were not amiss in those aiming for

88. Thomas Snagge, *Recollections of Occurrences,* ed. Harold Hobson (London: Dropmore Press, 1951), p. 106.

89. *The Life of Thomas Holcroft Written by Himself Continued . . . by William Hazlitt,* ed. Elbridge Colby (London: Constable, 1925), I, 154.

90. Petronius Arbiter, *Memoirs of the Present Countess of Derby* (London: Symonds, [1797]), p. 12.

91. On 3 March 1777, for instance, Maria Hunter was paid "for her Charges in coming from London to perform" at Norwich. *The Committee Books of Theatre Royal Norwich 1768–1825,* ed. Dorothy H. Eshleman (London: Society for Theatre Research, 1970), p. 52.

92. Sir St Vincent Troubridge, *The Benefit System in the British Theatre* (London: Society for Theatre Research, 1967).

93. Eshleman, p. 52.

a London career. Opportunities to build repertoires and to try different "lines" and specialties were often excellent, especially where specialists were an unaffordable luxury. The experience of Charles Macklin has often been cited as an example of extreme versatility: "Sometimes he was an architect, and knocked up the stage and seats in a barn; sometimes he wrote an opening Prologue, or a parting Epilogue, for the company; at others, he wrote a song, complimentary or adulatory to the village they happened to play in, which he always adapted to some sprightly popular air, and sung himself; and he often was champion, and stood forward to repress the persons who were accustomed to intrude upon, and be rude to the actors."[94] All that in addition to acting an extensive round of characters, comic and tragic. When James Gardner was with Mrs Baker's company on the Canterbury, Rochester, Maidstone, Tunbridge Wells circuit, he was the "stage manager, who played all the heroes, Falstaff, and the violoncello, set the accompaniment of the orchestra, taught the singers, and sometimes copied the parts."[95]

That there were appalling discomforts and dangers in incessant traveling in the British Isles in the eighteenth century is emphasized in every memoir. Samuel Foote complained in a letter to Wilkinson that on an excursion from Dublin to Edinburgh for seven nights of acting he had "encountered more perils than in a voyage to the Indies. Not to mention mountains, precipices, savage cataracts, and savage men, I was locked up for near a week in a village [Moffat], dirty, dismal, and desolate, by a deluge of snow."[96] Traveling from Bristol to Bath, the actor, manager, and dancer Joseph Glassington suffered a broken leg when his carriage overturned, and two actresses and the treasurer were "much bruised."[97] Drury Lane's comic repertory was crippled for months when Tom King's horse threw him and broke his leg.[98] Young Thomas Snagge's chaise horse fell on the road from Liverpool to London and his trunk of costumes

94. James Thomas Kirkman, *Memoirs of the Life of Charles Macklin* (London: Lackington, Allen and Co., 1799), I, 59–60.
95. *The Reminiscences of Thomas Dibdin* (London: Henry Colburn, 1827), I, 98.
96. Tate Wilkinson, *Memoirs of His Own Life* (York: Printed for the Author, 1790), IV, 246–47.
97. *Monthly Mirror*, May, 1801, p. 274.
98. *The Letters of David Garrick*, II, 549.

crushed his arm.[99] Rushing to join his company at Limerick, his "Tim Whisky" overturned when his horse ran away and he was *hors de combat* for three weeks. "The Dublin Newspapers announced [he] had been killed in the accident"[100] (one of many such false reportings).[101]

In the narrow playhouses and flimsy booths and barns, fire was a constant hazard.[102] A typical occurrence may be cited from John Palmer's "Memoirs." In Liverpool "one of the band, [snuffed] a candle with a piece of brown paper, which, unperceived, kindled into a flame as it laid under the music-desk:—The smell conveying itself to those who were near, a cry of fire immediately spread through the audience, whose apprehensions magnified the danger." A mate in an East Indiaman leaped from the gallery and was killed. Palmer ordered the band to play "God Save the King," which stilled the panic.[103] In 1753 the Bath Company were crossing Salisbury Plain when an ungreased wheel set their wagon afire and destroyed all their scenery and properties.[104] In 1760 Keasberry and Griffiths of the Bath Company built a temporary theatre near a camp of eight regiments. They played *Alexander the Great,* for which olive leaves "twisted and interwoven with little bits of wax were used for decoration." The stage lights ignited them: "The flames continuing to blaze, occasioned an intolerable stench, and an universal cry of fire, which was succeeded by a general panic; but none received so

99. Snagge, pp. 47–48.
100. Snagge, p. 101.
101. E.g., Thomas Hollingsworth by a Liverpool paper of 27 August 1798, William Keasberry by the *Morning Chronicle* of 12 August 1774, James Thomas Kear by the *Morning Post* of 17 June 1775, Miss Jarratt by the *Morning Chronicle* of 19 October 1780, and George Anne Bellamy by the *Daily Advertiser* of 17 May 1751.
102. Even in John Hippisley's Jacob's Wells Theatre, Bristol, "The accommodation for the players was so contracted that an actor who left the stage on one side and re-entered on the other had to walk round the outside of the house." John Latimer, *The Annals of Bristol in the Eighteenth Century* (Frome: Printed for the Author, 1893), p. 63.
103. "Memoirs of John Palmer, Esq.," *Thespian Magazine and Literary Repository,* 1793, reprinted in *17th and 18th Century Theatre Research,* 1 (1962), 49.
104. Sarah Ward wrote to West Digges on 28 June 1754: "I suppose you have heard the unhappy accident which has befall'n the Bath company; there cloaths, scenes, &c. &c. being consumed by one of the wheels of the waggon takeing fire, in there way to the Isle of Whight, which has reduced the poor people to great distress; from there unhappy circumstances, I doubt not but you may get both men and women on reasonable terms." *Letters Which Passed Between Mr. West Digges, Comedian, and Mrs Sarah Ward, 1752–1759,* [ed. James Maidment and William Hugh Logan] (Edinburgh: T. Stevenson), p. 108.

terrible a shock as the departed Clytus, who, at that time, lay *dead* before the audience. As by Galvanic impulse, he instantly revived, and, in his haste, o'erthrew the son of the immortal Ammon. . . . However, as soon as the cause was ascertained, all was restored to order, and the redoubted Clytus quietly returned, and (hard and uncommon lot) for the *second* time gave up the ghost."[105]

But the most dreaded danger was that incurred in the journeys by water, particularly the one across St George's Channel to Ireland from England and across the North Channel from Ireland to Scotland. Thomas Snagge crossed the Irish Sea many times "with perspirations and emetical operations that I conceived would be my death."[106] Once he was ten days between Bristol and the Cove of Cork, but at least he arrived. Others were unfortunate. Colley Cibber's son Theophilus, Michael Maddox the wire dancer, Franklyn the clown, and several others set out from Parkgate in the *Dublin Trader* on 27 October 1758, and the vessel foundered with all hands in a gale that night.[107] *The Hibernian Journal* of 17 January 1798 reported the sinking of the *Viceroy* out of Liverpool and the drowning of Mr and Mrs Fort and other members of a troupe on their way from London to Astley's Amphitheatre in Dublin.[108] Charles Benjamin Incledon the singer heroically saved several lives when the packet boat from Holyhead struck the Dublin bar in 1803 and sank in the night.[109] Miss Edgerton of Price's Irish Company was drowned crossing the Boyne in the spring flood of 1772.[110] Mrs Jane Storer Henry, her two children, her mother, and her sister Sarah, all performers, perished within sight of land after a voyage from Jamaica toward New York in August 1767 when a cabin boy, sent between decks to draw water, mistakenly broached a cask of rum and set it afire, sinking the brig *Dolphin*.[111]

105. Winston, *Theatric Tourist*, p. 71.
106. Snagge, pp. 45–46.
107. *Public Advertiser*, 28 November 1758.
108. Astley's performers were exposed to frequent water crossings. In addition to the London and Dublin hippodromes, there was one in Paris; Astley also went on extended excursions with troupes in Britain and abroad.
109. Winston, *Manager's Notebook*, pp. 218–20.
110. Newsclipping dated 1772, Burney Collection, British Library.
111. *Newport* [Rhode Island] *Mercury*, 24–31 August 1767, quoted by Richardson Wright, *Revels in Jamaica, 1682–1838* (New York: Dodd, Mead, 1937), pp. 345–46.

Even if performers came through their provincial journeys un-scathed by fire and flood and sound in wind and limb, life on tour was frequently harsh and exhausting. But it fostered a professional flexibility and begot a physical hardihood that were useful also in the demanding regimen of London.

IV The Actor's Art

Supposing that an actor was good enough, and lucky enough, to find a place in the legitimate London theatres, what was his acting like? That is a difficult question. R. B. Sheridan in his "Verses to the Memory of Garrick" reminds us that the early actor's art is writ on water: "Ev'n matchless Garrick's Art to Heav'n resign'd, / No fix'd Effect, no Model leaves behind."[112] Today's actor has inherited no system of notation with which he might hope to imitate the onstage presence of Garrick—nothing like that accurate system by which the modern harpsichordist can nearly duplicate Haydn at the keyboard, or even the far less exact scheme by which the dancer can divine the arabesques of Noverre. Critical speculation about acting has therefore been dependent on verbal description, often inexpert or full of rhapsodic or satirical subjective bias.[113]

The most elaborate and successful attempt to evoke the acting of the period and to discriminate various acting "styles," an essay by Alan Downer in 1943,[114] has been endorsed generally by most subsequent critics, and its conclusions will be incorporated here. But in the thirty years since Downer wrote, much evidence has accumulated in calendars and prefatory essays of *The London Stage,* in the volumes and files of the *Biographical Dictionary,* and elsewhere. Bertram Joseph in 1959 published 210 pages of description of the movements and voices of principal players from Betterton through the Kembles. Though further speculation is thus

112. *Verses to the Memory of Garrick. Spoken as a Monody, At the Theatre-Royal in Drury Lane* (London: T. Evans et al., 1779).
113. Joshua Steele, in his *An Essay Towards Establishing the Melody and Measure of Speech,* 1775, facsimile reprint (Menston, England: Scolar Press, 1969), created an excruciatingly elaborate system of notation, explained in 193 pages. But, even if it should be possible to master the symbols, Steele did not attempt to relate them to individual actors' voices.
114. "Nature to Advantage Dressed, Eighteenth-Century Acting," *PMLA,* 58 (1943), 1002–37.

irresistibly encouraged, we should admit that we are not much nearer actually visualizing either a "typical" or an individual acting performance than we have been.[115]

The finest actors and actresses of tragedy[116] across the whole span of the eighteenth century—Thomas Betterton, Barton Booth, James Quin, Charles Macklin, David Garrick, Spranger Barry, William Powell, John Philip Kemble, Susanna Maria Cibber, Hannah Pritchard, Sarah Siddons—shared an aim, professed and largely sincere, of holding the mirror up to nature. But the nature of "Nature" changed in histrionics as it did in poetry and philosophy. What was "natural" in acting altered under both personal interpretation and the influence of changes in the repertoire, in popular sentiment, and in the sizes of the playhouses.

The action and voice delivery of Thomas Betterton changed over the fifty years of his service but at its most mature was marked by restraint, dignity, and subdued fervor, varied as necessary by a passionate forcefulness. Betterton, like Elizabeth Barry and other stellar performers of his era, acted much with his eyes, and he practiced his action before a mirror.[117] In the time of the managerial triumvirate of Colley Cibber, Barton Booth, and Robert Wilks, and shortly afterward, when the most impressive actor was James Quin, there gradually developed a more exaggerated style. Though Barton Booth was relatively restrained and divided his soliloquies into "emotional components"—now loud, now soft, occasionally violent—other, lesser players were not only consistently extravagant but overattentive to detail. Meticulous overaction was en-

115. In addition to Downer, above, the curious reader should consult the following: John Harold Wilson, "Rant, Cant and Tone on the Restoration Stage," *Studies in Philology*, 52 (1955), 592–98; Earl R. Wasserman, "The Sympathetic Imagination in Eighteenth-Century Theories of Acting," *Journal of English and Germanic Philology*, 46 (1947), 264–72; Bertram Joseph, *The Tragic Actor* (London: Routledge and Kegan Paul, 1959), pp. 28–239; Cecil Price, *Theatre in the Age of Garrick* (Oxford: Basil Blackwell, 1973), chap. 2; Kalman A. Burnim, *David Garrick, Director* (Pittsburgh: Univ. of Pittsburgh Press 1961), passim; the sections on Acting and Actors in the critical introductions to the parts of the *London Stage*, and the *Biographical Dictionary*, passim.

116. Comic styles are almost impossible to discriminate for purposes of discussion today. They were imitated and inherited and were developed within confines of "type" just as were the broad "lines" of tragic heroes, heroines, and villains. But variations seem to have been much more numerous because even more susceptible to differences imposed by eccentric faces, forms, and personalities.

117. Downer, p. 1015.

163

demic during the middle years of the century and not even the much-admired reforms of Charles Macklin and David Garrick could persuade some players to abandon their gallery-pleasing excesses.

James Quin, whose active years ran virtually from Betterton's time until Garrick's maturity, was the most popular actor of tragedy between those two titans. He was rhetorically pompous and occasionally violent. John Hill admired his talent "in speaking the sublime,"[118] and he had a huge following in the audience. But by 1740 he was lamentably old-fashioned, a dinosaur left over from the tradition of which Dudley Ryder was already in 1716 complaining when he said "the manner of speaking in our Theatres in tragedy is not natural. . . . Persons would call it theatrical, meaning by that something stiff and affected. . . . as if they were reading a book."[119] Tobias Smollett cloaked his own disgust at Quin's style in the comments of a foreign visitor, in his novel *Peregrine Pickle* (1751): "His utterance is a continual sing-song, like the chanting of vespers, and his action resembles that of heaving ballast into the hold of a ship. . . . In almost all his most interesting scenes, [he] performs such strange shakings of the head, and other antic gesticulations, that when I first saw him act, I imagined the poor man laboured under that paralytical disorder, which is known by the name of St. Vitus's dance."[120] That critic ended by praising Quin's Falstaff, Sir John Brute, and other comic characters, saying that he "would be equal to many humorous situations in low comedy, which his pride will not allow him to undertake."

Charles Macklin was on the stage longer than any other performer in the whole period from 1660 to 1800, preceding Garrick and remaining for a few years after Garrick retired and died. He had roots in the Betterton period through his mentor Chetwood, the Drury Lane prompter. A passionate individualist, Macklin refused to deliver "in the hoity-toity tone" of Quin but aimed to speak "familiar." When in 1741 he brought his conception of Shylock to

118. *The Actor, a Treatise on the Art of Playing* (London: R. Griffiths, 1750), p. 99.

119. *The Diary of Dudley Ryder 1715–1716,* ed. William Matthews (London: Methuen, [1939]), p. 360.

120. Tobias Smollett, *The Adventures of Peregrine Pickle. In which are included, Memoirs of a Lady of Quality* (London: Printed for the Author, 1751), I, 139–40.

Drury Lane, he deliberately concealed his radical intentions from the manager and even from his fellow actors in rehearsal. His fierce, villainous, and unrepentant Shylock, with his "red hat . . . piqued beard, loose black gown" (Macklin's own description) was a complete departure from the comic Shylocks of the earlier tradition. George III is supposed to have spent a sleepless night after seeing him perform the character.[121]

As Professor Downer remarked, David Garrick "was more of a refiner than a reformer of previous acting techniques. From Macklin he took the natural speech and the broken tones of utterance, from the older school he took the fire of romantic acting and the careful attention to grace in posture and gesture."[122] Thus, though Garrick and Macklin were sometimes close friends and for a long period enemies, they were not the rivals in style that Garrick and Quin were. The playwright Richard Cumberland remembered seeing Garrick as Lothario and Quin as Horatio in *The Fair Penitent:*

I have the spectacle even now as it were before my eyes. Quin presented himself upon the rising of the curtain in a green velvet coat embroidered down the seams, an enormous full bottomed periwig, rolled stockings and high-heeled square-toed shoes: with very little variation of cadence, and in a deep full tone, accompanied by a sawing kind of action, which had more of the senate than of the stage in it, he rolled out his heroics with an air of dignified indifference, that seemed to disdain the plaudits, that were bestowed upon him. . . . But when after long and eager expectation I first beheld little Garrick, then young and light and alive in every muscle and in every feature, come bounding on the stage, and pointing at the wittol Altamont and heavy-paced Horatio—heavens, what a transition!—it seemed as if a whole century had been stept over in the transition of a single scene; old things were done away, and a new order at once brought forward, bright and luminous, and clearly destined to dispel the barbarisms and bigotry of a tasteless age . . . superstitiously devoted to the illusions of imposing declamation.[123]

121. See Appleton, chap. 3, "Shylock," for a complete discussion.
122. Downer, pp. 1013–14.
123. *Memoirs of Richard Cumberland* (London: Lackington, Allen and Co., 1806), pp. 59–60.

It is difficult to give Garrick his due as the foremost actor of his age, just as it is hard to praise him sufficiently as a manager and a benign social force, without at the same time diminishing the accomplishments of other performers and even falsifying history. Burke's remark that he raised his art to the rank of a liberal profession[124] was inspired by admiration for the artist. If it was meant to suggest that Garrick had done it all alone, it was as partial as Johnson's remark, inspired by admiration of his conduct, that Garrick had "made his profession respectable." But the great curve of accomplishment did coincide with Garrick's active years. It perhaps peaked around the year of his retirement, 1776, and then went into slow decline through the Kemble era.

Overtopping all other tragic actors from 1776 until the advent of Edmund Kean in 1814 were John Philip Kemble and his sister Sarah Siddons, whom Garrick had ushered onto the Drury Lane stage in the season of his retirement, 1775–76.[125] There was a family resemblance between the acting of the two leading Kembles, and they reinforced and complemented each other's personal styles. Their "school" was "a careful adaptation of those that had gone before. It was neoclassical in its accent on dignity, on carefully planned and minimal action, on rhetorical speech, on claptraps and addresses to the audience."[126] But it had also to accommodate the new vogue for romantic rodomontade and melodramatic gesture, the contrived *angst* of the flood of Kotzebue translations, for instance. And of course the cohorts of the Kembles had to "project" from larger and larger stages into larger and larger auditoriums.

Throughout the eighteenth century there was an implicit linkage between formal oratory and acting. When John Downes wished to compliment Barton Booth in 1708 he spoke of his "mellifluent Pronuntiation, having proper Gesticulations, which are Graceful Attendants of true Elocution" in a "Compleat Tragedian."[127] And in 1778, Burke rose in the House, with Garrick present, to praise him

124. William Windham, *Diary,* ed. Mrs H. Baring (London: Longmans, Green, 1866), p. 261.
125. The triumphs of Stephen Kemble (such as they were) were largely managerial and in the provinces. Charles achieved great success as a London manager in the nineteenth century.
126. Downer, p. 1021.
127. John Downes, *Roscius Anglicanus* (London: H. Playford, 1708), p. 52.

"who was the great master of eloquence; in whose school they had all imbibed the art of speaking, and been taught the elements of rhetoric. For his part, he owned that he had been greatly indebted to [Garrick's] instruction." Burke was "warmly seconded" by Fox and Townshend, who acknowledged Garrick "their old precep- tor."[128] Numbers of players taught "elocution"—for example Charles Macklin, Thomas Sheridan, George Stayley, and Francis Gentleman. Gentleman thought that "a professorship in oratory might be obtained for him" when he taught the art at Glasgow.[129]

Considering the preoccupation with oratory and the frequent analogies drawn between pulpit and stage, stage and Parliament, there is little wonder that the two rhetorical affectations "rant" and "cadence" persisted widespread so long after teachers and critical exponents of "natural" Garrickian acting pronounced anathema on them. If we are to believe Burke's compliment in the House, Garrick served to curb extravagance there as well as on the stage. Nevertheless, from the late seventeenth century until somewhat after the retirement of Booth and Cibber the ability to "cadence" or "tone" words was required of all actors; and the preference for doing so remained well into Garrick's period. "Toning" was an essential ability for orators and actors alike. A clue is offered by Betterton's remark, "For in all good Speech there is a sort of Music, with respect to its Measure, Time and Tune." Its companion device "rant" upset judicious critics even more. It persisted much longer also, since it was easy to learn, of surefire effect on the galleries, and actively encouraged by the fustian of some neoclassical tragedies. Partially subdued during the Garrick period, it burst forth anew toward the end of the century.

A comparable influence on bodily action is suggested by a com- parison of attitudes struck in formal paintings and sculpture of the eighteenth century and earlier (including those of the Renaissance and antiquity) with those in theatrical prints and in handbooks of instruction indicating the passions in action. Betterton recom- mended "The Studying history Painting" to "teach the Actor to vary

128. Davies, II, 358–62.
129. Preface to *The Modish Wife*, pp. 12–13.

and change his Figure."[130] Theophilus Cibber testified that Booth's "Attitudes were all picturesque.—He had a good Taste for Statuary and Painting, and where he could not come at original Pictures, he spared no Pains or Expence to get the best Drawings and Prints: These he frequently studied, and sometimes borrowed Attitudes from, which he so judiciously introduced, so finely executed, and fell into them with so easy a Transition, that these Masterpieces of his Art seemed but the Effect of Nature."[131]

In the middle of the century the critic Roger Pickering was offering the same advice;[132] and at the end Mrs Siddons was also endorsing such study.[133] Her son Henry Siddons at the beginning of the next century offered the most elaborate of all the attempts to describe the gestures appropriate for emotional reaction.[134] Over fifty states of mind—suspicion, contempt, pride, phlegm, hauteur, astonishment, terror, expectation, menace, servility, distraction, mirth and so on—were portrayed in his book-length treatise in minutely detailed drawings and were discussed. The attitudes in the drawings are not materially different from those found (for instance) in the marvelous *ad vivam* costumed depictions in John Bell's acting edition of Shakespeare in the 1770s or, for that matter, from the drawings in the Rowe Shakespeare of 1709. But of course they are—one and all—frozen attitudes, static and mute.

V Practicing the Profession

The qualities demanded by the stage do not change: voice, presence, striking appearance, and that indefinable quality (the eighteenth century would have said *je ne scai quoi*), which sends a personality winging across the footlights. The attribute most

130. *The History of the English Stage from the Restoration to the Present Time* (London: E. Curll, 1741), p. 50, quoted by Downer, p. 1028.

131. *The Lives and Characters of the Most Eminent Actors* (London: R. Griffiths, 1753), p. 51, quoted by Downer, p. 1028.

132. *Reflections upon Theatrical Expressions in Tragedy* (London: W. Johnston, 1755), cited by Downer, p. 1028.

133. See Thomas Campbell, *The Life of Mrs. Siddons*, 2 vols. (London: Effingham-Wilson, 1834), cited by Downer, p. 1028.

134. *Practical Illustrations of Rhetorical Gesture and Action, Adapted to the English Drama. From a Work on the Same Subject by M. Engel, Member of the Royal Academy of Berlin* (London: Richard Phillips, 1807).

criticized was voice, both its volume and its quality. Fielding praised Christiana Horton for "that clear Melody in her Voice, with Strength enough to express the Violence of some Passions, and Softness to subside into the Harmony of others, that no Actress now performing on either Stage can, in this Light, be compared to her."[135] Dennis Delane had a voice whose "loud Violence" was "useful to him when Anger, Indignation, or such enrag'd Passions are to be expres'd,"[136] but was not pleasant in young lovers.[137] The excellent actress Hannah Haughton got rid of a "Newcastle" manner of pronouncing her *r*'s but was always hampered by a lack of power.[138]

The finest male voices of the century, judging from the universal praise they drew, were David Garrick's and Spranger Barry's, Garrick's for range and flexibility and Barry's for sheer melody. But there were many others who also had what Garrick called "lemon" in their voices[139] as well as sinew, like West Digges and John Jackson. Thomas Cory had a voice, said the *Monthly Mirror,* "the most powerful we ever heard, or ever expected to hear, and not unsusceptible of pathos."[140] Sheer power began to dominate toward the end of the century as the larger theatres were built, and not a few good actors were, like both Maria Gibbs and R. W. Elliston, advised that their true histrionic home was the little Haymarket.[141] They both survived and prospered, presumably after voice exercises. Others could not. Elizabeth Edmead was despaired of by the *Monthly Mirror* in June 1799 because she wanted "powers of voice and of expression" for "a theatre [Drury Lane] of this vast extent."[142]

Some, realizing their limitations, adapted their roles rather than

135. *An Apology for the Life of T . . . C . . .* (London: J. Mechell, 1740), p. 142.
136. Fielding, p. 139.
137. John Hill, *The Actor, a Treatise on the Art of Playing* (London: R. Griffiths, 1750).
138. See *The Present State of the Stage,* 1753, cited in *LS,* Part 4, I, 364.
139. *The Diary of Sylas Neville,* ed. Basil Cozens-Hardy (Oxford: Oxford Univ. Press, 1950), p. 51.
140. November 1798. Charles Hulett "took too much Pride in the Firmness of his Voice; for he had an odd Custom of stealing unperceiv'd upon a Person, and, with a Hem! in his Ear, deafen him for some time. . . . the last Hem! he gave broke a Blood-Vessel, which was the cause of his Death in Twenty-Four Hours After." Chetwood, pp. 172–73.
141. *How Do You Do,* 10 September 1796.
142. P. 365.

their voices, Charles Farley, superb in certain Shakespeare parts—Cloten, Osric, Barnardine, Roderigo—was best in melodrama and eccentrics. His voice was so loud that he was called "Stentor." It had, said John Doran, "a curious bubbling sound, which he could less control as his very remarkable nose grew larger and larger."[143] There were some women who, like the incomparable singing actress Susanna Arne Cibber, combined fine speaking with great histrionic ability. But beauty and ability could do much to compensate for harshness of voice. When Elizabeth Hartley was scouted for Drury Lane by John Moody, he found "not the least harmony in her voice; but when forced (which she never fails to do) . . . is loud and strong, but such an inarticulate gabble, that you must be acquainted with her part to understand her."[144] But she had a ten-year career in leading parts before ill health forced her retirement, though "her beautiful figure and sweet face, made every auditor wish that nature had given her a voice less dissonant and monotonous."[145]

Not the least of Mrs Hartley's assets was that she was "tall and elegant" and "her carriage easy."[146] In the early and middle years of the century, cubits of stature had not seemed to matter so much. There are a few comments tending to show that massiveness was not amiss in Quin and Macklin and others habitually taking "heavy" parts, and John Hill in 1750 testified that "Our managers have more than once rejected persons who have offer'd themselves, not only for playing the first characters, but even the subordinate ones, merely for want of height," but Hill went on to say that "we have seen within these few years, that when Mr. *Johnson,* a person of considerable merit in tragedy, but of an enormous stature [came on] it was in vain that he attempted to bring the audience to approve him, even with the advantages of an expressive countenance, a sonorous voice, and a majestic deportment. He appear'd a giant among a nation of dwarfs; a *Gulliver* surrounded by a *Lilliputian* army: if he was engag'd in a quarrel, it was no merit for him to

143. *Notes and Queries,* 2nd ser., 7 (1859), 143–44.
144. James Boaden, *Private Correspondence of David Garrick,* 2 vols. (London: Henry Colburn and Richard Bently, 1831), I, 476.
145. *Covent Garden Journal,* February 1773.
146. *Macaroni and Savoir Vivre Magazine,* October 1773.

conquer a man whom he seem'd so vastly an over-match for; and if he made love, we had no idea but of a *Polypheme* and *Galatea*. . . . The disproportion between this gentleman's stature and that of *Mrs. Giffard,* with whom he usually play'd, was esteem'd to be such as no audience would ever be brought to bear."[147]

Garrick prudently doffed aside a few characters, like Othello, which did not seem to sort with his diminutive size, but in general his artistry made the question seem unimportant. He was not particularly bothered by the fact that his leading ladies were often a head taller. But as the century wore on into the era of the lofty Kembles, and theatres were enlarged, superior height began to be rewarded. More and more reviews, like that of the *Monthly Mirror*[148] of Nannette Johnson's Roxalana in *The Sultan* in 1798, gave approval to figures "tall and elegantly proportioned." The beautiful Margaret Cuyler may be cited. She advanced under Sheridan's management largely because of Junoesque proportions. Large or small, the charm of the female form divine, so overwhelming a novelty on the Restoration stage, never wore off. Though costume too revealing was quickly called to account by audiences and critics, Sir Harry Wildair in Farquhar's *The Constant Couple,* converted to a female role by Peg Woffington, was exploited by beauties throughout the century, and a figure fine enough to sustain the "breeches parts" of Shakespeare's heroines was almost a necessity for a young actress who aspired to leading roles.

Physical attributes determined to some extent which "lines"— heroes, rakes, ingenues, low comedians, chambermaids, old men, and so on—actors assumed, but many performers were capable of a wide variety.[149] Further, though few new "types" were invented (old maid or innkeeper, braggart soldier or fop) great variety within types was presented. At no time was the personality of a good actor submerged by his part. Life still instructed art. In 1711 John Dennis remarked that "most of the Writers for the Stage in my time, have not only adapted their Characters to their Actors, but these actors

147. Hill, p. 65.
148. September 1798, p. 172.
149. See Ben R. Schneider, "The Coquette-Prude as an Actress's Line in Restoration Comedy During the Time of Mrs. Oldfield," *Theatre Notebook,* 23 (1968), 143–47.

have as it were sate for them."[150] And in 1776–77, when Sheridan plotted his *School for Scandal,* he went straight to the actors he knew for the characters he drew. The devious John ("Plausible Jack") Palmer directly inspired the hypocritical Joseph Surface, and the personality of the suave sportsman William ("Gentleman") Smith furnished the loveable rake Charles—and so on down to the least member of the cast.[151]

Many players found popular following and artistic fruition in concentrating on one subordinate "line," or even part of a line. Increased commerce with Ireland, the southern emigration of Scots after the union, and the improvement of English post roads, all stimulated London interest in dialect characters. Stage Irishmen, who early stemmed from the footman Teague in Sir Robert Howard's *The Committee* (and John Lacy's interpretation) diversified in time: Irish officer, Irish countryman, Irish bully, melodious Irishman, drunken Irishman. But all required the brogue and were comedy characters—for the "Irish question" could not be staged. Some Anglo-Irish and English struggled to acquire the brogue while some Irish, aspiring to broader fame, set about divesting themselves of it.[152] Thomas Sheridan, for instance, with his aristocratic Irish background and avid interest in elocution had little brogue to lose.[153] For others it was a disabling difficulty. Lawrence Clinch, a native of Dublin, performed in Ireland, then made a gradual approach through Norwich to London. His debut role at Drury Lane (as "A Young Gentleman") was the title role in *Alexander the Great.* The prompter Hopkins reported that his performance was "a Little too much upon the Brogue."[154] He played in Cork and came back to London, but at Covent Garden was still not satisfactory in heroic leads.[155] He is thought to have saved Sheridan's *The*

150. In "Reflections . . . upon . . . an Essay upon Criticism," *The Critical Works of John Dennis,* ed. Edward Niles Hooker, 2 vols. (Baltimore: Johns Hopkins Press, 1939–43) I, 418.

151. See Christian Deelman, "The Original Cast of *The School for Scandal,*" *Review of English Studies,* NS 13 (1962), 257–66.

152. See the prompter Hopkins's comment in his diary, 16 May 1772, *LS,* Part 4, III, 1636: "Maj^r O Flaherty Mr Hurst—not enough upon the Brogue."

153. Esther K. Sheldon, *Thomas Sheridan of Smock-Alley* (Princeton: Princeton Univ. Press, 1967), pp. 10, 15, and passim.

154. Hopkins, 16 October 1772.

155. *Westminster Magazine,* October 1774.

Rivals when he stepped in to replace Lee as Sir Lucius O'Trigger on the third night, and Sheridan gratefully wrote for him the juicy part of Lieutenant O'Connor in *St Patrick's Day*. Clinch's career was long but not distinguished. He finally retreated to the Irish theatre where brogues were usual.[156]

There were comic Scots and Welsh and at least attempts to differentiate the accents of some English counties. John Emery was the last and finest of the "county characters" in the century. His Yorkshiremen were unsurpassable. James Winston was of the opinion that "Till Emery came to London, all our stage countrymen were from 'Zummerzetshire,' or rather from no shire at all, but of a bastard breed, a mongrel mixture of all. He introduced that fine, broad, rich, Yorkshire phraseology, with a naiveté so unaccountable, and effect so irresistibly ludicrous."[157]

A few "Jewish" comic characters were created, and played well enough when represented by actors like "Jew" Davis and Robert Baddeley (the first Moses in *The School for Scandal*). But it is possible that most foreign speech was more or less polyglot. For instance, *A Pin Basket to the Children of Thespis* (1797) suggests that stage Frenchmen were most "charmingly managed by [Ralph] WEWITZER, who is the only actor thoroughly acquainted with the idiom." But Wewitzer's father had been a Norwegian immigrant,[158] and Thomas Dutton commended him as "without exception, the first foreigner upon the stage," while praising him in the character of the German soldier Hans Molkus in *Of Age Tomorrow*.[159] The critic for *How Do You Do*[160] was "glad Wewitzer has returned again to Drury Lane.—We shall have no more apologies for foreigners."

156. See his entry in *BD*, III, 334–37. The rage for Irish characters grew especially strong in the last quarter of the century, with playwrights furnishing many comedies and musical farces featuring Irish life and managers reviving older plays. A selection: Tully in *The London Hermit*, O'Whack in *Notoriety*, Sir Callaghan O'Brallaghan in *Love à la Mode*, Dennis Brulgruddery in *John Bull*, Murtock Delany in *The Irishman in London*, Major O'Flahery in *The West Indian*, O'Rourke O'Daisy in *Hit or Miss*, O'Gallagher in *The Travellers*, Sir Sturdy O'Tremor in *What a Blunder*, Captain Macgallagher in *Bannian Day*, O'Carrel in *The Mountaineers*, O'Neill in *Abroad and at Home*, Michael in *Naples Bay*, and Liffey in *Ramah Droog*.
157. Winston, *Manager's Notebook*, p. 539.
158. *Hibernian Magazine*, January 1775.
159. I, 119, 188.
160. 24 September 1796.

George Gosling Davenport, who played native eccentrics and countrymen generally, was equally ready in the low Spaniard Alonzo in *Barataria,* the high Spaniard Don Juan in *The Castle of Andalusia,* and the Dutchman Captain Vansluisens in *The World in a Village.*

The personality quirks and foibles and the consequent tricks and nuances, which varied "styles" and underlined "types" from performer to performer in similar "lines," sometimes developed into specialties that became individual performers' personal theatrical signatures. Some entered the stream of stage tradition and were continued several generations. They involved not just bits of "business" but elaborate "turns" as well. Joe Haines at the end of the seventeenth century spoke his Epilogue from an Ass. It was adopted by Thomas Doggett, adapted, passed on to William Penkethman, and imitated by others all over Britain until the end of the century. Richard Wilson, for instance, spoke an Epilogue from an Ass at his benefit at Covent Garden on 18 May 1791.[161] The text varied according to the occasion, but in all probability the business was essentially the same.

George Alexander Stevens invented his comic farrago "A Lecture Upon Heads," which was later purchased by Charles Lee Lewes, who amended it and lived upon it for years. It was widely plagiarized and imitated. James Solas Dodd, a classicist "first designed for the Church," began his stage career by public dramatic delivery in the Great Room at Exeter 'Change and at Plaisterers' Hall of an entertainment published in 1767 as *A Satyrical Lecture on Hearts, to which is Added a Critical Dissertation on Noses.* The actor Creswick advertised in *The Morning Chronicle* of 28 October 1779 that on the same day at the Old Theatre, No 5, Portugal Street, his "Lecture on Elocution" would "be exemplified in reciting part of Dr. Young's Night Thoughts;/An Affecting Story from the Fool of Quality/Thompson's Palaemon and Lavinia/Several Passages from Shakespeare/A few extracts from the Lecture on Hearts;/Some Observations on Scandal and Defamation;/And Mr. George Stevens' Remarks on the origin of Lectures, and practice of snuff-

161. Playbill of date.

taking." An actress, Mrs Kennedy, at the Haymarket in 1782 proffered a monologue in brogue entitled *Phelimoguffinocarilo-carneymacframe's Description of a Man of War and a Sea Fight, with Explanations.*[162]

The vocal recitalist on the public stage was a typically eighteenth-century innovation, nurtured by audiences' interest in, and actors' abilities at, illustrated oratory. It led to the accomplished mimics of the century, like Tate Wilkinson and George Saville Carey, whose monologues typically took a mimical form. One was advertised in 1786: "A Lecture on Mimicry in three Parts, will be delivered by George Saville Carey [at York and Leeds], as repre-sented at the Theatres-Royal, Covent-Garden and Hay-Market, before their Majesties at Windsor, and at the Universities of Oxford and Cambridge. Characters Imitated . . . A Song, Mr. Ver-non. Othello, Mr. Barry. Jane Shore, Mrs. Hartley. Waterman, Mr. Bannister. Shylock, Mr. Henderson. Cymbeline, Mr. Hurst. Feignwell, Mr. Leoni. Juno in her Cups, Miss Catley. No Flower that Blows, Mrs. Baddeley. Etiquette, Mr. Edwin. Macbeth, Mr. Macklin . . . Prospero, in the Manner of the Late Mr. Mossop. The Examination of a Stage Candidate, after the Manner of the immortal Garrick. A New Dialogue in the Shades, between Messrs. Foote and Weston." Such bills of fare alone would serve to refute any argument that principal performers imitated so slavishly as to pro-duce mechanical, look-alike "styles" of acting. Mossop, Garrick, Foote, and Weston were long dead, but apparently their distinctive voices and mannerisms still rang and flashed in the memories of audiences.

VI The Corps

Performers' articles of employment were for limited periods; no one had permanent tenure. Yet a sizeable and very slowly changing number of durable favorites of the first three ranks went on revolv-ing the repertory year after year and largely in the same companies—passing along traditions, adapting to changes of fash-

162. 21 April 1782. See *LS*, Part 5, I, 506.

ion, honing skills, and developing before the second half of the century a high degree of professionalism. Even leaving aside as atypical Charles Macklin, who was on the stage for 66 years, one can illustrate this longevity from a (by no means exhaustive) survey of the first two letters of the alphabet only: Frances Abington, 38 years; James Aickin, 44; Francis Aickin, 48; Charles Bannister, 39; John Bannister, 37; John Barrington, 37; Spranger Barry, 32; Betterton, 50; Barton Booth, 30; Astley Bransby, 33; Mary Bradshaw, 37; William Bullock, 45; John Burton, 34.

The work was hard, even for established actors. For those just starting careers, and obliged to act, dance, sing, or serve in whatever capacity was needed, it was often grueling. Edward Cape Everard in his early Drury Lane years was an actor who was also obliged to serve as a figure dancer. He describes his day: "The porter, or call-man, used to come to my lodgings of a morning, and, knocking at my door, this little dialogue used to pass:—'Mr Everard!' 'Well, James.' 'At eleven, in the Green Room, to the reading of the New Play. . . . At twelve, to Much ado about Nothing,—Mr Garrick will be there.'—'Very well'—'At one, in the practising room below, Mr. Grimaldi's dances in the Tempest . . . At two, on the stage, Mr Slingby's dance, the Savage Hunters . . . At half-past two, Signior Dagueville's Double Festival . . . At three o'clock Mr Atkin's Sailors Revels' "—and more. Everard was busily learning dramatic roles, too. He was frequently at the theatre from ten in the morning until midnight.[163]

Actors were proud of the number of roles necessity obliged them to amass, and they went on adding repertoire until the end of their careers. James Winston wrote that in the later eighteenth century exactly four weeks was the time allotted to the rehearsal of a new play (while playing other works, of course). When Harris, the Covent Garden manager, asked Pope, whose part was the longest in a new comedy, if he could be ready in *three* weeks, and Pope replied yes, "He got into great disgrace with his brother-actors for being the cause of breaking through what they considered a good old custom that ought *never* to have been disturbed."[164] But there are many anecdotes of difficult parts learned overnight.

163. *Memoirs of an Unfortunate Son of Thespis* (Edinburgh: James Ballantyne, 1818).
164. Winston, *Manager's Notebook*, p. 226.

Garrick played 90 roles, but much of his energy went into refining them, and much more into the century's best job of management. Many actors and actresses had lists of 100 or more major roles. James Fearon probably had a repertoire running above 200 (to cite almost at random a typical second-rank actor). John Fawcett must have learned nearly 200 *major* roles, and he, like most others, was called upon to play a terrifying repertoire each season. For instance, in 1791–92, he acted 38 different characters and spoke a dozen prologues on 109 nights. In just 14 years on the stage, Charles Holland learned over 100 capital roles. In his 54 years on the stage Thomas Hull learned upward of 225. John Bannister's biographer lists some 425 roles for him. Some minor actors were assigned more parts and were on stage more frequently than major actors, albeit acting walk-ons or other roles not very taxing. Their contributions cannot be measured accurately by inspecting bills, for they were frequently not listed. For example, Ann Gaudry, who served faithfully for some 15 years in London, appears in fewer than twenty bills in the season of 1789–90. But the Drury Lane accounts[165] show that she was involved in performances on 101 of the 197 nights of that season.

Nearly every role added to the repertoire would be used at short notice at some time in any long future and so had to be kept in mind simultaneously with the growing list of others.[166] Feuds of heroic proportions arose between actors over parts, as in the epic contention in 1736 between Kitty Clive and Susanna Maria Arne Cibber over who should play Polly in *The Beggar's Opera*. Clive won, after the affair gave rise to three months of satire in the public prints. She maintained in a letter that there was "a receiv'd Maxim in the Theatre, *That no Actor or Actress shall be depriv'd of a Part in which they have been well receiv'd, until they are render'd incapable of performing it either by Age or Sickness.*"[167]

There were other causes of friction between performers, and

---

165. Folger Library Ms. W.b.295.

166. Size of role was measured in "lengths." See John Brownsmith, *The Theatrical Alphabet Containing a Catalogue of Several Hundred Parts . . . in Different Plays and Farces* (London: Rowland, 1767). Edward A. Langhans calculates that major roles ran 10 to 20 lengths (Hotspur, for instance, is a 12-length role; Romeo is 16 lengths). Minor roles ran usually below 10 (Rosencrantz is 3).

167. *London Daily Post and General Advertiser,* 19 November 1736.

between them and managers, and dozens of outbursts could be cited over the more than 100 years which this survey concentrates on. But when all is inspected, considering the talent and temperament involved, there were amazingly few disruptions. No good manager could tolerate protracted discord, and sensible players understood that. There developed a society hierarchical but fluid. A strong sense of camaraderie, formed at first partly in reaction to judgments of the outside world, contributed to solidarity. The solidarity as well as the hierarchy was commonly expressed in the military metaphor, with its extended conceits involving references to commanders, enlistments, campaigns, foragings, victories, spoils, scouts, and retreats. Henry Fielding puffed his company in the *Daily Advertiser* of 7 January 1737: He has "declar'd open War against Harlequin, Punch, Pierot" and "will open the Campaign next Week. . . . he makes head against a powerful Alliance," and so on. Thomas Snagge, on being enrolled in a country company, exulted: "Now blazoned forth the Ensign of Glory! The trumpet sounded to the charge, and to advance properly caparisoned became a duty" and "Only a few of the light Rangers of the Corps had filed off to their respective quarters. . . . A general review was to take place . . . if the Muster proved sufficient."[168]

The advancing century witnessed the growth of a real sense of professionalism even among minor performers of every kind. It arose out of the vital leadership of David Garrick to some degree, of course, and from that of the two Colmans, Samuel Foote, Tate Wilkinson, and many another artistically sensitive, commercially intelligent, and humane manager, in London and elsewhere. It was contributed to by the great musical organizers—Handel, J. C. Bach, Arne, the Ashleys in the oratorios, Salomon and his concerts. It also came from the leaders who rose from the ranks, like Kitty Clive and Thomas King and John Bannister and John Beard, who urged professional polish and personal decorum upon their associates.

Musicians took the lead in caring for their unfortunate fellows. When the oboist Jean Christian Kytch dropped dead in St James's Street in 1737, the violinist Michael Christian Festing and some

168. Snagge, p. 11.

others, observing the destitution of Kytch's children, organized the Decay'd Musicians Fund (which shortly became the Royal Society of Musicians). After the first meeting, on 23 April 1738, a system of yearly benefit concerts kept it growing and able to assume some care of the widowed, the orphaned, and the sick. Later, provincial funds were established.[169]

Thomas Davies wrote that, about 1759, William Pritchard the actor circulated a "scheme to relieve infirm players," and that John Arthur the actor "drew a plan of a large building . . . I suppose on the model of Dulwich College," a sort of home for indigent actors. But it was too grandiose for prospective subscribers.[170] Nothing like the Society of Musicians was available to dramatic performers until 1765, when Thomas Hull, moved by the plight of the old and impoverished actress Esther Hamilton, put in motion a scheme he had long deliberated by founding the Covent Garden Retirement Fund. The following year David Garrick and a committee of leading actors at Drury Lane followed suit.[171] After seven seasons of enrollment the members of a fund were entitled to an annuity at the onset of age or infirmity. Physicians' fees, drugs, annuities for widows and children, and funeral expenses (for indigents) were also provided.

The funds seemed to have been strongpoints around which all ranks could rally, and generations of performers served with pride on their directorates. The comedian Robert Baddeley, a member of the founding committee at Drury Lane, made its fund residuary legatee of an estate which included a country house in West Moulsey (for "Baddely's Theatrical Asylum") and a town house in New Store Street, as well as interest of a trust worth £650. But he is better remembered for his bequest of money to provide cakes and wine for the performers in the green room every Twelfth Night, a custom observed ever since.[172] Thomas Hull left a portrait to be

169. The manuscript records of the Royal Society of Musicians, still preserved and maintained, are the most complete repository of vital statistics for musicians of the period.
170. Davies, II, 331–32.
171. See *The Act of Parliament for the Relief of Indigent Persons, Belonging to His Majesty's Company of Comedians, of the Theatre-Royal, Drury Lane . . . 1777* (London: Jane Lowndes, 1824).
172. Will, PCC, PPR, PRO.

hung in the meeting room of the Covent Garden Fund "in humble hope that [it] may be considered as brotherly testimony of my ardent wish that the said institution may long continue to answer the salutary purposes for which it was intended."[173] Many other actors left amounts large or small to the funds.

But if the funds formed a practical center of the performers' sense of professionalism, the symbolic center came to revolve around Garrick (once he had died) and Shakespeare, from whose work Garrick became in the public mind inseparable. The leading actors of Garrick's time formed a loose association called The School of Garrick. Thomas Hull left to Jane Holman, wife of the actor John Holman, "my two small medallions carved indubitably on pieces of Shakespeare's Mulberry tree with the Heads of Shakespeare and Garrick."[174] When Oliver Carr was leading strolling players in the London suburbs it was said that he dressed his Richard III "in the same garments which were worn by Garrick" at his debut in that character, and that the "dress was held, by the strollers of his company, in high estimation."[175] The manager Samuel Jerrold, father of the playwright Douglas Jerrold, appeared on the stage each night in Greenwich in 1798 wearing shoes which he advertised as having belonged to Garrick.[176] Garrick himself had felt the weight of his history and the gathering tradition and the need for relics. At the end of his emotional final season, 1775–76, he wrote to Thomas King: "Dear King./Accept a Small token of our long & constant attachment to Each other—I flatter Myself that this Sword, as it is a theatrical one, will not cut Love between us, and that it will not be less valuable to You for having dangled at my side some part of the last Winter—. . . . *Farewell remember Me!*"[177]

173. Ibid.
174. Ibid.
175. Gilliland, II, 921.
176. Dibdin, p. 68.
177. *Letters,* No. 1028, III, 1112.

6
The Making of the Repertory

GEORGE WINCHESTER STONE, JR

WE MAY TAKE as axiomatic that repertories of established theatres exhibit a large degree of conservatism and a smaller one of innovation. The root of both lies, of course, in the basic economics of the theatre. Theatre is, and certainly in the eighteenth century was, a business. It brought some profit to managers, and provided a livelihood for hosts of actors, dancers, singers, and company servants. In entertaining a wide public it tapped the logistic support of hundreds of tradesmen and businesses in London. Every spectator was, in his or her peculiar way, a critic, and every playwright was a prima donna—hurt, angered, or confused when a draft of a *new* play was threatened by rejection or met with a demand for radical revision before acceptance.

But audiences actually loved excellently performed *old* plays—the best of the stock winnowed by trial and altered to suit updated conditions. Managers needed this stock of proven box-office appeal as their base of annual operation. Shakespeare, Jonson, Beaumont and Fletcher yielded a staple repertory nearly always sure to attract a good audience clear through the century. Periodically new and oncoming playwrights complained that they were being excluded, not because of the questionable quality of their pieces, but because of the mad rage for profit among venal managers who used old plays to save on author compensation. When one views the theatre system as a whole, however, one sees little truth in the complaints.

When theatres were failing in the 1680s, and hence united for survival, Downes noted that the company "Reviv'd the several old and Modern Plays, that were the Propriety of Mr. *Killigrew.*"[1] He lists eleven potential money-makers, six of which were by the long-dead dramatist John Fletcher, one by Ben Jonson, one by Shakespeare, and one by Richard Brome (d. 1652). Only the tenth and eleventh were by contemporaries—Dryden and Wycherley.[2] The sample is small, but indicative—nine plays by dramatists dead before 1652 and only two by contemporaries. George Powell in his "Preface to the Reader" of his *new* play *The Treacherous Brothers* (1690) noted about these ratios: "reviving of the old stock of Plays, so ingrost the study of the House, that the Poets lay dorment; and a new Play cou'd hardly get admittance, amongst the more precious pieces of Antiquity, that then waited to walk the Stage. And since the World runs all upon Extremes, as you had such a Scarcity of new ones then; 'tis Justice you shou'd have as great a glut of them now."[3] Hence he offered his play.

But competent contemporary playwrights were, of course as always, doing well, intermingled though their works were with those of their predecessors. Nicoll lists 129 new dramatists in the period 1660–1700, each of whom wrote from one to twenty-nine plays, most of which were ultimately performed in the period, though some waited long to walk the stage.

Half a century later the cry against managers came louder, oftener, and more poignently. One instances Oliver Goldsmith (successful dramatist though he became) writing on the English stage in his "Enquiry into the Present State of Polite Learning in Europe" (1759)—"Are [the plays in stock] sufficiently good? And is the credit of *our* Age nothing? Must our present times pass away unnoticed by posterity?"[4]

What about the repertory over a broad span in the century? What

---

1. *Roscius Anglicanus* (London: Playford, 1708), p. 39.
2. *Rule a Wife, The Scornful Lady, The Beggar's Bush, Rollo, The Humorous Lieutenant, The Double Marriage,* by Fletcher; *Bartholomew Fair,* by Jonson; *The Moore of Venice,* by Shakespeare; *The Jovial Crew,* by Brome; and *The Mock Astrologer,* by Dryden; *The Plain-Dealer,* by Wycherley.
3. London: James Blackwell, 1690. See also *LS,* Part 1, p. 316.
4. *The Collected Works of Oliver Goldsmith,* ed. Arthur Friedman, 5 vols. (Oxford: Clarendon Press, 1966), I, 323.

complex forces determined it? How accurate a chart was it of public taste? What emerges from a close study of performance frequencies (now calculable from the pages of *The London Stage, 1660–1800*)? In attempting to answer such questions one should say something about the economic forces, something about acting technique and actor personalities, something about trendsetters (i.e., audience demands), something about management policy, and something about results—changes over a period of time—for the century was certainly not all-of-a-piece in its tastes, interests, activities, acceptances and revolutions, emotional and intellectual responses, elegant and urbane though much of it seems to have been.

Having recently proofed and provided identifiers for some 140,000 items in eight volumes (1660–1776) of the forthcoming computerized *Index* to *The London Stage* I wish to share some findings and inescapable conclusions about repertory during that period. To give compass to the discussion I pitch for comparison upon two periods of about the same length in years—the Cibber period (1700–1728) which Professor Hume calls the Augustan, and the Garrick period (1747–76) embracing most of what Professor Hume calls the High Georgian period.[5] Firm believer as I am that dramatic impact comes not so much in the number of play titles as in the frequency of play performance, I have counted and cross-counted the performances in the two periods and have noted in passing the frequency and quality of commentary by spectators, as fleeting indications of impressions that the repertories made. My lists and charts are long and somewhat tedious. I shall, therefore, try to synthesize and provide briefed statistics.

But first the economics of it all. What did it cost, and what was involved in putting into rehearsal and performance a new play in each of the two periods? Extant account books and Lord Chamberlain's records are specific. Nicoll gives a breakdown of financial outlays for a year in the Augustan period, the totals of which are summarized in pounds per annum:[6]

5. Repertory in the Restoration period is difficult to analyze because of inadequate records. For changing repertory patterns at the end of the eighteenth century see Hogan's Introduction to Part 5 of *The London Stage*.

6. *A History of English Drama 1660–1900*, rev. ed., 6 vols. (Cambridge: Cambridge Univ. Press, 1952–59), II, 276–78.

Players	2,700
Dancers	500
Singers	320
Under officers	930
Rent, Candles, Managers	1,800
Remaining incidentals (as scenes, cloaths, printing, new plays, coals, musick)	1,950
Total	8,200

If these round figures are divided by 180 (the approximate number of nights which the company acted) the house charges to cover expenditures each night would come to £50. Professor Avery's closer calculation indicates a house charge of £40 billed to beneficiaries in this period.[7] Such charges rose to £63 and on to £80 late in the Garrick period.[8] The charges represented actual costs and were not padded. They had to support salaries, heating, lighting, ground rent, taxes, return to investors ("Renters") of at least 2s for each share each night of performing, wardrobe, scenery, upkeep of the facilities, and music. The specialized duties of the house servants required a large staff of ticket collectors, treasurers, barbers, dressers, candle women, guards, property men, scenemen, scene painters, machinists, charwomen, and janitors. Taxes included those for the land, a rate for the poor of the parish, for the rector, the scavanger, the watch, and the water supply. Doors could not open unless income could at least match the required expenditures. This fact the managers knew; of this fact some aspiring dramatists seemed ignorant.

Since the London season hardly got underway before mid-October, and since Lent, coming in February, closed the theatres for plays on Wednesdays and Fridays during that period of religious observance, and since "benefits" for prominent actors in the company began thereafter (during which time the house gained only its operating charges) managers throughout the century sought a rep-

7. *LS*, Part 2, I, xcvii.
8. *LS*, Part 4, "Theatrical Financing," I, xlv–lix, and Appendix D.

ertory which would meet its estimated expenses and provide some profit during the first 150 nights. Extant account books indicate that the major theatres did so, save for a number of bad years.[9] Repertory was basic in providing the income.

Income was the lifeblood of theatrical performance. At just about the mid-point of the century a Drury Lane or Covent Garden theatre counted a house bringing in £120 as a moderately full and successful nightly operation. By the end of the Garrick period (after the theatres had been enlarged) expectancy rose to a total box receipt of from £150 to £160 for an average full house. In reading and accepting a new play experienced actor managers (the Cibbers, Booths, Garricks, Riches, Beards, and Colmans) had to keep these contingencies in mind, as well as the quality of the writing, and the capacities of the acting company to perform the piece so as to give it a profitable run of six to nine nights, with some hope of its taking a place in the repertory thereafter.

One wishes not to belabor the fairly obvious, but I draw attention to two revealing items. The first is a table of costs and income for Covent Garden and Drury Lane at the beginning and then at the close of the High Georgian period, showing the great rise in both financial areas in that golden age of theatre performance. The figures may be compared with those listed above for the early Augustan period. Whereas the bottom line for the Cibber operation was £9,000 a year, that for Covent Garden in 1746 was £18,163, and that for Drury Lane for 1775 was £33,453. The itemized expenses show some relatively constant costs over the years, but indicate striking increase in expenditures for salaries, scenery, lighting and music.[10] The second item is a detailed analysis made by John Ballard, Covent Garden's treasurer in 1760, the year before manager Rich died.[11] By a sort of cost accounting, relative to income potential, Ballard showed what the house might yield (at current ticket prices of 5s 3s 2s and 1s for seats in the boxes, pit, gallery, and upper gallery). At full capacity in each area the income would be:

9. Ibid.
10. Ibid., Appendix D.
11. Ibid., I, l–li.

185

Boxes	729 s
Pit	357 s
First gallery	700 s
Upper gallery	384 s
Total	2,170 shillings

Converted to pounds a full house could bring in £320, of which full boxes would have yielded £182, or nearly 52 percent of the total. Ballard found, however, that during the 1760–61 season the actual receipts for the box section returned only 25 percent of the total income; yet Rich made a profit of £2,900 during the season. The main financial support was obviously coming from the pit and gallery occupants. The question we ask ourselves today, as managers probably did then, is what guideline this analysis may have signaled for the next year's repertory. Should one tailor it more to supposed taste in the boxes (the area of major income potential) or to the whims of the larger volume support among pit and gallery attendees?—supposing, that is, any discernible difference in taste existed among those who flocked to each section.[12] The thought of raising ticket prices may have crossed the managers' minds but was quickly ruled out.[13] In the succeeding decade the Covent Garden managers increased the proportion of comedy, pantomime, and musical shows in the repertory (presumably to continue attracting the pit and gallery folk) and somewhat reduced tragedy, history, and the serious.

The economic indicators suggest, therefore, that changes in repertory were made to keep audiences flowing into the theatres. As every theatre historian knows, when the theatres had reopened back in 1660 a wave of adaptations of old plays occurred alongside of the new ones. Adaptation actually constituted novelty in *text*— *Lear* via Tate gained a happier ending, *Romeo and Juliet* became in Otway's hands *Caius Marius. The Tempest* became an opera, and

12. General practice was to plan for balance, allowing special emphases to be determined by the quality and following of actors.
13. Unpleasant arguments, if not riots, accompanied price rises. See especially the "Half Price Riots" which were to occur in 1763. *LS,* Part 4, II, 947, 974 ff.

Coriolanus became *The Ingratitude of the Commonwealth*. Changes in text were thus often substantive and the audiences loved the resulting plays. Shifts in emphasis were attuned to contemporary currents of ideas. The emphasis in Tate's *Lear* shifts (and historians know why) from King Lear to Lear's kingdom.

Adaptations in the Garrick period, however, brought freshness and novelty not only by textual change—generally a swinging back to originals and much restoration of authentic dialogue—but perhaps more importantly by the infusion of a new acting style. A traditional comic Shylock became Macklin's fearsome character; an eloquently declamatory Tancred of Quin became Garrick's lively and passionate frustrate; a traditional minor comic Abel Drugger became, in Garrick's humorous depth-treatment, an idiosyncratic tobacconist. The double change—both in restored text and in a shift in acting style—is important. Style changed from often exquisite presentation of universals (the passions of love, fear, hate, anger, jealousy, and the like, in abstract) to individualistic treatments of the passions aligned with the characters and situations that produced them—Macbeth's fear (after killing Duncan), different from the fear of Drugger (after dropping a urinal); Lear's anguish in contemplating filial ingratitude, different from that of Romeo's contemplating Juliet in the tomb. Both the restored text and the new acting style made any of the older plays new to mid-eighteenth-century audiences. We note now with some surprise that Garrick, though eliminating the gravediggers from his 1772 text of *Hamlet* actually restored over 600 lines to the earlier part of the play, which theatregoers of the century had never heard on the stage. Any overall consideration of repertory must pay attention to the creative element involved in professional adaptations in each period, for the basic certainty is that audiences loved the plays both in altered text and in acting style. The quality of repertory cannot be determined by title or by text alone. To general changes in acting style must be added (in the High Georgian period) Garrick's increasing emphasis upon excellent ensemble performance.

While keeping in mind such generalizations and influences upon repertory building, one thinks naturally about the articulateness of the audiences themselves and wonders in what seats the trend makers sat. A remarkable resurgence of royal patronage, for example, exhibited itself after the death of Queen Anne under the aegis of the first two Hanoverians. Command performances for George I featured French farces, musicals, and pantomimes.[14] Close attention to names and titles of those attending the theatres in the Augustan period shows not only the presence of members of the royal families, but also particular requests on their parts, and on those of the earls, dukes, and viscounts who supported George, for entertainments which pleased him. One might make case that George I and George II enjoyed what was tantamount to an animated comic book in their predilection for 2,027 performances of pantomimes, farces, drolls, musicals, and nondescript "entertainments"—a number nearly equaling the 2,361 performances of tragedies, and about half the number (5,823) of performances of comedies.[15] Professor Avery makes special note of the fact that after-pieces, only sporadic in appearance before 1714, increase by leaps and bounds thereafter.[16]

The general theatrical public, however, warrants analysis and further comment as to its formative influence on repertory change. Two kinds of audience pressure asserted itself in the century. First came the impressionistic response of the audience sitting in the theatres nightly; second, the thoughtful afterresponse on paper of critics in the news media of the age. I have written at some length about the second influence in the eighteenth century, and the way in which actors took a leading part in moving a change in critical point of view from priority concern with plot structure (Farquhar's "a tale handsomely told") to character and characterization (Thomas Whateley's "there is a subject for criticism more worthy of attention [than the fable] . . . I mean the distinction and preservation of character, without which the piece is but a tale, not an action."[17] One notes the pertinent fact of a great increase after

14. See Louis D. Mitchell, "Command Performances during the Reign of George I," *Eighteenth-Century Studies*, 7 (1974), 343–49.

15. All figures for numbers of performances of plays, and genre popularity are obtained from an actual count by the author for the periods 1700–1728 and 1747–76 from Parts 2 and 4 of *The London Stage*.

16. *LS*, Part 2, I, cxvii.

17. See especially *LS*, Part 4, I, cxcix–ccx; and G. W. Stone, Jr, "David Garrick's Significance in the History of Shakespearean Criticism," *PMLA*, 65 (1950), 183–97.

about 1760 of periodical journalism and a concommitant expansion in the treatment of performed drama. Here, however, I wish to consider the first group—the paying guests in box, pit, and galleries. This critical group probably exerted the most potent direct pressure (on actors and acting texts) in its demands for entertaining and agreeable evenings. To discuss repertory apart from the composition of its regular spectators is to isolate and distort but one segment in the complex art of drama.

That ultraconservative critic Francis Gentleman (under the pseudonym Sir Nicholas Nipclose) called the audience in general "the loud-mouthed multitude," which rushed sweeping by, carrying its standards of new and therefore bad taste as a banner before it (1771).[18] A pleasanter view is suggested by an anonymous author of a set of verses in 1753 called "The Upper Gallery." And we, in a sense, enter Drury Lane Theatre with him as he comments on a typical group of people gathered to see a play, hear the music, enjoy the dance, and applaud the evening's afterpiece:

> Now fills the dome, they trim the languid flames
> And the glad tapers call forth all their beams.
> Wedg'd eager in front rows they throng, they squeeze,
> And fans soft waving, shed a gentle breeze.
> Pit, boxes, gallery shine in blended rows—
> Ladies and Bawds, and Cits, and Rakes, and Beaux,
> 'Tis smiling, curtsying all. The Fiddlers rise,
> The wing'd notes thicken, and the music flies.

A prompter peering from behind the curtain on such a cheerful scene might rub his hands in delight, anticipating a happy evening. But as the evening advanced even this audience might become very, very articulate—and darkeningly so—about what it was witnessing. The articulate audience (then much more so than now in our polite days) formed the most necessary element (along with text and actors) in the art of drama—the group for which all else was created. And eighteenth-century audiences in bulk reaction ran the gamut from quiet attentive acceptance of a play—such as the bland *Coun-*

18. *The Theatres: A Poetical Dissection* (London: J. Bell, 1771).

try Girl[19]—to vociferous damnation, and disruptive action, which they took against Noverre's *Chinese Festival* afterpiece in 1755. Half a dozen types of condemnatory groups and tinderbox situations had wrought havoc in the theatres throughout the century and had brought any house into an uproar—situations, for example prompted by quarrels among spectators (as sometimes happens in the stands at modern American football games); quarrels among actors spilling out onstage; quarrels between political factions; trampled personal loyalties and tensions; management errors; premeditated damnation; and spontaneous eruption.[20]

At issue was the tradition of British freedom of speech and action. The records show that about once every ten years in that century both patent houses had to redecorate because of audience riots, which spared neither drapes, benches, nor chandeliers. During the intervals minor eruptions came in the hiss or catcall, or the tossing of some fruit (purchased from the concessionnaire in the lobby) on the stage.[21] The Cross-Hopkins *Diaries* attest the care with which those two prompters followed and assessed each such disturbance. Theatrical prosperity required a successful repertory and an avoidance of costly outbreaks.

Disturbance could be and was initiated by persons in any class in society—lords, commons, or mob. At the seventh performance of *The Foundling* (22 February 1748) writes Richard Cross, "There was a report that my Lord Hubbard had made a party this night to hiss *The Foundling* off the stage, that the reason was it ran too long and they wanted variety of entertainment."[22] Garrick went onstage, negotiated with the potential rioters, and reached a compromise that peace would prevail until after the ninth night. An apple was thrown, and hisses resumed. Several nights later Garrick announced that *As You Like It* would replace the play under dispute, "But the Pit rose and insisted *The Foundling* should be given out [again], which was done, tho' the Lords who opposed it were in the House." On the following Monday "Great threatening," writes

19. Garrick's 1766 alteration of Wycherley's *The Country Wife*.
20. See discussions of audiences in the Introductions to the five parts of *The London Stage*.
21. Ibid., and "Theatre Riots in London," by Sir St. Vincent Troubridge, in *Studies in the English Theatre in Memory of Gabrielle Enthoven* (London: Society for Theatre Research, 1952), pp. 84–97.
22. *LS*, Part 4, under date.

Cross, "among the Lords, and the managers to prevent tumult gave out *Lear* for Tuesday."

Who precisely composed theatre audiences including both the riotous and the patient? Was there a nucleus of regular attenders? And even if we had their names and addresses, how can we tell now what their basic attitudes and biases were and what animated their acceptance or rejection of plays?[23] The gradually changing repertory helps us answer the last question, and some new source-hunting helps us to answer the first two.

Materials are now at hand from which we may identify by name, if not precisely by address, nearly 5,000 individuals who were constant spectators, especially in the latter period. In both periods, however, audiences flocked into the theatres from some ten identifiable sources. First came the parliamentary contingent who returned to London in October with wives, cousins, children and aunts.[24] Second came several hundred who subscribed to editions of plays, and books on the dance.[25] Third came students and lawyers from the four Inns of Court.[26] Then came, occasionally, apprentices from ninety-four trades listed in such a work as R. Campbell's *The London Tradesman* (1747),[27] and next the tradesmen and merchants themselves from some ninety companies who

23. For some basic assumptions about earlier Restoration audiences, see James R. Sutherland, "Prologues, Epilogues, and Audiences in the Restoration Theatre," in *Of Books and Humankind: Essays and Poems Presented to Bonamy Dobrée,* ed. John Butt (London: Routledge and Kegan Paul, 1964), pp. 37–55; Harry William Pedicord, *The Theatrical Public in the Time of Garrick* (1954; rpt. Carbondale and Edwardsville: Southern Illinois Univ. Press, 1966); Leo Hughes, *The Drama's Patrons* (Austin: Univ. of Texas Press, 1971); George Rudé, *Hanoverian London, 1714–1808* (Berkeley: Univ. of California Press, 1971); and Harry William Pedicord, "George Lillo and 'Speculative Masonry,' " *Philological Quarterly,* 53 (1974), 401–12.

24. See lists of 1,342 potential spectators in *History of Parliament* (Oxford: Oxford Univ. Press, 1970), by Romney Sedgwick.

25. See the names of 440 subscribers to Mrs Elizabeth Griffith's *A Wife in the Right* (London: E. and C. Dilly, 1772); and of 171 subscribers to Kellom Tomlinson's *The Art of Dancing* (London: for the author, 1744).

26. See Hugh H. L. Bellot, *The Inner and Middle Temple* (London: Methuen, 1902); W. Paley Baildon, *Records of the Honorable Society of Lincoln's Inn* (London, 1897–1902); H. H. L. Bellot, *Gray's Inn and Lincoln's Inn* (London: Methuen, 1925); and *A Prospect of Gray's Inn* by Francis Cowper (London: Stevens, 1951); also for 769 prospective spectators see *A Calendar of Inner Temple Records* (1750–1800), Vol. V, ed. R. A. Roberts (London: G. Barber, 1936).

27. Pertinent also are Defoe's *The Compleat English Tradesman* (London: Charles Rivington, 1727), I, 6–14, 40, and Letters 8–10; also Samuel Richardson, *The Apprentice's Vademecum* (1734; rpt. Los Angeles: Augustan Reprint Society, 1975).

did business with the theatres and whose names appear in the comment sections of *The London Stage* (Parts 2 and 4).[28] Sixth came the renters (investors and stockholders) who were entitled to a free seat each performing night.[29] Seventh were the hosts of visitors to London who arrived over the years; many of whose names are listed in diary, letter, and newsprint, especially in the early years when the Georges were counting on the theatres as instruments of public relations for envoys from Morocco, Tripoli, Spain, and the Americas.[30] In the latter period one may add names, from the parish registers of Westminster and St Martins and Covent Garden, who rubbed elbows in the street with their neighbors Garrick, Mrs Pritchard, the Barrys, Macklins, Rich, and other actors.[31] A ninth source of audience names is the *Monthly Review*, for which intellectuals wrote after 1749,[32] and a tenth may be found among the several thousand persons with whom Garrick corresponded.[33] The spectrum was broad and the assembly mixed. This nucleus gave continuing support not only to Drury Lane and Covent Garden but to the Opera House, the summer Haymarket, and the dozens of booths at the London Fairs.

One cannot talk usefully about repertory without considering its relevance to the spectators and their demands (when they demurred at Johnson's Irene's being garroted onstage, the action was changed in the next performance), but still the catalytic agent in the two periods under consideration was the actor-manager who was running the business, and upon whose shoulders devolved the responsibility for dispensing theatrical fare, and for keeping the

28. In the Garrick period alone appear some 616 individuals and trades including 7 bankers, 67 printers, 54 taverners, 53 coffeehouse keepers, along with many haberdashers, perukiers, coal and oil merchants, carpenters, mercers, drapers, florists, glaziers, smiths, etc.

29. See Comment sections in Parts 2 and 4 of *LS*, where from 40 to 60 are listed.

30. Ibid.

31. The Westminster Records list the names of 442 of Garrick's neighbors (and their occupations) who took part in a by-election (1749), and G. C. Lichtenberg, *Visits to England, as Described in Letters and Diaries*, trans. Margaret L. Mare and W. H. Quarrell (Oxford: Clarendon Press, 1938), pp. 6–7, comments on Garrick's relation to them.

32. Some 127 names are listed by Benjamin C. Nangle, *Index to Contributors to The Monthly Review, 1749–1789* (Oxford: Oxford Univ. Press, 1934).

33. See *The Letters of David Garrick*, ed. David M. Little and George M. Kahrl, 3 vols. (Cambridge: Harvard Univ. Press, 1963), hereafter referred to as Kahrl; and *The Private Correspondence of David Garrick*, ed. James Boaden (London: Henry Colburn and Richard Bentley, 1831–1832).

business healthy for all. Why, for example, did William Mickle's "Siege of Marsailles," and Elizabeth Ryves's "Adelaide" not make it to Garrick's stage and to the Drury Lane repertory, to mention but two, and how many drafts did others such as Home's *Agis* and *Fatal Discovery* have to go through before Garrick accepted them?

The Garrick correspondence gives us the clue. Of Mickle's play Garrick wrote to Boswell, "Speeches and mere poetry will no more make a play, than planks and timbers in the dockyard can be called a ship. . . . It is Fable, Passion and acting which constitute a tragedy, and without them we may as well exhibit Tillotson's Sermons."[34] Elizabeth Ryves had sent her play under a covering letter bewailing the pathetic circumstances of her life. Garrick replied, "Let me assure you that I want no application to my humanity to do justice as far as in me lies to every Lady and Gentleman who are pleased to send me their performances; but on the other hand it would not only be an act of cruelty to the author, but a great injury to myself, should I not judge plays from the little knowledge I have of such performance, more than from the circumstances of the writer. The tragedy 'Adelaide' in my opinion could not answer the ends proposed by it, and the consequences would hurt both the author and the managers. I am sorry that I cannot accept of that play for representation."[35] Garrick asked Home to come for a conference to see what could be done to relieve the heaviness, to perfect the timing, and to strengthen the motivation as well as the probability in his *Agis*. When a dozen years later Home submitted *The Fatal Discovery* he had learned what a play needed. "The construction of your Fable," wrote Garrick, "is excellent. . . . You leave the audience at the end of every act with a certain glow, and in the most eager expectation to know what is to follow—it drew tears in great plenty last night from my wife and a very intimate friend of ours."[36]

During his term of management Garrick read (and often more than once) the manuscripts of at least 162 new plays and afterpieces which were put on at Drury Lane. He also read and rejected at least 83 more, along with revisions and second submissions of a number

34. Kahrl, Letter 677.
35. Ibid., 595.
36. Ibid., 509.

of them.[37] His readings were responsible, and so, one must believe, were those by Cibber and John Rich, by Colman and Beard. Anecdotes suggest that managers from whim, or pique kept some manuscripts overly long, and submerged others. But despite a human turn for arrogance here and intolerance there (though direct evidence is lacking), one might well remember that each manager had to choose in terms of the probable success of a piece. It required no small effort to cast a play, put it into rehearsal for at least two weeks, procure scenes, freshen wardrobes, and provide musical accompaniment. Success meant continuance of the theatre and the livelihood of all those from sceneshifter to premiere ballerina employed by the company, as well as profit to the author and manager. Failure put a whole business in jeopardy.

The process, the cost, the pressures, the standards for choice: What now can the pages of *The London Stage,* with their daily accounts of what went on, tell us overall about results—repertory in the first and third quarters of the eighteenth century? The answers suggest the shifts in taste and the name and nature of genres and of plays that counted, and hence might bear closer attention by English professors and theatre historians.

First the genres. In the Augustan period audiences saw 11,837 performances of 876 different plays, including musicals, puppet shows, entertainments, and acrobatic displays put on in the theatres. Comedy preponderated (5,823 performances of 350 different pieces). One should add to this lighter side of entertainment 813 more performances of 76 pantomimes, 592 of 104 French farces, 263 of 19 musicals, 54 of 7 ballad operas, 24 of 17 drolls, and 275 of some 36 pieces called by their contemporaries simply "entertainments." Tragedy reached 2,361 performances of 145 different plays, to which on the serious side might be added 25 of 5 tragicomedies, 139 of 3 history plays, 1,206 performances of serious opera, and 152 of 11 masques. The remaining are miscellaneous forms of puppetry, tumbling, and pastorals.

In the High Georgian period quantity moved up apace. Londoners were bombarded in the Garrick phase with 24,870 perfor-

37. Evidence from a count in Kahrl and Boaden.

mances of 929 different plays, operas, oratorios, pantomimes, and entertainments. One need not be submerged here by statistics, but an overview, similar to that of the earlier period, provides comparison. Of the 24,870 total, comedy was performed 11,365 times; tragedy, 3,802; pantomime, 3,586; comic opera, 1,703; serious opera, 1,070; musicals (mostly comic but not formal operas), 1,225; farce, 584; entertainments such as processions, 519; oratorios, 500; burlettas (comic), 289; and masques, 237. Though sometimes called a sentimental period the age as a whole was overwhelmingly a laughing one. Proportions among the genres seem not far different than in the Augustan period, but some new ones gain prominence—the oratorio, the burletta, and the comic opera.

The sheer mass when both periods are added up cries out for more refined and accurate definition of types than we have long been accustomed to. But by using the familiar terms for genres, behold what an analysis of the plays and performances yields.[38] First the Cibber period:

100 or More Performances			40 to 99 Performances			Totals	
10	comedies	1,292	45	comedies	2,890	55	4,182
5	tragedies	598	13	tragedies	822	18	1,420
2	operas	219	7	operas	400	9	619
2	pantomimes	239	7	pantomimes	365	9	604
1	musical	144	2	musicals	161	3	305
1	masque	100		- - -		1	100
			2	farces	149	2	149
			3	entertainments (including puppetry and tumbling)	150	3	150
			2	history plays	117	2	117
Totals 21		2,592	81		5,054	102	7,646

The totals are worth a note or two. Of those plays performed over 100 times, none was exceedingly popular, but Farquhar's *The Recruiting Officer*, with a record of 164 performances, *Hamlet* with

38. Figures derived from a count in the computerized *Index* to *The London Stage*, comp. Ben Ross Schneider, Jr. (Carbondale and Edwardsville: Southern Illinois Univ. Press, 1979).

151, and Farquhar's *The Beaux Stratagem* (145) led the way with Gay's *Beggar's Opera* (in existence only a year) coming close with 144. All, save Gay's, had been popular over a long period of years, and contributed to a repertory pleasing to and called for by a very mixed audience. All received the bulk of their performances at the major theatres Lincoln's Inn Fields, Drury Lane, and the King's Haymarket.

These 102 plays (about 11.5 percent of the total) in amassing 7,646 performances made up about 64 percent of the total battery of performances. One wonders about the opposite end of the scale. Did the plays that had but a single performance (and their number was 279) plus those that made it only twice (and 87 such are recorded) fall into any different pattern? One considers a minimally successful play to have come on at least three nights, in order to have provided the author one benefit. This group of relative failures, amounting to 41 percent of the total titles, may best be seen according to types:

Single Performances	*Twice Only*	
90 comedies	34 comedies	68
33 tragedies	7 tragedies	14
38 pantomimes	7 pantomimes	14
45 farces	23 farces	46
36 entertainments	6 entertainments	12
12 operas	1 opera	2
9 musicals	4 musicals	8
11 drolls	5 drolls	10
2 masques		
2 interludes	1 interlude	2
2 puppet shows		
Totals 280	88	176

A note of caution in judging these apparent failures: the sixty-eight farces with only one or two performances came largely from limited showings during several seasons of a wide repertory by companies of French actors, in which most of the dialogue was in

French. Some of the others were one-shot affairs at Great Rooms, or at the Fairs, yet the bulk occurred at Lincoln's Inn Fields, Drury Lane and the Little Haymarket theatres. Some, of course, were revived especially for a single time for an actor's benefit. But the pattern, though a little wider in range, and the ratios among types of play seem not radically different, or excessively experimental, from those of the successes.

What now can one say about public taste as evidenced by the twenty-one specific plays most often called for in the Augustan period? These, the brightest and the best, include eighteen main-pieces, and three afterpieces, all credited with 100 or more performances: *The Recruiting Officer* (164); *Hamlet* (151); *The Beaux Stratagem* (145); *The Beggar's Opera* (144); *Macbeth* (132); Howard's *Committee* (131); Dryden's *Spanish Fryar* (128); Congreve's *Love for Love* (127) and *Old Batchelour* (120); Cibber's *Love Makes a Man* (121); Haym's opera *Camilla* (114); Southerne's *Oroonoko* (108); Mrs. Centlivre's *The Busie Body* (106); Motteux's operatic *Island Princess* (105); *Julius Caesar* (105); Rowe's *Tamerlane* (103); the operatic *Tempest* (102); Cibber's *The Careless Husband* (100); and the three afterpieces—*Harlequin Dr. Faustus* (129); *The Necromancer* (110); and John Hughes's masque of *Apollo and Daphne* (100).

These twenty-one were followed hard on by twenty-three pieces that enjoyed more than 70 performances—eighteen were main-pieces and five were afterpieces: Betterton's *Amorous Widow* (98); Addison's *Cato* (98); Mrs Behn's *The Rover* (93); John Banks's *The Earl of Essex* (92); Farquhar's *Constant Couple* (89); *King Lear* (87); Vanbrugh's *The Relapse* (87); Fletcher's *Rule a Wife* (87); *1 Henry IV* (85); Betterton's operatic *Prophetess* (85); Cibber's *Love's Last Shift* (83); Shadwell's *Squire of Alsatia* (81); *Othello* (80); Fletcher's *The Royal Merchant* (80) and *The Pilgrim* (77); *The Merry Wives of Windsor* (74); *King Henry VIII* (72); and Crowne's *Sir Courtly Nice* (74); and the five afterpieces—Mrs Behn's *Emperor of the Moon* (98); Farquhar's cutdown *Stage Coach* (98); Doggett's *Hob* (97); Gay's *What D'Ye Call It* (93); and Aaron Hill's *The Walking Statue* (72).

These listings suggest the taste of Augustan audiences. Significantly, all but three of the mainpieces (the two operas and *Sir*

Courtly Nice) carried on into the Garrick period, though only seven remained among the top billings with the High Georgians. Among the after pieces only one, *The Emperor of the Moon,* was dropped in the Garrick period. The rest remained but were less often performed. Comparatively speaking, performances in each period are as follows:

Play	Genre	Augustan Period	High Georgian Period	
Recruiting Officer	C	164	116	
Hamlet	T	151	203	up
Beaux Stratagem	C	145	211	up
Beggar's Opera	OP	144	395	up
Macbeth	T	122	139	up
Committee	C	131	64	
Spanish Fryar	C	128	43	
Love for Love	C	127	84	
Old Batchelour	C	120	36	
Love Makes a Man	C	119	71	
Camilla	OP	114	0	
Oroonoko	T	108	75	
Busie Body	C	106	175	up
Island Princess	OP	105	0	
Julius Caesar	T	105	27	
Tamerlane	T	103	85	
Tempest	OP	102	90	
Careless Husband	C	100	71	
Harl. Dr. Faustus	P (A.P.)	129	157	up
The Necromancer	P (A.P.)	110	17	
Apollo and Daphne (Hughes's masque)	M (A.P.)	100	(Theobald's Pantomine) 174	up
Amorous Widow	C	98	5	
Cato	T	98	31	
Rover	C	98	20	
Earl of Essex (Banks)	T	92	(Jones & Brooke) 210	up
Constant Couple	C	89	66	
King Lear	T	87	141	up
Relapse	C	87	49	
Rule a Wife	C	87	102	up
1 Henry IV	C	85	72	
Prophetess	OP	85	23	
Love's Last Shift	C	83	45	

Squire of Alsatia	C	81	18	
Othello	T	80	124	up
Royal Merchant	C	80	27	
Pilgrim	C	77	12	
Emperor of the Moon	F (A.P.)	98	0	
Stage Coach	F (A.P.)	98	7	
Hob	Mus (A.P.)	97	47	
What D'Ye Call It	F (A.P.)	92	52	
Merry Wives	C	74	82	up
King Henry VIII	H	72	81	up
Sir Courtly Nice	C	74	0	
The Walking Statue	F (A.P.)	72	2	
	44 Totals	4,517	3,449	

Tables for the Garrick-High Georgian period (1747–76) show 76 plays that came on the boards 100 times or more, and 72 that received 50 to 59 performances. These 148 (i.e., 15 percent of all plays performed) account for 17,031 (or about 68 percent) of the total performances. They would seem to be the plays to reckon with. The Garrick period is as follows:

100 or More Performances		*50 to 99 Performances*		*Totals*	
33 comedies	4,834	41 comedies	2,974	74	7,808
13 pantomimes	2,322	6 pantomimes	454	19	2,776
12 tragedies	1,967	11 tragedies	801	23	2,768
10 musicals	1,648	3 musicals	240	13	1,888
4 farces	569	1 farce	71	5	640
3 entertainments	380	8 entertainments	514	11	894
1 oratorio	108	2 oratorios	149	3	257
Totals 76	11,828	72	5,203	148	17,031

A note about the table: Of those plays in the over 100 category, three were extremely popular—*The Beggar's Opera* with a record of 395; the pantomime *Harlequin Sorcerer* with 347; and the tragedy *Romeo and Juliet* with 335. Under "musicals" I have grouped comic operas at the King's, burlettas heavily laden with song, ballad operas, and musical pieces such as Bickerstaff's *Love in a Village* and *The Padlock*. These successful plays totaled their performances over a period of many years. None was a single-season phenomenon.

199

Hence all were major contributing elements to a repertory that the mixed audiences called for and enjoyed again and again. All (after the Licensing Act) received the bulk of their performances at Drury Lane, Covent Garden, the King's Opera House, and the summer Haymarket.

What of the obverse in the Garrick period? Do the plays that had but one or two performaces (and their numbers are respectively 175, or 17 percent, and 66, or 7 percent of all the titles) fall into a new or different pattern? The answer, again, is no. Hence one concludes that bad acting, rainy nights, inappropriate timing, or poor managerial choice may account for the proportions. The types that failed in the Garrick period are as follows:

Single Performances		*Twice Only*		
90	comedies	33	comedies	66
17	pantomimes	4	pantomimes	8
10	tragedies	5	tragedies	10
21	musicals	13	musicals	26
12	farces			
11	operas	4	operas	8
10	oratorios	5	oratorios	10
4	entertainments	2	entertainments	4
175		66		132

But before concluding categorically that bad acting, bad choice, or London rain caused these apparent failures, one must note that causes were many. Some, as in the former period, were one-night revivals requested by actors for special benefit performance; some were written just for such a performance; some failed on political grounds. One remembers that a number of Mrs Clive's plays were composed by her for her own benefits, that Mrs Griffith's *Wife in the Right* failed because of Shuter's inebriation, that Henry Bate's *Blackamoor Wash'd White* suffered from bad timing, and that Hugh Kelly got caught up in political disfavor.

Yet who can account for public taste? Lord Hervey writing to Stephen Fox commented on the first performance of Fielding's *The*

Lottery (4 January 1732): " 'Tis a play ill written, ill acted, and ill sung, but *well* attended, and *well* applauded." The failures, as I have called them, were nearly all staged at the patent theatres—Drury Lane with 42, Covent Garden with 44, the Haymarket with 35, and the Opera House with 18. Another 35 had but a single performance at the fair booths, Marlybone, at hired halls and schools.

So much for types. What about public taste as indicated in great support for the forty-four plays most often presented? They fall, in this period, evenly between main and afterpiece—twenty-two of each—showing a marked change from the Cibber period in growing affection for the amusement at the end of the evening. Each of these top-billed forty-four plays received 126 performances or more during the twenty-nine-year period. The mainpieces in order of performance frequency were *The Beggar's Opera* (395); *Romeo and Juliet* (335); *Richard III* (223); Farquhar's *Beaux Stratagem* (211); Pergolesi's *La Serva Padrona* (204), mostly performed on the fringes; *Hamlet* (203); Bickerstaff's *Love in a Village* (201); Vanbrugh and Cibber's *Provok'd Husband* (195); Mrs Centlivre's *The Busie Body* (175); Hoadley's *The Suspicious Husband* (167); Lee's *The Rival Queens* (166); Rowe's *Jane Shore* (166); Foote's *The Minor* (162); Jonson's *Every Man in his Humour* (157); *King Lear* (141); *Cymbeline* (141); *Macbeth* (139); Rowe's *Fair Penitent* (138); Otway's *The Orphan* (137); *Othello* (134); Vanbrugh's *Provok'd Wife* (134); and *The Merchant of Venice* (126). The genres called for en masse were a ballad opera, a musical, ten tragedies, and ten comedies.

One notes the seven carry-overs from the Cibber era—plays by Gay, Farquhar, Shakespeare, and Mrs Centlivre. One can hardly fault the taste of audiences that enjoyed the whole group, nor for their popular accompanying afterpieces: *Harlequin Sorcerer* (347); Coffee's *The Devil to Pay* (272); Woodward's *Queen Mab* (259); Garrick's *Miss in her Teens* (256); Bickerstaff's *The Padlock* (247); Garrick's *Lethe* (239) and *Lying Valet* (210); *The Genii* (207); Theobald's *Perseus and Andromeda* (177); *The Necromancer* (174); Murphy's *The Citizen* (180); Garrick's *Harlequin's Invasion* (164); Foote's *The Mayor of Garrat* (169); Theobald's *Apollo and Daphne* (164); Bickerstaff's *Thomas and Sally* (164); Ravenscroft's *The*

Anatomist (163); Woodward's *Fortunatus* (161); Garrick's *The Jubilee* (153); Edward Phillips's *Harlequin Skeleton* (148); an anonymous *Orpheus and Eurydice* (147); Foote's *Englishman in Paris* (143); and James Townley's *High Life Below Stairs* (140). The genres most in demand were two entertainments, two musicals, two petite comedies, six straight farces, and ten pantomimes.

Who is to say (amid the complex elements composing theatre presentation) what particularly called these main and afterpieces forth? Was it text—plot, characterization, dialogue? Was it apposite theme or underlying idea? Was it more likely presence and actor popularity and skillful ensemble performance?

Professor Avery has shown that the two decades before 1720 were a period of great experimentation in repertory patterns. Indeed he identifies ten varieties of groupings of plays with additional attractions.[39] Prior to that time an afterpiece was added only occasionally; then came a sizeable sprinkling, as the pattern took hold; and finally the double billing became standard. Little wonder then, that the list of most popular plays in the Cibber period includes a preponderance of mainpieces, and but a sampling of continuous runs of pantomime and farce, droll and musical interlude. The upsurge in afterpiece frequency of performance becomes fixed in the Garrick period. It opened the way for a brilliant sequence of farces, as well as pantomimes.

The continuing performance of older plays bridging two periods tells us something about public taste.[40] The runs of new titles, and the increasing performance of new adaptations of old plays tell us more. But when one looks into causes for the popularity of certain plays (rather than of the broad spectrum of types and genres) the finger inevitably points away from class structure in audiences and toward actor personalities and casting. That *The Rival Queens,* which rose from 66 performances in the Augustan period to 166 in the High Georgian, and *Jane Shore* from 59 to 166, *The Fair Penitent* from 31 to 135, and *The Orphan* from 0 to 137 may, of course, be tied in with an overall change in sensibility, but more surely related

39. *LS,* Part 2, I, cxvi.
40. See Shirley Strum Kenny, "Perennial Favorites: Congreve, Vanbrugh, Cibber, Farquhar, and Steele," *Modern Philology,* 73 (1976), S4-S11 (Arthur Friedman *festschrift* special issue), for an account of the lasting popularity of work by comic writers active c. 1700.

to the particular quality of new styles of acting of certain actors and actresses. With a Mrs Pritchard, a Mrs Hopkins, a Miss Younge as Roxana, and a Mrs Bellamy, Mrs Ward and Mrs Yates as Statira, *The Rival Queens* was bound to succeed. Likewise with Garrick as Chamont and Mrs Cibber as Monimia *The Orphan* could not fail, nor could *Jane Shore* go anywhere but up in the ratings with Garrick as Hastings, Mrs Pritchard as Jane, and Mrs Cibber as Alicia. Just so with *The Fair Penitent* when Garrick established a pattern for Lothario and audiences flocked to see Calista rendered by Mrs Cibber, Mrs Yates, or Mrs Anne Barry. The influence of Garrick the actor (not the manager) is inescapable in the dramatic rise, in repertory frequency between the two periods, of *Richard III* (in Cibber's adaptation) from 47 to 166; *The Provok'd Husband* from 49 to 195; *Lear* from 87 to 141; *The Provok'd Wife* from 70 to 134; *Romeo and Juliet* from 32 to 335. Betterton, Booth, Wilkes, and Quin had carried similar powers for making certain plays popular in their own eras. Quin made Falstaff his own, as he did Sir John Brute. When he quit the stage both *Henry the Fourth* (Part 1) and *The Merry Wives* suffered, and only Garrick, with a fresh approach to the Brute, could account for its emerging popularity.

Were modern students to read (or better to see) the forty-four most popular plays of each period rather than study the two dozen that have regularly appeared in classroom anthologies during the past fifty years, how different would their perception of the period be? Perhaps not greatly so, but surely their vision of the dominant entertainment would be considerably widened. The managers in the century did not pitch performances for any long period to a particular segment of the house (box, pit, or gallery), and they constantly reminded spectators, in prologues and epilogues at the openings of seasons of the need for balance. Garrick's Prologue at the opening of Drury Lane in his last year (1775) but rang another change on a concept of repertory policy that he had enunciated time and again:

> You Tragedy, must weep and love and rage
> And keep your turn, and not engross the stage;
> And you, Gay madam, gay to give delight,

Must not, turn'd prude, encroach upon her right.
Each sep'rate charm; you grave, you light as feather,
Unless that Shakespeare bring you both together; . . .

For you, Monsieur [to Harlequin] whenever Farce or Song
Are sick and tir'd—then you without a tongue,
Or with one if you please—in Drury Lane
As Locum Tenens, may hold up your train.[41]

A balanced offering was basic, as it had been in the earlier period
of London stage history. But despite Garrick's public relations
stance in a number of prologues (reminding Britons how fortunate
they were to admire roast beef more than fricassee in entertainment
taste) his own responsibility for fine artistry and fine content was
much on his mind. His manuscript note, now in the Folger Library,[42] leaves no doubt that he felt an important shared responsibility: "There are no hopes of seeing a perfect stage, till the public as
well as the managers get rid of their errors and prejudices: the
reformation must begin with the first. When the taste of the public
is right the managers and actors must follow it or starve."

Cibber knew this and hinted at the same relationship between
actor, manager, author, and audience again and again in his *Apology.*[43] Both managers, if they thought reform to be really necessary
in the drift of theatrical presentations, were mainly concerned with
the *quality* of performance in the repertory. *What* was played was,
of course, of general interest, but since nearly every spectator knew
the plot line of *Macbeth* and of *The Provok'd Wife, how* it was played
became the crucial factor in drawing audiences again and again to
the playhouse.

And how did the public respond to the *quality* of performance?
People came by the hundreds to see, but as the century progressed
they also reveled in reading the critical commentary which was
burgeoning in the press. C. H. Gray has pointed out that full critical

41. *LS,* Part 4, I, clx.
42. Pasted in I, 1, of Joseph Knight's *Life of Garrick,* extra-illustrated and extended to four volumes.
43. *An Apology for the Life of Mr. Colley Cibber* (1740), ed. B. R. S. Fone (Ann Arbor: Univ. of Michigan Press, 1968), pp. 126–29, 279–83.

articulateness became widespred only after the mid-century,[44] but a pen or two from the earlier period shows how some playgoers were responding. Steele (*Tatler* 167) wrote of "the wonderful agony which [Betterton] appeared in, when he examined the circumstance of the handkerchief in *Othello;* The mixture of love that intruded upon his mind, upon the innocent answers Desdemona makes, betrayed in his gesture such a variety and vicissitude of passions, as would admonish a man to be afraid of his own heart, and perfectly convince him that it is to stab it, to admit that worst of daggers, jealousy. Whoever reads in his closet this admirable scene will find that he cannot . . . find any but dry, incoherent and broken sentences; but a reader that has seen Betterton act it, observes there could not be a word added; that longer speeches had been unnatural, nay impossible, in Othello's circumstances." And Cibber was also moved by some *particulars,* as well as by Betterton's communication of *general* passions in his acting Hamlet. On viewing the Ghost, "he open'd with a Pause of mute Amazement! then rising slowly, to a solemn, trembling Voice, he made the Ghost equally terrible to the Spectator as to himself! . . . his Expostulation was still govern'd by Decency, manly, but not braving; his voice never rising into that seeming Outrage, or wild Defiance of what he naturally rever'd."[45]

Later in the century as the press printed more and more commentary, audience appreciation became keener. The descriptions of a Garrick performance in comedy (as Ranger, as Benedict, as Sir John Brute, as Archer) whetted and rewhetted the appetites of all readers to see him again. This delight the repertory theatre provided. Opportunities for comparison, not only of Garrick with Barry, but of Garrick with himself, occurred for thirty-five years, during which he appeared on stage 2,500 times in ninety different parts. He did Sir John Brute (and the rest) over a long period of time, and each time with a subtle difference, and each time with a differently individualized ensemble.

Let one description of a comic instance suffice here, that of

44. See Charles Harold Gray, *Theatrical Criticism in London to 1795* (1931; rpt. New York: Blom, 1971).
45. Cibber, *Apology,* p. 61.

Garrick's scene of Sir John Brute's falling asleep in *The Provok'd Wife*. Quin's rendering had bred instant detestation among the ladies, wrote an anonymous critic for the *London Chronicle*, but "with Mr. Garrick it is quite a different case: the Knight is the greatest favorite in the play; such a joyous, agreeable wicked dog that we never think we can have enough of his company, and when he drinks confusion to all order there is scarce a man in the house who is not for that moment a reprobate at heart."[46] Particularly enjoyed by all spectators from apprentice to advocate, from literary critic to his lordship, was the realistic and detailed sequence of Sir John's return from an evening's revelry: "Whoever has seen Mr. Garrick sit down in his chair," wrote one, again for the *London Chronicle*, "must acknowledge that sleep comes upon him by the most natural gradations; not the minutest circumstance about a man in that situation escapes him: the struggle between sleep and his unwillingness to give way to it is perfectly just. The lid depressed, yet faintly raised; the change of his voice from distinct articulation to a confused murmuring; the sudden oppression of his senses and the recovery from it; his then beginning his broken chain of thoughts, and the malicious smile that unexpectedly gleams from him till he is at length totally overpowered, are all such acknowledged strokes of art that they keep the whole house agitated at once with laughter and admiration."[47]

Among his tragic roles King Richard III won him instant acclaim when he was only twenty-four years old, and he stamped a new and marvelous interpretation on Macbeth, Hamlet, Romeo and Jaffeir. But his greatest role was probably that of King Lear, which he grew into (also when he was young) by listening to audience response, and by heeding the advice of many onlookers, including that of his severe contemporary Charles Macklin, who commented finally with delight, that the curse upon ungrateful Goneril "exceeded imagination, and had such an effect that it seemed to electrify the audience with horror. The words 'kill—kill—kill' echoed all the revenge of the frantic king, whils't he exhibited such a sense of the

46. *London Chronicle*, 14 October 1758.
47. *London Chronicle*, 3 March 1757. The virtues of a small house are seen in such close observations.

pathetic discovering his daughter Cordelia, as drew tears of comis-
eration from the whole house."[48]

Such acting gave the touch of class that began to pervade performance *throughout* the profession and to all segments of the whole
show in the High Georgian period. One theatregoer wrote for the
Theatrical Monitor (21 November 1767) concerning equally artistic
performing of theatrical dance: "Sir: as Dancing has ever been
received by the greatest dramatic writers with encomiums suitable
to its distinguished merit please [express in your paper] the satisfaction I met with from Mr. Aldridge in the *Merry Sailors;* his stature,
strength, agility and swiftness are beyond anything I ever saw on
Covent Garden theatre. He stands tiptoe upon the very pinnacle of
perfection, and gives us an idea of Homer's pyrrhic dance de-
lineated on the shield of Achilles." Another wrote for the *Theatrical
Review* (11 March 1772) on the cellist Duport's performance in
entr'acte music: "His execution is masterly, his tone very brilliant,
his taste pleasingly delicate and chaste. What he performs on this
instrument is wonderful." Ticket prices doubled for attendance at
the Oratorios during Lent, yet for Handel's *Messiah* (on 13 March
1761) fourteen hundred people crowded in to listen. Love of
religious music was strong. So, likewise, was love for secular music,
as evidenced by the thriving business done by music publishing
houses from the Strand up to Oxford Street, which printed and sold
sheet music for songs from the plays. Repertory, one must remember, was seated like a jewel in a gold ring of the evening's
complete offerings.

The press, after Garrick engaged Philip De Loutherbourg
(1772), is replete with excited comment (some derogatory, but
most plauditory) on the pictorial features of stage presentation that
were abloom. In De Loutherbourg's staging of Garrick's ex-
travaganza *A Christmas Tale* (1773), a magic garden appeared
where colors of leaves changed before the eyes of the audience.
Nigromant's castle sank into a lake of fire, and a beautiful prospect
of sea and castles developed before a glorious rising sun in the
distance.

48. William Cooke, *Memoirs of Charles Macklin* (London: Asperne, 1804), p. 107.

207

Whenever acting, interpretation, and the sense of art were excellent, when the ingredients of music, and dance, and scenic effect were equally so, as they often were in the Augustan and High Georgian periods, stage performance fascinated and inspired, stimulated and pleased. The varying repertory simultaneously *led* the way and in turn *responded* to public desire for pleasurable entertainment. "Pleasure upon the whole," said Dr Johnson, voicing the attitude of the people, "consists in variety." The offerings and the attitudes of reception come clear in the records. What can one conclude about audience taste? Who is to say that the lords and their ladies wanted a steady diet of *Hamlets* and *Messiahs,* and *Beaux Stratagems,* that tradesmen needed the moralizing of *George Barnwell* steady on, that apprentices and servants, shareholders, lawyers, and coachmen did not sense an evening of rich enjoyment when *King Lear* and three songs and a dance were followed by *Tom Thumb,* all offered in a skilled ensemble performance at both patent theatres? Often, remark the prompters in their extant *Diaries* (and they were there at the time), the *whole house* was dissolved in tears, or convulsed with laughter.[49]

What can one conclude about repertory? The obvious is corroborated by our analysis. The well-being of the theatre as a business required a stock repertory of acceptable plays. We must remember, however, that these proven pieces always carried in their presentation something new—in ensemble, in shifting nuance, in an addition or an excision. Repeated plays in the season's basic fifty or sixty different pieces were in no way comparable to our television reruns, where every scene is a frozen duplicate of the original performance. The repertory audience in the eighteenth century enjoyed the pleasures both of recognition and of discovery, and the fare in the periods under study was nearly always satisfying, and often brilliant. If the audience was left unsatisfied it would not return. If it felt sufficiently bored or antagonized, the audience in this articulate period was quite ready to make its disapproval vocal—going so far as to riot in a few celebrated instances. These sensational uproars, rare as they were, serve as a reminder that the repertory reflects the

49. See particularly notes by prompters Richard Cross and William Hopkins as reproduced in *LS,* Part 4, *passim.*

daily taste of a large and disparate audience. In the commercial theatre of the eighteenth century, writers wrote and managers presented what the audience wanted to see.

7
Music as Drama

CURTIS A. PRICE

THE LONDON STAGE was a thoroughly musical theatre in the late seventeenth and eighteenth centuries. Between 1660 and about 1705 scarcely a play was mounted that was not accompanied by vocal and instrumental music—often in abundance—newly composed by the best masters. Henry Purcell, of course, was the greatest of the Restoration theatre composers. Who besides a handful of drama historians would have heard of *The Indian Queen, The History of Dioclesian,* or *The Gordian Knot Untied* if not for his splendid incidental music and sensitive settings of often less than splendid poetry? Ironically, Purcell, a born opera composer, wrote for a theatre that did not spawn its own operatic style. Within fifteen years of his death in 1695, when the London audience finally seemed willing to accept the absurdity of people conversing in recitative, the Restoration musical play gave way to the Italian operas of George Frederick Handel and Giovanni Bononcini. Music remained an important feature of English plays throughout the new century, but native art music rarely graced plain spoken drama, and audiences turned mostly to foreign wares to satisfy their "concupiscence of jig and song."

Much that drama historians and critics have written about the musical features of the Restoration and early eighteenth-century London stage is downright condemnatory.[1] They have pointed out

1. Notable exceptions are Robert E. Moore's *Henry Purcell & the Restoration Theatre*

210

that extraneous music and dance were injected into already shaky spoken dramas, often in fatal doses, simply to please an audience enamored of the accoutrements rather than the business of the stage. Admittedly music was exploited throughout the period. As early as 1663 Dryden remarked sarcastically (and hypocritically) that a play might be poorly designed if it were not "but one continued Song, Or at least a Dance of 3 hours long."[2] And in the decade around 1700, playwrights and managers exploited native as well as foreign singers and dancers in the great battle for audiences, a bitter competition that nearly caused the collapse of the English theatre. Yet many of the best plays of the period show a judicious and skillful use of music and dance to enhance their plots, and a few are remarkably innovative in the way music is allowed a narrative—I might say operatic—role in the drama. In this essay I will discuss the many functions of music in the plays of the period and examine in detail three masterly works in which lengthy musical scenes advance plots in significant ways, occasionally imparting levels of meaning to the drama that spoken dialogue alone cannot. They are Elkanah Settle's *The Empress of Morocco* (1673), Purcell's operatic version of Dryden and Sir Robert Howard's *The Indian Queen* (c. 1695), and Thomas Durfey's *Massaniello* (two parts, 1699). Since these works are dramaturgically so extraordinary, we need first to look at two plays whose musical scenes are more typical of late seventeenth-century stage practices.

Like many plays produced by the United Company in the early 1690s, William Congreve's comedy *The Old Batchelour* (1693) has music by Purcell, the theatre's chief composer.[3] As early-comers waited in unreserved seats for the play to begin, two sets of two pieces each (called the first and second music) were played to ease the tedium. Following Anne Bracegirdle's delivery of the prologue

(Cambridge, Mass.: Harvard Univ. Press, 1961) and the several studies by Robert Gale Noyes, especially "Conventions of Song in Restoration Tragedy," *PMLA*, 53 (1938), 162–88. The various complete editions of dramatic works prepared by Montague Summers, and his *The Restoration Theatre* (London: Routledge & Kegan Paul, 1934), for all the criticism they have sustained, are also usually sympathetic in their treatment of theatre music, largely, it seems, because Summers had the good sense to rely on the expertise of the music historian W. Barclay Squire.

2. Prologue to *The Wild Gallant* (published 1669).
3. *The Works of Henry Purcell*, 32 vols. (London: Novello, 1878–), XXI, 19–37.

(a plea to the critics to look favorably on Congreve's "first-born play"), the orchestra would have rendered Purcell's overture or "curtain tune," an expansive piece in A minor, whose somber close is a rather incongruous prelude to Ned Bellmour and Frank Vainlove's early-morning banter in the street. During the rest of the play the orchestra would have sat idle, except to play a short tune at the end of each act, save the last.

Purcell set two songs in *The Old Batchelour*. The first, "Thus to a ripe consenting maid" (II.ii), is organic to the play, although frequently cut from modern revivals. Araminta is counseling the affected Belinda about her suitor, Bellmour. When the gentleman comes to call, the conversation between the standoffish lovers turns nasty, and in an attempt to stave off further unpleasantness, Araminta asks her music master, Mr Gavot, to sing a song apropos the situation. In Purcell's ballad-like setting of Congreve's lyric, an experienced shepherdess (Araminta?) tells a young girl (Belinda?) never to let a man discover too much about her, for if he does, he will find that "Every woman is the same." When asked how he liked the song, the rakish Bellmour applauds Gavot's performance but not the words.

As is often the case in comedies of the 1680s and 1690s, Purcell reserved his best music for a lyric of little importance to the plot. The fourth scene of Act III opens with a sexy, diverting ditty only remotely related to the action ("As Amoret and Thyrsis lay"). Heartwell (the old bachelor) has purchased the music to entertain and, he hopes, impress Silvia. Purcell set the lightweight lyric as a languishing duet, with seductive suspensions and expressive dissonances; it is followed by an unspecified "Dance of Antics." Songs and dances of this sort constitute most musical scenes in late Restoration comedies: music obviously introduced for its own sake rather than to enhance the plot; it is not completely incidental to the action, of course, being worked into the drama on some pretense. Such scenes proliferate in the poorer comedies of the period— Edward Ravenscroft's *The Anatomist: or, the Sham Doctor* (1697) or the third part of Thomas Durfey's *Don Quixote* (1696), to name two extreme examples—making the actors mere masters of ceremonies for musical shows.

The only other music required is for the obligatory dance in celebration of recent and anticipated weddings at the end of the last act. Most final dances in plays produced before about 1690 were cast dances, executed by the pairs of lovers. But in *The Old Batch-elour* the dramatis personae stood by while professional dancers entertained them. Toward the end of the century, final dances frequently yielded to long, paradramatic musical scenes; they would be indistinguishable from afterpieces (also starting to gain popularity at this time) if not for the fact that the actors had to remain onstage to "hearken to the music" and afterward deliver a few lines of dialogue and the final rhymed couplet, a ludicrous anticlimax, but one necessary to maintain histrionic convention. Quasi-operatic scenes were encouraged, but only as plays within plays. Compared with other comedies of the 1690s *The Old Batch-elour* requires modest amounts of music and dance. And all but the brief song in Act II could be cut without disrupting Congreve's plot, as many modern directors have unfortunately discovered. In several tragedies of the period, however, music is frequently elevated to an active participant in the drama. To omit it would be unthinkable.

Such a play is Dryden and Nathaniel Lee's *The Duke of Guise* (1683), so thinly disguised a parallel to the 1681 Exclusion crisis involving the Duke of Monmouth that the play was banned for a time in 1682. One might ask what place song and dance have in the politics of revolution, the Huguenots, and the Council of Sixteen. Not much, to be sure, but Dryden and Lee successfully weave eerily effective music into the main subplot, which centers on Malicorne, a necromancer and secretary to the treasonous Duke of Guise. This minor character has made a pact with an agent of the Devil, Melanax, who hopes to throw France into anarchy by commanding Malicorne to assassinate the king. Restoration playwrights rarely missed a chance to have music accompany scenes of the supernatural; accordingly, in III.i, when the Guise insists on pleading his case before the king, a spirit sings a song, heard only by Malicorne, warning the duke that he will lose his head if he goes to the palace. Heeding the message, the conjurer cum secretary persuades the Guise not to seek an audience with the king. The lyric thus influences the course of events. But the song is merely a vehicle for the supernatural message, and the spirit could have conveyed the same information in ordinary speech. The song in the bloody fifth act of *The Duke of Guise,* however, is more operatic.

A quality essential to opera is that the music impart a meaning to the drama that the words alone cannot. In the middle of Act V Malicorne is discovered at a private banquet celebrating the twelfth anniversary of his hellish pact with Melanax. But the magician suddenly becomes melancholy, and he asks his servants to sing a song to raise his spirits (literally, as it turns out). The lyric ("Tell me Thyrsis, tell your anguish") is a light bit of pastoral stuff, but Simon Pack's music foreshadows a dread event.[4] As is more fully explained below, Restoration theatre composers frequently used two musical devices to allude to death: the key of G minor and a stepwise bass line descending from the tonic. Both of these musical ill omens are seen in Pack's plaintive song (as shown in the example on the next page). Immediately after the music, a loud knock is heard at the door, and Melanax enters to claim Malicorne's soul, dragging him down to hell in the best Faustian tradition.

Though an effective way to dispose of a minor character, this scene is a brief episode in Dryden and Lee's political play. As in most Restoration tragedies, the protagonist does not participate in musical scenes, nor is he much influenced by them. Only spirits, fairies, court jesters, witches, and the like are given singing roles. For kings and queens, generals and ministers, to express themselves in music would violate histrionic conventions and push the play into the realm of *dramma per musica.* Yet this occasionally happened in the late seventeenth-century theatre, producing not true opera, but an exciting kind of music drama nevertheless.

The Empress of Morocco

The first Restoration play in which a long musical episode advances the plot is Settle's heroic tragedy *The Empress of Morocco*

---

4. The music is reprinted from the 1683 quarto in *Dryden: The Dramatic Works,* ed. Montague Summers, 6 vols. (London: Nonesuch, 1931–32), V, 293–95.

Shepherdess.

Tell me Thyr-sis, tell your an-guish, why you sigh, and why you lan-guish; when the nymph whom

[6] [6] [6]

you a-dore, grants the bless-ing of pos-sess-ing what can love and I do more?

[#] [#] [6] [♮] [#] [#] [6/5] [#]

(1673), a controversial yet successful work, which weathered a brutal attack by John Crowne, Thomas Shadwell, and Dryden in their famous *Notes and Observations on the Empress of Morocco* (1674). Most critics have awarded Settle a victory for his defense of a "confus'd heap of false Grammar, improper English, strain'd Hyperboles," and incoherent plot "full of absurdities."[5] True, Crowne, Shadwell, and Dryden stoop very low in their line-by-line dismantling of the play (by ridiculing Settle's stammering, for instance), but their critique is as devastatingly accurate as it is funny. The plot *is* fragmented and convoluted; the dramatis personae do in fact "all speake alike, and without distinction of Character"; and many of the rhymed couplets *are* "incorrigibly lewd." But the play is blessed in one respect; it is powerfully dramatic. And the climax

5. From the preface to *Notes and Observations*.

occurs in a musical scene, something that happens in almost no other play of the period.

The evil Empress of Morocco, the queen mother, has killed her husband, and with the help of her lover, the villainous Crimalhaz, she hopes to dispose of her son Muly Labas, the new king. The latter begins to sense that something is amiss only in the fourth act, when Crimalhaz robs the treasury of its gold and flees to the mountains with the Moroccan army. The queen mother, in laying a trap for her son, suggests that he seek out the villain in his hideaway in order to learn his motives. By the third scene, the king has managed to find the outlaw's camp, where all seems calm; in fact, Crimalhaz has even prepared a masque to entertain his guest (perhaps to be paid for with the king's filched gold). King Muly Labas is quite prepared to accept this unexpected hospitality when Hametalhaz, one of Crimalhaz's henchmen, warns him that he will be killed during the masque. To bait the trap further, he whispers that Crimalhaz was his father's assassin. The king is finally convinced of Crimalhaz's treachery but sees no way out of his dilemma. The queen mother, however, has a plan. The evening's masque is to be Orpheus's descent into Hades to fetch Euridice. She has secretly arranged with the masquers to have the king himself play Orpheus, and his queen Morena, now apparently Crimalhaz's captive (a predicament not fully explained by our playwright), will be dressed as Euridice. After Orpheus retrieves his bride from the stygian shores and the happy pair have marched out of hell, they can just keep marching past the guards and out of Crimalhaz's hellish camp and thereby escape. A good plan and good drama, but not the whole story.

After instructing her son in the intricacies of the masque, the queen mother gives Morena different stage directions. Yes, she is secretly to play Euridice but is told that Crimalhaz, not her beloved husband, is to be dressed as Orpheus. Furthermore, Crimalhaz will use the last scene of the masque as an excuse to carry off "Euridice" and ravish her. To save herself and her king, she must stab "Orpheus" at the appropriate moment. With the doubly deceptive plot thus laid, the entertainment begins with "all the Court in Masquerade."

The masque itself is not in fact a very ambitious affair musically or dramatically. But one must keep in mind its double meaning. Orpheus makes his usual plea for the return of his beloved. Pluto scoffs at the mere mortal's request. Proserpine intervenes, touches a sentimental nerve in her husband, and he finally releases the fair Euridice. Rejoicing follows and Orpheus is spared the test of faith (that is, not looking back at Euridice). Crowne, Shadwell, and Dryden objected particularly to Orpheus's weak response to Pluto's first question: "Whence Mortal does thy Courage grow, / To dare to take a Walk so Low?" He answers, "To Tell thee God, thou art a Ravisher" who commits "Rapes on Souls." The critics dryly observe that "Orpheus came a long Journey to tell Pluto very great news, viz. that he was a Ravisher, as if he did not know that before" (p. 45). But they have missed a subtle point. King Muly Labas is under the mask of Orpheus; perhaps his fears that Morena may be ravished indeed by her real captor are creeping into his lines. Unfortunately Settle did not complete the irony by having Crimalhaz act Pluto, but this felicitous arrangement may have been prevented by the fact that the villain was portrayed by Betterton, who could not sing.

At the end of the masque after a dance of celebration by infernal spirits, Orpheus advances to claim his bride (see Figure 37). Thinking it is Crimalhaz about to abduct her, Morena stabs him. When the masks are removed, the catastrophe is apparent, and Muly Labas dies as the deceitful Crimalhaz sends for doctors. The impact of this *Pagliacci*-like scene on Restoration audiences can only be guessed, but the niggling critics, although unremitting in their attacks on Settle's poetry, are silent about the *coup de théâtre*.

The masque was set to music by Matthew Locke, at the time a composer for the King's Violins. One of the earliest examples of English dramatic recitative, it survives in Oxford, Christ Church Mus. Ms. 692. On the whole the music is disappointing stuff from a composer who gave us wildly innovative consort suites and a brilliant, programmatic overture to Shadwell's 1674 version of *The Tempest*. The music is characterized by a stiffness of declamation, having none of the passions of a Purcellian recitative. And it is archaic in the way it frequently breaks into triple-meter melodies to punctuate rhythmically freer sections, a trait seen in the recitatives

217

37. The Masque in Act IV of *The Empress of Morocco* from the quarto of 1673. *Left to right:* King Muly Labas ("Orpheus"), attendant, Pluto, Proserpine, and Queen Morena ("Euridice"). Courtesy of the Harvard Theatre Collection

of Monteverdi and Cavalli forty years earlier. Yet for all its tentativeness, it achieves moments of beauty, as when Orpheus pathetically repeats the name of his beloved to an intransigent Pluto. Better music had certainly been heard on the Restoration stage, but none had been put to such effective dramatic ends.

The Empress of Morocco must have presented a casting problem for an early Restoration theatre company: namely, to find an actor who could both render the role of the protagonist, King Muly Labas, and sing the part of Orpheus in the masque in Act IV. Actor-singers were common in the playhouses from the earliest years of the restored theatre, but most of the hybrid Thespians, Elizabeth Knepp and Moll Davis, for instance, took only minor speaking roles. Not until Anne Bracegirdle and Richard Leveridge began acting in the early 1690s did playwrights create major speaking parts for professional singers. Muly Labas was acted by Henry Harris, who is known to have sung in a few plays and who even undertook to teach Pepys a song on one occasion.[6] He may have attempted Locke's recitative or simply mimed the part;[7] but Pluto was almost certainly sung by a professional singer, because Crimalhaz (the logical choice among the dramatis personae to sing this part) was portrayed by Thomas Betterton, who never sang a serious song during his entire career. In any case, the music was not well received. Roger North, writing many years after the event, remembered that it was "scandalously performed."[8] Settle's imaginative attempt at music drama had apparently taxed the resources of the Duke's Company.

The Indian Queen

During the twenty years following the première of *The Empress of Morocco,* the London stage became increasingly musical, and by

6. See *The Diary of Samuel Pepys,* ed. Robert Latham and William Matthews, 11 vols. (Berkeley and Los Angeles: Univ. of California Press, 1970–), IX, 195, 11 May 1668. Harris sang in the following plays: William Davenant, *The Rivals* (1668), III.ii; George Etherege, *She wou'd if she cou'd* (1668), II.ii; and Robert Stapylton, *The Slighted Maid* (1663), I.i.
7. Earlier in the scene, the queen mother tells Muly Labas that he should "in dumb show enter in *Orpheus* Roome."
8. *Roger North on Music,* ed. John Wilson (London: Novello, 1959), p. 306.

1690 a special kind of play had emerged, one specifically designed to accommodate long episodes of music and dance as well as spectacular scenic effects. This is, of course, the much-criticized and misunderstood dramatic opera, the best examples of which are by Dryden and Purcell. Many historians have seen the dramatic opera as corrupt, a kind of half-spoken, half-sung play that never quite blossomed into true opera. Even Allardyce Nicoll describes it as "prose or blank verse dialogue breaking into song."[9] But Dryden and Purcell chose not to follow the lead of Settle and Locke, who cleverly showed how a chunk of opera could be worked into a play. Rather they almost completely avoided integration of music and spoken dialogue in their works; only rarely does a scene involving protagonists (King Arthur, Dioclesian, and Montezuma) blubble over into song à la Broadway musical comedy. In the dramatic operas music is nearly always introduced into detachable scenes of magic, celebration, and solemnity—most often appearing purely as entertainment for the dramatis personae. Perhaps blinded by Purcell's magnificent music, drama historians have overlooked a crucial point: It is in ordinary plays, not lavish dramatic operas, that the links between spoken drama and music are closest. *The Empress of Morocco* and *The Duke of Guise,* despite their modest requirements for music, come far closer to opera than do *The Fairy Queen* and *Dioclesian.*

The most brilliant operatic scene in a late seventeenth-century English play is found in Dryden and Howard's *The Indian Queen.* This heroic tragedy had little music in its first production of 1664: a dance in III.i; a song and perhaps a recitative for the conjurer in III.ii; a duet for aerial spirits in the same scene; and a song of sacrifice for a priest in V.i. In 1694 or 1695, however, Purcell composed about an hour of music for a revival of the tragedy, turning it into what has been dubbed a dramatic opera,[10] but what is really a musical intensification of the play: It has less music than his dramatic operas (none at all in Act I and only one song in Act IV),

9. *A History of English Drama 1660–1900,* rev. ed., 6 vols. (Cambridge: Cambridge Univ. Press, 1952–59), II, 225.

10. See, e.g., Franklin B. Zimmerman, *Henry Purcell 1659–1695: An Analytical Catalogue of His Music* (London: St. Martin's Press, 1963), p. 630. The music is in *The Works of Henry Purcell,* Vol. XIX.

and most of it is substituted for the original songs. Unlike nearly all of the full-fledged "semi-operas," Purcell's *Indian Queen* has a musical scene of crucial importance to its plot.

Most of the music is so tangential to the action that little purpose would be served here by recounting the complex story in detail. Briefly, the Peruvians (Incas) and the Mexicans (Aztecs) are at war, each side being helped in turn by Montezuma, a warrior of unknown race. The Mexican queen, Zempoalla, is a usurper, and at the end of the play, the rightful empress, Amexia, regains her crown. The masque of "Fame and Envy" in II.ii is Purcell's only major interpolation. It is offered as a throne-room entertainment for Zempoalla, and although not directly related to the plot, it is mildly allegorical. Fame (representing Zempoalla) routs Envy (representing the queen's various detractors). But Purcell's music adds another dimension. The aria and chorus "I come to sing great Zempoalla's story," in brilliant C major with trumpets and endless repetitions, is pompous and full of glitter but with little musical substance. However, the trio for the followers of Envy, "What flat'ring noise is this" (in the darker key of C minor), with its sinuous violin parts and madrigalistic depiction of hissing snakes, is engaging. When the chorus is repeated at the end of the masque, Fame's victory sounds hollow indeed.

In transforming the rather conventional incantation scene in III.ii into a celebrated moment of music drama, Purcell simply used Dryden and Howard's text as it stands. Zempoalla recounts a rather ominous dream. She has seen herself standing before an altar holding a mighty lion by a twisted strand. A dove descends, embraces the lion with its wings, and cuts the thread with its beak. The freed lion then attacks and kills her. This dream hardly needs interpreting, but Zempoalla asks her conjurer, Ismeron, to explain its meaning. He demurs, believing the vision to be "too full of fate / Without the Gods assistance to expound." He offers to call up the God of Dreams for an expert opinion. Ismeron, played by Leveridge, a great bass singer who was also capable of acting small but demanding speaking roles, then sings the famous recitative "You twice ten hundred Deities." When the music produces no result, Zempoalla becomes impatient, threatening to withhold sac-

221

rifices to the gods. After a few lines of spoken dialogue, Ismeron sings the macabre incantation aria, "By the croaking of the Toad," during the middle strains of which the God of Dreams arises to a chromatically ascending line. Although Ismeron will not reveal *in words* what fate awaits the queen, Purcell's music offers the careful listener a clear foreshadowing.

The recitative, one of his most graphic in its depiction of individual words such as "doom'd" and "discord," is in G minor. In other theatre works Purcell and his contemporaries used this key in scenes associated with death.[11] At the crucial words "what strange Fate must on her dismall Vision wait," he quotes the most potent symbol for death known to middle baroque composers, a chromatic tetrachord descending in the bass from tonic to dominant (as shown in the example on the next page). In the long aria sung by the God of Dreams,[12] in which he also refuses to reveal the future (because if man knew his destiny, "He wou'd not live at all, but always dye"), Purcell avoids strong cadences in G minor at expected places, delaying the definitive determiner of the death key until the words "always dye."

Purcell's music is operatic because it tells us unequivocally something the poetry does not: that the Indian queen is doomed. In Act V her dream is played out. Montezuma is the bound lion, who, when Zempoalla cuts his bonds, kills the villain Traxalla. Under the weight of unrequited love for the hero, the death of her son, and the return of the banished Amexia (all precipitated by the ambivalent Montezuma), she kills herself. The conjurer's scene of Act III is operatic in another significant way. Ismeron, a speaking character, expresses himself in song, thereby drawing the Indian queen deeply into this musical episode. Purcell has transformed Dryden and Howard's spooky excursion from the plot into the turning point of the tragedy.

---

11. In *Dido and Aeneas,* for example, the heroine's lament is in G minor; and in IV.ii of *King Arthur,* when the protagonist is being lured to his death by sirens and illusory nymphs and sylvans, the long musical scene is entirely in this key. See also John Blow's masque *Venus and Adonis,* in which G minor is similarly threnodic.

12. Because it is not set in italic type in the first edition, this verse was apparently spoken in the 1664 production.

Ismeron.

You twice ten hun-dred De-i-ties, to whom, to whom we dai-ly Sac-ri-fice; Ye pow'rs, ye pow'rs that

dwell with Fates be-low, and see what Men are doom'd to doe; where E-le-ments in dis-

- cord dwell, thou God of sleep a-rise and tell; tell great Zem-po-al-la, what

strange, strange Fate must on her dis- mall, dis- mall Vi- sion wait.

223

The conjurer's scene is as close as Purcell got to opera during his career as a composer for the professional stage. Yet he wrote one true opera, *Dido and Aeneas* (c. 1689). Historians have long wondered why this masterpiece was not performed on the public stage during his lifetime. The most frequent answer is that the late seventeenth-century English audience would not accept all-sung opera, preferring instead that their music drama be confined to the more rational environment of a play within a play. *Dido* is indeed a foundling among the dramatic operas and other musical plays of the 1690s. This miniature opera could have been accommodated by the existing theatrical organization only as a masque to be presented with a spoken play as host. And this is in fact how it made its public debut in 1700—as paradramatic entertainments grafted awkwardly onto Charles Gildon's adaptation of *Measure for Measure*.[13] In the context of the London theatre world of 1700, the finest music drama of the era is not an opera at all but a series of masques.

A vindication of the theatre managers and dramatists who apparently banished *Dido* from the professional stage, then dismembered it for its first public performance, is in order. As audiences demanded increasing amounts of music on the stage, playwrights had to look for ever more novel ways of incorporating such scenes into their dramas. Here they faced a dilemma. If the musical scenes were to be made integral to the plots of the parent play (as is the masque of Orpheus in *The Empress of Morocco*), then such episodes had to be brief. If not, the dramatists risked turning the play into a ridiculous series of disconnected scenes. The solution (which prevented the further deterioration of English drama) was to make the longer excursions of music and dancing unabashedly incidental to the plot. The play was left more or less intact, and the singers and dancers were thus provided with an expansive forum in which to display their talents. This trend is especially apparent between about 1695 and 1706. But in this wasteland of music drama between the death of Purcell and the arrival of Handel, one masterly musical play was produced.

13. See Eric Walter White, "New Light on 'Dido and Aeneas,'" *Henry Purcell, 1659–1695, Essays on His Music,* ed. Imogen Holst (London: Oxford Univ. Press, 1959), pp. [14]–34.

Massaniello

Thomas Durfey was as responsible as anyone for the rot of interpolated music and dance attacking the dramatic substance of late Restoration plays. Some of his comedies—the third part of the *Don Quixote* trilogy, for example—are rackety, pasted-together vehicles for the bawdy, occasionally witty lyrics, collected in his mammoth *Wit and Mirth: or Pills to Purge Melancholy*. But recent criticism has discovered in his large dramatic output unnoticed genius; Durfey is certainly the most underrated playwright of the era. His masterpiece is *The Famous History of the Rise and Fall of Massaniello* (1699). In this "isolated freak, an experiment not re-peated,"[14] we find the most skillful and ambitious employment of music and ballet of any play of the period. Nowhere in this long, two-part prose tragedy is there a scene as operatic as Ismeron's in *The Indian Queen*, but neither is music added simply for its own sake. In *Massaniello* the lyrical elements are carefully marshaled, all working together toward the chilling, musical climax.

The special nature of this play is signaled by the prologue deliv-ered by Will Pinkethman, who appeared holding a song in manu-script. He carps that the theatre managers are ignoring his widely recognized comedic abilities by requiring him to learn to sing and dance.[15] But he admits that times are so bad for the theatres that actors must perform songs in order to attract audiences. Accord-ingly, he promises that the tragedy to follow will be "Mixt with good Humour, and good Musick too."

The play is a riveting story about the uprisings of the common people of Naples against their corrupt rulers. The revolution is led by the lowly fisherman Massaniello, who has studied politics in his spare time. His provisional dictatorship becomes even more cor-rupt than the aristocratic one it replaces, and his destruction is moralistically assured by his love of drink and lust for the captive Duchess of Mataloni. Durfey writes the lion's share of his powerful dialogue in the low language of the common people, reserving

14. See Robert D. Hume, *The Development of English Drama in the Late Seventeenth Century* (Oxford: Clarendon Press, 1976), pp. 456–57.
15. He did not, however, act in *Massaniello*.

elevated poetry for scenes among the gentry and clergy. Cleverly woven into the main plot are persistent comic elements, centering mostly on Massaniello's fat and obscene wife, Blowzabella. Helping to weld these divergent elements into a coherent dramatic structure is music of all sorts.

The verisimilitude of the main plot is shattered in two places by deus ex machina appearances of St. Genaro, the overseer of the fortunes of the main characters. In II.i of the first part of the play, he appears in the cathedral and sings to Massaniello, asleep under the altar, of violent revolutions to come. He predicts that Naples will be made free, "Yet he that does the Deed, / For doing it must bleed." The tuneful appearance of a saint, spirit, or conjurer predicting or at least hinting at the future is a stock scene in plays of the period. But, atypically, Durfey chooses to reintroduce St. Genaro at another structurally important place. In the second part of the tragedy, Massaniello has been convinced to surrender his power to the Viceroy of Naples in exchange for a marble monument in recognition of the various reforms his revolution has accomplished. His followers, however, are reluctant to give up their lucrative cabinet posts, and they incite Massaniello to drink and violence. In III.ii, after ruffians have abducted two gentlewomen to use as hostages in the power struggle, St. Genaro appears in the clouds and sings a song of comfort to the Viceroy and Cardinal Fillomerino, predicting an end to the revolution. The saint has his sword drawn, which the Viceroy interprets as a signal to stop further negotiation with the rebels and meet violence with violence.

Other musical scenes integral to the plot include the songs delivered by Fellicia in Part 2, IV.ii, in a desperate and futile attempt to forestall her rape by Don Pedro, and the ceremony in the cathedral in II.i (of Part 2), in which Massaniello transfers his power to the Viceroy. But these scenes constitute only a fraction of the total musical requirements of the play. And at first glance the rest of the music and dance seems to be of the paradramatic type: entertainments of little importance to the plot. Yet Durfey has tried something radically new in these seemingly extraneous episodes.

The banquet in Part 2, II.ii, is typical of the miscellaneous "shows" that infest many comedies of the 1690s. Extremely bawdy dialogues between a gambler and "his Hostess" and a chimney sweep and a cookmaid are preceded by "Mimicking Dancing at a Ball with Clowns, Morrice-dancers and Tumblers mixt." The songs have no bearing on the action and the dances appear to have been inserted simply to provide the professionals with an excuse to display their talents. A greater contrast with the solemn cathedral scene immediately before this would be difficult to imagine. But Durfey is spinning a clever plot. The banquet has been prepared by the vulgar Blowzabella for a captive audience of noblewomen. She does her best to impress them (by serving beer in sack glasses, for example) and offers the choicest music she knows. In the last act, the noblewomen return the favor.

To give the aristocratic counterrevolutionaries easy access to Massaniello so they can carry out the deed suggested by St. Genaro, their wives have arranged for Blowzabella to be out of the way at a masque in her honor. Without knowing that her husband has been assassinated, she arrives at the entertainment in all her garish finery. The masque is a simpleton's allegory of her rise to power: A fisherman and his wife dance; then they are dressed in fine clothes and strut about. But Blowzabella does not understand the mime, and a servant is appointed to explain it to her scene by scene. After a song by Rebellion, a dance is performed by Death, the Hangman, and the Devil. She has still missed the point when Death emerges from among the masquers, seizes her, and carries her off struggling. The grisly purpose of this remarkable ballet is seen a few minutes later when the shutters are drawn to reveal the headless torso of Massaniello and the body of his wife impaled upon gibbets.

This choreographic climax is an effective means of reconciling the serious main plot of the play with its comic subplot. Massaniello, hardly a tragic or even sympathetic villain, is summarily shot in the preceding scene. Blowzabella, a thoroughly detestable yet truly funny character, is disposed of in a crude, somewhat whimsical masque. Durfey observed convention by avoiding music in scenes involving the active participation of the protagonist, but he brilliantly exploited the musical potential of the theatre in those involving a person incongruous to the tragedy. Blowzabella, an

227

extraordinary character in any context, could hardly exist here without her musical trappings.

The vocal music of *Massaniello* is typical of post-Purcellian efforts. At least three undistinguished composers shared responsibility for the songs, which are scattered in various collections and single sheets brought out around 1700. Ironically, most of the lewd dialogues survive, while nearly all of the music crucial to the plot (such as Rebellion's song in Part 2, V.iv) does not.[16] The play was a failure, and judging from the number of songs that were published, the music was probably its most successful feature. Two of the finest singers of the era performed in *Massaniello*: Leveridge (Ismeron in *The Indian Queen*) and the great countertenor, William Pate. The 1690s saw not only the rise of the actor-singer (such as Leveridge and Mrs Bracegirdle) but also the advent of the professional stage singer (one could say "opera singer" had England had that genre). Pate, for instance, sang as often between the acts of plays as within them. And following the drift of musical taste, he had studied abroad. John Evelyn writes on 30 May 1698 of an evening at his friend Pepys's house: "I heard that rare Voice, Mr. Pate, who was lately come from Italy, reputed the most excellent singer, ever England had."[17] But by broadening his musical experience, Pate had also planted the seeds of his own destruction. With the "rare Italian Recitatives" he brought with him from the Continent soon came larger fragments of opera and eventually Italian singers, especially the castrati, whose intoxicating silvery tones rendered native male altos unfashionable. But the introduction of Italianate opera into London between 1705 and 1710 has been too much blamed for the near-destruction of the spoken play. By the mid-1690s English drama had already begun to decay from within.

Don Quixote

Despite undistinguished music, Durfey's *Massaniello* shows the Restoration musical play at its best, while his *Don Quixote* trilogy

16. For a list of the printed songs, see Cyrus L. Day and Eleanore Boswell Murrie, *English Song-Books 1651–1702: A Bibliography* (London: Bibliographical Society, 1940).
17. Quoted from *LS*, Part 1, p. 496.

(1694–96), with its remarkably fine music, graphically illustrates what was most rotten in the late seventeenth-century London theatre—not (as most critics would have it) that plays had become shabby vehicles for lengthy, extraneous musical scenes (indeed the dramatic opera proved how successful that combination could be), rather that the musical scenes themselves had begun to outgrow and outshine the spoken ones around them.

The main plot of Durfey's *Don Quixote* is, like the original, episodic: A series of slapstick scenes (most having music) in which the Don and Sancho are tricked, beaten repeatedly, and otherwise humiliated is held together by sketchy, romantic subplots involving the perpetrators of the cruel humor. Inserted into this inside-out comedy is some of Purcell's greatest music. The second act of Part 1 illustrates this peculiar mixture. In the first scene the innkeeper performs the sham knighting of Don Quixote, who is entertained by Purcell's duet "Sing all ye Muses" and a dance of knights errant killing a dragon.[18] The foolish ceremony is followed immediately by a funeral for the late Chrysostome, a young Englishman who has killed himself after being spurned by the beautiful Marcella. Tone is often difficult to assess in late seventeenth-century plays, and one might suspect that Durfey's extravagant funeral oration is a send-up. But John Eccles's elaborate dirge for two soloists and three accompanying recorders is without doubt serious music.[19] And the following passage (as shown in the example on page 230), with its boldly ascending harmonic progressions, produces a truly moving moment worthy of Eccles's more famous collaborator.

The centerpiece of Act IV of *Don Quixote,* Part 1, is "Let the dreadful Engines of eternal will," perhaps Purcell's greatest baritone aria. It is sung by Cardenio, who has taken to the hills after having been treacherously deprived of Luscinda, his betrothed. This seven or eight-minute "mad cantata," which shifts rapidly from pathos to humor, from dissonant recitatives to gentle, lilting tunes, tells us infinitely more about Cardenio than all his subsequent spoken lines. Later in the play, when the romantic subplot dries up

18. Purcell's complete music is in *The Works of Henry Purcell,* Vol. XVI.
19. In *The Songs to the New Play of Don Quixote:* Part 1 (London: J. Heptinstall, 1694), pp. 9–18.

230

and the subtleties of his character have not been further exploited, the drama is left horribly out of balance. This masterpiece may have been cut from the original production, supposedly to reduce its running time,[20] but one suspects that Purcell did his job too well.

By far the most popular piece from Durfey's *Don Quixote* was Eccles's "I burn, my Brain consumes to Ashes," in Part 2, V.ii. It too is a mad song but, unlike Cardenio's famous aria, is introduced for flimsy dramatic reasons, being essentially a showpiece for the great Mrs Bracegirdle. In the preface Durfey acknowledges her help in the success of the play, remarking that the song (which is full of virtuosic passagework but little musical substance) was "incomparably well sung, *and Acted*" (italics added). Sadly, the third part of *Don Quixote* is thoroughly degenerate. The playwright makes little attempt to rationalize the interpolated music, even Purcell's last song, the beautiful "From Rosie Bowers" (Act V). Near the end of the play, after the Don has made his will and is dying, he is entertained by a tasteless duet about a brother and sister's incestuous relationship. Nothing could better illustrate how desperate British drama was for reform.

The Reform of the Drama

This "thoroughly musical theatre," whose potential for true opera was at least as great as Italy's in the 1590s, seems to have done everything wrong in the decade around 1700. Henry Purcell, perhaps the greatest operatic composer between Monteverdi and Mozart, was confined to writing masques for dramatic operas and brief, though more operatic, songs for ordinary plays. The amount of music heard in the playhouses increased significantly after his death, but instead of using music to enhance spoken dialogue, playwrights and theatre managers found it more efficient to confine music to intervals and afterpieces. A letter written around 1706 by a Drury Lane actor to a friend in Nottingham understates the situation:

20. The *Daily Courant,* 14 June 1703, reports that "the mad Song in *Don Quixote*" was omitted from the play. For speculation about the reason see *BD,* II, 199.

Our stage is in a very indifferent condition. There has been a very fierce combat between the Haymarket and Drury Lane, and the two sisters, Music and Poetry, quarrel like two fishwives at Billingsgate. . . . Though Farquhar meets with success, and has the entire happiness of pleasing the upper gallery, Betterton and Wilks, Ben Jonson and the best of them, must give place to a bawling Italian woman, whose voice to me is less pleasing than merry-andrew's playing on the gridiron. "The Mourning Bride," "Plain Dealer," "Volpone," or "Tamerlane," will hardly fetch us a tolerable audience, unless we stuff the bills with long entertainments of dances, songs, scaramouched entries, and what not.[21]

The player mentions almost in passing a factor that finally disrupted the delicate balance between music and spoken drama on the London stage: the foreign singer. Leveridge, Pate, and Bracegirdle could sing incantations and mad songs in plays, and native as well as French dancers might advance plots in allegorical ballets; but foreign singers were singularly useless to the early eighteenth-century English theatre, except, of course, as entr'acte attractions. Their Italian arias may have been effective weapons in the battle for audiences; dramaturgically, however, the imported music was in the same category as tumblers and rope dancers.

The foreign singers were the advance guard of the dreaded Italian opera, which most actors, playwrights, and critics believed would be the final straw in the collapse of the London theatre.[22] But the string of Italianate operas in English translation and, later, the bilingual *pasticci* produced between 1705 and 1711 had quite a different effect. At first they did give plays stiff competition. The theatre managers soon discovered, however, that they could not afford the tremendous added expense of prima donnas and

21. The letter is printed without date in Percy Fitzgerald, *A New History of the English Stage,* 2 vols. (London: Tinsley, 1882), I, 240. The Italian woman is perhaps Margarita de l'Epine, who is first recorded as performing on the London stage in 1703.

22. For a sampling of these fears expressed in prefaces, prologues, and epilogues to contemporary plays, see Nicoll, *A History of English Drama,* II, 227–33, and Curtis A. Price, "Musical Practices in Restoration Plays," Diss. Harvard (1974), pp. 301–10. See also John Dennis, *An Essay on the Opera's After the Italian Manner,* "Which are about to be Establish'd on the English Stage: With some Reflections on the Damage which they may bring to the Publick" (1706), rpt. in *The Critical Works of John Dennis,* ed. Edward Niles Hooker, 2 vols. (Baltimore: Johns Hopkins Univ. Press, 1939–43), I, 382–93.

castrati, and the opera had to be artificially sustained by large injections of aristocratic money and by changes in theatre management.[23] But the predicted destruction of the London stage never happened. Instead, the play was able to shed the musical burden it had borne since 1660, and dramas with little or no music, such as Farquhar's *The Beaux Stratagem* and Cibber's *The Lady's Last Stake* (1707), were able to compete successfully with the all-sung opera. Music finally had its own medium in the English theatre, albeit a foreign one. Even the opera's harsher critics were relieved. Joseph Addison, writing in *The Spectator* (1711), found the "Transition from an Air to Recitative" in Italian opera more "natural" than the awkward "passing from a Song to plain and ordinary Speaking," which had been the practice in Restoration musical plays.[24] He did not mean that the works of Durfey and Purcell were unsatisfactory simply because they mixed music and spoken dialogue. Rather, he believed that if protagonists were to converse in music at all, then they should do so entirely, dispensing with the play-within-a-play rationale.

The reform of the play precipitated by the success of the Italianate opera seems to have been welcomed by almost everyone,[25] but the position of native music on the London stage was permanently altered. English theatre composers were soon unemployed and unemployable, and the actor-singers variously retired (as did Mrs Bracegirdle), concentrated on singing (as did Leveridge), or turned principally to acting (as did Mrs Cross). During the 1706–8 seasons, the Lord Chamberlain even prevented the mounting of musical plays and dramatic operas by transferring all musical forces to the opera company, leaving the playhouse with no singers and only a small orchestra to perform the overtures and act tunes.[26] The conventions that had allowed English art music to enhance the scenes of spoken plays were soon forgotten, and Purcell's miniature music dramas, such as the conjurer's scene from *The Indian Queen*,

23. These developments are outlined in Curtis A. Price, "The Critical Decade for English Music Drama, 1700–1710," *Harvard Library Bulletin,* 26 (1978), 38–76.
24. *The Spectator,* ed. Donald F. Bond (Oxford: Clarendon Press, 1965), I, 120.
25. See Price, "The Critical Decade," p. 65.
26. Ibid., pp. 54–69.

resurfaced a few seasons later as entr'acte entertainments or after-pieces, rarely appearing with their original plays.

Colley Cibber, an actor, manager, and playwright who benefited greatly from the theatrical reforms of the first decade of the eighteenth century, explains in his autobiography how difficult it was for the reformed companies to revive Restoration musical plays. He recalls that William Mountfort, whom most people remembered as a fine actor and defender to the death of Mrs Bracegirdle's honor, was also an accomplished countertenor. Cibber admired his handling of roles in which "Singing was a necessary Part," and he particularly envied Mountfort his performance in Crowne's *Sir Courtly Nice* (1685), "which I, alas! could only struggle thro' . . . under the Imperfection of a feign'd, and screaming Trebble."[27] Even dancing, which had been a necessary skill of many Restoration actors—particularly those who specialized in minor roles—was not common among the Thespians in the reformed theatre. In 1712 Steele remarked that "it would be a great Improvement, as well as Embellishment to the Theatre, if Dancing were more regarded, and taught to all the Actors."[28]

The history of music in the London theatres in the first half of the eighteenth century is really the history of Handel's Italianate opera. True, by 1715 music had begun to creep back into plays, where it remained in varying amounts throughout the century. But the new musical plays differ fundamentally from the Restoration types discussed above. In both, music was governed by histrionic rather than operatic coventions, but during the eighteenth century, song and dance were rarely allowed narrative roles in spoken plays; and no composer of Purcell's stature supplied the Augustan stage with music. With the foreign opera providing the London audiences with the finest music of the time, plays no longer had to include art music.[29] That Handel would have composed masques or mad songs for plays is inconceivable. His dramatic muse required a large canvas, unsullied by competing genius. When the Italianate opera

---

27. *An Apology for the Life of Colley Cibber* (1740), ed. B. R. S. Fone (Ann Arbor: Univ. of Michigan Press, 1968), p. 76.

28. *The Spectator*, III, 395.

29. For a comprehensive survey of English dramatic music in decline, see Roger Fiske, *English Theatre Music in the Eighteenth Century* (London: Oxford Univ. Press, 1973).

bubble burst in London in the 1730s and he was urged to create an English style of opera,[30] Handel, probably with a keen awareness of the subservient position music had traditionally held in the English theatre, turned instead to writing unstaged operas: the dramatic oratorios.

Old Roger North was right, of course, in believing that "by an error of mixing 2 capitall enterteinements," the late seventeenth-century musical play "could not stand long. For some that would come to the play, hated the musick, and others that were very desirous of the musick, would not bear the interruption that so much rehearsall gave, so that it is best to have either by itself intire."[31] But it was not simply the mixing of music and spoken dialogue that led to the demise of this stage form. The fatal flaw in the lyrical plays of Dryden, Durfey, Eccles, and Purcell was that music and drama were made equals, and that, as any Wagnerian knows, can happen only in opera.

30. See Aaron Hill's letter of 5 December 1732, printed in Otto Erich Deutsch, *Handel: A Documentary Biography* (New York: W. W. Norton, 1955), p. 299.
31. *Roger North on Music*, pp. 353–54.

8
The Changing Audience

HARRY WILLIAM PEDICORD

ANY APPRAISAL of English drama and stage history from the Restoration until the close of the next century has to take into account theatre attendance, the composition of the audience, and patrons' taste, all of which changed greatly during a span of 140 years. Critics in general have agreed in interpreting the social categories, behavior, and the general taste of the public,[1] but certain problems remain to perplex us. Critics agree that the restoration of the playhouses attracted a new constituency, but they are still divided about the composition of that audience, what it demanded, and how it evolved.

When the eighteen-year prohibition of playhouses under the Commonwealth came to an end in 1660 the newly constituted patent companies had to woo an almost entirely new public. Richard Southern,[2] in explaining why Killigrew and Davenant both had to seek temporary quarters on the sites of tennis courts while planning and constructing new theatres, remarks: "It is perhaps significant to note that neither turned to one of the surviving

---

1. See Emmett L. Avery, "The Restoration Audience," *Philological Quarterly*, 45 (1966), 54–61; Leo Hughes, *The Drama's Patrons: A Study of the Eighteenth-Century London Audience* (Austin: Univ. of Texas Press, 1971); Harold Love, "The Myth of the Restoration Audience," *Komos*, 1, No. 2 (1967), 49–56; James J. Lynch, *Box, Pit, and Gallery: Stage and Society in Johnson's London* (Berkeley: Univ. of California Press, 1953); John C. Whitty, "The Half-Price Riots of 1763," *Theatre Notebook*, 24 (1969–70), 25–32.

2. *The Revels History of Drama in English*, ed. T. W. Craik, Vol. V: *1660–1750* (London: Methuen, 1976), p. 84.

Elizabethan playhouses; that era was ended." But he does not explain further. The surviving playhouses were old and incommodious and their stagehouses could not accommodate to the new vogue for elaborate scenery and machines. The Red Bull in St. John Street was partially open to the weather and its plays had to be acted by daylight. The Cockpit and Salisbury Court houses were not large enough to suit the ambitious plans of the new managers for more spectators and elaborate *mise en scène*.[3]

We do not know the seating capacity of the late seventeenth-century theatres with any precision. The best estimates suggest that even Drury Lane and Dorset Garden held under 1,000 at this time, perhaps well under. In the years 1682–95 only one theatre was active, and when a second company was reestablished in 1695 it used the cramped little "second" Lincoln's Inn Fields building. We may guess, therefore, that as late as c. 1700 no more than a maximum of 1,800 people could have attended the theatre on a given day, or 10,800 per week (making no allowance for repeat attenders, who were numerous). London's population was then about 540,000,[4] so no more than 2 percent of the population could have attended the theatre in any given week. Probably nothing like that number of different persons ever did attend.

Not only was a significant core of the audience composed of habitués, but we know that attendance was poor a great part of this time. James Wright in his *Historia Histrionica* (1699) has Lovewit, speaking of the pre-Commonwealth period, marvel: "That the Town much less than at present, could then maintain Five Companies, and yet now Two can hardly Subsist."[5]

Until recently it was the custom to assume that Restoration theatre audiences were drawn primarily from the upper class. A closer look, however, has shown that this was not always the case. True, the decisive group from 1660 to 1672 seems to have been the court of Charles II. As John Loftis reminds us,[6] Dryden thought so,

3. See James Wright, *Historia Histrionica* (1699), rpt., Preface by Arthur Freeman (New York: Garland, 1974), p. 7.

4. Gregory King's estimate. See David Ogg, *England in the Reigns of James II and William III* (Oxford: Clarendon Press, 1955), pp. 30–31.

5. Wright, p. 5.

6. *The Revels History*, V, 4.

and considered his works as courtiers' dramas derived from the taste, example, and particular advice of noblemen such as Buckingham, Dorset, Howard, Rochester, and Sedley, patrons of the stage and craftsmen in the art of playwriting, whose arbiter was none other than the young king himself. James Wright is careful to distinguish between audiences before the Commonwealth and after the restoration of the monarchy. Always sensitive to class distinctions, his Truman remarks: "The two last [The Fortune and the Red Bull] were mostly frequented by Citizens, and the meaner sort of People."[7] When Lovewit seems surprised at the small attendance in 1699, Truman explains: "Do not wonder, but consider, That tho' the Town was then, perhaps, not much more than half so Populous as now, yet then the Prices were small (there being no Scenes) and better order kept among the Company that came; which made very good People think a Play an Innocent Diversion for an idle Hour or two, the Plays themselves being then, for the most part, more Instructive and Moral."[8]

The implication seems to be that prices determined the audiences by the time of the Restoration, that ordinary citizens could not afford to attend the theatres. And yet we find Samuel Pepys complaining as early as 1662 that he was "not so well pleased with the company at the house [Duke's Theatre] today, which was full of Citizens, there hardly being a gentleman or woman in the house, but a couple of pretty ladies by us, that made sport at it, being jostled and crowded by prentices."[9] Five years later he is still complaining: "Here a mighty company of citizens, prentices, and others; and it makes me observe that when I begin to be able to bestow a play on myself, I do not remember that I saw so many by half of the ordinary prentices and mean people in the pit, at 2s-6d apiece, as now; I going for several years no higher then the 12d, and then the 18d places, and though I strained hard to go in then when I did—so much the vanity and prodigality of the age is to be observed in this perticular."[10] And yet he is impressed on 12 February 1667

7. Wright, p. 5.
8. Ibid.
9. *The Diary of Samuel Pepys,* ed. Robert Latham and William Matthews, 11 vols. (Berkeley: Univ. of California Press, 1970–), III, 295–96.
10. Ibid., IX, 2.

by a talk with Thomas Killigrew: "He tells me how the Audience at his House is not half so much as it used to be before the late fire. . . . Now, all things civil, no rudeness anywhere; then, as in a bear-garden. . . . [Before 1642] the Queen seldom and the King never would come; now, not the King only for state, but all civil people do think they may come as well as any. . . . And he tells me plainly that the Citty Audience was as good as the Court—but now [since the Great Fire] they are most gone."[11]

James Wright's Truman described how the audience had changed by 1699: "Whereas of late, the Play-houses are so extreamly pestered with Vizard-masks and their Trade, (occasioning continual Quarrels and Abuses) that many of the more Civilized Part of the Town are uneasy in the Company, and shun the Theater as they would a House of Scandal. . . . the present Plays with all that shew, can hardly draw an Audience, unless there be the additional Invitation of a *Signior Fideli,* a *Monsieur L'abbe,* or some such Foreign Regale exprest in the bottom of the Bill."[12] John Dennis, early in the eighteenth century, differs in his impression. Looking back, he declares: "That was an age of Pleasure," the implication being that audiences were made up of privileged persons who had the leisure to attend and "had that due application, which is requisite for the judging of Comedy."[13]

Modern critical attitudes are divided on the subject. K. M. P. Burton, D. R. M. Wilkinson, and A. S. Bear, all favor a continuing coterie audience to appreciate the witty conversation and suggestive situations in Restoration comedies.[14] Harold Love, John Loftis, and Robert D. Hume have opted for an opposite view: the nonhomogeneous nature of the spectators from 1660 to 1700.[15] Hume sums up his argument for change: "The heyday of the

11. Ibid., VIII, 55–56.
12. Wright, pp. 5–6.
13. *The Critical Works of John Dennis,* ed. Edward Niles Hooker, 2 vols. (Baltimore: Johns Hopkins Univ. Press, 1939–43), I, 294.
14. K. M. P. Burton, *Restoration Literature* (London: Hutchinson, 1958); D. R. M. Wilkinson, *The Comedy of Habit* (Leiden: Universitaire Pers, 1964); A. S. Bear, "Criticism and Social Change: The Case for Restoration Drama," *Komos,* 2, No. 1 (n.d.), 23–31.
15. Harold Love, "Bear's Case Laid Open; Or, A Timely Warning to Literary Sociologists," *Komos,* 2, No. 2 (n.d.), 72–80; John Loftis, *Comedy and Society from Congreve to Fielding* (Stanford: Stanford Univ. Press, 1959); Robert D. Hume, *The Development of English Drama in the Late Seventeenth Century* (Oxford: Clarendon Press, 1976).

Carolean Court circle vanished with the Popish Plot: to suppose
that Congreve and Farquhar, who were small children at that time,
wrote for a Court audience is ridiculous."[16]

There are sufficient grounds for thinking that audiences did
change in quality and taste during these forty years, especially in the
1670s and 1690s, though the change might also be thought as one in
which the stage educated its public. The courtly audience was
enthralled by such plays as Sir Samuel Tuke's *Adventures of Five
Hours* (LIF, 1663), Thomas Porter's *The Villain* (LIF, 1662), John
Dryden's *The Rival Ladies* (Bridges St., 1664), and the rhymed
heroic drama as represented by Dryden and Sir Robert Howard's
The Indian Queen (Bridges St., 1664) or the Earl of Orrery's *The
History of Henry the Fifth* (Bridges St., 1664). All of these dramas
were based on a code of righteous conduct and their plots were
filled with intrigue and high-spirited women. But in three years'
time the new breed of spectators, men of business and even the
ordinary citizens so abhorred by Pepys, preferred such entertainments as the Duke of Buckingham's *The Chances* (Bridges St.,
1667) and Sir George Etherege's *She wou'd if she cou'd* (LIF, 1668).
Eight years later the same spectators were enjoying a spate of
comedies in the spirit of Etherege. In two glorious seasons they
were treated to William Wycherley's *The Country-Wife* (DL, 1675),
Etherege's *The Man of Mode* (DG, 1676), Thomas Shadwell's *The
Virtuoso* (DG, 1676), and Wycherley's *The Plain-Dealer* (DL,
1676).

At the outset of the second great era in the century's drama,
another segment of the broadening audience became noticeable.
John Dennis, writing in 1702, deplored three types of persons in
the audience by this time. These were patrons who had had no
education and were "unheard of in the Reign of King Charles the
Second." He describes them as

A great many younger Brothers, Gentlemen born, who have been kept at
home, by reason of the pressure of the Taxes. Several People, who made
their Fortunes in the late War; and who from a state of obscurity, and

16. Hume, p. 25.

240

perhaps of misery, have risen to a condition of distinction and plenty. I believe that no man will wonder, if these People, who in their original obscurity, . . . could never attain to any higher entertainment than Tumbling and Vaulting and Ladder Dancing, and the delightful diversions of *Jack Pudding,* should still be in Love with their old sports, and encourage these noble Pastimes still upon the Stage. But a 3d sort of People, who may be said to have had no education at all in relation to us and our Plays, is that considerable number of Foreigners, which within these last twenty years have been introduc'd among us; some of whom not being acquainted with our Language, and consequently with the sense of our Plays, and others disgusted with our extravagant, exorbitant Rambles, have been Instrumental in introducing Sound and Show, where the business of the Theatre does not require it, and particularly a sort of a soft and wanton Musick, which has used the People to a delight which is independent of Reason, a delight that has gone a very great way towards enervating and dissolving their minds.[17]

In any event, this new breed demanded and got a more diversified bill for its entertainment, complete with expensive scenery, entr'acte features, and, beside the best of the older dramas, new ones such as William Congreve's *The Old Batchelour* (DL, 1693), *The Double-Dealer* (DL, 1693), *Love for Love* (LIF, 1695), Sir John Vanbrugh's *The Relapse* (DL, 1696) and *The Provok'd Wife* (LIF, 1697). But here we are inferring change in audience from change in popular fare. Harold Love is correct when he insists: "there is no hard evidence whatsoever for any current view of the composition of the Restoration audience."[18]

   During the first third of the eighteenth century this new audience began to include an ever greater diversity of playgoers. While the theatres were always fashionable places of entertainment, they became less fashionable c. 1700, due in part to the lack of interest of royalty in support and attendance. After the brief reign of James II the playhouses were to lose their association with the court almost entirely. William and Mary had their special political problems and evidenced little enthusiasm for the theatre, and Queen Anne

17. *Critical Works,* I, 293–94.
18. Love, p. 74.

241

perhaps even less. In fact, it was not until the advent of the first Hanoverian king, George I, in 1714 that royal patronage was again a prime factor in theatregoing. As early as 21 September 1714, at the opening of the season at Drury Lane, before a performance of Farquhar's *The Recruiting Officer,* Robert Wilks spoke an occasional prologue by Sir Richard Steele saluting "His Majesty's Publick Entry." Even though His Majesty had just landed in England, theatre management was anticipating royal attendance once more. George I did indeed visit Drury Lane and the King's Theatre, even Lincoln's Inn Fields on occasion, and royalty was represented even more often by the Prince and Princess of Wales. Thus royalty once more gave prestige to playhouses, which now welcomed not only persons of quality and fashion but also merchant citizens, their apprentices, the clergy, and members of the nation's armed forces, all of them anxious to bask in the royal presence.

A growing population and a broadening audience are evidenced in the growth of fringe theatres prior to the Licensing Act of 1737. Adding audiences at the Opera House (1,400), the Little Theatre in the Haymarket (800), Goodman's Fields (700), Drury Lane (1,001), and Covent Garden (1,335), A. H. Scouten conjectures that as many as 14,300 people could have attended the theatre during Christmas week 1732.[19] This is some 2.8 percent of the metropolitan population.

An increase in population inevitably brought less fashionable people into the playhouses and led to certain groups distinguishing themselves more by their behavior than by any social position. The Mohocks who vandalized London in the early years of the century brought their catcalls into the theatres and became the scourge of players, only to be supplanted in later years by the young Templars, students of law, who came to openings to insist on their own brand of criticism not only of the repertoire but the acting of it. The early years also brought the rise in influence of the Freemasons, a social phenomenon yet to be thoroughly explored. These patrons brought appreciation and a certain decorum to the pit and first galleries, and, on occasion, to the front boxes. Even the arch-enemies of Freemasonry, the Gormogons (1724), the Gregorians

19. *LS,* Part 3, I, clxi–clxii.

(1741), the Mercurians (1741), and the "Scald Miserables" (1741), appear to have behaved themselves when the play began.[20] The Freemasons were in part responsible for the initial success of George Lillo's *The London Merchant* (DL, 1731) and its long record of performances throughout the century and beyond. A dedicated playwright, two actor-managers (Theophilus Cibber and Henry Giffard) both active Masons, a cast drawn from a theatrical lodge, the Bear and Harrow in Butcher Row (now St. George's Lodge and Corner Stone No. 5), including Rodger Bridgewater, William Mills, and Robert Wetherilt, and audiences representing a Masonic cross-section of London's most substantial citizens helped give this drama a record of 236 performances from 1731 to 1800.[21]

Another factor determining attendance and the quality of spectators in the early part of the century was a growing spirit of partisanship. The initial performance of Joseph Addison's *Cato* (DL, 1713) and subsequent ones, at which political parties loudly vied with each other to demonstrate their partisan love of liberty, and the 1716 revival of Nicholas Rowe's *Tamerlane* (LIF, 1701), with its virtuous hero (William III) and the vicious Bajazet (Louis XIV), are cases in point. Both served notice on the public that some theatres were more loyal than others, namely, Drury Lane as opposed to Lincoln's Inn Fields. Rowe's occasional prologue to the *Tamerlane* production (DL, 5 November 1716) celebrated loyalty to the government and began the custom of playing this drama every 4 or 5 November for many years in honor of William III and subsequent monarchs.

Slowly there developed the typical distribution of theatre audiences, which by this time exactly paralleled box office tariffs and in turn imposed rigid social distinctions: persons of quality in the front and side-boxes; the pit and first gallery occupied by wealthy tradesmen, their wives and families; the upper gallery inhabited by "the Mob" at a shilling apiece. Such an arrangement was categorized by Theophilus Cibber as the "Noble, Gentle, or Simple, who fill the

20. Harry William Pedicord, "White Gloves at Five: Fraternal Patronage of London Theatres in the Eighteenth Century," *Philological Quarterly*, 45 (1966), 270–88.
21. Harry William Pedicord, "George Lillo and 'Speculative Masonry,'" *Philological Quarterly*, 53 (1974), 408.

Boxes, Pit, and Galleries . . . as K——ng, L——rds and COM-
MONS . . . make that great body the Nation."[22] As early as 1704
Jonathan Swift was including a humorous survey of playhouse
audiences in his *A Tale of a Tub*. The pit is situated below stage,
"that whatever *weighty* Matter shall be delivered thence (whether it
be *Lead* or *Gold*) may fall plum into the Jaws of certain *Criticks* (as I
think they are called)." The ladies sit in boxes, because "That large
Portion of Wit laid out in raising Pruriences and Protuberances, is
observ'd to run much upon a Line, and ever in a Circle." He
characterizes the inhabitants of the first gallery as having "frigid
Understandings," and dismisses the upper gallery as "a suitable
Colony, who greedily intercept them [bombast and buffoonry] in
their Passage."[23]

The following year Richard Estcourt's speaking of the epilogue to
Mrs Centlivre's *The Basset Table* (DL, 1705) again alluded to such
distinctions.

> This goodly Fabrick to a gazing Tar,
> Seems Fore and Aft, a Three Deckt Man of War:
> Abaft, the Hold's the Pit, from thence look up;
> Aloft! that's Swabber's Nest, that's the Main-Top.
> Side Boxes mann'd with Beau, and modish Rake,
> Are like the Fore-castle and Quarter-Deck.[24]

John Macky described the audience of 1714: "The Parterre, commonly called the Pit, contains the gentlemen on benches; and on the
first story of boxes sit all the ladies of quality; in the second, the
Citizens Wives and daughters; and in the third, the common people
and footmen."[25] As late as 1776 the prologue for the opening of
Drury Lane went thus:

> Another simile, we mean to broach—
> A new one too!—The stage is a stage coach.—

22. "Preface to the Town," *Two Dissertations on the Theatres* (London: Griffiths, 1756),
p. 5.
23. *The Prose Works of Jonathan Swift,* ed. Herbert Davis, 16 vols. (Oxford: Blackwell,
1939–74), I, 36–37.
24. *Works,* 3 vols. (London: John Pearson, 1872), I, 201.
25. *A Journey through England,* 4th ed., 2 vols. (London: J. Hooke, 1724), I, 165.

Here *(boxes)* some take Places, and some mount basket. (gall.)
Our cattle too, that draw the stage along,
Are of all sorts and sizes—weak and strong,
Brown, gray, black, bay, brisk, tame, blind,
    lame, fat, lean, old and young!
If as we're jogging on, we sometimes stop,
Some scold within, and some asleep will drop.
While sailors and their doxies sing and roar a'top.[26]

Such were the patrons in the period which gave birth to four new forms of drama—the ballad opera, the oratorios of Handel, the satirical and political comedies of Henry Fielding, and the strange allurement of domestic tragedy.

The second half of the eighteenth century brought with it not only increased attendance at the legitimate theatres but also enlargement of those houses to accommodate increased patronage. (See Edward Langhans's essay, above.) The metropolis, the cities and liberties of London and Westminster together with the Borough of Southwark and adjacent parts, is estimated to have included 676,250 citizens by 1750, rising to 900,000 by the end of the century.[27]

If both patent theatres had operated each night at peak capacity, we can assume the maximum number of spectators in metropolitan London to have been 2,336 nightly, 1732–47; 2,603, 1747–62; 3,697 from 1762 to the enlargement of Covent Garden in 1782. Such figures, always adjusting for repeat attenders, afford a maximum weekly potential of 14,016 from 1732 to 1747; 15,618 from 1747 to 1762; and 22,182 from 1762 to 1782. Actual attendance figures, however, may be calculated as follows: daily average of 1,410, weekly 8,460 for the two patent houses, 1740–42; 1,878 daily and 11,268 weekly, 1746–48. In fifteen years these averages had become 1,979 a day and 11,874 a week, 1758–60.[28] Samuel Foote, a shrewd manager, offers corroboration in *A Treatise on the*

26. *Town and Country Magazine,* October, 1776, pp. 551–52.
27. M. D. George, *London Life in the Eighteenth Century* (New York: Knopf, 1925), pp. 24–38.
28. Harry William Pedicord, *The Theatrical Public in the Time of Garrick* (New York: King's Crown Press, 1954), p. 16.

Passions by saying: "Upon the least favourable Calculation, the Number of those called Play-Followers, cannot be rated at less than twelve thousand in this Metropolis."[29]

The composition of these audiences continues to broaden substantially, even though there are no further noticeable changes in their quality before the end of the century. Behavior again becomes the only distinguishing feature, but by now this behavior is expressed in terms of entire audiences. For the most part the performance evenings were relatively quiet, and, given a good series of entertainments and performance, most spectators behaved themselves once the first music sounded. Archenholz, who visited Drury Lane in 1769–70, reported that "When the play begins, all noise and bombardment ceases, unless some especial provocation gives rise to further disturbances; and one is bound to admire the quiet attentiveness of such an estimable folk."[30] There was, of course, the noisy freedom expressed before the curtain rose and during intermissions. But it was now a matter of articulate audiences. Spectators called for prologue and epilogue when they were omitted after the ninth night; they called for particular tunes from the orchestra; they demanded and got explanations and apologies from actors and their management. To all of which those behind the scenes wisely responded as best they could.

The Freemasons continued to bring reason and courtesy to their special nights and were treated to the likes of the pantomime *Harlequin Freemason* (CG, 29 December 1780). Other groups likewise patronized the theatre. Between 1768 and 1773 The Grand Order of the Bucks bespoke many nights at the theatres. This anti-Masonic group and its guests even relished Thomas King's popular epilogue "Bucks Have At Ye All" (first spoken at Drury Lane on 18 April 1768).[31]

> Ye social Friends of Gallantry and Wit!
> Where'er dispers'd in merry Groupes ye sit;

29. (London: Printed for C. Corbet, et al., n.d.) Sig. A₂. This treatise is usually attributed to Foote.

30. John A. Kelly, *German Visitors to English Theaters in the Eighteenth Century* (Princeton: Princeton Univ. Press, 1936), p. 55.

31. (Oxford: Printed for The Bodleian Library, 1971), pp. 10–12.

> Whether ye gild the glitt'ring Scene below,
> Or midst yon *Upper Tribes,* your Fun bestow,
> Ye Bucks, assembled at a *Brother's* call,
> By Heav'n I know ye—and have at ye all.
> ·
> Each *Buck* point out his Likeness to another,
> With Temper see, with Candor spare a Brother.

Since this epilogue was also billed from time to time as "A Picture of the Playhouse," it contained a candid look at the behavior of the familiar categories in the audience.

> For Instance now—to charm th' admiring Croud,
> Your *Bucks i' th' Boxes* sneer, and talk aloud.
> Thence to the more *commodious Seats* they run,
> (*Illo! Illo! my* Bucks! *well, what's the* Fun?
> ·
> Your *Bucks* i' th' *Pit* are—Miracles of Learning!
> Who point out Faults—to shew their own discerning.
> ·
> The *Middle Row,* whose keener Views of Bliss
> Are chiefly center'd in a fav'rite Miss;
> A Set of jovial *Bucks* who there resort,
> Flushed from the Tavern—reeling ripe for Sport—
> Whisp'ring soft Nonsense in the fair One's Ear,
> And wholly ignorant—what passes *here;*
> Wak'd from their Dream, oft join the House Applause,
> *Bravo! Bravo! &c.—what was it?*
> Thus shew their *Taste*—unconscious of the Cause.
> Or missing that, behold another Row,
> Supplied by Citizens, or smirking Beau;
> ·
> High over all, supremely wise are they
> Who, Insect-like, together swarm, to prey
> On the fresh Carcase of each newborn Play.
> In various kinds of Fun, the Hours they chase,
> Careless alike of *Action, Time,* or *Place.*—

Some the shrill Trumpet, some the Cat call try,
Some Broomstickado's softer Harmony—
Others in nobler Mimickry excell,
You'd think 'em Beasts, they act the Beast so well.
Here mews a *Cat*—there barks a snarling *Dog*—
Here crows a *Cock*—there grunts a bristled *Hog*.
   First with the noise some rusticated Clown
Roars from his empty Stomach—*Knock him down.*
Here *Nosey, Nosey,* merry *Witlings* cry—
There *Taylors! Taylors!* echoing *Smarts* reply—
Till mingled Shouts & Screams pierce thro the vaulted Sky.

How was the audience changing? Allardyce Nicoll described the eighteenth-century theatre world as beginning in rowdyism, riot, and brutality, traced a gradual softening of this barbarity through the influence of middle-class social pretensions, to arrive at the end of the period in what he called an "equitable calm." Such a contrast is too broad, and the facts simply do not justify it. Nicoll does note that "no decided cleavage can be traced between the audiences of the early and those of the late eighteenth century"; but he goes on to say, "slowly the main features of the typical body of spectators were changing during these years. In spite of recurring riots, in spite of rowdyism during and after the performance of plays, the playgoers of 1770 were quieter and less uproarious than their predecessors of 1730."[32]

The record of serious disturbances at Drury Lane Theatre alone contradicts such a view. Of the seven riotous occasions extending over a thirty-three-year period, only a two-day altercation involving parties favoring Charles Macklin in his resentment of Garrick's apparent desertion in a decision to rejoin Fleetwood's company (DL, 6–7 December 1743) took place in the earlier years. The other six were more prolonged and took place in the period characterized as leading to an "equitable calm." On 22 January 1750 the audience rioted against the popular actor Henry Woodward for satirizing Samuel Foote in Otway's *Friendship in Fashion.* According to the

32. *A History of Late Eighteenth-Century Drama 1750–1800*, rev. ed. (Cambridge: Cambridge Univ. Press, 1955), p. 5.

prompter, Richard Cross, Woodward "was forc'd to desist ye 4th and 5th Acts were much hooted." When the play was given out again for the next evening, Cross writes: "the Audience . . . call'd loudly for Garrick, but as he was not this Night at the House, they pull'd up the Benches, tore down ye King's Arms, & wou'd have done much more mischief had not Mr Lacy gone into the Pit, & talk'd to 'em, what they resented was giving out a piece again after they had damn'd it—the Gallery resented ye Guards being sent in."[33]

Five years later came the six-day riot against Garrick's *The Chinese Festival* (DL, 8–15 November 1755), when patriotic fervor protested the engagement of French dancers. Excerpts from the Cross Diary tell the story in part:

[12 November] A great deal of Hissing—but the Boxes being on our Side some swords were drawn, & several turn'd out of the Pit & Galleries. The Officers of the Army are very busy in this Affair, on Account of their hissing when ye King was there . . . the King did turn his back to the Audience.

[13 November] More noise against the Dancers, wch so enraged My L^d that with a Number of Gents: he went in the upper Galleries & took out a very noisy person—who prov'd to be Cap: Venor's Brother; he resisted & was not brought behind the scenes without much Difficulty, sadly beat, yet still obstinate . . . but all was adjusted without further Mischief.

[15 November] A great Noise, the whole House against us—When Garrick appear'd one from the Slips cry'd out Monsieur, & great Numbers Hiss'd—the play went on—wch done, the Mutiny began, amazing noise. . . . Some benches were pull'd up, & Mr Lacy gave up the Dance to appease 'em.[34]

In 1763 Garrick endured his share of the general Half-Price Riots (25–26 January) when the audience demanded and obtained admittance at half price after the third act of a mainpiece except at

33. *LS*, Part 4, I, 169–70.
34. Ibid., II, 505–8.

the run of a new pantomime. Cross notes: "A Riot to demand admission at ½ price . . . wch. not agreed to, the Mob broke Chandeliers, &c. No Play."[35] Two years later there occurred an unusually violent first-night of Mrs Griffith's *The Platonic Wife* (DL, 24 January 1765). In 1770 there was a three-day riot against Hugh Kelly's *A Word to the Wise* (DL, 3–5 March) because the author was anathema to the followers of John Wilkes. Cross writes: "As soon as the Curtain was drawn up they began to hiss—a party was made against it—because he was suspected of Writing for the Court party. Much hissing. Mr. Garrick call'd for. No Play &c. Cry'd out, at last the play was got thro' with much hissing and Groaning When the play was given out again One Party was for it no more and Kelly's party was for it again so that no play at all was given out." The next performance was received in much the same manner and, "at Length the House was dismiss'd about Nine O'Clock."[36] The management was obliged to return the customers' money. And in Garrick's last season as manager there was a four-day riot (2–5 February 1776) against Henry Bate's *The Blackamoor Wash'd White* (DL, 1–5 February) in which London citizens were criticized in lines such as "O that I should ever live to see the day when white Englishmen must give place to foreign blacks."[37] The title of this afterpiece was quickly shortened to *The Blackamoor!*

Most of these events cannot be blamed on the general public, but they do make it difficult to subscribe to a gradually changing process toward peaceful evenings at the playhouse. While agreeing with the thought of change, I object to the tendency to overstress the bad behavior of early audiences and to credit later playgoers with a higher degree of decorum than facts warrant. George Winchester Stone, Jr, rightly warns: "One should always count to twelve thousand, of course, before drawing conclusions upon audience behavior based upon such concentration of rowdy response. . . . More often than not their reaction was favorable, else the business could not have prospered as it did. Often they demonstrated appre-

35. Ibid., pp. 974–75.
36. Ibid., III, 1458–59.
37. Ibid., pp. 1948–49.

ciation of having the most brilliant theatre in Europe to amuse them."[38]

One thing is certain: These audiences went to the theatre for *amusement*. They delighted in comedy rather than tragedy, old comedies altered to suit the taste of the times, such as *Every Man in His Humour* (DL, 1751), *The Chances* (DL, 1754), *The Gamesters* (DL, 1757), and *The Country Girl* (DL, 1766), perhaps even more than new comedies by Colman, Murphy, Garrick, Cumberland, and Goldsmith. The only sentimental pieces they tolerated were those that were at the same time soundly constructed, amusing, and stageworthy. Out of a total of 376 productions during Garrick's management only 35 plays belong to the sentimental vogue; and of these 35 sentimental plays only 25 can be considered successful. Only a handful were popular; the public soon rid themselves of the others. Despite Garrick's enthusiasm as an alterer-champion of Shakespeare, only his personal performance could win continued audience approval. If we are to credit the word of G. F. A. Wendeborn, a German visitor, English audiences were only lukewarm toward Shakespearean drama—if one of them was featured on the bill it had to be brilliantly staged and interspersed with songs, dances, and other diversions between the acts in order to keep the audience awake. And even then it had to be propped up by a really sparkling afterpiece. Wendeborn writes: "I have seen various Shakespeare plays performed before audiences which were conspicuously bored, although a Garrick or a Woodward employed his talents to make them pleasing."[39] Such audiences reserved their severest criticisms for farces and afterpieces, while maintaining the greatest tolerance for ballad operas, comic operas, and other musical extravaganzas. Their love for the English pantomime and spectacle was proverbial.

The enlargement of Drury Lane and Covent Garden in the 1790s increased daily capacity above 6,600.[40] With London's population up to 900,000, this raised the potential weekly audience to 4.4

38. Ibid., I, cxc.
39. Kelly, p. 122.
40. *LS,* Part 5, I, xliii–xliv.

percent (up from 3.2 percent in the 1780s). Thus although the number of theatres could not increase while population rose, the percentage of the population that could attend the theatre more than doubled in the course of our period. We should scarcely be surprised that the enormous and heterogeneous group required to fill the later theatres remained loyal to perennial favorites like *The Beggar's Opera, Hamlet,* and *The School for Scandal* among mainpieces. Charles Beecher Hogan, who has totaled performances for the last quarter of the century, points out the preponderance of comedies, particularly musical pieces, and notes that only four plays of a serious nature are to be found in the dozen mainpieces and a like number of afterpieces most often performed before 1800.[41]

The commercial nature of theatre operations was solidly established when the Licensing Act of 1737 made management of small theatres catering to small audiences impossible. George Winchester Stone, Jr, has detailed the nature of profits in the two patent theatres during the Garrick period and concluded that there were "ups and downs in profits," but that there was "a gradual trend after 1757 toward larger volumes of business, continued solvency, and steadily increasing profits."[42] Judge Samuel Curwen of Boston, who had no taste for the spectacles at Covent Garden in 1781, could deplore the theatre repertoire "as a proof among many others of the depravity of the present day";[43] nevertheless theatre managers were compelled to please an ever-increasing and diversified number of spectators—and they reaped enormous profits from their efforts.

41. Ibid., pp. clxxi–clxxiii.
42. *LS,* Part 4, I, xlvi. For details of large budgets and profits at the end of the century, see Hogan, Introduction to *LS,* Part 5, and chap. 1 above.
43. *Journal and Letters 1775–1784,* ed. G. A. Ward (New York: C. S. Francis, 1842), pp. 299–300.

9
Political and Social Thought in the Drama

JOHN LOFTIS

DRAMATISTS from Shakespeare to Sheridan have alluded, mockingly yet not ironically, to the drama as a record of the society that produces it. Their mockery provides a caution against an overliteral reading of the drama as social or political history; their avoidance of irony provides a reminder of the usefulness, a limited usefulness, of the printed drama as a voluminous (and partially unexplored) source for the student of history.[1] In creating the imaginary and self-contained worlds of their plays, the dramatists imposed an order on the experience they depicted, and in doing so they revealed widely held attitudes toward social and political relationships. The drama may tell us more about the habits of thought of its authors—and those of the audiences on whose favor they depended—than about the world that provided its subject. Yet it is worth knowing how a large group of intelligent and articulate persons who lived two or three hundred years ago thought about politics and society.

In one of their historical dimensions, the plays may be read as a series of efforts by men and women of the Restoration and

1. In an earlier essay I considered "The Limits of Historical Veracity in Neoclassical Drama," *England in the Restoration and Early Eighteenth Century: Essays on Culture and Society,* ed. H. T. Swedenberg, Jr. (Berkeley: Univ. of California Press, 1972), pp. 27–50. In this essay I examine a complementary aspect of the subject: the usefulness, within carefully circumscribed bounds, of the large body of printed drama in the historical study of the era.

eighteenth century to bring to the articulation of dramatic form their conceptions about relationships among individuals in the society in which they lived. The subject of drama is an interaction among a group of individuals, and because English society was organized in well-defined social classes, the dramatists could not portray their characters without identifying the social rank to which they belonged and without accepting social rank as one, though by no means the only, determinant of the implied evaluations of them. The fact that the dramatists, with a few exceptions in the final years of the period under review, accepted the traditional class relationships as a condition of life (even when they wrote about non-European societies)[2] provides a measure of their conservatism and that of the relatively affluent audiences for which they wrote. To be sure, they occasionally depict foolish characters of high rank in their comedies and wicked characters of high rank in their tragedies, but they show little inclination to question the justice of a distribution of wealth and privilege in patterns determined by social rank and, beginning under the Hanoverians, success in commerce. The theatrical monopoly established by Charles II soon after his restoration, as well as supervision of the stage by the Lord Chamberlain and his subordinates, helped keep such egalitarian thought as had been engendered by the mid-seventeenth-century civil wars from finding expression in drama.

Yet if conservative in depicting class relationships, the dramatists were not silent, within the limits imposed by governmental supervision of the theatres, about controversial political personalities and constitutional issues. The tragedies more than the comedies reveal changing patterns of political thought. Although the comedies of certain periods, notably those of the nine years separating *The Beggar's Opera* of 1728 and the Stage Licensing Act of 1737, include pungent political satire, the dramatists turned to tragedies for sustained and coherent exposition of political thought. Because of the conventional limitation of the subjects of tragedy to the concerns of leaders of states—customary despite such experiments as those of George Lillo—dramatists were confronted in the imaginary worlds

2. As in Dryden and Howard's *The Indian Queen* (1664) and in Dryden's *The Indian Emperour* (1665).

they created with fundamental problems of sovereignty and administration, and they made use of their characters and fables to provide expositions of systems embodying principles resembling the systematic formulations of political theorists. Many of the less successful tragedies, and occasionally a very good one such as Nathaniel Lee's *Lucius Junius Brutus,* can be regarded as cognate expressions of political theory expressed by contemporary philosophers.

Convictions about political issues had—and still have—social corollaries. We look to tragedy for political ideology; to comedy for social assumptions that followed from the dramatists' political convictions. Much of the comedy was intended to be, and was sometimes stated by contemporaries to be, an accurate portrayal of the life of the times. Polonius's comment about the drama as history (meaning tragedy as well as comedy) found similar expression in the hundred and forty years after the Restoration in application to comedy more frequently than to tragedy. Dennis, for example, defended Etherege's *Man of Mode* from Steele's moralistic criticism of it with the argument, among others, that it was an accurate portrayal of the life of courtiers during Charles II's reign.[3] Soon after the play's first performance, Etherege had in fact been criticised for writing an unimaginative transcription, with literary heightening, of the conversation he heard about him.[4]

The epistemological preoccupations of literary criticism in our part of the twentieth century provide forceful admonitions against assuming that the drama or any other form of imaginative literature can provide a faithful representation of life as we experience or observe it. So much might be assumed about the drama, in any event, conditioned as it is by the necessity of focusing attention for a short space of time on an intelligible and coherent sequence of events leading to an ending that is aesthetically satisfying. Yet there is an oblique relationship between the drama of an era and the life, which provides its subject, that repays study.

3. "A Defence of Sir Fopling Flutter . . . ," *The Critical Works of John Dennis,* ed. Edward Niles Hooker, II (Baltimore: Johns Hopkins Univ. Press, 1943), 244.
4. Alexander Radcliffe, *News from Hell,* in *The Ramble* (1682), p. 5. Quoted from H. F. B. Brett-Smith, ed., *The Dramatic Works of Sir George Etherege,* 2 vols. (Oxford: Blackwell, 1927), I, lxx.

I The Reigns of Charles II and James II

The drama of the early years of the Restoration bristles with the convictions and the prejudices of the Cavaliers. The triumph of Charles II in 1660 could not erase the bitter memories of the previous eighteen years, memories exacerbated by present realities, above all by the inability of many who had suffered financial losses in the king's service to regain their fortunes. Although Church and Crown land and much of the land of prominent Royalists that had been confiscated rather than sold was restored, the land of Royalists that had been sold, often to pay heavy fines levied on them, could not be restored. Royalist memoirs dealing with the early 1660s reveal in poignant detail futile efforts by persons, rich before the wars, to regain their wealth. Lady Fanshawe provides a brief statement in her memoirs that conveys in epitome the social dislocations that were a consequence of the wars. In 1667, she writes, the head of her late husband's family, the second Viscount Fanshawe, found it necessary to sell the family seat "to Sir Thomas Bide, a bruer of London."[5] Intelligible motives led the dramatists, who without significant exception were Royalists, to include satirical characterizations ridiculing those social groups they considered responsible for the Cavaliers' misfortunes.

The temper of some of the early attacks on the alleged hypocrisy, financial opportunism, and dishonesty of the Parliamentarians is conveyed in Sir Robert Howard's *The Committee* of 1662. The action takes place before the Restoration, but close enough to that event for the prudential members of the Committee of Sequestration (of the play's title) to anticipate the possibility of that event and to attempt defensive measures. The principal butts of the satire are the chairman of the committee, Mr Day, a petty but dangerously avaricious tyrant, and his wife, formerly a kitchen maid who is now absurdly proud of her social position. The husband and wife are conceived not as characters possessing individualized foibles but as

5. *The Memoirs of Anne, Lady Halkett and Ann, Lady Fanshawe*, ed. John Loftis (Oxford: Clarendon Press, 1979), p. 191. She writes that her own father, Sir John Harrison, claimed to have lost over £130,000 "by the rebells" (p. 110). Lady Halkett comments severely on the financial consequences for Royalists of the Act of Indemnity passed by the convention Parliament in 1660 (p. 85).

representative types of persons whom Sir Robert Howard, the son of an earl and a man who had won his own knighthood on the battlefield, detested as upstarts whose rise to power and affluence had been made possible, not so much by their unscrupulous dishonesty and hypocrisy, as by the prolonged mid-century turmoil produced by war. In Howard's comedy, to be sure, two Royalist couples of rank preserve their property by trickery, depicted as justifiable trickery, but the old order is not restored.

The play closes before the Restoration, and so does another notable play of similar political bias, Abraham Cowley's *Cutter of Colman Street,* produced the preceding year. Cowley specifies the time and place of his dramatic action: "The Scene LONDON, in the Year 1658"—presumably to make capital of the growing political uncertainties in the protectorate in that year of Oliver Cromwell's death. The uncertainties had led unscrupulous men to hypocritical misrepresentations of their past actions and present convictions. The title character is identified in the preliminary list of "The Persons" of the play as "A merry sharking fellow about the Town, pretending to have been a Colonel in the King's Army," and his companion, bearing the descriptive name "Worm," is identified as "such another fellow, pretending to have been a Captain." Yet Cowley is honest enough to represent a Royalist, Colonel Jolly, "whose Estate was confiscated in the late troubles," as sufficiently opportunistic to regain his estate by marriage to a Puritan, Mistris Barebottle, "A Sopeboyler's widdow, who had bought Jolly's Estate, A pretended Saint." The satirical review of London in the climactic year of 1658, however, is not incompatible with the successful intrigue of a young couple to marry despite opposition from a guardian and a father.

The social and political animosities, which animate these early comedies, persist, if with diminished emphasis, to the end of the century and beyond. The dramatists were sensitive to the dislocations of class relationships. Etherege's *Comical Revenge* (1664) includes among its large number of characters one whose surname describes both the individual and his role in the play, "*Sir* Nicholas Cully. Knighted by *Oliver.*" Cully is, we learn in the final act, the son of a dairy maid. For his next play, *She wou'd if she cou'd* (1668),

257

Etherege chose the surname of Sir Oliver Cockwood for the knight's wife, whose undiscriminating lust is epitomized in the title; but Sir Oliver's Christian name, resonant politically ten years after the Protector's death, is all his own. The Duke of Newcastle and Dryden provide a glimpse of the deprivations suffered by Royalists when in the dénouement of *Sir Martin Mar-all* (1667) they reveal that the title character's clever servant Warner is a kinsman of a lord, a gentleman by birth whose father's estate was ruined during the troubles.

The animosities surviving from the interregnum find expression in comedy most frequently in portrayals of merchants of the City of London, many of whom had supported Parliament in opposition to Charles I. Remembering the execution of the reigning king's father by Nonconformists who had derived strength from the financial community, dramatists provided an oversimplified and essentially inaccurate portrayal of businessmen, creating the long-lived type character of the "cit," used indiscriminately in the depiction of overseas traders on a large scale and petty shopkeepers. The persistence of such characters in comedies written after the revolution of 1688—and cits are not uncommon in plays written as late as Queen Anne's reign—no doubt owed more to dramatic tradition and lack of inventiveness on the part of the dramatists than to resentments arising from the civil wars. Not until George I's reign were many of the dramatists willing to acknowledge that successful merchants constituted, in Steele's phrase, a "Species of Gentry."[6] With a few exceptions, comedies of the later seventeenth and eighteenth centuries are preoccupied with the affluent and the fashionable to the exclusion of portrayals—except in satirical or subordinate roles—of characters representative of a much larger part of the nation.[7]

The Royalist and aristocratic bias of the Restoration theatre is well represented in the work of the most important of all the late seventeenth-century dramatists, John Dryden, Poet Laureate from

6. Steele, *The Conscious Lovers*, IV.ii. For an account of changes in the attitudes of dramatists toward merchants, see John Loftis, *Comedy and Society from Congreve to Fielding* (Stanford: Stanford Univ. Press, 1959).

7. For an account of the sufferings of the Nonconformists during the Restoration, of which the drama does not provide a record, see Gerald R. Cragg, *Puritanism in the Period of the Great Persecution, 1660–1688* (Cambridge: Cambridge Univ. Press, 1957).

1668 until the revolution twenty years later. His two-plot tragicomedies, his rhymed heroic plays, his tragedies, his operas, as well as such of his nondramatic poems as "To My Honoured Friend, Dr. Charleton," reveal a reverence for an anointed king, quasi-religious in nature, that was central to what in the later years of Dryden's life may be called the "Tory" position. All this has been the subject of extensive commentary in our time and does not require detailed discussion here. Suffice it to say that his employment of a two-plot structure in his tragicomedies enabled him to introduce witty couples onstage and allow them free use of their uninhibited tongues without affronting the dignity of characters of higher rank, who appear in separate scenes until all characters are brought together at play's end. His heroic plays won the patronage of the royal family—for intelligible reasons the plays celebrate a conception of the great man as the shaper of events in a manner compatible with the Stuart conception of their role. "Heroic poesy," he writes to the Duke of York in his dedicatory epistle prefixed to *The Conquest of Granada,* "has always been sacred to princes, and to heroes." He refers in the epistle to the duke's conduct in battle as a youth, his valor having proved him a hero as well as a prince. In the preface to his last—and arguably finest—tragedy, *Don Sebastian,* he refers to his achievement, in a climactic scene in the play (IV.iii), in which a renegade Portuguese nobleman is brought to submission by the force of character of his king. Dryden asks his critics *"whether I have not preserv'd the rule of decency, in giving all the advantage to the Royal Character."*

Dryden was the last great poet to celebrate the Stuart conception of kingship, articulated by James I and perpetuated by his son and his two grandsons. His devotion to the House of Stuart survived even the revolution of 1688, though in the reign of William III he could perforce give only muted expression of it.

His devotion was not shared by all his countrymen. Disaffection grew after it became known in 1673 that the heir to the throne, the Duke of York, had failed to take the Anglican sacrament on Easter of that year. The Earl of Shaftesbury joined with other members of Parliament in advising the king to divorce the Catholic Queen Catharine of Braganza. By June news of hostility between the Duke of York and Shaftesbury had become public. At about the same time the king began to suspect, probably unjustly, that Shaftesbury had entered into traitorous intrigue with the Dutch, with whom the English were then engaged in a war of which Shaftesbury had earlier been one of the most forceful parliamentary advocates. As a result of all this the Achitophel of Dryden's famous poem of 1681 received conspicuous satirical attention from the dramatists.

The animosity between the Duke of York and Shaftesbury and the alleged treacherous negotiations between Shaftesbury and the Dutch during the war, which he had earlier supported, provide the subject, in transparent allegory, of Henry Nevil Payne's *The Siege of Constantinople,* produced at court and, in November 1674, at Dorset Garden Theatre. If twentieth-century historians of the drama, as Shaftesbury's most recent biographer has argued,[8] have been over-ingenious in identifying characters in Restoration drama with Shaftesbury, there can be no doubt in this instance that Payne had Shaftesbury in view. Portraying the Duke of York as the emperor's brother, Thomazo, Payne employs him in the opening scene as spokesman for the Stuart distrust of democracy:

> This Rule of most Appears to me stark madness;
> > when that most
> Are plainly prejudic'd, and led by faction.

Thomazo quickly identifies the leader of "faction," referring to Shaftesbury who had been Lord Chancellor:

> That Damn'd Chancellor
> Romes Pentionary lately, now the Turks.

With an audacity unusual even in that outspoken era, Payne depicts friction between the royal brothers, allowing Thomazo to comment on the jealousy of his brother and sovereign toward him, in a passage that could not have been misunderstood by courtiers famil-

8. K. H. D. Haley, *The First Earl of Shaftesbury* (Oxford: Clarendon Press, 1968), pp. 212–14. I base my account of Shaftesbury's political career on this biography. See, in particular, Haley, pp. 299–335.

iar with the latent jealousy between Charles and James, which had origin before their father's execution in 1649. But the focus of the dramatic action lies in the emperor's unsuccessful attempt to defend Constantinople against the Turks despite the refusal by the senate, led by the chancellor, to vote supplies. This is an allegorical attack on Shaftesbury, who is depicted, as he was often to be depicted later, as wanton and lascivious as well as insubordinate and treacherous.[9]

Other alleged attacks on Shaftesbury—some no doubt intended by the dramatists, others not—have been cited, too many of them for systematic discussion. Yet the most famous of them requires consideration, that by Thomas Otway in *Venice Preserv'd,* first performed on 9 February 1682.

Traditionally Shaftesbury has been identified with two corrupt characters in the play, the elderly and lascivious senator Antonio of the "Nicky-Nacky" scenes, and the elderly, treacherous, and lustful Renault, leader of the conspirators who plot to overthrow the senate and assume control of Venice. Shaftesbury's biographer, K. H. D. Haley, questions the identification with the two different characters, who represent opposing political positions: "There is plainly a difficulty here, from which some authorities try to escape by saying that Otway portrays him . . . both as Antonio, the fool, and Renault, the knave, and trying to provide explanations for his presence on both sides at once in the play. But this is surely a *reductio ad absurdum.*"[10]

My admiration for Haley's biography notwithstanding, I disagree on this issue. If Otway had been writing systematic allegory, it would indeed have been absurd to represent a single historical figure by two different characters in a situation of political opposition. But Otway was writing a play with the suggestive second title "A Plot Discovered" less than four years after the allegations con-

9. Harold Love refers to Payne's satirical portrait of Shaftesbury as "The first dramatic caricature" of him: Love, "State Affairs on the Restoration Stage, 1660–1675," *Restoration and Eighteenth-Century Theatre Research,* 14 (1975), 5. Elsewhere in his article (pp. 1–9), Love comments on a number of the political plays produced during the first fifteen years of the Restoration. For a review of the subject concerned with a longer time span, 1660–1698, see Allardyce Nicoll, "Political Plays of the Restoration," *Modern Language Review,* 16 (1921), 224–42.

10. Haley, p. 214.

cerning a Popish Plot. He was writing just as the Exclusion crisis, which had come when Shaftesbury's party attempted to enact legislation barring the Duke of York from succession, had passed. When *Venice Preserv'd* was first performed, the Duke of York was still in diplomatic exile in Scotland. Otway's play could not have been performed had it been a systematic political allegory. Had he employed allegory in this play, which includes criticism of the "Venetian" government by leading characters who are neither malicious nor foolish though they may be misled, *Venice Preserv'd* would have been promptly and permanently banned, as Lee's *Lucius Junius Brutus* had been banned little more than a year before.[11] Rather than systematic allegory Otway employs a satirical technique akin to that Gay used later in *The Beggar's Opera:* establishing briefly a parallel between a character and his satirical target, rapidly replacing that parellel with another. Peachum, the receiver of stolen goods and thief-taker, and Macheath, the gallant highwayman, both represent Walpole, even though they become antagonists, Peachum coldly plotting to have Macheath hanged.

The characterizations of Antonio and Renault, as well as the circumstances of the early performances of *Venice Preserv'd,* support the traditional conception of the play as hostile to Shaftesbury. Royalist propaganda directed against him from at least 1674 had established a conception of his personality, almost formulaic in detail, to which Dryden had given classic expression in *Absalom and Achitophel,* published just three months before the premiere of *Venice Preserv'd.* In its descriptive and evaluative dimensions the Tory conception of the man cannot be regarded as historically accurate. But the Tory conception of him was sufficiently well known in February 1682, a time when Shaftesbury had lost power

11. J. M. Armistead has recently denied that Lee's Brutus embodies "Whig propaganda" ("The Tragicomic Design of *Lucius Junius Brutus," Papers on Language and Literature,* 15 [1979], 38–39). Armistead quotes Gildon's comment in 1703 that the play was "antimonarchical," but he ignores the Lord Chamberlain's actual order of suppression, 11 December 1680: "Whereas I am informed that there is Acted by you a Play called Lucius Junius Brutus . . . wherein there are very scandalous Expressions & Reflections upon ye Government these are to require you Not to Act ye said Play Again." P.R.O. LC 5/144, p. 28 (quoted from Allardyce Nicoll, *A History of English Drama 1660–1900,* Vol. I, rev. ed. [Cambridge: Cambridge Univ. Press, 1952], p. 10n.). To understand the political meaning of the play at the time of its first performance, and the significance of the term "Whig" then coming into common use, one must study closely the history of the Exclusion crisis, 1678–82.

and was soon to flee the country, for a Royalist audience to recognize both Antonio—who shared the earl's Christian name (Anthony), who was within a year of his age, who was lascivious even if allegedly impotent; and Renault—who was an aged lecher, a treacherous friend, and a leader of a conspiracy against the state—as caricatures of the hated earl. Both the king and the Duke of York attended performances of the play, the former on Otway's benefit day and the latter in April, not long after his return from Scotland. For all the dramatic power of this, the best of Otway's tragedies, it is to be numbered among the propaganda pieces engendered by the Popish Plot and its aftermath in the Exclusion crisis.

II The Reigns of William III and Anne

Most of the years of King William's reign, as well as those of his sister-in-law, Queen Anne, were war years—of large-scale wars by contemporary standards (if emphatically not by those of the twentieth century). The War of the League of Augsburg, begun in 1689 and terminated inconclusively by the Treaty of Ryswick in 1697, was followed after four years of military uncertainty by the War of the Spanish Succession, begun in the year before Queen Anne succeeded to the throne and, despite the brilliant successes of the armies led by the Duke of Marlborough, not terminated, by the Treaty of Utrecht, until 1713, the year before the queen died. It is to be expected that the drama of the two reigns, in its national and political dimensions, should have been dominated by war.

The years just after the revolution were in the theatres ones of cautious circumspection in matters political. The drama only gradually became as vehemently Williamite as it had earlier been Tory; and only in the final year of the king's life, in Rowe's allegorical *Tamerlane* of 1701, the escape from tyranny (as Whig dramatists envisaged the revolution to have been) reached a definitive statement. But throughout the 1690s plays appeared that reveal the change in political temper. Veneration for an anointed sovereign gives way to veneration of the abstraction "liberty"; jibes at Catholics and Jacobites are frequent in dialogue and even more frequent in prologues and epilogues; support for the king's war becomes a dramatic commonplace.

Plays by the Whig Shadwell, after having been kept off the stage for seven years, were produced again, and so were those of his Tory rival Dryden, who in political expression was perforce cautious, yet not timeserving—and at times surprisingly outspoken. Shadwell's Whig convictions appear in his work produced after the revolution, and so do, in less overt form, Dryden's Tory convictions in his own work.

Shadwell lived only four years to enjoy his new prosperity, but they were productive years, crowded with the performances of new plays, two of which are among his best. *The Squire of Alsatia* was produced in May 1688, five months before the Prince of Orange's invasion in November but after the Whig position had improved as a corollary of James II's rapidly deteriorating fortunes. Popular in its first run, the comedy remains in our time the most widely read of Shadwell's plays, providing as do few plays of the era a dramatist's imaginative rendering of the underworld of London life. But in May 1688 Shadwell could scarcely introduce political comment. In *Bury Fair,* produced in the spring of 1689, he could afford to be bolder. Even so, political comment, though unmistakable in its Whiggish thrust, is confined to occasional conversational references hostile to the French as well as to the high Tory doctrine of nonresistance, and laudatory of English freedom. By the time the play was published later that year, Shadwell had succeeded Dryden as Poet Laureate, an appointment to which Shadwell alludes with gratitude in his dedicatory epistle to the Earl of Dorset, who as Lord Chamberlain had determined the selection. In the epistle he refers to the "kind reception" the play had met except from "some of the late loyal poets." It would be a reasonable guess to think that he had Dryden in mind. In his two comedies of 1690, *The Amorous Bigot* and *The Scowrers,* Shadwell's political convictions are again apparent, in the former in his reintroduction on stage of the satirically conceived Irish priest Teague O'Divelly from his *Lancashire Witches* (1681); in *The Scowrers,* more vehemently political than the earlier comedies, in a harsh depiction of the Jacobites.

Dryden's writings in the years just after 1688 provide convincing rebuttal to those critics who, recalling his conversion to Catholicism in 1685, have doubted his courage or the sincerity of his religious and political convictions. He had to be circumspect and he had to take defensive measures, of course; in the interval between William's landing in November 1688 and the destruction of the French fleet by the English in May 1692, the direction that military and political events would take was uncertain indeed, and Dryden as a prominent Roman Catholic long associated with the House of Stuart had reason to fear for his safety. His circumspection and defensive measures seem in retrospect less surprising than his audacity.

His Jacobitism receives most forthright expression in comic idiom—in a prologue he wrote for an operatic adaptation of Fletcher's *Prophetess* performed in May 1690. The date is significant: James II was soon to go to Ireland, which had been in armed rebellion against the English since February 1689. "Early in 1690," writes David Ogg, "William decided that he must go in person to Ireland to retrieve a situation now doubly desperate—in Ireland, where Protestantism was again on the defensive, and in England where disgust and discontent were steadily mounting."[12] At this time when the new king's affairs were at low ebb, two months before the English victory in the Battle of the Boyne, Dryden sarcastically alludes to William's Irish campaign and to the taxation in England required to support it.[13]

Dryden is scarcely less bold in political expression in his tragedy *Cleomenes, the Spartan Hero.* His protestations of the inoffensiveness of the play in the preliminaries to the first edition must be regarded as disingenuous in view of the external evidence that contemporaries regarded it as subversive and, even more convincingly, of the internal evidence provided by the play itself. It was at first prohibited the stage, as Narcissus Luttrell wrote on 9 April 1692: "By order of the queen, the lord chamberlain has sent an order to the playhouse prohibiting the acting Mr. Drydens play called the

12. Ogg, *England in the Reigns of James II and William III* (Oxford: Clarenden Press, 1955), p. 253.
13. *The Works of John Dryden*, Vol. III, ed. Earl Miner and Vinton A. Dearing (Berkeley: Univ. of California Press, 1969), pp. 255, 507–10, 563.

tragedy of Cleomenes, reflecting much on the government."[14] Yet by 16 April the play had been acted, as Luttrell states, "with great applause, the reflecting passages on the government being left out."[15] If Dryden is truthful in writing, as he does in his preface, that the play was "printed as it was acted," not all the "reflecting passages" were left out—as a reading of the opening soliloquy by the title character with an awareness of the state of affairs in April 1692 will reveal.

In that month William and Mary's difficulties were scarcely less grave than they had been two years earlier, when Dryden wrote his prologue for *The Prophetess*. Although William had decisively defeated James at the Boyne on 1 July 1690, the English had just one day before, on 30 June, suffered a severe naval defeat at Beachy Head. James had returned from Ireland to France and by the spring of 1692 was known to be planning an invasion with the support of his French allies. Simultaneously, William was preparing to invade France during the summer of 1692. At this juncture, a month before the English destruction of the French fleet at the Battle of La Hogue made an invasion by James impossible, *Cleomenes* was performed.

At such a time could a London audience have failed to be reminded of James and the Battle of the Boyne when Cleomenes alludes to a defeat which had forced him into exile?

> I fought the battle bravely, which I lost;
> . . . .
> I fled; and yet I languish not in exile;
> But here in Egypt whet my blunted horns,
> And meditate new fights, and chew my loss.

Dryden's assertion in his preface "that here is no Parallel to be found" lacks credibility. That the play, despite the initial prohibition, reached the stage was apparently owing to the influence of Laurence Hyde, Earl of Rochester, to whom Dryden addressed his

14. Luttrell, *Brief Historical Relation of State Affairs* (Oxford: At the Univ. Press, 1857), II, 413.
15. Ibid., p. 422.

dedicatory epistle. Although the uncle of Queen Mary, Rochester was a nobleman of Jacobite sympathies.[16]

Dryden cannot be acquitted of dishonesty in what he wrote about *Cleomenes*, though it was no doubt a dishonesty forced on him by circumstances. Yet like his Whig antagonist Shadwell, he did not change his political allegiance with the revolution. Lesser dramatists—Crowne, Settle, and Durfey—did so, writing Williamite plays after 1688 as they had earlier written Stuart ones. Dryden must be credited with a courageous adherence to his convictions in difficult times.

But Dryden was an exceptional figure. As in nearly all wars against formidable enemies in which a large part of the articulate portion of a nation supports a concerted military effort, the wars of William and even more of Anne led to the performance of many plays that are chauvinistic and militaristic. Referring to the political temper of the theatres in Queen Anne's reign prior to the Tory rise to power in 1710, George Macaulay Trevelyan aptly remarked that "One peculiarity of the stage at this time was that nearly all the dramatists were Whigs, and that consequently the army, during the Marlborough wars, was represented in a sympathetic light, instead of being pursued with the rancour which Tory writers like Swift so often showed in speaking of a red-coat. Congreve, Addison, Rowe, Mrs. Centlivre and Colley Cibber were Whigs, and Farquhar, Vanbrugh and Steele were not only Whigs, but Soldiers." He added, however, that the "audience was by no means entirely Whig."[17]

Not until the three years prior to the Treaty of Utrecht, in a period when the Tory ministry led by Lord Oxford and Lord Bolingbroke was attempting—with the aid of Jonathan Swift, among others—to win support for a peace treaty, are there more than hints in theatrical history of reduced support for war. The archetypal Williamite—and Whig—play, Rowe's *Tamerlane*, was not acted from 1710 to 1715;[18] in 1711 a satirical "Interscenium"

16. *The Works of John Dryden*, ed. Sir Walter Scott, rev. George Saintsbury, VIII (Edinburgh: William Paterson, 1884), 213.

17. Trevelyan, *England under Queen Anne* (London: Longmans, Green and Co., 1930), I, 86.

18. John Loftis, *The Politics of Drama in Augustan England* (Oxford: Clarendon Press, 1963), p. 54.

directed against the war hero, the Duke of Marlborough, was performed at the Haymarket;[19] in 1712 the managers of Drury Lane refused to allow an epilogue by Mrs Centlivre which included a compliment to Marlborough to be recited.[20] Even so, no dramatizations of the older Tory constitutional position appeared during the four years, 1710–14, of Tory ascendency. Apart from the work of Dryden, the only play performed that will bear a Jacobite interpretation in either William's or Anne's reign is an obscure tragedy by an obscure man, Bevill Higgons's *The Generous Conqueror,* produced at Drury Lane about December 1701.

The circumstance that Whig and Tory leaders alike found it possible to endorse *Cato,* a dramatic celebration of the freedom of people and of heroic resistance to threatened encroachments on that freedom by a central authority, provides a measure of the ideological ambiguities of the Whig and Tory positions in the year before Queen Anne died.[21] The Whigs from the time of their emergence as a political group during the Exclusion controversy had identified themselves with opposition to tyranny. In *Cato* Addison expressed long-held themes of Whig dramatists as well as nondramatic writers. The Tory position had changed since the revolution, when they significantly failed to support James.[22] They could no longer espouse legitimacy, and particularly when they were in opposition they found it expedient to celebrate "liberty." Tory differences from the Whigs are expressed in drama by silences. As already noted, *Tamerlane* disappeared from the repertories during the four last years of the queen. Bolingbroke, who kept a watchful eye on the stage from 1710 until the queen's death,[23] presumably thought it impolitic to allow Rowe's Williamite and militaristic play to be performed. He, and to some extent

19. *London in 1710 from the Travels of Zacharias Conrad von Uffenbach,* trans. and ed. W. H. Quarrell and Margaret Mare (London: Faber and Faber, 1934), pp. 138–39. See also *LS,* Part 2, I, 227.

20. Mrs Centlivre describes the episode in the preface to the first edition of her play, *The Perplexed Lovers* (1712).

21. On the ideological positions of the Whigs and the Tories after 1688, and the changes in those positions, see J. P. Kenyon, *Revolution Principles: The Politics of Party, 1689—1720* (Cambridge: Cambridge Univ. Press, 1977).

22. B. W. Hill, *The Growth of Parliamentary Parties, 1689–1742* (London: Allen and Unwin, 1976), p. 25.

23. Loftis, *The Politics of Drama,* pp. 50–51.

Oxford, had stronger sympathies with the Stuart cause than Rowe, Addison, or even Swift knew. But *Cato,* unlike *Tamerlane,* includes no allegorical reference to the dynastic rivalry, and it could serve Bolingbroke's purpose in 1713 to be known as a patron of a play celebrating political liberty.

III The Walpole Era

With the death of Anne in August 1714, the peaceful accession of George I, and the new king's dismissal of Tories from office, the alternative interpretations of *Cato* as a Whig or Tory play (which in 1713 had prompted a spate of partisan pamphlets) became obsolete. With the absence of Tories from office the meaningful divisions in English political life became those among Whigs of varying shades of political ideology and personal association, above all, for nearly a generation beginning in 1721, between the supporters of Sir Robert Walpole and the opposition to his ministry. What, we may ask, was the connection between *Cato,* which retained its popularity, and the many tragedies revealing ideological similarities with it—some intended as opposition propaganda, some not so intended—of this new era?

Before attempting to answer this question, I must give brief attention to the plays of Gay and Fielding: brief attention only, not at all commensurate with their literary quality or effectiveness as partisan propaganda. Too much has been written about the relationships of these two major figures to Walpole for it to be profitable to undertake an extended discussion.

There is general agreement now, as there was in the eighteenth century, about the political meaning of *The Beggar's Opera.* If any doubters remain who believe that the interpretation of it as hostile to Walpole is the invention of overingenious scholarship, let them read the comments on the play in the opposition press—in, for example, the *Craftsman,* 17 February 1728. There was not unanimity in Gay's time, and perhaps there may not be in our century, that *Polly,* prohibited the stage by the Lord Chamberlain, does indeed carry a satirical burden not unlike that of the earlier musical play. Yet a familiarity with the idiom of the opposition should remove

269

uncertainty that it does so. Walpole may have erred politically in ordering the Lord Chamberlain to suppress it, but he did not err in his interpretation of its political meaning.[24]

Fielding's political stance, in the years between his first play in 1728 and the Licensing Act of 1737 which silenced him, presents a more subtle problem.[25] Some of his two dozen plays obviously do not treat partisan themes; others may or may not do so; still others include unmistakable hits at Walpole. In the early years of his brief though extraordinarily productive career as a dramatist, he reveals a certain indecision, perhaps calculated expedience, in introducing political subjects in his plays. *The Author's Farce* of 1730, primarily a satire on literary abuses in the manner of Pope's *Dunciad,* includes only such political overtones as were inherent in an attack on Colley Cibber, already identified in that year in which he became Poet Laureate as a symbol of the cultural degeneracy popularly associated with Walpole's ministry. *Tom Thumb* of the same year would seem to invite a political reading because of the emphasis on the title character's "greatness," a quality sardonically attributed to Walpole. Yet the absence of journalistic comment on the subject has led me to believe that the political dimension of this burlesque of absurdity in tragedy is minimal, if indeed it exists. There can be no doubt about the political audacity of *The Grub-Street Opera* of 1731, a loosely allegorical depiction of the royal household as that of a Welsh squire. Recognizable portraits of the king, the queen, and the Prince of Wales appear, inadmissible subjects of satire at the time.[26] Compounding his offense Fielding alludes—in extraordinarily bold innuendo—to the prince's alleged impotence. In comparison with this, Fielding's portrait of Walpole—Robin, the squire's butler—is, by the standards of opposition propaganda, good humored. Fielding had overstepped permissible bounds, and the play was suppressed.

24. Bertrand A. Goldgar, *Walpole and the Wits: The Relation of Politics to Literature, 1722–1742* (Lincoln: Univ. of Nebraska Press, 1976), pp. 80–84.

25. J. Paul Hunter is surely justified in remarking that "the question of Fielding's attitudes toward Walpole is far from settled": Hunter, *Occasional Form: Henry Fielding and the Chains of Circumstance* (Baltimore: Johns Hopkins Univ. Press, 1975), p. 232, n. 1. However, the responses of the partisan press provide aid in interpreting the political bias of the plays.

26. On the political meaning of the play, see Edgar V. Roberts's Introduction to his edition (Lincoln: Univ. of Nebraska Press, 1968).

The Modern Husband, a five-act comedy in his darkest vein of social criticism, presents a problem of political interpretation only by indirection. After the play was produced at the Theatre Royal, Drury Lane, early in 1732, Fielding published it, with a dedicatory epistle in the customary vein of flattery to Walpole. Opinions on the meaning of the dedication differ. Is it to be read as an exercise in irony? Or is it to be read literally, as an effort by Fielding to gain Walpole's patronage? Although J. Paul Hunter has presented a cogent argument for an ironical reading of the dedication,[27] I find Bertrand A. Goldgar's argument for a literal reading more convincing, in part because of the nature of the response to the play by the partisan press.[28] Furthermore, Fielding would scarcely have dedicated the play to the king's first minister without permission. Four years after Gay's *The Beggar's Opera* and a year after *The Grub-Street Opera,* Walpole had reason to be cautious in accepting a compliment from Fielding. If he lacked the time or inclination to attend a performance or read the play himself, he had others, attuned to the subtleties of political innuendo, to do so for him.

Fielding's open association with the opposition began in 1734 with *Don Quixote in England,* significantly produced not at Drury Lane but at the Little Theatre in the Haymarket. Don Quixote's improbable candidacy in a rural election for a seat in the House of Commons provides occasion for a mocking review of bribery in elections. But it is not in the text of this genial play but in the dedication prefixed to the first edition addressed to the Earl of Chesterfield, who had recently gone into opposition, that Fielding makes his own allegiance unmistakable. His final pair of important political plays, the very popular *Pasquin* of 1736 and *The Historical Register* of the following year, include satire directed at Walpole, the later play (and the afterpiece presented with it, *Euridice Hissed*) stronger and less ambiguous satire than the earlier.[29] Then came the Licensing Act, as everyone knows, and Fielding turned his immense energy to new endeavors.

In comparison with the best of the comic dramas of Gay and

27. Hunter, p. 56.
28. Goldgar, p. 112.
29. Ibid., pp. 151–53.

Fielding, the tragedies of the literary opposition to Walpole are unimpressive. But a number of them appeared, and they reveal with clarity the theoretical objections to Walpole's administration. These plays have a thematic relationship, cogently described by an anonymous journalist writing in 1731, to Addison's *Cato.* His praise of *Cato,* nearly twenty years after its premiere, suggests its continuing force in the theatre. Addison, he writes, "by a single Performance, plac'd himself on the Level, at least, with the greatest Authors that went before him."

But *Cato* itself has increased the Evils of the present Time, how many Poetasters have since then infested the World with wild Notions of Liberty and Patriotism! What strange romantick Whims have they had of Freedom, and Independency from Power! As if, as Mr. *Dryden* says,
> *They led their wild Desires to Rocks and Caves,*
> *And thought that all, but Savages, were Slaves.*

And how justly may it be said of some modern Authors, that while they describe to us their *Heroes,* they are endeavouring to paint a Non-entity, a Thing that never had a Being, or as a late elegant and noble Author expresses it:
> A Faultless Monster that the World ne'er saw.[30]

There is oversimplification in these brief and partisan remarks, but a reading of the tragedies written during the long ascendency of Walpole, after as well as before the publication of this essay, reveals that the critic had isolated a legitimate target. Addison's celebration of an uncompromising opposition to the usurpation of power by a central authority offered precedent for dramatists who wrote in political circumstances very different from those of 1713. The later dramatists drew on convictions about political relationships that were widely held before Walpole in 1721 rose to first place in the ministry.[31]

The Walpole era produced numerous plays that dramatize what Isaac Kramnick has aptly called "the politics of nostalgia." As

30. *Universal Spectator, and Weekly Journal,* 10 April 1731.
31. G. P. A. Pocock, *Politics, Language and Time: Essays on Political Thought and History* (New York: Athenaeum, 1971), pp. 124–26.

Kramnick explains, Bolingbroke's tract, *The Idea of a Patriot King* (not published until the 1740s but written in 1738 or 1739 and expressing ideas widely disseminated much earlier) provides aid in understanding the convictions of the opposition to Walpole—and indeed of many persons prior to Walpole's rise to first place in the king's government: "The *Idea of a Patriot King* opens with a description of corruption that pervaded all ranks in England from the vulgar to the highest in the land. All of Walpole's crimes were catalogued and the general rapaciousness after wealth described. The dying spirit of liberty in England could be revived only by a return to original principles, the principles of the constitution. According to Machiavelli, all governments degenerate and need to be drawn back to their original principles. The best way to achieve this return was through the emergence of a great man. A Patriot King was England's only hope."[32] Even before Walpole rose to first place, Edward Young had provided in *Busiris* (1719), which has a setting in ancient Egypt, a tragedy depicting contemptible tyranny and a noble defiance of tyranny. Using a setting in ancient Spain, Philip Frowde followed a similar pattern in *The Fall of Saguntum* (1727). And so did other dramatists who wrote about political "corruption"—that is, about a tyrant's usurpation of power and damaging or destroying constitutional liberties.

The satirical burden of some of the tragedies of the literary opposition may be suggested by the title of an anonymous one, printed in 1734 though never performed—and perhaps not written to be performed, so palpable and gross are the political parallels included: *Majesty Misled; or, The Overthrow of Evil Ministers,* "As intended to be Acted at one of the Theatres, But was refus'd for CERTAIN REASONS." Nominally a play about Edward II, described in the *Dramatis Personae* as "A weak Prince, misguided by his depraved Favourites," the play dramatizes the evil consequences of a sovereign permitting (as the dedicatory epistle puts it) "over-grown Courtiers to enslave a Nation." Less emphatic renderings of the theme, all written with Walpole in view, appear in *The Fate of Villainy* of 1730, *The Fall of Mortimer* of 1731, *The Fall*

32. Kramnick, *Bolingbroke and His Circle: The Politics of Nostalgia in the Age of Walpole* (Cambridge, Mass.: Harvard Univ. Press, 1968), p. 33.

of the Earl of Essex of the same year, and—after censorship of certain passages—William Havard's *King Charles the First* of 1737. Although James Thomson was a better poet than the dramatists who wrote most of these plays, in *Agamemnon* (1738) and *Edward and Eleanora* (published in 1739 after the Examiner of Plays had denied a license for it) he followed the familiar pattern of "Majesty Misled."

Yet by 1745—the year of Walpole's death, three years after he had resigned his places in government—all was different. Thomson's *Tancred and Sigismunda* of that year includes passages of dialogue that invite application to contemporary political issues, but they are different issues from those of the Walpole era. Along with a loosely disguised defense of a change in political alliance of his patrons, George Lyttelton and William Pitt,[33] Thomson includes lines that could be interpreted as loyal to the elderly George II or, surprisingly, as supporting the Stuarts' claim to the throne.[34] Thomson's calculated ambiguity of political meaning contributed to the success of the play.

The invasion led by Prince Charles Edward came four months later, demonstrating to all that the threat to the Hanoverian dynasty had been and remained real. The result in the theatres was an intensified vigilance by managers and Examiners of Plays alike to prevent plays hostile to the government and reigning dynasty from appearing.

IV The Mid-Eighteenth Century

Walpole's withdrawal from government in 1742 followed by his death three years later, the two years of leadership by Lord Granville (Carteret), the rise of Henry Pelham and his brother the Duke

33. Letter by Benjamin Victor printed in the *Daily Post,* 26 April 1745; reprinted in Alan Dugald McKillop, ed., *James Thomson (1700–1748): Letters and Documents* (Lawrence: Univ. of Kansas Press, 1958), pp. 178–81.

34. In *London in the Jacobite Times* (London: R. Bently and Son, 1877), John Doran writes at length about the play and its contemporary reception: "Pitt and Lyttelton were present at a private reading of the play, which, therefore, had a certain political significance, and Whigs and Jacobites sat in judgment on it. Thomson's cunning, however, enabled him to please both parties." Doran continues, with every appearance of working from contemporary sources, to describe the passages which the separate parties applauded (Doran, II, 108–10). Unfortunately, however, he provides no documentation for his account. I have thus far been unable to find the sources he presumably used.

of Newcastle in 1744 to what was to prove a long period of ascendency in government, all this and the suppression of the Jacobite Rebellion of 1745 and 1746 led to a relative stability in mid-century politics—and to a quietening of political comment in the theatres.

The enforced silence of the mid-century dramatists on controversial subjects[35] may be illustrated by the suppression of Charles Macklin's *The Man of the World,* performed in Dublin (with the title *The True-born Scotchman*) in 1764 but denied performance in London until 1781.[36] This play reveals no hint of Jacobitism, though its satirical thrusts at the Scots would in 1764 have been interpreted as having application to George III's partiality for the Scot, Lord Bute. (Years before, in 1746, Macklin had revealed his own firm Hanoverian convictions in his first play, a tragedy, *King Henry VII; or, The Popish Imposter,* written, Macklin states in the preface to the first edition, "as a Kind of Mirror to the present Rebellion.") The prolonged exclusion of *The Man of the World* from the London stage would seem to have been occasioned, not by its anti-Scottish bias, but by a pervasive though generalized arraigment of "corruption" in English political institutions. What would have been dramatic commonplace in the interval between *The Beggar's Opera* and the Licensing Act was for many years inadmissible. The political temper of the play may be succinctly suggested in a contemptuous description by Egerton, a young man of integrity, of the lord whose daughter his own father has selected as his intended bride (I): "A trifling, quaint, haughty, voluptuous tool—the mere lackey of party and corruption; who, for the prostitution of near thirty years and the ruin of a noble fortune, has had the despicable satisfaction, and the infamous honour—of being kicked up and kicked down—kicked in and kicked out,—just as the insolence, compassion, or convenience of leaders predominated." The Examiners of Plays wanted no criticism of English institutions, or of English policy, to receive a hearing—and except in a few notable instances they succeeded in delaying it or suppressing it altogether.

35. Considered in detail by L. W. Conolly, *The Censorship of English Drama, 1737–1824* (San Marino: Huntington Library, 1976), pp. 73–74.
36. Dougald MacMillan, Introduction, Macklin, *The Man of the World,* Augustan Reprint Society (1951), p. i.

One of the most important instances came in 1779—a year in which John Larpent, then the Examiner, denied *The Man of the World* a license (two years before he granted one for it)—in Richard Brinsley Sheridan's *The Critic.*[37] One cannot follow the workings of Larpent's mind. Yet it would seem to be significant that he had at most one day to read Sheridan's farce, in which political satire, though audacious in the extreme, is carefully concealed in what is ostensibly literary burlesque only. Although the Licensing Act required that manuscripts of new plays be sent to the Lord Chamberlain at least two weeks before performance, Sheridan did not submit a copy of *The Critic,* first produced on 30 October, until the day before, 29 October.[38] It would be interesting to know what Larpent's thoughts were when he came to recognize the full import of Puff's "The Battle of Hastings," the "tragedy" in rehearsal to which Sheridan's second and third acts are devoted.

And Larpent, as well as other members of the first audiences who read the newspapers, could scarcely have failed to understand the import after the farce was in performance. A journalist writing in the *Morning Post,* 1 November 1779, remarked, referring to Lord Burleigh's brief and mute appearance in "The Spanish Armada" (III.i), that "Puff's interpretation of that Prime Minister's *thoughts* [was not] by any means an ill-timed stroke of political satire." Puff had replied to a question from Dangle about Burleigh's silence "that a Minister in his situation, with the whole affairs of the nation on his head," did not have time to talk. Lord North was then suffering from what, in modern terminology, we would call "depression"—presumably occasioned by major reverses sustained by Britain under his leadership as well as by personal sorrow over the recent death of a son. His state of mind had led to an alarming paralysis of leadership during a period when vigorous leadership was needed. In the summer preceding the premiere of *The Critic,* there had been serious danger of an invasion of England supported by the combined French and Spanish fleets, and the defensive

37. For an account of the political significance of *The Critic,* see John Loftis, *Sheridan and the Drama of Georgian England* (Oxford: Blackwell, 1976), pp. 119–23.

38. On the date when Sheridan submitted his manuscript to the Examiner of Plays, see Conolly, p. 20.

measures taken—which Sheridan mocks in "The Spanish Armada," a stage burlesque having more to do with the events of 1779 than with those of 1588—were grossly inadequate. Despite Sheridan's conventional call for loyalty to king and country at the close of *The Critic,* his is a severe arraignment of Lord North's ministry. It is scarcely surprising that he was elected to the House of Commons the following year as a member in opposition.

Even Samuel Foote, the most persistent and unscrupulous of the dramatic satirists of mid-century, had introduced nothing on stage so audacious as Sheridan's burlesque of Lord North's ineptitude and incapacity in preparing the nation to repel a threatened invasion. An irritant on the London theatrical scene for over thirty years, Foote at first by subterfuge and after 1766 by royal favor evaded the limitation of theatrical production to Drury Lane and Covent Garden. His activities frequently brought him to the attention of the Lord Chamberlain, who suppressed two of his plays and who was urged by influential persons to suppress still another.[39] Yet Foote's satirical targets were prominent persons or types of persons—the Methodist George Whitefield, the actor and father of Richard Brinsley Sheridan, Thomas Sheridan, financial profiteers who had made fortunes during the Seven Years War—not the institutions of society nor governmental policy. An acerbity in caricature of individuals was not in his case, at least not overtly, inconsistent with the social conservatism of drama in mid-century. Yet the pungent bite of his plays, characteristically short pieces of two or three acts, reminds us that not all drama of the Garrick era was bland.

Foote's plays were an anomaly in Georgian drama; Sheridan's were not, except in the sense that they were better than those of his contemporaries. The boldness of his cleverly disguised attack on Lord North and his ministry notwithstanding, Sheridan's plays reveal in their genial relish for the social institutions of England a conservatism typical of mid-century drama and indeed of the later drama written before the final decade of the century, when, despite the vigilance of the censor during the French Revolution and the

39. Ibid., pp. 114, 117–18.

277

English war with France that was its aftermath, occasional plays of humanitarian protest against social injustice appeared.

Consider Sheridan's plays as representative of the social attitudes apparent in the comedies of the principal dramatists who wrote in the generation before his *The Rivals* was first performed in 1775: Benjamin Hoadly, David Garrick, George Colman the Elder, Arthur Murphy, Richard Cumberland, Hugh Kelly, and Oliver Goldsmith. Sheridan's predecessors, like Sheridan himself, wrote about the affluent, usually the wealthier gentry, introducing persons in subordinate positions on stage merely in minor roles, often as servants. Sheridan includes no lords in his plays (leaving out of account the burlesque tragedy in *The Critic*), though his predecessors sometimes did so. The social rivalry between impoverished peers and wealthy businessmen in fact provides some of the most effective comic scenes in Georgian drama: in, for example, George Colman and David Garrick's *The Clandestine Marriage,* in which the effete Lord Ogleby and the ostentatiously rich Mr Sterling are depicted with an impartiality of satirical disdain. Mr Sterling's social ambitions are ridiculed, but he is no latter-day "cit" cut to the model of that long-lived character type established soon after the Restoration and appearing in comedies written in the early eighteenth century. Affluent businessmen had come into their own in drama; it is easy to find admiring portrayals of them, such as Mr Freeport in Colman's *The English Merchant,* whose name recalls Addison and Steele's Sir Andrew Freeport of the *Spectator,* a periodical written in the closing years of the War of the Spanish Succession, when pointedly sympathetic portrayals of moneyed men had indeed been controversial, and Whiggish. The rich Sir Oliver Surface of *The School for Scandal,* the pivotal character in the play who astutely assesses the moral qualities of his nephews, is after all a man who has made a fortune in commerce—in India, a circumstance that acquires irony when we recall Sheridan's impassioned arraignment of British exploitation of India a decade after the play's premiere, in the impeachment and later the trial of Warren Hastings.

The comedies are "genteel," in the eighteenth-century sense of being preoccupied with the affairs of the gentry and, sometimes, in the modern pejorative sense of being excessively preoccupied with the decorums of fashionable society, as in Hugh Kelly's *False Delicacy*. (In the preface to the first edition of *The Good Natur'd Man*, first acted in competition with *False Delicacy,* Goldsmith objects to the restriction of comedy to the world of fashionable society.) Yet if the social range of comedy was not broadened from that customary in the late seventeenth and early eighteenth centuries, the range of geographical locales was broadened to include more frequent and more sympathetic depictions of life in provincial towns and in the country. With a few exceptions, notably Shadwell in the seventeenth and Farquhar in the early eighteenth century, the dramatists who wrote before the accession of the Hanoverians revealed a marked urban bias in placing their comedies in London and in introducing contemptuous allusions to life in the country. In contrast, two of Sheridan's three full-length comedies have settings in or near provincial towns, *The Rivals* in Bath and *A Trip to Scarborough* near the town named in the title. Sheridan's choice of setting for the latter play was presumably occasioned by dramatic expediency in that it enabled him to give greater unity to the action of Vanbrugh's *The Relapse,* of which *A Trip to Scarborough* is an adaptation. But the Bath of *The Rivals* is scarcely less important in conditioning the impact of the play than is the rustic mansion of Mr Hardcastle in Goldsmith's *She Stoops to Conquer.* Sheridan and his beautiful young wife had lived in Bath, and no doubt one of the reasons for his choice of the setting was a prudential desire to take advantage of public curiosity in his wife's and his own romantic adventures, which had been well publicized in the newspapers and in Samuel Foote's *The Maid of Bath.* But he provides a gallery of provincial characters—"fighting" Bob Acres, booby squire, would-be wit, and reluctant duellist; Mrs Malaprop, classic exemplar of a country gentlewoman with intellectual aspirations; Sir Anthony Absolute, astute intellectually but a father whose lack of self-knowledge makes him a domestic tyrant—as genial as those in *She Stoops to Conquer.* The zeal for social reform that Sheridan later displayed in the House of Commons is not evident in his comic celebration of life in rural England.

V The End of the Century

The French Revolution and the war between England and France that followed, beginning in 1793, reenforced the disinclination to criticize the government or the structure of English society that had been apparent in drama since the fall of Walpole. The audiences that attended the theatre were in the main affluent; more persons attended the theatre as the century advanced but only in proportion to the growth of London. The percentage of those attending, about 1.7 percent of the residents of London, remained remarkably constant;[40] and those few had reason enough to take alarm at what they heard and read about what was happening across the Channel. Censorship exercised in the form of audience preference, to which Goldsmith and Sheridan had both alluded many years earlier,[41] ensured the Examiner of Plays that his restrictive decisions would meet no widespread disapproval.

John Larpent held the office for nearly half a century, from 1778 until 1824. A file of the manuscripts submitted to him for licensing is preserved in the Huntington Library, enabling us to determine with precision what plays or passages in plays he judged inappropriate for performance. In a recent book on stage censorship and the Larpent Collection, L. W. Conolly includes a chapter on "The Suppression of Political Comment on the Stage During the French Revolution and Napoleonic Wars";[42] he demonstrates in convincing detail the diligence with which the Examiner kept out of the theatres most if not all of what could be judged subversive in that period of national danger from a formidable enemy. It is unnecessary to review Dr Conolly's findings. Suffice it to say that Larpent's censorship, reenforced as it was by the attitudes of the audiences, prevented plays, with a few controversial exceptions, that were critical of English social institutions from being performed.

Rather than give attention to the overwhelming majority of the plays that were supportive of governmental policy, I shall refer to a

40. Harry William Pedicord, *The Theatrical Public in the Time of Garrick* (New York: King's Crown Press, 1954), pp. 16–17.
41. Goldsmith in the preface to *The Good Natur'd Man* (1768); Sheridan in *The Critic*, I.i (1779).
42. Conolly, pp. 83–112.

few of the exceptions—several of them translations or adaptations from German drama—and the criticism they evoked. The criticism tells much about the conservatism of the era, which was so intense at times as to seem in retrospect an expression of paranoiac fear. These plays are not overtly critical of the government or the social structure; they are rather drama of humanitarian emotion—that is, drama with a focus on human suffering in which social criticism is sometimes implicit.

George Colman the Younger's *The Iron Chest,* acted at Drury Lane in 1796, provides a notable example. The play is a dramatization of William Godwin's *Things as They Are; or, The Adventures of Caleb Williams,* a "thesis" novel published in 1794, thematically related to Godwin's *Enquiry Concerning the Principles of Political Justice,* published the year before, a tract so vigorous in its criticism of English institutions as to have placed Godwin in danger of prosecution for seditious writing.[43] Colman undertook the dramatization of the novel at the request of Sheridan,[44] proprietor of Drury Lane and a leading member of the parliamentary opposition to Pitt's government. (One may reasonably speculate whether Sheridan's motive in encouraging Colman to write the dramatization was primarily political or financial.) The play did not succeed, in part owing to faults in the performance of the actors; and it was subjected to severe journalistic criticism. Faults in the play itself and in the mounting of it may at first have deflected criticism from the ideological burden of it. In any event, James Boaden a generation later, in 1825, expressed astonishment that Larpent was so "blind" as to allow such "libellous mischief" on the stage.[45] We need not concur in Boaden's assessment of the danger posed by Colman's play to wonder with Boaden why the play was licensed. In the anti-Jacobin temper of 1796, the association with Godwin's *Things as They Are* would seemingly have been enough to have prompted suppression.

43. George Sherburn, Introduction, Godwin, *Caleb Williams* (New York: Rinehart and Co., 1960), p. xv.
44. Jeremy Felix Bagster-Collins, *George Colman the Younger, 1762–1836* (New York: King's Crown Press, 1946), p. 83.
45. Boaden, *Memoirs of the Life of John Philip Kemble* (London, 1825), II, 154–55. (Quoted from Conolly, p. 191, n. 94.)

In the dramatization of the novel, Colman perforce omitted much and changed much, but until the episode of the arrest of Caleb, renamed Wilford in the play, Colman followed Godwin's plot line.[46] Yet despite the emotional distance provided by the songs and comic episodes Colman interpolated, Godwin's thesis of persons in high place exploiting their social inferiors remains. Colman's emphasis on injustice arising from social inequality may in fact be stronger than Godwin's: It replaces as focus of interest the psychological duel in the novel between Falkland and Caleb Williams.

Prominent among the humanitarian dramatists is to be counted Mrs Elizabeth Inchbald, novelist as well as the author of original plays and of adaptations from the German of Kotzebue. Her career illustrates the relationship between the vogue of Kotzebue late in the decade and English liberal thought as it found expression in the drama. Even before the Revolution in France she had written, in 1787, *Such Things Are,* a topical drama presumably written in response to public interest in British colonial policy in the East Indies, aroused by the impeachment that year of Warren Hastings.[47] It is significant that Mrs Inchbald and Sheridan, she in this play and he in a speech in the House of Commons, should both in 1787 depict brutality in the East Indies and that they should both a decade later, she in *Lover's Vows* of 1798 and he in *Pizarro* of 1799, employ adaptations of Kotzebue for dramatic protests against inhumanity. The German plays, written in a foreign dramatic tradition and without intended reference to British political life, were found by English liberals to be effective vehicles for the expression of opinion about human relationships in a time of active stage censorship and occasional prosecution of overbold writers.

The success of *Lover's Vows* and, more generally, the popularity of Kotzebue—twenty of whose plays were produced in England between 1796 and 1801[48]—may in considerable measure be attrib-

46. Bagster-Collins, p. 85.
47. Gary Kelly, *The English Jacobin Novel, 1780–1805* (Oxford: Clarendon Press, 1976), p. 46n.
48. Michael R. Booth, Richard Southern, Frederick and Lise-Lone Marker, and Robertson Davies, *The Revels History of Drama in English,* VI (London: Methuen, 1975), 110. For an analysis of the reasons for the popularity of Kotzebue in England, see Theodore

uted to the German dramatist's willingness to address social and
even sexual themes that English conservatism had kept off the stage
for generations before the French Revolution. Kotzebue rejected
the English literary convention that a female character who had lost
her chastity had forfeited her claim on the sympathy of the audience. Of more obvious political relevance, he rejected as well the
convention barring social misalliances in drama.[49] It is difficult
indeed to find in English drama of the Restoration and of the
eighteenth century prior to the 1790s unambiguous instances of
marriage between persons who are neither foolish nor villainous
and who are very different from one another in both fortune and
rank. Kotzebue and, after him, Mrs Inchbald in *Lover's Vows* depict
an extreme instance of marriage between persons in dissimilar
stations and in doing so write with compassion about a woman who
is the mother of an illegitimate child. That child, a son grown to
adulthood and become a soldier, finds his mother, a chambermaid
who because of illness cannot work, in the utmost poverty. From
her he learns that he is the son of a baron who had deserted her
before his birth. Out of desperation he sets out to beg and ultimately to steal. Having been arrested, he learns that the man whom
he had attempted to rob is his father, now a widower. The son
reveals to the baron his own identity and the condition to which his
mother has been reduced. In part owing to the intercession of a
benevolent clergyman, the baron agrees to marry his son's mother,
with whom he is reunited at play's end.

The political implications of *Lover's Vows* were not permitted to
pass unremarked. "It is the evident tendency of this piece," a critic
wrote in a journal the title of which reveals its political bias, the
Anti-Jacobin Review and Magazine, October 1798, "as, indeed, of
most of the pieces of the modern German school, and of its disciples in this country, to render the upper classes of society, objects
of indignation or contempt; and to confine all virtue, and every

---

Grieder, "The German Drama in England," *Restoration and Eighteenth-Century Theatre
Research,* 3 (November 1964), 40–41.
49. It is relevant to recall that one of the motives that led Fielding to write his novelistic
attack on Richardson's *Pamela* was Richardson's seeming approbation of a misalliance: see *An
Apology for the Life of Mrs. Shamela Andrews* (London: A. Dodd, 1741), p. 6.

noble quality, to the lower classes of the community; and, at the same time, to propagate and diffuse the principles of the *new philosophism.*"

The most illustrious of the "disciples in this country" "of the modern German school" of drama was Sheridan. In 1798, even before the production of Mrs Inchbald's *Lover's Vows,* he had assisted Benjamin Thompson with *The Stranger,* an adaptation from Kotzebue, not in this instance a play concerned with class relationships but rather with a domestic problem. A husband forgives a repentant wife who had in fact, not merely in appearance, been unfaithful. The play was subjected to political criticism, notably in the *Anti-Jacobin, or Weekly Examiner,* to which George Canning, later to become foreign secretary and prime minister, contributed.[50]

It was in his own immensely popular *Pizarro* of 1799, adapted from Kotzebue's *Die Spanier in Peru,* that Sheridan made his principal contribution to the vogue of German drama. Consistent with the liberal principles that he had long expressed in speeches in Parliament, Sheridan employs Kotzebue's dramatization of the notorious "black legend" of Spanish atrocity in sixteenth-century America to protest European exploitation of native peoples. The play has, and was recognized by contemporaries to have, a close relationship to Sheridan's speeches in 1787 and 1788 in the impeachment and trial of Hastings.[51] Yet it includes, in the form of an address by a Peruvian leader to his followers, a patriotic appeal to the English to prosecute vigorously the war against Napoleon Bonaparte. After an earlier position in Parliament of sympathy for the French, Sheridan had in 1797 and 1798 become convinced of the reality of the military threat they presented and had reversed his stand. His support of the English war against the French is reflected in Pizarro. But Sheridan had not altered his position as defender of oppressed peoples, a fact noted with emphasis by journalists supporting the government of William Pitt.[52]

50. Cf. L. Rice-Oxley, ed., *Poetry of the "Anti-Jacobin"* (Oxford: Blackwell, 1924).

51. Loftis, *Sheridan and the Drama of Georgian England,* pp. 128–29.

52. The most vigorous and detailed explication of the alleged seditious meaning of *Pizarro* was written by William Cobbett: *The Political Proteus, a View of the Public Character and Conduct of R. B. Sheridan, Esq.* (London: Budd, 1804), pp. 84–85.

The adaptations from Kotzebue and certain other plays such as Colman's *The Iron Chest* carry a liberal burden. Yet the drama of the 1790s, viewed in its entirety, is not liberal. The hundred and forty years of dramatic history that has provided my subject ended as it began—with a period of social and political conservatism.

10
Dramatic Censorship

CALHOUN WINTON

I Backgrounds

CENSORSHIP, in the minds of academic folk at least, is a concept without redeeming qualities. When two or three scholars are gathered together for a panel on the subject, it is safe to assume that one will not hear a kind word about censorship. In the twentieth century "censorship" raises images of *Ulysses* in the courtoom, of H. L. Mencken handing over a copy of the *American Mercury* to a Boston sheriff, of blacklists and ugly days in Hollywood. Censorship is identified with the enforcing power of civil government, with small-minded pressure groups in society, and is widely held to be, prima facie, wrong.

M. I. Finley, the distinguished historian of ancient Rome and Greece, has recently complained that this modern attitude has prevented our understanding important aspects of the classical past: "The semantic field of the word 'censorship' tends to be a narrow one today, and its emotional overtone is negative."[1] The same narrowness, I will argue, has wrought difficulties in understanding dramatic censorship in the period 1660–1800 and has produced some simplistic analyses of what took place. To put the matter directly: Most segments of British society with anything approaching political or social influence believed in dramatic censorship in

---

1. "Censorship in Classical Antiquity," *Times Literary Supplement,* 29 July 1977, p. 923.

one form or another. This is not to say that a given author was happy when his play was censored; it is to say that society as a whole was quite willing to accept the process, usually without comment.

What are we to make of an attitude so foreign to our own experience? L. W. Conolly, author of an important book on censorship covering the latter half of our period, expresses the modern liberal scholar's dilemma with amusing frankness: "My discussion of the censorship of drama is based firmly on the conviction that literary censorship of any kind is usually indefensible, and that the precensorship unique to the drama is an especially pernicious kind of censorship. . . . [But] I have . . . been persuaded to recognize that practically all levels of opinion in the eighteenth and early nineteenth centuries accepted the censorship of dramatic literature as an essential control of a powerful social and political force."[2] Many literary historians, it is fair to say, have been unwilling to accept the insight forced on Professor Conolly by his close study of the evidence. Instances of censorship are often described in partisan terms, Whig versus Tory, or in terms of liberty and tyranny; Sir Robert Walpole has been an especially attractive tyrant to cast against his opponents the playwrights, friends of liberty, in the drama of the Licensing Act of 1737.[3]

There are, of course, some crumbs of truth here. Without doubt part of Walpole's motivation for passing the Licensing Act was increased political control—though one should remember that various individuals and groups had by then for decades been demanding "theatre reform," for strikingly differing reasons.[4] Donald Thomas has shown that ministries, Whig and Tory alike, in the eighteenth century did not hesitate to prosecute printers if prosecution suited their purposes,[5] and there is no evidence to support the conclusion that Tory governments were more favorable to, or less

2. *The Censorship of English Drama 1737–1824* (San Marino: Huntington Library, 1976), p. 10.
3. For a temperate and informed discussion of Walpole's relations with writers, see Bertrand A. Goldgar, *Walpole and the Wits* (Lincoln: Univ. of Nebraska Press, 1976).
4. See *LS*, Part 3, I, xlviii–lx; and Calhoun Winton, "Sentimentalism and Theater Reform in the Early Eighteenth Century," in *Quick Springs of Sense,* ed. Larry S. Champion (Athens: Univ. of Georgia Press, 1974), pp. 97–112.
5. "Press Prosecutions of the Eighteenth and Nineteenth Centuries: The Evidence of King's Bench Indictments," *The Library,* 5th ser., 32 (1977), [315]–32.

disposed to censor, the drama and stage than Whig. It is true that there was less—much less—direct governmental interference with the stage during the last thirty years of the period than during the first thirty, but this probably reflects the increased self-censorship of drama and stage rather than the diffusion of libertarian sentiments. Only twice during the entire one hundred and forty years was there a sustained effort at political censorship: during the Exclusion crisis in the early 1680s and shortly after the passage of the Licensing Act of 1737.

The theory and practical means of censorship possessed already, of course, a long history at the restoration of Charles II in 1660. In theory the Master of the Revels, a member of the royal household under the general jurisdiction of the Lord Chamberlain, was empowered to regulate rather strictly what the theatre companies produced. In practice, before the interregnum, he had done so. G. E. Bentley has summarized the relationship in this way: "All plays presented in the London theatres throughout the period [1590–1642] required approval by the Master of the Revels, whose censorship seldom admitted of any appeal. Every dramatist knew this, every manager, every player, and every factotem of the company."[6] Edmund Tilney, Master under Queen Elizabeth, possessed a patent of 1581 authorizing him to commit offending "party or parties" to prison without bail for as long as he thought fit, and the patent was reissued to his successors under James I and Charles I.[7]

It is well to keep in mind that the function of censor involved, at least through the eighteenth century, not only the power to take away but also—as the theatre companies were acutely aware—the power to give. Tony Tanner has pointed out in a perceptive essay that the power to grant and to deny are closely related, even linguistically. "The office of Censor itself is rooted in paradox. . . . There is a curious meeting and merging of permission and prohibition involved in the activity and office of Censor-ing."[8] License, he notes, refers to the granting of permission but also to conduct which

6. Gerald Eades Bentley, *The Profession of Dramatist in Shakespeare's Time 1590–1642* (Princeton: Princeton Univ. Press, 1971), p. 145.

7. Bentley, p. 148.

8. "Licence and Licencing: To the Presse or to the Spunge," *Journal of the History of Ideas*, 38 (1977), 3.

is beyond the bounds of the permissible, a distinction M. I. Finley traces back to the Greek word *parrhesia,* freedom to speak one's mind openly, which Plato interpreted as signifying "irresponsible speech."[9]

The Master of the Revels who succeeded to the office in 1623, Sir Henry Herbert, exemplified in word and action this dual nature, the function of granting and denying. A bureaucrat of formidable guile, tenacity and ambition, Herbert made the post an office of profit indeed, raising the fee for licensing a new play, which had been seven shillings under Tilney, to two pounds. He also managed to extract benefit performances for himself from the theatre companies, obliged theatre musicians to pay an annual license fee, even charged "a Dutchman" a pound to show two dromedaries for a year. For a time Herbert attempted to establish authority to license the printing not only of plays but of poetry in general. Herbert denied: In 1642 he noted, "Received of Mr. Kirke, for a new play which I burnte for the ribaldry and offense that was in it, 2$. 0. 0."[10] (The reaction of the chagrined Mr. Kirke who lost his play *and* his two pounds is not recorded.) But Herbert also granted. A group of actors were awarded protection in 1624 under his seal from being "arrested, or deteyned vnder arest, imprisoned, Press'd for Souldiers, or any other molestation."[11]

This was a Master of the Revels with an expansive notion of the office, and King Charles II reappointed Sir Henry Master upon his restoration. It was clear almost from the outset, however, that matters were going to be different under the new Stuart king. In July 1660, only a few weeks after the restoration, a royal warrant ordered a patent issued to Thomas Killigrew under the Great Seal to establish an acting company and build a theatre, recognized Sir William Davenant's rights to establish his company under a patent issued by Charles I, and ordered all other companies of actors suppressed.[12] With a bureaucrat's instinct, Herbert recognized

9. Finley, p. 923.

10. *The Dramatic Records of Sir Henry Herbert,* ed. Joseph Quincy Adams (New Haven: Yale Univ. Press, 1917), pp. 43 (benefits), 46 (musicians, dromedary), 39 (Kirke).

11. *Dramatic Records,* pp. 74–75.

12. F. H. W. Sheppard, ed., *Survey of London,* Vol. XXXV: *The Theatre Royal Drury Lane and the Royal Opera House Covent Garden* (London: Athlone Press, 1970), p. 1.

immediately that this represented an encroachment on his authority. He dispatched a petition to the king protesting his lack of knowledge of the proceedings and requesting that the warrant be revoked, it being "of very ill consequence, as your petitioner is advised, by a new graunt to take away and cut off a braunch of the antient powers graunted to the said Office vnder the great seale."[13]

The action was certainly of ill consequence to Herbert, when he compared his powers to those he exercised in the heady days of the first Charles. Charles II's personal role in this is a matter for speculation. It seems likely that he had in mind clipping Herbert's wings somewhat. At any rate, the patents subsequently granted to Killigrew in 1662 and Davenant in 1663 stipulated that they enjoyed their rights "peaceably and quietly without the impeachment or impediment of any person or persons whatsoever,"[14] those persons including the Master of the Revels. About 4 June 1662 Herbert concluded an agreement with Killigrew under which Killigrew would pay him a pound for licensing old plays and two pounds for new. I cannot determine to what extent Herbert was able to hold the companies to any such agreement; the evidence that remains is inconclusive.[15] When Thomas Killigrew succeeded to the office of Master of the Revels in 1673 and was himself succeeded by his long-lived son Charles in 1677 it became virtually assured that little initiative for censorship would come from the Revels Office. The office which had exercised great power under the early Stuarts gradually became a cipher, a true sinecure, as everyone apparently tacitly recognized. The Walpole ministry undertook to give statutory authority to the censoring function by the Licensing Act of 1737, which specified the powers of the Lord Chamberlain. The following year the Lord Chamberlain created the office of Examiner of Plays and in the process simply ignored the Revels Office.[16]

13. *Dramatic Records*, p. 86.
14. As quoted in *Survey of London*, p. 2.
15. Herbert, *Dramatic Records*, p. 138, lists fees received for some twenty-odd plays licensed, but the fees were apparently received in 1663–64. On the other hand, Herbert certainly licensed plays in 1667 and 1672. See Judith Milhous and Robert D. Hume, "Two Plays by Elizabeth Polwhele: *The Faithfull Virgins* and *The Frolicks*," *The Papers of the Bibliographical Society of America*, 71 (1977), 7.
16. Conolly, p. 15.

If the power of the Master of the Revels was declining to zero after 1700, what other forces existed which exercised to some degree the censor's function, determining what should and what should not be played? One force was of course the sovereign himself or herself and members of the royal family; these had power in their own persons to influence the conduct of the theatre companies and the practice of the dramatists: by granting or influencing the granting of patents and licenses, by ordering—or failing to order—command performances, by requesting certain plays or the plays of certain dramatists, and so on. What was granted to one was withheld in effect from someone else; this was a form of censorship. The censorial office of denying was, as a matter of custom, usually exercised through the Lord Chamberlain and, in the beginning, the Master of the Revels, but this was not invariably so. King William III, for example, perhaps personally alarmed by the spread of immorality and profaneness at least once chose to include a call for reform in an address to Parliament from the throne, which he wrote himself.[17]

To generalize, no monarch in the period except Charles II evinced much interest in the drama or stage, other than the musical stage. One piece of evidence for this generalization, at least through the reign of Anne, is the declining number of command performances.[18] It could be argued of course that Charles's interest in the stage was exceptional by any standard, that no other British monarch has ever been such a theatre buff, that the attitude of his successors is the "normal" attitude for British royalty. At any rate, although the monarch had the authority to influence what should and what should not be played, after the death of Charles II the monarch rarely did so, beyond issuing exordia to stamp out immorality and profaneness.

These royal exordia influenced and were influenced by another, major censoring force, though one that is very difficult to define, the force of public opinion. The public whose opinion carried any

17. See Calhoun Winton, "The London Stage Embattled: 1695–1710," *Tennessee Studies in Literature*, 19 (1974), 11.
18. Louis Mitchell, "Command Performances during the Reign of Queen Anne," *Theatre Notebook*, 24 (1970), 111–17.

weight in the world of the London theatres was still relatively small in this period, but it was markedly larger than the analogous public before the interregnum, and of course with the rise of the periodical press and of printing generally, much more self-conscious. One way public opinion could make itself felt on the stage was through the medium of the various courts.

While the patent theatres were in themselves generally beyond the reach of the courts, individual members of the companies were not, nor were the various transient theatrical performances that were set up at neighborhood fairs. The courts could serve as an effective censor indeed; Cibber once remarked that nothing made him as nervous as a "Presenting *Middlesex* jury."[19] Prosecution could be brought under various statutes. For example, under the Act for Reducing the Laws relating to Rogues, Vagabonds, Sturdy Beggars, and Vagrants, into One Act of Parliament (12 Anne, stat. 2, cap. XXIII) "Common Players" were included among said sturdy beggars and vagrants, along with fencers, bear-wards and jugglers. The habitual offender, that is, one who persisted in his acting or juggling, could be transported and "imployed in some of her Majesties Plantations" for seven years.[20] The attacks of the Societies for the Reformation of Manners on the stage around the turn of the century relied on this association of actors with vagrants and vagabonds. Actors who ventured away from the relative safety of the patent theatres to act in the provincial or in transient London parochial theatres—and most actors at one time or another did so—were subject to prosecution under these laws. The Middlesex Court of Quarter Sessions, for example, was informed in July 1718, that booths had been erected in Tottenham Court and "several drolls" played there "to the debauching & ruineing of Servants Apprentices & others," and ordered all such players "deemed & declared Rogues & vagabonds." If any such players remained in their evil ways, the court directed that they be seized by the constables and brought before the nearest justice of the peace.[21] Decade

19. Dedication to *Love Makes a Man* (London: R. Parker, 1701), sig. A2[r].

20. *Anno Regni Annae Reginae Magnae Britanniae, Franciae, & Hiberniae, Duodecimo* (London: John Baskett, 1714), p. 417.

21. Greater London Record Office (Middlesex Records), Court Order Books, MJ/OC 1, fol. 34[r].

after decade, the Middlesex records bear witness to the efforts of the court to suppress these small-time theatrical operations. With a fine irony, the supposed principal victim of the Licensing Act of 1737, Henry Fielding himself, was engaged in 1751 as a magistrate and member of the court in suppressing a "Notorious House called Goodmans Fields Wells . . . wherein Plays Interludes and other Disorders are often Acted."[22]

Fielding's presence on the bench might serve as a reminder of what has already been argued, that during the period under discussion public opinion emphatically approved of dramatic censorship in theory and ordinarily did not object to censorship in practice. Occasionally, one must admit, the pursuit of plays and players seems reminiscent of a butterfly hunt with an elephant gun, as when in 1724 the office of Sir Philip Yorke, the attorney general of the realm, prepared an information for prosecution at the Court of King's Bench against Tony Aston and several other well-known London actors who had the temerity to erect a booth in the parish of Saint Sepulcher and to act there "a Certain impious prophane and obscene Droll or stage Play intituled or called The Prodigall Son or Libertine reclaimed."[23] The play as described in the information, far from being obscene, seems innocuousness itself to a modern eye, but the attorney general, with what one might term considerable self-assurance, pronounced the acting as being "to the great displeasure of Allmighty God." The play, on a Scriptural subject, was *ipso facto* blasphemous. Such an attitude would have put a quick end to traditional English drama in the fifteenth century.

If public opinion was a powerful though amorphous censoring force in this period a decisive change in attitude toward what should be represented on the stage must be recognized as occurring around the turn of the eighteenth century. This is usually referred to as the Jeremy Collier crisis or controversy, although scholars have long understood that Collier was a symptom rather than the principal cause of the shift in attitude. Exactly why the shift should

22. Greater London Record Office (Middlesex Records), Court Order Books, MJ/OC 5, fol. 222ʳ.

23. Cambridge University Library, Cholmondoley (Houghton) MSS, Lists 81/20. These are the papers of Sir Robert Walpole. I am editing the information for publication.

have taken place in such a precisely defined time span—the fifteen years between 1694 or 1695 and 1709 or 1710 cover the process quite adequately—has never been satisfactorily explained. The rise of the bourgeoisie? But why should those everrising shopkeepers levitate more successfully between 1695 and 1710 than in any other fifteen-year period? The ultimate replacement of the libertine court of Charles II with—what? The refined circle of George II, as described by Lord Hervey? At any rate, a change in attitude did take place, toward what was represented on the stage, but not toward the printed page itself. The same audience that would boo and catcall a play for "low" dialogue would read, discuss, and approve *Tristram Shandy.* The shift in attitude, which made playwrights and theatre managers cautious, encouraged the self-censorship that would eventually render the official censor almost superfluous.

II Censorship in Action

With these backgrounds in mind, let us examine specific instances of censorship in the period, as an aid to understanding what theatrical performances seemed reprehensible. Gerald Bentley, in his account of the censor in Shakespeare's era, has summarized the grounds for censorship as follows: 1) Critical comments on the policies or conduct of the government; 2) unfavorable presentation of friendly foreign powers or their sovereigns, nobles, or subjects; 3) comment on religious controversy; 4) profanity, i.e., blasphemous or obscene language; 5) personal satire of influential people.[24] As we will see, censorship was invoked on each of these grounds at one time or another in the period 1660–1800, but without any consistent pattern.

Sir Henry Herbert attempted in the early years of the reign of Charles II to restore some or all of the very considerable powers he had exercised as Master of the Revels before the interregnum. One incident of censorship in those years illustrates some of the forces involved in determining what should or should not be represented on the stage.

Sometime early in 1663 Thomas Killigrew, patentee of the

24. *The Profession of Dramatist in Shakespeare's Time,* p. 167.

King's Company, submitted a manuscript prompt copy of a new play by John Wilson, entitled *The Cheats,* to Herbert for inspection before production.[25] This was in accordance with the agreement of June 1662 mentioned earlier. Herbert set about his work with his usual zeal, underlining for deletion objectionable words, phrases, and whole speeches. These deletions principally have to do with blasphemous language, or swearing as it would have been termed in the period,[26] and religious controversy. Wilson had written a lively city comedy in which the Puritans are severely mauled, especially in the person of the Nonconformist preacher, Scruple, who calls on his followers to keep up their courage: "A giue not ouer this good old Cause, wch yo^w haue Contended for wth soe much Treasure and Blood—A—beare vp yet but a little while and yo^w shall See dagon will fall." Herbert apparently felt that even the presentation of Puritan ideas, exaggerated as that presentation may have been, was a danger to the fragile new regime. As he had been for the earlier Charles, he was a zealous, indeed, a learned foe of blasphemous language, excising "odds niggs," "good faith," and even "The Diuell take 'em." At the end of the amended manuscript Herbert penned his approval: "This Comedy, of the Cheates, may be Acted, As Allowed for the stage, the Reformations strictly obserued, to the Kings Company of Actors by Henry Herbert. Master of the Reuells."[27]

In spite of his zeal complaints were voiced when the play appeared and the king himself ordered it withdrawn until it could be examined by the poets Denham and Waller. Their comments have not survived, but Wilson prepared the play for publication and it was published under Roger L'Estrange's license in 1664, with Herbert's excisions restored. The play went to four editions before 1700 and William Winstanley in 1687 referred to it as having "passed the Stage and Press with so general an applause."[28]

25. The manuscript, now in the library of Worcester College, Oxford, has been edited with full annotation by Milton C. Nahm, *John Wilson's The Cheats* (Oxford: Blackwell, 1935). For a detailed discussion, see Edward A. Langhans, *Restoration Promptbooks* (Carbondale and Edwardsville: Southern Illinois Univ. Press, forthcoming).
26. See Ashley Montagu, *The Anatomy of Swearing* (New York: Macmillan, 1967), pp. 154–86.
27. *The Cheats,* pp. 188, 233.
28. *The Lives of the most Famous English Poets* (London: H. Clark, 1687), p. 215.

What generalizations about censorship can be drawn from this instance, the circumstances of which are preserved in unusually full detail? In the first place, although he had duly censored a play presented to him, the authority of the Master of the Revels had been undermined—in this case by the direct intervention of the king in appointing Waller and Denham, in effect to censor the censor. Second, Herbert's attempt to assert the Master's control over printed plays had failed; thus, third, the act of censorship concerned what was represented on the stage, not what was printed. Fourth, the principal objects of censorship are profane and blasphemous language and political themes, two of the five grounds for censorship which existed before the interregnum and the two most often to be invoked in the years to come.

In Bentley's category of censorship on the grounds of "personal satire of influential people" there is perhaps no better example than the case of the Howard and Villiers *The Country Gentleman* (1669).[29] In that instance Villiers, the Duke of Buckingham, inserted a scene into Howard's comedy which satirized a very recognizable Sir William Coventry, Buckingham's political foe. The King's Company had the play in rehearsal when Coventry got wind of the scene and "told Tom Killigrew," Pepys records, "that he should tell his actors, whoever they were, that did offer at anything like representing him, that he would not complain to my Lord Chamberlain, which was too weak, nor get him beaten, as Sir Ch. Sidly is said to do, but that he would cause his nose to be cut." As the modern editors of the play remark, the threat "reduced the actors' enthusiasm for the play to the vanishing point"[30] and it never opened. The incident provides an amusing example of the most direct sort of dramatic censorship imaginable: the threat of physical violence.

When Sir Henry Herbert died in 1673—a rich man—more than half a century had passed since his appointment to the office of Master of the Revels. There was no reason to think that his succes-

29. Sir Robert Howard and George Villiers Second Duke of Buckingham, *The Country Gentleman*, ed. Arthur H. Scouten and Robert D. Hume (Philadelphia: Univ. of Pennsylvania Press, 1976).

30. *The Country Gentleman*, p. 7; *The Diary of Samuel Pepys*, ed. Robert Latham and William Matthews, IX (London: G. Bell, 1976), 471–72.

sor, Thomas Killigrew, actor, playwright, theatre manager, the King's Jester, would be as zealous as old Sir Henry in ferreting out bawdry and blasphemous language, and every reason to think that he would not. I am not aware of evidence that he ever censored anything. He did, however, collect two hundred pounds annually for "divers things necessary to be provided in the office of the Revels."[31]

His son Charles, who succeeded his father as Master in 1677, inherited a sturdy constitution, one which would keep him in the post for more than forty years. He also inherited the political troubles of the last years of King Charles's reign, the years of the Exclusion crisis and its aftermath. Most of what censoring took place—and not much in the aggregate, even in those troubled times, did take place—had to do with politics. Charles II was attempting to hold off the various opposition factions grouped under the Whig label by any means available to him, including influencing public opinion.[32] Nathaniel Lee's *Lucius Junius Brutus* (1680), with its implied reflections on monarchy, was silenced for its "Scandalous Expressions & Reflections upon ye Government."[33] *Brutus* was a victim of poor timing, for the legend was susceptible of nonpolitical treatment, as a number of dramatic authors later demonstrated.[34] In the case of John Crowne's *City Politiques* (1682), a stinging satire on Charles's Whig opponents, permission to produce was granted, then withdrawn, then restored, apparently on the direct orders of Charles II.[35] This was an instance of the censoring power, the sovereign himself, granting rather than denying.

Although politics was the censoring authorities' primary concern

31. *Calendar of Treasury Books, 1672–1675,* ed. William A. Shaw (London: H. M. S. O., 1909), p. 453.

32. See James R. Jones, *The First Whigs: The Politics of the Exclusion Crisis 1678–1683* (London: Oxford Univ. Press, 1961), pp. 115–210; and John Miller, *Popery and Politics in England 1660–1688* (Cambridge: Cambridge Univ. Press, 1973), pp. 154–95.

33. See Arthur F. White, "The Office of Revels and Dramatic Censorship During the Restoration Period," *Western Reserve Univ. Bulletin,* NS 34, No. 13 (September 1931), 5–45. This is still the best study of censorship in the period (by "Restoration" White means 1660–1700), based on a study of primary materials. It badly needs updating.

34. See Calhoun Winton, "The Roman Play in the Eighteenth Century," *Studies in the Literary Imagination,* 10 (Spring 1977), 79–82.

35. See Arthur F. White, "The Office of Revels," p. 36; and *City Politiques,* ed. John Harold Wilson (Lincoln: Univ. of Nebraska Press, 1967), pp. ix–xix.

during the Exclusion crisis, they appear to have been more active in other areas as well. No doubt this had to do with the fact that the Master necessarily had to read the plays with greater care; looking for political issues he found other objectionable qualities. Killigrew cut drastically the parts of Smerk, an Anglican priest, and Tegue O Divelly, an Irish Roman Catholic priest, in Shadwell's *The Lancashire Witches* (1681). Shadwell contended that he was the victim of the "Clamours of a Party (who can support themselves by nothing but falshood)," and he may have been so, but criticism of the clergy would be a sensitive issue during the "immorality and prophaneness" controversy fifteen years later.[36]

In the turbid atmosphere of the Exclusion crisis and its aftermath almost any theme was potentially dangerous. Plays involving English history were suspect. Nahum Tate's adaptation of *Richard II* was ordered closed by the Lord Chamberlain in 1680, presumably because it dealt with a successful usurpation, and John Banks's *The Island Queens: or, The Death of Mary, Queen of Scotland* suffered a similar fate in 1684, because, Banks contends, "evil Spirits . . . incens'd the King with a wrong Interpretation of the Scenes."[37]

During the long reign of Charles II the king himself often acted as the censoring force. This was characteristic of a monarch who was both a lover of the stage and an ambitious politician. After his death royal interest and influence decline; there are almost no instances of direct intervention by the monarch after the reign of Charles II. Agents of the Crown act in the sovereign's name.

The powerful attacks on the stage during the reigns of William and Anne have been interpreted, since the early eighteenth century, as reactions to the licentiousness of the Carolean period. This was Steele's analysis, and Pope's. It is now recognized that Jeremy Collier was only part of a widespread atmosphere of hostility toward the stage, signs of which were clearly evident several years before the appearance of the *Short View*.[38] The movement certainly

36. "To the Reader," (London: John Starkey, 1682), sig. A2ʳ. Shadwell prints the excised parts of the text in italics.

37. John Banks, *The Island Queens: Or, The Death of Mary, Queen of Scotland* (London: R. Bentley, 1684), Dedication, sig. A1ʳ⁻ᵛ.

38. The older view, presenting Collier as the principal motivating force in the attacks on the stage, is set forth in J. W. Krutch, *Comedy and Conscience after the Restoration*, rev. ed. (New York: Columbia Univ. Press, 1949) and Sister Rose Anthony, *The Jeremy Collier Stage*

had support at various levels of society; it is a distortion to represent the hostility as a manifestation of bourgeois morality, whatever that may be. Daniel Defoe, always singled out as the quintessential bourgeois, deplored immorality and prophaneness, it is true, but so did Jonathan Swift and King William. For that matter, King George III as one of the first acts of his new reign issued a royal proclamation calling for the "punishing of vice, profaneness, and immorality."[39] Part of the difficulty the authors attacked by Collier had in replying to him derived from the fact that they did not know who their opposition was. A nonjuring clergyman? A Middlesex grand jury? The bishop of Rochester? The queen?

The theatre companies at least knew where they stood with Collier. Actors, he had written in the *Short View,* in his characteristic sardonic tone, "have no relish of Modesty, nor any scruples upon the Quality of the Treat. The grossest *Dish* when 'twill down is as ready as the Best. To say Money is their Business and they must *Live,* is the Plea of *Pick pockets,* and *Highwaymen.*"[40] The practical effect of the Collier controversy as far as the theatres were concerned was increased activity on the part of the censoring authorities, if we may rely on Colley Cibber. The Master of the Revels, Cibber recalls,

who then, licens'd all the Plays, for the Stage, assisted this Reformation, with a more zealous Severity, than ever. He would strike out whole Scenes of a vicious, or immoral Character, tho' it were visibly shewn to be reform'd, or punish'd. A severe Instance of this Kind falling upon my self,

Controversy 1698–1726 (1937; rpt. New York: Benjamin Blom, 1966), the latter of which should be supplemented by the list of publications in the controversy in *The Critical Works of John Dennis,* ed. Edward Niles Hooker, 2 vols. (Baltimore: Johns Hopkins Press, 1939–43), I, 468–70. More recent scholarship treating the attacks on the stage includes *LS,* Part 1, pp. lxiv–lxv and cxlviii–cxlix; A. H. Scouten, "The S.P.C.K. and the Stage," *Theatre Notebook,* 11 (1957), 58–62; Winton (n. 17 above). Aubrey Williams, in an important article, presents a reasoned analysis of Collier's charges and the replies to them in "No Cloistered Virtue: Or, Playwrights versus Priest in 1698," *PMLA,* 90 (1975), 234–46. For a recent, informed summary of the scope of Collier's influence on the drama, see Robert D. Hume, *The Development of English Drama in the Late Seventeenth Century* (Oxford: Clarendon Press, 1976), pp. 487–94.

39. J. Steven Watson, *The Reign of George III 1760–1815* (Oxford: Clarendon Press, 1960), p. 7.

40. *A Short View of the Immorality, and Profaneness of the English Stage* (London: S. Keble, 1698), p. 285.

may be an Excuse for my relating it. When *Richard the Third* (as I alter'd it from *Shakepear*) came from his Hands, to the Stage, he expung'd the whole First Act, without sparing a Line of it. This . . . occasioned my applying to him, for the small Indulgence of a Speech, or two, that the other four Acts might limp on, with a little less Absurdity. No, he had not Leisure to consider what might be separately inoffensive. He had an Objection to the whole Act, and the Reason he gave for it was, that the Distresses of King *Henry the Sixth,* who is kill'd by *Richard* in the first Act, would put weak People too much in mind of King *James,* then living in *France;* a notable Proof of his Zeal for the Government![41]

Cibber's statement notwithstanding, little evidence has survived of actual censorship by the Master or other court officials during the early years of the eighteenth century. The epilogue to Susanna Centlivre's *The Perplex'd Lovers* (1712) was licensed by the vice-chamberlain's office only after a delay,[42] and twenty-three lines in Rowe's *Jane Shore* which referred to the royal succession were excised during the Succession crisis of 1714.[43] The production of Thomas Baker's *An Act at Oxford* (1704) was stopped by someone in authority—the vice-chamberlain?—apparently because of complaints from the university.[44]

There was plenty of incidental harassment, not only from enemies of the stage like Collier, Arthur Bedford, and Defoe but also legal action by the occasional magistrate, egged on, perhaps, by the Societies for the Reformation of Manners. For example, the luckless actor George Bright was fined the very large sum of ten pounds for speaking the words "a' Gods name" in *The Man of Mode* at Lincoln's Inn Fields, though Bright argued that he "did humbly

41. *An Apology for the Life of Colley Cibber,* ed. B. R. S. Fone (Ann Arbor: Univ. of Michigan Press, 1968), pp. 151–52.
42. *The Perplex'd Lovers* (London: Owen Lloyd, 1712), Preface, sig. [A3ʳ]. Centlivre contends that the delay was caused by a rumor that it was a "notorious whiggish Epilogue. . . ." The rumor was true.
43. Nicholas Rowe, *Poems on Several Occasions* (London: E. Curll, 1714), sig. E [4ʳ&ᵛ]: *The Exceptionable Passages left out in the Acting and Printing of the Tragedy of Jane Shore.*
44. [Thomas Baker], *An Act at Oxford* (London: Bernard Lintott, 1704), Dedication, sig. [A2ᵛ], declares himself "resign'd to the Authority that put it by, and pleas'd it was thought worth so Honourable a Period." He goes on (sig. [A3ʳ]), referring to Oxford University, to deny having "rudely treated that LEARNED BODY for which I have the highest Deference and Esteem." The play was revamped as *Hampstead Heath* and acted in 1705.

conceive, y^t there was neither imorality or prophainess therein."[45]
A member or members of the audience had brought the complaint.

Treading warily, the theatre companies and dramatic authors
were censoring themselves. Steele advertised his *The Lying Lover*
(1703) as "no improper Entertainment in a Christian Commonwealth."[46] The author of the prologue to Farquhar's *The Constant
Couple* (1699) observed: "The Ladies safe may smile: for here's no
Slander,/ No Smut, no lewd-tongu'd Beau, no double Entendre."
The play was one of the most successful comedies of the century.[47]
Cibber contended that the new plays helped attendance: "Indecen-
cies were no longer Wit; and, by degrees, the Fair Sex came again to
fill the Boxes, on the first Day of a new Comedy, without Fear or
Censure."[48]

With the change of administration on Queen Anne's death and
the securing of a theatrical patent by Richard Steele, Drury Lane
simply declared its independence of the Revels Office, refusing to
submit plays to the Master for examination.[49] The Duke of Newcastle's attempt in 1719 and 1720 to reassert the authority of the
Lord Chamberlain is certainly an example of government intervention, but the motivation was partly political—to even scores with
Steele for opposing the ministry in the Peerage Bill controversy—
and had almost nothing to do with what was to be presented on the
stage.[50] The fact that the Master of the Revels played no part in the
proceedings signals, however, for practical purposes the total end
of his authority. Henceforth, until the establishment of the
Examiner's office under the Licensing Act of 1737, the Lord Cham-

45. From Bright's petition quoted in J. W. Krutch (n. 38 above), p. 174. Krutch presents
other examples of legal harassment during this period, on pp. 166–74. See also T. C. Duncan
Eaves and Ben D. Kimpel, "The Text of Congreve's *Love for Love*," *The Library*, 5th ser., 30
(1975), 334–36.

46. *The Plays of Richard Steele*, ed. Shirley Strum Kenny (Oxford: Clarendon Press, 1971),
p. 115.

47. Sig. A2^v. For its popularity, see Shirley Strum Kenny, "Theatrical Warfare, 1695–
1710," *Theatre Notebook*, 27 (1973), 130–45.

48. *Apology*, p. 151.

49. See John Loftis, *Steele at Drury Lane* (Berkeley: Univ. of California Press, 1952), pp.
48–50.

50. See *Richard Steele's The Theatre 1720*, ed. John Loftis (Oxford: Clarendon Press,
1962), pp. ix–xvii; and Calhoun Winton, *Sir Richard Steele, M.P.* (Baltimore: Johns Hopkins
Univ. Press, 1970), pp. 169–78.

berlain would take whatever action he felt called for directly, without employing the Master.

In view of the heated nature of party politics during the Walpole administration the Lord Chamberlain, the Duke of Grafton, took surprisingly little action with respect to the patent theatres and much of what he did was beneficial, the bestowing rather than the denying function of the censor: ordering the companies in 1730 not to receive actors without "especial leave, or licence from ye Lord Chamberlain," for example.[51] Or ordering silenced the theatre in Goodman's Fields in the same year, on the grounds that the Lord Mayor and Aldermen of the City of London had by petition "Represented to His Ma^ty that many ill Consequences have and may arise from Plays being Acted" there.[52] Bad for Goodman's Fields, good for Lincoln's Inn Fields and Drury Lane.

The Lord Chamberlain could give and he could of course take away when he wanted to. The most celebrated incident of censorship during the decade of the 1720s, the suppression of Gay's *Polly* (published 1729), provides a good example of a dramatic writer trying his luck, seeing what he could get away with. The enormous success of *The Beggar's Opera* ensured that its sequel would be the center of attention in the London theatre world, and Gay's association with the opposition wits raised the expectation that the sequel would contain attacks on Walpole even more trenchant than those in the *Opera*. Perhaps Gay expected the suppression; certainly he and the London printers looked forward to profiting greatly from the sale of the printed play: The first two authorized quarto editions in 1729 alone ran to 10,500 copies and the pirated editions of this play about pirates no doubt ran to thousands more.[53] It is interesting that no scrap of documentary evidence concerning the suppres-

51. Public Record Office, L.C. 5/160/138, dated 2 November 1730.

52. P.R.O., L.C. 5/160/130. The order was not, however, obeyed, illustrating the decreasing power of the Lord Chamberlain to enforce his own commands. See P. J. Crean, "The Stage Licensing Act of 1737," *Modern Philology*, 35 (1938), 239–55; and *LS*, Part 3, I, xlviii.

53. James R. Sutherland, " 'Polly' Among the Pirates," *Modern Language Review*, 37 (1942), 291–303. See the letter of Gay to Swift of 2 December 1728: "I am sure I have written nothing that can be legally supprest, unless the setting vices in general in an odious light, and virtue in an amiable one may give offence." In the context of Swift and Gay's friendship this surely amounts to a knowing wink. *The Letters of John Gay*, ed. C. F. Burgess (Oxford: Clarendon Press, 1966), p. 78.

sion has ever been found. Politicians do not like to reduce their threats and promises to writing if they do not have to do so, and in all probability Grafton's secretary simply materialized at Lincoln's Inn Fields and told Rich the eighteenth-century equivalent of "The Boss says don't do it." Walpole, of course, may have had nothing personally to do with the suppression; Grafton may have acted on his own political instincts.[54]

Henry Fielding was a more resourceful man of the theatre than John Gay, the decade of the 1730s was more turbulent politically than that of the 1720s, and Walpole's government was gradually losing its power even as it appeared to be gathering strength. Also involved in the theatrical history of the decade was the increasing independence of the Little Theatres in the Haymarket and Goodman's Fields. These theatres provided outlets for the work of new playwrights but at the same time exemplified by their existence how ineffective the government's control of stage entertainments had become since the days when Sir Henry Herbert demanded and received a fee for displaying dromedaries.

Fielding's place in opposition politics during the years before the passage of the Licensing Act is too complex to be reviewed here in detail. Certainly it would be misleading to portray Walpole's sponsorship of the Licensing Act as solely a response to Fielding's dramatic satire, although some scholars have argued in that vein.[55] Fielding's was only a part, and a relatively minor part, in the orchestrated opposition chorus. With the applause of the Prince of Wales, symbolic leader of the opposition, and of his followers ringing in his ears, Fielding became increasingly daring in his productions at the Little Theatre, Haymarket. The phenomenal success of *Pasquin* (1736), which is not a party play, was followed in March 1737 by

54. Our knowledge of Walpole's role in the suppression is based entirely on Lord Hervey's account in his memoirs. See John, Lord Hervey, *Some Materials Towards Memoirs of the Reign of King George II,* ed. Romney Sedgwick (London: Eyre and Spottiswoode, 1931), p. 98. It should be noted, however, that Hervey was living in Italy from July 1728 until October 1729 and thus necessarily received his information at second hand.

55. The question of Fielding's attitude toward Walpole, as Paul Hunter remarks, is far from settled, and so, it might be noted, is the reverse. Perhaps the best way through the tangle of scholarship on the subject is to begin with the extensive bibliographic footnotes in his book: J. Paul Hunter, *Occasional Form: Henry Fielding and the Chains of Circumstance* (Baltimore: Johns Hopkins Univ. Press, 1975), pp. 232–35.

The Historical Register and *Eurydice Hissed,* which emphatically are. As if underscoring his dare, Fielding proposed in the spring of 1737 to present a version of the play John Gay had taunted the ministry with, *Polly,* "much taken, if not improv'd from the famous Sequel of the late celebrated Mr. Gay."[56] Fielding did not realize the season was to be the last for his company in the Little Theatre, Haymarket.

Walpole was taking his dare. The pretext was not one of Field-ing's productions, although the Little Theatre, Haymarket, as a center of opposition propaganda, was surely one of the targets of Walpole's proposed Licensing Act. Fielding's plays were powerful satires but clean. The pretext was provided by an obscene play, *The Golden Rump,* never performed and since lost, of which Walpole obtained a copy. The provenance and authorship of the play have never been resolved. No matter. The satire, involving Walpole and his followers worshiping the gilded posterior of King George II, was sufficiently offensive for Walpole to convince Parliament that regulation of the stage was needed.

The arguments of the Earl of Chesterfield and of Samuel Johnson, which associated freedom of dramatic performance with freedom of the press, have been justly celebrated in discussions of libertarian thought but they were of course quite unavailing.[57] Backbenchers were not going to be caught voting for obscene plays, and the bill sailed comfortably through Parliament to enactment in June 1737.

The Licensing Act (10 George II, cap. XXVIII) was an amend-ment to the act mentioned earlier of Queen Anne's reign relating to rogues, vagabonds, and actors. It was intended, essentially, a) to protect and strengthen the position of the two patent theatres by restricting the opening of rival theatres, and b) to provide a specific and required mechanism for the approval of all theatrical perfor-mances presented in those theatres or anywhere else. The Lord Chamberlain was charged with enforcing the act—the Master of the Revels was simply ignored—and he was authorized to prohibit any

56. *Daily Advertiser,* 25 May 1737, as quoted in John Loftis, *The Politics of Drama in Augustan England* (Oxford: Clarendon Press, 1963), p. 136.

57. See the discussion in Conolly, pp. 15–16; Tanner, pp. 10–12; and Frank Fowell and Frank Palmer, *Censorship in England* (London: Frank Palmer, 1913), pp. 134–42.

play or other stage entertainment, or any part thereof, an authority that he of course already possessed and had exercised. In practice, the manager who wished to produce a new representation would send a true copy of the acting text to the office of the Examiner of Plays, a subordinate of the Lord Chamberlain, at least fourteen days before the opening night.[58] The Examiner could then indicate his objections (if any) to the manager in time to see that they were corrected. Fortunately for the history of the London stage, the Examiner always kept the copy of the play submitted—even though there was nothing in the law authorizing him to do so.[59]

On the whole, although the theatre managers complained from time to time, the Licensing Act probably granted them more than it denied. Cibber argues the case for the act, from the point of view of the companies, quite effectively in his *Apology.* Its effect on individual playwrights is of course another question.

For a few years, while the opposition to Walpole flourished, a handful of playwrights chose to test the new act by writing plays that were in the context of the time clearly attacks on the government. In Henry Brooke's *Gustavus Vasa* for example, Trollio, the vice-regent to Cristiern, usurping king of Sweden, obviously is meant to represent Walpole. A delegation of peasants complain to Cristiern of the tyranny of his subordinates. We are, they say,

> bow'd beneath a Host of Tyrants,
> Task-Masters, Soldiers, Gatherers of Subsidies
> . . . .
> Will-doing Potentates, the Lords of Licence.[60]

The references to the Excise Tax and the Licensing Act would have been tolerably intelligible to readers of the *Dunciad,* even though Brooke proclaimed when the play was suppressed in 1739 that his "Attachments were only to Truth, I was conscious of no other Principles, and was far from apprehending that Such could be

58. Conolly, pp. 14–20. For a good discussion of the effects of the act, see Loftis, *The Politics of Drama,* pp. 147–53.
59. He was not legally entitled to do so until 1912: Conolly, p. 19.
60. *Gustavus Vasa* (London: R. Dodsley, 1739), p. 17 (II, ii).

offensive."[61] The list of subscribers reads like a roll call of Walpole's opposition: Lord Chesterfield, Sir William Wyndham, the Earl of Oxford, Jonathan Swift (who bought ten copies), and so on.[62] James Thomson's *Edward and Eleonora* was banned a week later than *Gustavus Vasa* but Thomson did not adopt Brooke's air of innocence in his defense. His printers were prepared with a large edition, and Professor Conolly has directed our attention to an article in a Dublin magazine that contended Thomson added three speeches after he had completed the play "in order to induce the Licenser to prohibit its representation: hoping thereby to render the new Stage-Act, and the Ministry that had procured it, more unpopular."[63] After the banning of William Patterson's *Arminius* later in 1739, however, the Examiner's office effectively withdrew from censorship on political grounds until the era of the French Revolution at the very end of our period. In 1760, for example, during the tensions of the Seven Years War, Garrick presented John Home's *The Siege of Aquileia* which was immediately recognized as propaganda for Scottish nationalism, disguised in Roman dress. Garrick's prefatory note dated 7 February 1760 on the copy he submitted says merely, "We intend to perform this Tragedy if it meets with the approbation of the Lord Chamberlain." There is no comment or alteration at any point by the Examiner.[64]

From time to time the Examiner took action against cases of personal satire, especially when it concerned prominent members of society. This had been grounds for censorship, of course, in the sixteenth and seventeenth centuries. A principal offender after 1737 was Samuel Foote. His comedy *The Author* was licensed and produced in 1757 but suppressed in 1758 when a Mr. Apreece, a Welshman satirized as Cadwallader in the play, complained to the Lord Chamberlain. On the other hand Foote's celebrated attack on Whitefield and the Methodists, *The Minor,* was not suppressed,

---

61. Sig. [a2ᵛ].

62. See R. W. Chapman, "Brooke's *Gustavus Vasa*," *Review of English Studies*, 1 (1925), 460–61; and *RES*, 2 (1926), 99.

63. *Gentleman's and London Magazine* of June 1762, quoted in Conolly, p. 58.

64. Huntington Library, Larpent Collection LA 170. See James Malek, "John Home's *The Siege of Aquileia*: A Revaluation," *Studies in Scottish Literature*, 10 (1973), 232–40; and Winton, "The Roman Play," p. 86 (n. 34 above).

even though the Countess of Huntingdon and the Archbishop of Canterbury personally intervened to stop it.[65] But again, Gen. John Gunning received authority in 1791 from the Lord Chamberlain to censor a play himself which supposedly referred to a scandal involving his, Gunning's, daughter.[66] Censorship on the grounds of personal satire was, then, infrequent but capricious and unpredictable. It depended, one might say, on whose ox was gored and the outcry the ox could make.

Governmental interference on the grounds of "prophaneness and immorality" was even less of a problem for the theatre companies. Only three plays were denied approval by the Examiner on moral grounds between 1737 and 1800 and all three were granted permission after revision. As Professor Conolly has pointed out, censorship of Kane O'Hara's farce, *The Golden Pippin* was much more severe in 1772 than had been that of Fielding's *The Wedding Day* in 1743. Fielding's play in its original version contained dialogue with the vital qualities he would soon transfer to his novels. His aging procuress, Mrs Useful, for example, urges Clarinda to leave her husband for a lover. Clarinda: "What! with the loss of my honour?"

Mrs. Useful. The Loss of a Figg.—I would as soon grieve at the loss of a Queen Elizabeth Ruff—they have both no value but when in Fashion.—pray what do you think this Honour was—Why it was a Specious Covering for an Intrigue—as the other was for the Neck. But the present Age desires no covering for either—Besides you may keep your Honour still—for every woman has it till she is discover'd.[67]

This is dialogue worthy of Parson Tickletext or Mrs Slipslop, and though the Examiner forced Fielding to tone it down he allowed much to remain—so much that the audiences complained. In 1772

65. Conolly, pp. 114–22. This work, based on a study of the Larpent Collection, supersedes all previous work on dramatic censorship for the period which it discusses. There is no general treatment comparable to White's and Conolly's for the period 1700–1737.

66. Conolly, pp. 132–34. During 1789 three productions having to do with the French Revolution were censored, partly to spare the feelings of the French aristocrats, a rare example of Bentley's category of censorship on grounds of unfavorable presentation of friendly foreign nobility. See Conolly, pp. 87–93.

67. As quoted in Conolly, p. 142.

O'Hara was compelled to substitute for Paris's lines to Juno: "Gad, Ma'am, let's cuckold Jove! 'tis what he merits," "Gad, Ma'am let's use your husband as he merits."[68] After this the Examiner did not find it necessary to refuse licenses for bawdry.

For by then, theatre managers, actors, authors, and audiences were doing their own censoring. Plays which had been fully acceptable in 1715 became only marginally acceptable in 1755 and disappeared from the repertory in 1790. Far more influential in the long run than any Master of the Revels or Lord Chamberlain was an audience that was changing its mind about the propriety of stage performances. The difference in expectations between the audience that could applaud Dryden's *Amphitryon* in 1690 and that which needed to be shielded from the word "cuckold" in O'Hara's farce is very great, but the change had been a gradual one. By 1800 the London writers and managers had learned to steer a safe course.

68. Ibid., p. 149.

11
The Publication of Plays

SHIRLEY STRUM KENNY

PUBLICATION of plays in the Restoration and eighteenth century flourished as a business venture. From the Restoration onward, publishers—and pirates—showed considerable interest in plays; by the eighteenth century, regular publication and republication indicate that drama texts were indeed profitable. Modern scholarship on play publication in this period, however, has been limited; although some excellent spade work has been completed, much needs to be done. In the following discussion, inevitably skewed to some extent toward the early period because of the present state of scholarship, I will suggest the progression from manuscript to first and later editions, including piracies; will show relationships between author's papers, acting versions, and printed versions; will sketch the role of playwright, printer, and bookseller in the metamorphosis of play script to printed text; and will suggest mercantile aspects of the trade. This essay must of course be considered a preliminary view of publication in the period. The definitive explanation lies well in the future.

I

Play publication from 1660 to 1800 was not, as a rule, remarkably lucrative for playwrights, although it yielded enough return to authors and booksellers to interest both. There are some "lost plays," that is, plays produced but not published, but most plays acted in London in this period were printed.

Playwrights clearly felt greater concern for the staging of their productions than for publication, a fact explicable not only by the author's desire to see his play fully incarnated but also no doubt in part because he had a chance to gain considerably more by third-night benefits than by publication contracts. For example, Colley Cibber received the remarkably high sum of £105 for publication of *The Non-Juror* in 1718;[1] however, within fifteen days of the premiere on 6 December 1717, Cibber had cleared nearly £1,000 in the playhouse, which had "not been so crowded for many years."[2] Impressive as the payment from Lintott was, it was dwarfed by his playhouse receipts. Richard Steele, similarly, sold his rights to *The Conscious Lovers* to Jacob Tonson, Jr, for £40 and "divers other good Causes and Considerations"; although the legal phrasing often disguises much larger sums, Rodney M. Baine believes the sum was accurately recorded, and indeed it would not have been out of line with other sums paid playwrights.[3] But Steele received £329 5s for his three third-night benefits and £300 more for his share as a patentee,[4] a sum of course not available to most authors. Although these plays are unusual in their theatrical success, other playwrights also hoped for and sometimes got big returns from box office receipts.

But the theatre was risky—audiences were fickle, and consequently authors faced considerable uncertainty about the size and number of their third night benefits—if indeed a play lasted three nights. By contrast, they found some security in the hard cash settlements, limited though they were in size, offered by publishers, regardless of whether the texts sold or not. In 1691, for example, John Dryden assigned the rights to *Cleomenes* to Jacob Tonson for 30 guineas;[5] the play was printed in a single early

1. John Nichols, *Literary Anecdotes of the Eighteenth Century* (London: The Author, 1812–1815), VIII, 294–95. The date of the agreement must have been 1 October 1717, not 1718 as Nichols states.

2. Applebee's *Original Weekly Journal*, 21 December 1717.

3. Rodney M. Baine, "The Publication of Steele's *Conscious Lovers*," *Studies in Bibliography*, 2 (1949–50), 170.

4. George A. Aitken, *The Life of Richard Steele*, 2 vols. (London: Isbister, 1889), II, 314.

5. Folger Shakespeare Library manuscript, C.c.1(7).

edition. In 1705 Cibber bargained up to £36 11s for *Perolla and Izadora,* which only had one early edition. By contrast, in 1705 George Farquhar sold his rights to *The Recruiting Officer* to Lintott for a mere £16 2s 6d; three editions appeared within a year and a fourth the year after; by 1708, the comedy was included in Lintott's edition of Farquhar's collected works. In 1707, Farquhar sold *The Beaux Stratagem* to Lintott for £30,[6] and it too proved enormously successful in print. As the years passed, authorial profits from publication grew, but published texts did not offer the potential afforded by successful productions for either income or artistic gratification. One obvious exception is Gay's *Polly;* forbidden onstage, it brought Gay more than £1,000 in print, but he himself had been involved in financing the edition.[7]

One additional way to profit through publication lay with the ability to write dedications that successfully flattered the right people. Sometimes a well-received dedication meant money: Cibber received £200 from the king, to whom he had dedicated *The Non-Juror,*[8] and Steele received a munificent 500 guineas from the king for *The Conscious Lovers* (1722). At other times it meant other kinds of patronage, a fact that explains why a man like the Duke of Ormonde was the dedicatee of several plays in the year he was raising a troop. Dedications carried no guarantee, but at times they were considerably more profitable than the selling of copyright to a publisher.

Before the Copyright Act of 1710, copyright had resided with members of the Stationers' Company or with other persons given the privilege and authority to print books. The Printing Act of 1662 confirmed the authority of patent and license holders and of Stationers' copyright. Although the Stationers' *Register* proved, in fact, to be ineffective as a record of copyright, the general notion that copyright resided in the printer or bookseller was upheld in litigation. Later acts poorly patched the old regulations, and in 1695

6. Lintott's agreements with Cibber and Farquhar are listed in Nichols, VIII, 294–96.
7. James R. Sutherland, " 'Polly' Among the Pirates," *Modern Language Review,* 37 (1942), 291.
8. Richard Hindry Barker, *Mr. Cibber of Drury Lane* (New York: Columbia Univ. Press, 1939), p. 107, citing Applebee's *Original Weekly Journal,* 28 December 1717 and 4 January 1718; Colley Cibber, *A Letter from Mr Cibber to Mr Pope* (London: Lewis, 1742), p. 24.

311

the Printing Act lapsed permanently.[9] Booksellers clung—without the authority of a new act—to their publication rights, but new legislation was obviously required. It came in an unexpected form. The Copyright Act of 1710 provided that copyright of all works published before 10 April 1710 continued with the present owner for twenty-one years but not perpetually; for all works published on or after that date, copyright resided in the author for a period of fourteen years, renewable for fourteen more.[10] One effect of the legislation seems to have been that booksellers began to pay higher fees to authors to acquire the copyright now vested in the writer. If an author was reluctant to sell his copyright, he might not manage to publish his book; if he did get it published, his profits might well suffer either from the terms of his contract with the bookseller or from lack of promotion.[11] Although many authors sold their rights for what seems little, they must have been to some extent overpowered by the booksellers. One illustration of an incipient argument between author and publisher emerged in an advertisement in the *Daily Courant* on 10 December 1708 for Thomas Baker's *The Fine Lady's Airs,* to be "speedily" published. The advertisement concluded, "The Booksellers are to know that at present the Author is in his Airs, and designs to sell his Copy once more," obviously for a better price. Baker's enterprise was soon squelched by his publisher's announcement; the next day the advertisement read, "Note, All Differences between the Author and Booksellers are amicably Accomodated." Baker may have made a deal for more money, but his publisher had, through the advertisement, effectively cut off the possibility of his seeking a higher fee elsewhere.

Playwrights regularly sold their copy outright to booksellers. Although the statute read that after the expiration of the first fourteen years, "the sole Right of Printing or Disposing of Copies shall Return to the Authors thereof, if they are then Living" for another fourteen years, booksellers usually bought all title to the

9. Cyprian Blagden, *The Stationers' Company: A History 1403–1959* (Cambridge: Harvard Univ. Press, 1960), p. 175.

10. Harry H. Ransom, *The First Copyright Statute* (Austin: Univ. of Texas Press, 1956), pp. 76–109. Lyman Ray Patterson, *Copyright in Historical Perspective* (Nashville, Tenn.: Vanderbilt Univ. Press, 1968), pp. 114–79.

11. Patterson, p. 152. See also A. S. Collins, *Authorship in the Days of Johnson* (London, 1927; rpt. Clifton, N.J.: A. M. Kelley, 1973).

works for the future. Therefore, once an author had traded his rights for cash, his interest in later published editions usually diminished. Authorial profits from publication were immediate but seldom long-term. Cyprian Blagden reports that there were instances in eighteenth-century publishing in which authors or their families retained a share of the copyright, for example, Warburton's share in Pope's *Works;* there are also instances of authors being paid for revisions. These, however, are the exceptions rather than the rule.[12]

Although play publication in the early decades was erratic, by the turn of the century most plays saw print almost immediately— publication was delayed only long enough to insure a first run. Judith Milhous and Robert D. Hume find little consistency in the time lag between production and publication in the 1660s; of fifty-eight plays considered, twenty were published within three months to a year and a half, but another fifteen waited more than four years, and nine of that fifteen were printed from ten to thirty-one years after production. By the 1670s, the normal time lapse had shortened, first to six–twelve months, then to six months, then to three. The normal lapse in the 1680s was three months; in the 1690s it dropped to one month, and shorter periods were common.[13] During the next decade, the usual time lapse shrank yet again. Although no comprehensive examination of this period has been completed, a few examples will indicate the change: The three plays by Farquhar for which we have precise dates indicate a common spread of slightly more than two weeks: *The Twin-Rivals,* fifteen days; *The Recruiting Officer,* sixteen; *The Beaux Stratagem,* nineteen. The same kind of span seems typical of plays by other authors; for example, during the 1708–9 season, *The Fine Lady's Airs* was published thirteen days after the opening (despite Baker's feud with the publisher); Cibber's *Rival Fools,* eighteen days; John Dennis's *Appius and Virginia,* fourteen days.[14]

There was an intentional correlation between the length of the

12. Cyprian Blagden, "Booksellers' Trade Sales 1718–1768," *The Library,* 5th ser., 5 (1951), 251.

13. Judith Milhous and Robert D. Hume, "Dating Play Premières from Publication Data, 1660–1700," *Harvard Library Bulletin,* 22 (1974), 374–405.

14. Premiere dates are taken from *LS,* Part 2, passim. Publication dates are taken from the *Daily Courant.*

run and the date of publication. Drury Lane manager Christopher Rich contracted with Cibber for *Woman's Wit* (1696)[15] and with Richard Steele for *The Tender Husband* (1705) and probably with others not to publish for a month after the first performance. *The Tender Husband,* however, was offered for sale six days short of that time,[16] perhaps because the comedy only ran five nights. Of course some plays took longer.

Musical dramas, however, could reach print far sooner—the opera *Pyrrhus and Demetrius* opened 14 December 1708 and appeared in print by 17 December; *The Beggar's Opera* was published sixteen days after the opening and long before the end of the first run, despite the complexity of engraving the music. Operas were in fact sometimes published simultaneously with the premiere.[17] Libretti were often sold within the playhouse, perhaps because of the difficulty of understanding the words in the theatre.

Later in the century, the tendency to delay publication until after the first run decreased. Fielding's *Author's Farce* (1730) saw print one day after the premiere. Goldsmith's *The Good Natur'd Man* (1768) was published the sixth day of a ten-day run. Early copies of plays were even peddled at the theatre. On 25 March 1773, at 4:00 P.M., ten days after *She Stoops to Conquer* opened, F. Newbery published the text. That night, when the play was performed for the fourth time, copies abounded in the theatre; the *Morning Chronicle* the next day marveled: "It is very remarkable, that almost every one present had the play in their hands, insomuch that the Orangewomen acknowledged they never sold so many of any new piece during its whole run, as they disposed of yesterday evening in less than half an hour."[18] Sales were, in fact, so healthy that two days

15. Allardyce Nicoll, *A History of English Drama, 1660–1900,* 6 vols., Vol. I: *1660–1700,* 4th ed., rpt. (Cambridge: Cambridge Univ. Press, 1961), pp. 381–82.

16. "The Answere of Christopher Rich Esq[r] Deft to the bill of Complaynt of Richard Steele gent Complaynant," 9 November 1707, quoted in Aitken, *The Life of Richard Steele,* I, 118. Rich said "the Complaynant was not to print the said play untill a month should be expired from the ffirst day it should be acted and three of the printed Books in Marble paper Covers and Gilt edges were to be delivered into the office for the use of the patentees assoone as the same should bee printed."

17. Milhous and Hume, p. 402.

18. Quoted in Arthur Friedman, ed. *The Collected Works of Oliver Goldsmith,* 5 vols. (Oxford: Clarendon, 1966), V, 93.

later "A New Edition," actually a second impression, graced the market. Obviously theatrical sales benefited the publisher.

Early publication, then, remained the rule, but there are exceptions; Sheridan's *A Trip to Scarborough* (acted in 1777) was first published four and a half years after the premiere, and *The Critic* (acted in 1779) waited two years. Obviously many factors, personal, political, and commercial, affected publication schedules; yet in general, a short period from production to print seemed to predominate throughout the century.

One reason for the shrinking time lag was the growing interest of booksellers in drama. As publication became increasingly profitable, booksellers began to arrange in advance for rights. Lintott, for example, paid Farquhar for *The Twin-Rivals* twelve days before the premiere, for *The Recruiting Officer* fifty-six days before, and for *The Beaux Stratagem* forty days before. Tonson bought the rights to *The Conscious Lovers* eighteen days before the premiere and within a week reassigned a half share to Lintott. Other plays found less demand; Steele's *The Lying Lover* (1703) was purchased more than a month after the premiere; publication postdated performance by eight weeks.[19] Once play publication became well established as a financial venture, booksellers bought rights early, often before performance, enabling them to publish as quickly during or after the first run as possible.

II

The nature of the manuscripts from which plays were printed remains a subject of considerable speculation. In at least some cases, playhouse copies were surely sent to the printshop; scholars have identified thirty printed plays of the Restoration period which show traces of prompt book copy.[20] Edward A. Langhans speculates that prompt copies for failed plays might well have been sent to the printer, although successful ones would have been considered too valuable to be loaned out. Traces of the prompter's hand would enter the printed text only through individual compositors' negli-

19. Nichols, VIII, 301, inaccurately dates the payment 13 June 1703–4; the date should be 13 January, according to publication ads in the *Daily Courant*.
20. Edward A. Langhans, *Restoration Promptbooks* (Carbondale and Edwardsville: Southern Illinois Univ. Press, forthcoming).

gence, according to Langhans, and as a result, such traces tend to appear in clusters. Some promptbooks, however, would be messy enough to precipitate such unintentional printing of prompter's marks. As Langhans points out, in many cases one cannot know whether the source of a printed play was a promptbook or not. "Call" and "Ready" notes are undeniable evidence; notes on props *("Niece's Lodgings, two Chairs and Table"* or *"A Table, Chairs, Pen, Ink, and Paper")* might come from a prompter, but they might also come from an author.

In all probability, however, the printer's copy was most often not a promptbook, but rather a separate copy intended for the printshop; otherwise, more traces of prompter's marks would probably have infiltrated the printed texts. Commonly printer's copy, while doubtless closely resembling the script sent to the playhouse, did not reflect the cuts and revisions made during rehearsals and early runs. Since censorship imposed on plays to be licensed for presentation did not extend to the printed text, expunged passages could be and were published. Cibber's *Richard III* was staged minus the first act, but the entire text was published. Thomas Shadwell not only printed the censored passages in *The Lancashire-Witches* (pub. 1682); he italicized them. But ordinarily copies were probably sent to the printer without deliberate consideration by the author of stage cuts and revisions. Of course the revised text was sometimes used; for example, Thomas Durfey's *The Old Mode and the New* (1703), shortened by at least an hour for the second performance, was printed in the truncated version. But often authors were reluctant to cast aside their pearls; in *The Critic* Sheridan, in satirizing the battles of actors and authors over the text, shows the author's tendency to cling to his cut lines in the printed text:

Underprompter. Sir, the carpenter says it is impossible you can go to the Park scene yet.
Puff. The Park scene! No—I mean the description scene here, in the wood.
Underprompter. Sir, the performers have cut it out.
Puff. Cut it out!

Underprompter. Yes Sir.

Puff. What? the whole account of Queen Elizabeth?

Underprompter. Yes Sir.

Puff. And the description of her horse and side-saddle?

Underprompter. Yes Sir.

Puff. So, so, this is very fine indeed! Mr. Hopkins, how the plague could you suffer this?

Hopkins, from within. Sir, indeed the pruning knife—

Puff. The pruning knife—zounds the axe! why, here has been such lopping and topping, I shan't have the bare trunk of my play left presently.—Very well, Sir—the performers must do as they please, but upon my soul, I'll print it every word.

Sneer. That I would indeed. . . .

Puff. To cut out this scene!—but I'll print it—egad, I'll print it every word![21]

Despite the exaggeration, the scene depicts a situation recognizable to the audience; authors did, in fact, tend to "print it every word," and companies did tend to cut for production. According to Cecil Price, Sheridan's printed version of *The Critic* shows that "he was more concerned to put out a text that read well than one that represented exactly the lines spoken in the most recent stage performances."[22] Often, however, authors did not decide between acting and reading versions; after the time lag had been reduced and publication contracts often predated performances, they probably sent the original version to the printer and did not revise what they sent unless there was significant cause. If one assumes from the short time lag that at least frequently two sets of papers were involved, one sent to the playhouse, another to the printer, it is likely that a second manuscript would be completed before the play went to rehearsal. If this supposition is correct, and the lack of prompt traces as a frequent feature of published plays suggests that it is, the two would probably have agreed in every detail except for those errors and additions introduced by the transcriber. But the

21. *The Dramatic Works of Richard Brinsley Sheridan*, ed. Cecil Price, 2 vols. (Oxford: Clarendon, 1973), II, 536–37.

22. Ibid., I, 24.

manuscript that was sent to the printer would not incorporate those additions, deletions, and revisions produced through rehearsal or introduced during the first run. Colley Cibber specifically states in the preface to *The Provok'd Husband,* dated seventeen days after the premiere and four days before publication, that the reader will "find here a scene or two of the lower humor that were left out after the first day's presentation."

Variations from the playhouse version are not always announced—many are unintentional—but they can sometimes be detected. One such case occurs in Farquhar's *The Twin-Rivals.* The bawd-midwife in that play is called "Mandrake" in the first edition, which was published fifteen days after the opening. Although no playbill exists, a number of bits of evidence suggest that the character was called "Midnight" onstage, even during the first run. In a Folger Shakespeare Library copy of the first edition, shelf-marked Prompt T33, printed on fine paper, and containing emendations in two eighteenth-century hands, "Mandrake" is consistently emended to "Midnight" except for one emendation to "Mother." Since "Mother-Midnight" was a cant term for "a Midwife (often a Bawd)"[23] and since "Mandrake" lacked these cant connotations, obviously "Midnight" is more appropriate as a tag-name for the character. No Drury Lane cast lists exist for performances before 29 November 1725, according to *The London Stage,* but then and subsequently, the midwife is listed as "Midnight." At Lincoln's Inn Fields, however, where the promptbook would have been a purchased copy, she is consistently "Mandrake." She continues to be called "Mandrake" in the printed editions of 1714 and 1718 and the Dublin edition of 1726. However, in the *Comedies* of 1728 and the *Dramatick Works* of 1736, which contain some theatrical revisions, as well as in later editions including Bell's of 1777 "Regulated from the Prompt-Book" of Covent Garden, she is "Midnight." Similar discrepancies between acting version and printed text were probably the rule rather than the exception.

Few Restoration and eighteenth-century playwrights showed concern for the texts of their published works. Curt A. Zimansky

23. B.E., *A New Dictionary of the Terms Ancient and Modern of the Canting Crew* (London: Hawes, Gilbourne, and Davis, [1690]).

described a typical author when he said of *The Relapse*, "Nothing suggests that Vanbrugh paid the slightest attention to any printing—not even to the first."[24] Although first editions vary, obviously, as widely as playwrights and printers vary, most plays of the period have the appearance of hasty and careless printing. Often they have been divided between two or more compositors. As a result, a single character may be labeled by more than one speech prefix, or abbreviations may vary according to the compositor. Dividing the manuscript between compositors leads to the introduction of all sorts of errors. Either through authorial carelessness or compositorial ineptitude, a character may have more than one name, "Tom," for example, in some parts, "Tim" in others, or two characters with similar abbreviations may become confused. Both accidental and substantive errors and awkwardnesses are common.

In most plays only the most obvious errors are stop-press corrected—for example, errors in pagination, catchwords, and running titles. By contrast, errors in the text are often ignored. The kinds of error corrected most frequently suggest that printing-house personnel, not authors, read proof, and they did so in a decidedly casual manner. The object of printing a play was, as a rule, to publish it as soon as possible after performance so that playhouse publicity would encourage sales. The important thing was not neatness or accuracy but speed.

There is little evidence of playwrights actually reading proof. Edward Filmer, in the preface to *The Unnatural Brother* (1697), offers "but one word more to the Reader, . . . And that is, that he would not charge me with any Errors of the Press. The Bookseller in my absence, has undertaken the care of inspecting it, and therefore he only ought to be accountable for all such faults." Whether Filmer's statement suggests that playwrights usually proofread is doubtful, at least judging from the kinds of errors that creep through, for example, mistakes in speech prefixes, nonsense phrases probably derived from interlineated manuscripts or careless composition, words misread from the manuscript.

Playwrights must have had an opportunity to correct copy for the

24. Curt A. Zimansky, ed. *The Relapse*, Regents Restoration Drama Series (Lincoln: Univ. of Nebraska Press, 1970), p. xiii.

first edition, for they often brought to the printer prefatory material that postdated early performances. Authors frequently commented in prefaces on the reception in the theatre, as well as any objections raised against the play. Sometimes other post-premiere material would be included, such as an additional prologue to Cibber's *The Careless Husband* "design'd for the Sixth Day, but not spoken." Steele printed "A Song Design'd for the Fourth Act, but not Set" with *The Tender Husband,* and in the preface to *The Conscious Lovers* he included a song "omitted for want of a Performer" and replaced by Carbonelli's violin "sonata." In the first edition of Farquhar's *The Inconstant,* the heading to the prologue explains: "The Prologue that was spoke the first night receiv'd such additions from Mr——who spoke it, that they are best if bury'd and forgot. But the following Prologue is literally the same that was intended for the Play, and written by Mr *Motteux.*" All of these materials, of course, were printed in the preliminary gatherings, the sheets ordinarily printed last. Authors who brought their prefaces and dedications to printers sometimes, probably often, did so after some or even most of the text was in print; thus they could add to the prelims at a time too late to change (except by cancellation) the text of the play, which was already set.

Nor did playwrights ordinarily show great concern for revision of later editions. Edmond Malone said of Dryden that once his works were published, "he in general seems to have dismissed them from his thoughts, and to have been little solicitous about rendering them more perfect."[25] When authors did revise, their changes were often based not on aesthetic considerations but on other interests dictated by a developing prudishness, an author's concern for his reputation, and sometimes a financial gain. For example, Steele revised only one of his plays for republication; in the second edition of *The Funeral,* he changed some vaguely suggestive wording, omitted a line, and made minor corrections of a single sheet. But he made the significant changes as an afterthought, by cancellation, in an edition that was being printed at exactly the time he was publishing the *Spectator* with the same bookseller, Tonson, and therefore

25. Edmond Malone, "Account of the Life and Writings of John Dryden," in *The Prose Works of John Dryden* (London: Baldwin, Cadell, and Davies, 1800), I, Part i, pp. 143–44.

had almost daily contact with him. Furthermore, he added a dedication to the Duchess of Hamilton at the same time and named the Duke of Devonshire in a passage in the preface, which had formerly read "a very great Man."[26] His primary interest in the revision was patronage; his second, reputation. Verbal revisions were an afterthought. The revised 1710 texts of Congreve's *The Old Batchelour* and *The Double-Dealer* prudently omitted oaths and references to God.

Sometimes, of course, authors made more important revisions for better cause. Farquhar revised the second edition of *The Constant Couple,* published less than two months after the first, during a year in which the play reputedly played more than fifty times. The revision consisted of the substitution of a different version of the scene in which Sir Harry Wildair discovers that Angelica is not a prostitute and asks for her hand (V.i). The scene was revised either during rehearsal or early in the first run, doubtless to strengthen and enhance the character of Wildair; the original script proved inappropriate to the character as portrayed by Wilks, and the change was probably made for consistency and thus greater appeal.[27] Farquhar himself must have been responsible for the change in the second edition, but his revision of the text ran no farther than submitting to the printer the new material, showing him where to insert it and what to delete. Otherwise, the second edition is a mere reprint of the first, with no textual authority. In an uncharacteristic manner—for an uncharacteristically successful play—Farquhar or perhaps Ralph Smith, the bookseller, showed continuing interest in the publication of the third edition, a little more than six months later, in which a new prologue was added. The prologue had been written to counteract an attack on Farquhar in John Oldmixon's prologue to Charles Gildon's alteration of *Measure for Measure.* On 13 July 1700, an author's benefit of *The Constant Couple* at Drury Lane featured Farquhar's new prologue; the prologue was added to the third edition, dated 1701 but published on 20 August 1700.[28]

26. Shirley Strum Kenny, ed., *The Plays of Richard Steele* (Oxford: Clarendon, 1971), pp. 9–13.

27. Shirley Strum Kenny, "Farquhar, Wilks, and Wildair; or, the Metamorphosis of the 'Fine Gentleman,' " *Philological Quarterly,* 57 (1978), 52–53.

28. *Post Man,* 17–20 August 1700.

Again, Farquhar's only revisory action was to forward the new prologue to the printer, and one cannot even be sure the initiative lay with him. The text of the third quarto was printed from the second, the only other difference being that the epilogue was moved to the end and the type was crowded so that the printing of no additional leaves was necessary despite the addition of the new prologue. The fourth edition, dated 1704, is a hasty reprint of the third, with no additional revisions. Farquhar was typical of his fellow playwrights in the casualness with which he sent copy to the printer; not only did he not regularize accidentals, he did not even bother to correct obvious errors when he revised or sent additions to the press. Similarly Steele, for example, changed what had been brought to his attention as offensive in *The Funeral,* corrected the sheet in proof at the time he was in the printshop, but did not, at the same time, correct the name "Sharlot" to "Harriot" in a passionate love scene in which Campley addresses his beloved by the wrong name (III.iii).

Despite the common lack of interest in revising plays for later editions, there are cases in which authors revised on artistic grounds. Congreve's revisons of *The Mourning Bride* (1697) in the first edition of his *Works* in 1710 were, by his own statement, literary in origin: "The Tragedy of the *Mourning Bride,* in this Edition, is reformed in its *Numbers,* and by several little Variations and Transpositions in the Expression, intirely cast into Blank Verse; in respect of which Measure, it was before, in many Places, defective. Some few Verses are also, in one or two places, inserted, or substituted in the Room of others, it is hoped for the better."[29] Oliver Goldsmith made a few substantive revisions in *The Good Natur'd Man* without an unusual cause such as Steele and Farquhar had, although he made none in *She Stoops to Conquer.*[30] Henry Fielding proved more unusual when he revised *The Author's Farce,* first published in 1730, for an edition twenty years later. Sheridan's *The Rivals* (1775) appeared in a third edition (1776) corrected to the acting version, including the Serjeant-at-Law prologue slightly

29. William Congreve, Preface, *The Works of Mr. William Congreve* (London: Tonson, 1710), I, A3.
30. Friedman, V, 9, 96.

revised, the Prologue Spoken on the Tenth Night, a few verbal revisions, and a number of actors' cuts.[31] There are, of course, numerous other examples of revisions, and one could point to authors who cared about accidentals as well as substantive changes, although they are few in number. Nevertheless, the attitude most commonly exhibited by playwrights was one of relative disinterest in revision.

III

Although playwrights stood to gain little from publication after selling their rights, booksellers stood to gain a good deal after buying them, and the publishing of plays became a strong interest of some. Although play publication interested booksellers as soon as the theatres reopened in 1660, the number and size of editions grew greatly by the turn of the eighteenth century; ten or twenty years later, the industry had expanded and developed to another dimension—and so throughout the period. The history of play publication in this period is one of expanding runs of plays, accelerating republication of successful plays, increasing interest on the part of booksellers, and ever-growing numbers of partners in the publication of old plays as booksellers divided, sold, or willed their copyrights.

Although booksellers could as a rule make substantial profits only on successful plays, most plays produced in London, successes and failures, were printed. Booksellers learned to advertise not only newly published plays but also stock plays that were running in the theatre. Advertisements regularly followed the playhouse advertisements in the *Daily Courant,* announcing that the plays could be purchased from booksellers. Sometimes texts, particularly libretti, were sold in the playhouse itself, in some instances during the first run. A successful revival sometimes provided impetus for a new edition of an old play.

In play publication three general patterns can be discerned. First, plays that were unsuccessful onstage might see a single edition,

31. J. Q. Adams, "The Text of Sheridan's *The Rivals," Modern Language Notes,* 25 (1917), 171.

usually a quarto, casually set and never reprinted. A second common pattern is exemplified by the publication history of Otway's *Venice Preserv'd* (1682): "The first quarto was carelessly set; the second follows the first closely but corrects numerous errors; the third was set from the second but introduces several unnecessary emendations; and the text in the *Works* was derived from the third quarto."[32] In such cases, a play, either a repertory piece or the work of a popular author, was reprinted at intervals as copies ran out; compositors corrected obvious errors, but the play was never extensively or intensively revised. Sometimes derivation of the text was completely orderly, as with *Venice Preserv'd*, but sometimes it was not: A fourth edition could derive from a second if that was the edition available to the printer. Expanded to greater proportions for longer-lived plays, this lackluster seriatim printing could extend to many editions continuing for decades or throughout the eighteenth and perhaps nineteenth century.

Finally, with the few great successes a pattern emerges of an immediate need for many thousands of copies; such demand was often but not always followed by a long period of frequent reprintings. In the Restoration and well into the 1710s, first editions were usually quartos; by the late 1710s or early 1720s, octavos had become the usual format for first editions. Immediate reprints tended to follow the format of the first editions; later reprints, however, were most frequently economical duodecimos.

A prime example of the final pattern is *She Stoops to Conquer;* 4,000 copies sold in three days, a fact that caused the *Morning Chronicle* (1 April 1773) to observe that "No piece was ever honoured with so rapid a sale." In all, six impressions were printed in 1773, variously labeled through the "Fifth Edition." It was, of course, for these few plays that booksellers hoped, but there is every indication that they could also profit modestly by less successful ones.

Immediate sales following a successful opening must have been gratifying. Box office and bookseller were, in a sense, linked in financial success or failure. On the occasion of great theatrical

32. Malcolm Kelsall, ed., *Venice Preserv'd,* Regents Restoration Drama Series (Lincoln: Univ. of Nebraska Press, 1969), p. xi.

successes, printers saw their profits multiply. When a strong reception was expected, a large number of copies could be printed even during the stage run; if it was printed afterward, the run helped gauge sales. When *The Conscious Lovers* was puffed as the best play that ever came upon the English stage and played eighteen nights without interruption, "many thousand" copies were printed and "a good part" immediately sold.[33] By contrast, upon the suppression of one play, Gay's *Polly,* the printing probably exceeded the size it might have attained with a stage run; William Bowyer published two big editions, a total of 10,500 copies.[34] Ordinarily far fewer copies would be printed, but if the play was an unexpected success, the run could be enlarged.

For rapid publication of additional copies of a successful play, printers had several alternative methods. An unusually large first edition could be printed, and by the cancellation of the title page and substitution of a new one and perhaps new prelims, could be reissued as one or more new editions. The first edition of Hugh Kelly's *False Delicacy* (1768) was reissued several times, so that the "Fifth Edition" and those that preceded it are actually new impressions of the first. Cibber's *Papal Tyranny* (1745), for which John Watts paid £80 on 20 February 1745,[35] five days after the opening of a nine-day run, was metamorphosed to a "second edition" by the cancellation of leaves A1 (the title page) and A4 and the resetting of a1^r and a2^v. Lintott issued the first edition of *The Non-Juror* on 2 January 1718. Its popularity led him to reissue the same setting, labeled first as the second, then the third edition within the month; and before the end of the year, he reissued the same setting again, labeled as the fourth and fifth editions.[36] Sometimes, after printers acquired sufficient amounts of type in the shop, set type could be tied and stored, then reimpressed without the necessity of recomposing. If popularity of a play was established after some but not all sheets had been through the press, printers often extended the run for sheets not yet impressed; as a result, some "second" editions

33. G. A. Aitken, "Steele's *Conscious Lovers* and the Publishers," *Athenaeum,* 5 December 1891, p. 771, citing Chancery Pleadings, Winter 1714–58, No. 690.
34. Nichols, I, 404.
35. Folger Shakespeare Library manuscript, Y.d.467(5).
36. Copies examined are in the Folger Shakespeare Library.

are, in fact, only partially new editions, containing some sheets from the first edition. Sometimes, alternately, more than one printing of a play would be issued with seemingly identical title pages, when the publisher recognized the need for a longer run after type had been distributed; the illusion of one edition rather than two or more was thereby created.

A few other examples will illustrate the economies of the printing house in enlarging runs or storing type; they also illustrate how rapidly additional copies were needed for the most popular plays. Addison's *Cato* opened 14 April 1713; Tonson had bought the rights for £107 10s, "one of the best investments of his publishing career," according to Kathleen M. Lynch.[37] By 29 April the third "edition" was advertised in the *Daily Courant;* by the end of the year, eight "editions," six quarto and two duodecimo, had appeared, the fourth by 9 May, the fifth by 22 May, the sixth by 1 June, the seventh by 26 June. The play was also printed at Edinburgh, Dublin, and The Hague. It was translated into French by Abel Boyer and into Italian by Antonio Maria Salvini (1715). By 27 April 1713 there had been a piracy in London "wherein are numberless great Faults and several Scenes left out."[38] The play continued to be published with astonishing frequency throughout the century. The first eight "editions" were, in fact, fewer than eight; the first three were separate issues of a single edition, as were the two duodecimos, labeled seventh and eighth.

Within a year William Griffin published five impressions of Goldsmith's *The Good Natur'd Man* (1768), four of them in less than three weeks. The first two carried no designation on the title page; the third and fourth were labeled "A New Edition," and the last, "The Fifth Edition." Six impressions of *She Stoops to Conquer* were issued within a year.[39]

The scope of the business operation for the publication of plays

37. Kathleen M. Lynch, *Jacob Tonson Kit-Cat Publisher* (Knoxville: Univ. of Tennessee Press, 1971), p. 87.

38. I am deeply indebted to Professor Donald F. Bond for information on the publication of *Cato,* including information from advertisements in the *Daily Courant,* 29 April 1713 and 19 November 1715, and from the *Guardian,* 27 April, 9 May, 22 May, 1 June, and 26 June 1713.

39. William B. Todd, "The First Editions of *The Good Natur'd Man* and *She Stoops to Conquer,*" *Studies in Bibliography,* 11 (1958), 133–42.

suggests that publishers might not be particularly concerned with the authenticity of the text or the relationship between printed and acting versions without some incentive. Although authors did sometimes revise early editions, few publishers thought about relating their texts to current theatrical practice. But in at least two periods such revisions did occur. Around the 1730s a number of editions were published in which seeming relationships to the theatre can be observed. For example, the 1728 edition of Farquhar's *Beaux Stratagem* was a revised text. A note explained that the revision reflected changes made in the theatre during the first run. *The Stage-Coach* was printed in a completely new version in 1735 that had nothing to do with either of the first two quartos, one published in Dublin (1704), one in London (1705); it must have derived from a promptbook. Although these editions, and editions of other plays related in printing history and unusually interesting for their revisions, have not been studied systematically yet, the bookseller William Feales seems to have been involved with them.[40]

The other period of theatrical editions that claimed to be corrected from the promptbook occurs later in the century, with the well-known *Bell's British Theatre,* the *New English Theatre,* and other editions. Current casts were regularly listed, sometimes, as in *The Beaux Stratagem* of 1776 (Lowndes, Caslon, Nicoll, and Bladon), giving current casts in more than one theatre. Other changes were made. For example, in that edition lines originally spoken by the Count were given to Foigard, as they were in the 1728 edition, along with appropriate revision of the dialogue. The full text of songs is printed, rather than a couple of lines. Texts such as the *New English Theatre* were innovative popular editions which, for the most part, tried to reproduce both the reading and the acting texts, at least as far as stage cuts were concerned.

For booksellers, the play texts could remain remunerative for many years, as long as copyright lasted, as long as pirates could be prevented from stealing too much business—and often much longer. The usual reason for multiple editions of a play was continu-

40. Shirley Strum Kenny, "The Mystery of *The Stage-Coach* Reconsidered," *Studies in Bibliography,* 32 (1979), 231.

ing popularity in the theatre. There are many instances of new productions of old plays precipitating new editions, even many years after the original production. However, other considerations could also affect republication. A poor play by a noted playwright might reappear frequently because the author's collected works continued to be reprinted—*The Lying Lover,* the total stage life of which consisted of six nights in 1703 and four more in 1746,[41] was published five times during Steele's lifetime, in 1704, 1711, 1717, 1723, and 1725 (Dublin), and continued to be published fairly frequently after his death, not because of its merit but because buyers wanted copies of Steele's collected plays.

Throughout the eighteenth century, collections of the "best" English plays, that is, the most famous and most popular, proved of interest to publishers. Sometimes they included specially printed new editions of plays; at other times entrepreneurs purchased remaindered stock and patched together collections with the addition of a title page. Thomas Johnson's *Collection of the Best English Plays,* first published in 1712 and reissued in 1720, printed at the Hague, was really a combination of the two methods—he had printed twenty-five of the forty plays in the ten-volume set in 1710, twelve in 1711, and three more in 1712. Henry Scheurleer bought remaindered stock from the second printing and reissued the collection in 1750 as *A Select Collection of the Best Modern English Plays.* William Feales in the 1730s pieced together *The English Theatre* by buying remaindered copies of plays, then supplementing with newly printed editions when the old were exhausted. His collections carry the imprints of the original editions but are covered by a title page for the collection, which carries his imprint. In the second half of the century, collections proliferated in editions such as *The English Theatre* of 1765 in eight volumes and the *New English Theatre,* dated 1776–77, in twelve. *Bell's British Theatre* expanded still more—the 1776–81 edition ranged to twenty-one volumes, that published in 1791–1802 to thirty-six. The nineteenth century continued the tradition with editions such as Mrs Inchbald's, Oxberry's, and Cumberland's.

Booksellers also learned the advantages of sharing rights in plays.

41. *The Plays of Richard Steele*, p. 105.

If one house had published one of a man's plays and one or more others had published the others, the two—or three or four—might well join to publish the works. Such agreements would, ordinarily, involve shares that correlated with the relative percentages of the copyrights the individuals held. These agreements eventually made for some remarkable fractions—Blagden lists a one-quarter share of Young's *Busiris* (1719) producing in 1759 a total of 32⅔ copies of a run of 1500 copies of Young's *Works,* and one-sixth of five-ninths share of four of Otway's plays producing 41 copies of the three-volume edition of his *Works.*[42]

Agreements between booksellers often became far more complex than a simple sharing of one author's works. They could involve works by more than one author. They could involve both copyright and stock. Tonson and Lintott agreed on 16 February 1718 to go equal shares in all plays they bought during the next eighteen months.[43] Although that agreement must have been unusual at the time, as the century progressed, booksellers shared in agreements involving growing numbers of participants.

At least as early as 1690, a conger, a cooperative association of booksellers for the publishing and/or marketing of books, was established.[44] Congers were perceived as associations of strong booksellers to shut out the weaker ones. Although the etymology is suspect, congers were supposedly named for the large conger eel, devourer of small fry. *The New Dictionary of the Terms Ancient and Modern of the Canting Crew* (1690) defined a conger as "a Set or Knot of Topping Book-sellers of *London,* who agree among themselves, that whoever of them Buys a good Copy, the rest are to take off such a particular number as (it may be) Fifty, in Quires, on easy Terms. Also they that joyn together to Buy either a Considerable, or Dangerous Copy." Not only did congers divide printings at wholesale prices, they also banded together in copyright in some cases.

Another common way of attaining shares was through auctions, held often at taverns, dinner or refreshments provided. When a

---

42. Blagden, "Booksellers' Trade Lists," p. 251.
43. Nichols, VIII, 303.
44. Blagden, "Booksellers' Trade Lists," p. 257.

bookseller died, his stock and copyright holdings were often sold through auction; a shortage of cash could also lead to auction, which was a common means of selling printed stock and copyrights.[45] With auctions, as with congers, lesser booksellers complained of being excluded.

Obviously, through individual agreements, congers, and auctions, the copyright of both individual and collected works could be widely distributed, the fractions complicated. A few examples of Thomas Lowndes's acquisition of copyright in Farquhar's plays will illustrate the point. After the initial quartos were published by Standfast and Coggen (*Love and a Bottle*), Smith and Banbury (*The Constant Couple*), Knapton (*Sir Harry Wildair*), Knapton, Strahan, and Lintott (*The Inconstant*), and Lintott (*The Twin-Rivals, The Recruiting Officer, The Beaux Stratagem*),[46] Lintott seems to have acquired the rights to all seven full-length comedies or made some arrangement with the other copy holders. He began publishing editions of the *Comedies* and the *Works* (the *Comedies* plus the miscellany, *Love and Business*) under his imprint. The third through fifth editions (1712–21) were shared by Lintott, Knapton, Smith, and Strahan. By the sixth (1728), Clark had replaced Smith, and Knapton's heirs carried his share. In the seventh edition, called the *Dramatick Works* (1736), Feales became involved as a bookseller, though apparently not a copy holder. By the eighth edition (1742), Bernard Lintott had passed his holdings to Henry Lintott. By that point copyright had shifted somewhat between sharers: *Love and a Bottle* was printed for Lintott and Clark; *The Constant Couple,* Clark; *Sir Harry Wildair,* the Knaptons; *The Inconstant,* the Knaptons, Strahan, and Lintott; and the other three plays, Lintott (Bernard Lintott had owned rights to them from the beginning). Strictly speaking, the copyright had, in fact, expired, but the powerful booksellers obviously continued to act as if they held it. By the ninth edition in 1760, the imprint lists Clark, John and James Rivington, Fletcher, Crowder, Caslon, Lowndes, Woodgate, and Brooks. William Upcott's record of "Original Assignments of

45. Ibid., pp. 243–47; Terry Belanger, "Booksellers' Trade Lists 1718–1768," *The Library,* 5th ser., 30 (1975), 281–302.

46. The first London edition of his farce, *The Stage-Coach,* was probably unauthorized. See Shirley Strum Kenny, "The Mystery of *The Stage-Coach* Reconsidered," 226–31.

copyrights of books and other Literary Agreements"[47] shows how Lowndes gradually bought into the Farquhar copyright. At an auction at the Queens Arms on 26 April 1759, he purchased from Catherine Lintott, Henry's widow, one-fourth of the copyright of *The Beaux Stratagem* for £7 15s, and, in four lots, four quarters of *The Twin-Rivals* for prices rising from £3 to £4 10s. On 7 October 1760 he bought quarter shares in *Sir Harry Wildair* and *The Twin-Rivals* for 10s 6d each, then sold a third of each to Caslon and another third to Kearsley. On 6 November 1760 he bought from Thomas Caslon one-twelfth of *The Recruiting Officer* for 16s 8d and a twenty-fourth of *The Beaux Stratagem* for £1 1s 8d at the sale of Woodgate and Brooks. On 23 February 1763 he bought from Caslon 25 copies of *The Constant Couple* plus one-fourth of the copyright, the latter costing £5 18s 6d. He then sold half of his share to Corbet. On 5 June 1763 he bought from Caslon at an auction at the Globe Tavern in Fleet Street five-twenty-fourths of *The Beaux Stratagem* and 1333 (of 3,000) copies of *The Recruiting Officer*. He acquired a twenty-fourth of *The Beaux Stratagem* from Nicoll on 6 December 1763. On 16 October 1764 at an auction at the Queens Arms, he bought one-twelfth of *The Recruiting Officer* and sold off part of it to Nicoll; the copy, which had belonged to George Kearsley, who was bankrupt, had been sold by his assigns.[48] In the ninth edition of the *Works* Lowndes is listed with three to seven other booksellers in the imprints of five of the seven individual plays, *Sir Harry Wildair, The Inconstant, The Twin-Rivals, The Recruiting Officer,* and *The Beaux Stratagem*.[49] By the tenth edition in 1772, only John Rivington, Crowder, Caslon, and Lowndes remain from the partners in the ninth, the others having been replaced by Johnston, Nicoll, Bladon, Corbet and Baldwin. Some of Woodgate's and Brooks's stock had passed to Lowndes; some of what he bought in various auctions had been sold to Nicoll and Corbet. Obviously each of the other sharers bought into the rights in similar ways. But in fact perpetual copyright had expired in 1731—and was thereafter maintained only by pure bluff.

47. British Library, Add. MS. 38,730, dated 1825.
48. Add. MS. 38,730, fols. 117b, 204, 39, 42, 47b, 131, 104b.
49. *The Stage-Coach* is not included in this edition.

Farquhar provides an unusually rich example because his plays were so popular and so frequently reprinted. However, the ways in which shares in a work split between multiple holders was a common pattern, increasing, as in Farquhar's case, when the original publishers, such as Tonson and Lintott, shared agreements with others, often in congers, and then accelerating when the old copy holders died and their copyrights and stock were auctioned.

IV

Although booksellers managed to protect their copy long after legal copyright had expired, they often had considerable difficulty keeping new plays safe from the pirates. The story of play piracy is a long and elaborate one; the scope of this paper allows for no more than a suggestion of the ways in which pirates plied their trade.

First of all, English copyright law only applied to copies printed in England and Scotland. Copies printed at The Hague or in Dublin and sold in England were not, strictly speaking, piracies, although the publishers certainly had no claim to copyright. One of the most talented exporters of English plays to English book-buyers was Thomas Johnson, an English printer who began his remarkable extralegal activities at The Hague in 1710, the year of the Copyright Act. According to Giles E. Dawson, although some of Johnson's imprints gave London as the place of publication, there is unmistakable evidence that all were printed in the Netherlands: The paper is consistently Dutch, the workmen were "at least mainly" Dutch as shown by certain misspellings and also by Dutch methods of bookmaking. Johnson first published plays in 1710–12, then reprinted them in 1720–21. His texts are remarkable for their clarity, care both in setting and in emending cruxes, and faithfulness to the text. In 1712 he began marketing his ten-volume *Collection* of plays by Shakespeare, Dryden, and the most popular contemporary dramatists. The twenty-five plays he published in 1710 omitted his name and either had a false London imprint or omitted the place of publication. Later he occasionally used an imprint with his name, the true place of publication, or both. After trying other title-page ornaments, he adopted an elaborate monogram, his initials mirrored and entwined, so as possibly to be read as J. T. for Jacob

Tonson. When the plays in the first *Collection* began to run short, he reprinted in 1720–21 those which were exhausted.[50] Johnson is one of the most interesting invaders of English copyright in the century, not only because he published so many plays, but also because he printed extremely good texts, useful, oddly enough, to modern editors because of intelligent, careful emendations of cruxes, speech prefixes, and other errors in the authorized editions.

Dublin editions were also exported to England and sold, often in the provinces, without any copyright expenses for the entrepreneurs. Dublin publishers were quick to print the plays that were most successful onstage, in order to compete with first or early editions, but they also produced editions long after the first run. With the Dubliners, the number of plays printed varied—in the 1720s, for example, there were large numbers of Irish editions because of the industry of printers like S. Powell and booksellers like William Smith. Dublin editions tended to be cheaply printed on poor paper; they offer little to the modern editor except an additional unauthorized edition to collate.

Actual piracies occurred in London and occurred with considerable frequency. The reopening of the theatres at a time when the stock of printed plays was minimal made piracy of popular plays especially attractive. According to Johan Gerritsen, Francis Kirkman, a specialist in publishing drama, who advertised that he could supply "all the Playes that were ever yet printed," was responsible for at least ten piracies as early as 1661; although he denied the allegation, his stock was seized and he never got redress.[51] Another notorious pirate, Henry Hills, Jr., was probably printing piracies as early as the 1690s and had become infamous by 1709 for cheap piracies; he probably included plays among his illegitimate publications, although he is best known for poems and sermons.[52]

Ordinarily, pirates sought anonymity, but they made no attempt to disguise their wares as legitimate editions. The imprint might

---

50. I am greatly indebted to Giles E. Dawson for access to his unpublished research on Thomas Johnson.

51. Johan Gerritsen, "The Dramatic Piracies of 1661: A Comparative Analysis," *Studies in Bibliography,* 11 (1958), 117–31.

52. John W. Velz, " 'Pirate Hills' and the Quartos of *Julius Caesar,*" *Papers of the Bibliographical Society of America,* 63 (1969), 177–93.

well read simply "Printed for the Booksellers in Town and Country" or "Printed in the Year 1709." But in the 1730s an altogether remarkable anonymous pirate was at work, one who imitated authorized editions with exquisite care and included imitated woodcut ornaments and frontispiece engravings to compound the deceit. Even though sometimes the texts of these piracies vary slightly from the text being copied, the general appearance is so deceptive that for two centuries they went undetected.[53] No one to this day has figured out a rationale for such relentless accuracy in detail, nor in all probability has all of this pirate's handiwork been identified.

The biggest threat from pirates, however, arose not from printing later edition of works but from ignoring copyright as soon as the first editions of a very successful play was printed. Pirates could buy a copy of the play as soon as it went on sale, print with great speed, and have a competing edition on the streets within days. In such cases, court action might well ensue. Tonson, for example, having published an edition of "many thousand" copies of *The Conscious Lovers* on 1 December 1722, managed to prevent a London piracy advertised for 8 December, first by a restraining order, then an injunction against Francis Clifton, Robert Tooke, John Lightbody, and Susanna Collins. Tonson claimed that these printers had entered a confederacy to defeat his rights by procuring a copy of the play and having several hundred copies printed. He was not, however, able to stop the immediate publication of editions in Dublin and at The Hague, which were imported to compete with the legitimate octavos.[54] George Lillo's *The London Merchant* (1731), which underwent five different printings by John Gray the first year and four more by 1740, was printed in Dublin the first year, then pirated in London in 1733, twice in 1737, and again in 1739. An advertisement in Lillo's *Christian Hero* of 1735 complains that the town "swarms" with "incorrect pyrated" copies of *The London Merchant.*[55]

53. Giles E. Dawson, "Three Shakespeare Piracies in the Eighteenth Century," *Studies in Bibliography*, 1 (1948), 49–58; D. F. Foxon, "A Piracy of Steele's *The Lying Lover*," *The Library*, 5th ser., 10 (1955), 127–29; Shirley Strum Kenny, "Piracies of Two Plays by Farquhar," *Studies in Bibliography*, 28 (1975), 297–305.

54. Rodney M. Baine, "The Publication of Steele's *Conscious Lovers*," 170–71; Aitken, "Steele's *Conscious Lovers* and the Publishers," p. 771.

55. William H. McBurney, ed., *The London Merchant*, Regents Restoration Drama Series (Lincoln: Univ. of Nebraska Press, 1965), pp. ix–xi.

One of the most heavily pirated plays of the century was *Polly,* greatly in demand because it had failed to appear onstage. At least three London piracies, one in at least two issues with the second labeled as the second edition, and a Dublin import were hawked in London very shortly after Gay's own six-shilling edition, complete with music, appeared. Gay's edition was published 5 April 1729.[56] By 11 April the *Daily Post* carried an advertisement to announce that certain booksellers were being prosecuted for spurious editions; seventeen printers and booksellers were enjoined on 17 June 1729, and at least four more had been included by summer.[57] Once again the pirates acquired a legitimate copy upon publication and immediately had printers—in some cases more than one house—set it as quickly as possible so that their ware could be in the stalls to compete while the play was strongly in demand. Because the pirates tended to undersell, price wars resulted, to the advantage of none of the booksellers.

James R. Sutherland records the wages of piracy, or at least those claimed by some of *Polly's* abductors. James Watson testified that he shared with Thomas Astley the expense of printing an edition falsely labeled "Printed for T. Thomson," in a first edition of 2,000 and a second of 1,000. He charged the public 1s 6d, making a profit of 10d per copy, and he sold copies to the trade at 1s, for a profit of 4d per copy. In all, he estimated he had made £20 on the two editions; Astley estimated £15.[58] One may suspect both men of estimating modestly in such courtroom proceedings; however, they could not have succeeded in quoting figures grossly out of proportion with the profits that might be expected. The wages of piracy were not, it would seem, remarkably high, but, we must conclude, piracy at least provided steady work.

Play publication, like piracy, in fact, must often have brought profits in the tens of pounds, sometimes in the hundreds, but seldom in the thousands. The great money-makers were rare, but the consistent moneymakers were more numerous. Since booksellers and their assigns or those who bought their copies tended to

56. *Whitehall Evening-Post,* 3–5 April 1729, "This Day is publish'd," quoted in Sutherland, p. 293.

57. Sutherland, p. 292.

58. Ibid., p. 295.

claim rights to plays long after there were legal grounds to do so, a play could, by large or multiple early editions immediately yield a sizeable profit for the publisher and, over the decades, continue as a steady moneymaker. Prices shifted, format and quality of paper changed, but the text itself rarely varied by more than the multiplication of errors until the 1770s, when some interest in correcting editions according to the promptbook emerged and generated new interest in old plays. Frontispieces, often reused in later editions or copied for later use, were then modernized; cast lists of recent casts were introduced. If one recognizes such attention to the theatre as purely commercial enterprise, one feels nevertheless some satisfaction in knowing that these plays, of such continuing, steady benefit to booksellers, occasionally touched, however lightly, the stage that had launched them as literary properties.

12

The London Theatre at the End of the Eighteenth Century

JOSEPH DONOHUE

IN HIS 1819 essay on the drama Sir Walter Scott looked back over the long history of Western dramatic literature and the circumstances of its theatrical performance. Closing with a sustained critical analysis of the decline, as he saw it, of serious dramatic art in Britain over the years, Scott laid the blame for this sad debilitation directly at the portals of the London patent theatres, identifying three unfortunate results from the traditional exercise of patent rights: the huge size of contemporary theatres, the unfavorable conditions affecting performers and authors, and the seemingly calculated encouragement of prostitution and consequent loss of a substantial segment of the audience. Scott's solution to the problem was to do away with patent privilege altogether and replace the current two immense houses, Covent Garden and Drury Lane, with several theatres of moderate size which would specialize in either tragedy, comedy, or musical pieces, thus regularly employing the slighted or wasted talents of many playwrights and actors, the hours of performance at one theatre being suited to the habits of the upper class, while at another the "middling classes" might assemble "after the business of the day."[1] Scott's analysis of licensed privilege addresses the ills of his own time, but it offers a convenient perspec-

1. "Essay on the Drama," in *The Miscellaneous Prose Works of Sir Walter Scott, Bart.*, 3 vols. (Edinburgh: Robert Cadell, 1850), I, 615–16.

tive on the complex, paradoxical nature of the London theatre as the late eighteenth century gave way to the early nineteenth. For the conduct of the patent theatre monopoly and the consequent relationship of the great major houses to the minors are crucial to understanding the essential character of theatrical entertainment in the age of Sheridan and Kemble.

Ironically, Scott's ideal of relatively small, specialized houses had already been intimated over a quarter century before in the development of musical and theatrical entertainment in the "minor" theatres, circuses, and pleasure gardens of late eighteenth-century London. Even as he wrote, the house specialties so characteristic of nineteenth-century London theatrical performance were beginning to emerge in the pantomimes, burlettas, melodramas, equestrian spectacles, and comic operas performed at such minor houses as Astley's, the Sans Pareil (soon to become the Adelphi), the Surrey, the Olympic, the Royal Coburg, and the English Opera House (formerly the Lyceum). Patent rights would wither away by 1832, when Edward Lytton Bulwer's Select Committee of Parliament inquired into the decline of dramatic literature, and would be officially abolished by the Theatres Act of 1843.[2] But that was in another age. The earlier period on which Scott looked back in his retrospective critique was one in which the managers of the patent theatres behaved as the despotic entrepreneurs they were, but also one in which the other houses where theatrical or quasi-theatrical activity took place were laying claim to a substantial local or even metropolitan audience and were developing certain kinds of entertainment that extensively imitated, augmented, or even inspired the type of fare available at the patent houses.

This situation was the ultimate result of theatrical legislation enacted at the Restoration of King Charles II and revised in the mid-eighteenth century. The patents for theatrical performance issued by Charles to Sir William Davenant and Thomas Killigrew were both highly restrictive and boldly permissive in tenor. They asserted the exclusive rights of the patentee to the erection of a

2. *Report from the Select Committee on Dramatic Literature: With the Minutes of Evidence* (House of Commons, 2 August 1832); "An Act for regulating theatres," 6–7 Vict. c.68 (1843). See Dewey Ganzell, "Patent Wrongs and Patent Theatres: Drama and the Law in the Early Nineteenth Century," *PMLA*, 76 (1961), 384–96.

playhouse and the mounting of theatrical performances on its stage and further guaranteed those rights in apparent perpetuity to the "heirs, executors, administrators and assigns" of the principal.[3] Far from defining the exact norms or limits of theatrical performance, the language of the documents seems deliberately vague and all-embracing in regard to the stated types of performance allowed, which include "tragedies, comedies, plays, operas, musick, scenes and all other entertainments of the stage whatsoever." For all their concern with the reestablishment of what came to be known as "legitimate" drama, the letters patent issued to Davenant and Killigrew encompass the rich assortment of entertainment, from opera, spectacle, and concerts of music to entr'acte and incidental dancing, singing, juggling, tumbling, and ropedancing, that ultimately became part of the variety regularly available to London playgoers. The intent appears to have been to give the two patentees license to perform anything that might be mounted on a stage and to forbid the same to all others. In 1752 that intention was reasserted in the Act of 25 George II "for the better preventing Thefts and Robberies, and for regulating Places of publick Entertainment, and punishing Persons keeping disorderly Houses." The act expresses concern that "the lower Sort of People," victims of "the Habit of Idleness," spend their money "in riotous Pleasures" in a "Multitude of Places of Entertainment," and therefore directs that the proprietors of any such place "kept for publick Dancing, Musick, or other publick Entertainment of the like Kind" in London or Westminster or for twenty miles around must obtain an annual license at the Michaelmas quarter sessions, or else the establishment will be declared a disorderly house.[4] The Theatres Royal in Drury Lane and Covent Garden, of course, as well as the King's Opera in the Haymarket, are explicitly exempted by virtue of letters patent, as are any entertainments carried on under license from the Crown or the Lord Chamberlain (whose powers were greatly strengthened by the Licensing Act of 1737 controlling the performance of plays).

---

3. The text of Davenant's patent is reprinted as Appendix I in the *Report from the Select Committee* (1832), pp. 237–38.
4. Act of 25 G2. c.36. See Ganzell, pp. 386 ff.

Presumably, the authors of the 1752 act took the view that what cannot be suppressed must be regulated. But in regulating the activities of such houses as Sadler's Wells they were unavoidably legitimizing the existence of those houses, and in allowing such places the performance of "publick Entertainment" licensed by any local magistrate within twenty miles of London or Westminster they unwittingly paved the way for the development of various species of entertainments available in and around London in the last quarter of the eighteenth century. Such entertainment proved to offer substantial competition to Drury Lane and Covent Garden as well as to the summer theatre in the Haymarket, whose patent dated from 1766 and which enjoyed from mid-May to mid-October the same privileges as the winter houses.

Over the entire period of the late eighteenth century the proprietors of these officially sanctioned theatres remained unstintingly devoted to the cause of self-preservation. Although competitors day-by-day, Richard Brinsley Sheridan and Thomas Harris as proprietors respectively of Drury Lane and Covent Garden became long-standing cohorts united against any effort that might deprive them of their "just monopoly."[5] As early as 1777 Sheridan and Harris conceived of a scheme to build a third winter theatre under their joint control. The plan came in response to widespread agitation for a third theatre and the consequent fear of Sheridan and others that a new structure "for some species or other of Dramatic Entertainment" might be erected by some opposing interest and that the resulting competition would quickly effect "the absolute ruin" of one of the present theatres. Sheridan's proposal identified four strong reasons why another theatre was justified: the presence in London of many higher-class people who because of various inconveniences seldom attended the theatre; the distance of the present two theatres from fashionable districts; the small number of

5. Agreement between Sheridan and Harris, British Library Add. Ms. 42,720, fol. 5, quoted in *The Letters of Richard Brinsley Sheridan,* ed. Cecil Price, 3 vols. (Oxford: Clarendon Press, 1966), I, 215n. Originally one of three purchasers of Garrick's half share of Drury Lane in 1776, Sheridan gained a nine-fourteenths share by 1780; see *Survey of London,* ed. F. H. W. Sheppard, Vol. XXXV: *The Theatre Royal Drury Lane and The Royal Opera House Covent Garden* (London: Athlone Press, 1970), p. 16.

side boxes at Drury Lane and Covent Garden (an oblique reference to the numerous prostitutes in the other boxes); and the early time of performance (soon after six o'clock), an inconvenience for members of Parliament and for all who dined at the currently fashionable hour.[6]

Nothing immediately came of the idea, but well into the 1780s Sheridan's proposal for a third theatre hung fire. And his consistent double purpose of preventing all competition and of catering especially to fashionable audiences remained evident. Sheridan's plan was to use the extra, "dormant" patent held by Covent Garden to license the new theatre, described in a document dating from 1784 found among the architect Henry Holland's papers as "a Spacious, elegant Edifice, to be called (By Authority) The Prince of Wales Theatre with a grand assembly Room, and other Rooms for Suppers, Balls, and Concerts." The "theatrical and other Exhibitions" would begin at a later hour—an arrangement "more accommodated to Persons of Rank and Fashion than can now be effected at any other Place of Publick Entertainment."[7] Sheridan and Harris's scheme cleverly exploited the preference of fashionable London for the varied facilities of the pleasure gardens of Ranelagh, Vauxhall, and elsewhere. In an application to the Lord Chamberlain Harris described the proposed edifice, planned for Hyde Park Corner, as "a Theatre with an adjoining Grand rotunda with contigious [*sic*] lesser Rooms for Balls, Concerts, etc. . . . surrounded with Gardens of great extent."[8] The same pursuit of monopolistic rights and of the patronage of fashionable audiences appears in Sheridan's and Harris's purchase of the King's Theatre early in 1778, which gave them control of both legitimate drama and opera in London for several years. And these intentions emerge once again in a change of plan, by 1786, in which the theatre scheme was replaced by an

6. Proposal directed to proprietors of Drury Lane and Covent Garden, 1777, in *Letters of Sheridan,* I, 116. Although the normal dinner hour in the late eighteenth century was 4:00 P.M., most people of fashion dined later and took longer to eat, and so were seldom able to arrive at the theatre before 8:00 P.M.; see *LS,* Part 5, I, ccxv, and sources cited there.

7. Manuscript quoted in Ian Donaldson, "New Papers of Henry Holland and R. B. Sheridan: (II) The Hyde Park Corner Operas and the Dormant Patent," *TN,* 16 (1962), 117–25; see p. 119. At this time the Covent Garden proprietors held two patents, one of which was unused, or "dormant"; see Donaldson, p. 119, and *Survey of London,* XXXV, 2–6.

8. Undated document (1784–85?) quoted by Donaldson, p. 120.

opera house, with an auxiliary theatre on the same site to serve as a nursery for burgeoning talent.[9]

The last thing the patent house proprietors could be accused of was shortsightedness. When at length the idea of a third theatre was abandoned (as it seems to have been by 1791) in favor of the enlargement or reconstruction of the two existing houses, Sheridan stood firm in his view that patent privilege was to be jealously guarded in order that "the exclusive right to exhibit Dramatic Entertainments is maintained and continued to the two Theatres."[10] When it appeared that financing of the new Drury Lane Theatre (opened in 1794) was impossible to obtain without the security of a permanent patent (the current twenty-one-year patent being considered insufficient), Sheridan promptly arranged to buy the dormant Killigrew patent from Harris, at an exorbitant price.[11] Even when the threat was apparently no more formidable than that of a group of socially prominent amateurs who proposed to fit out a theatre for occasional performances, the patent houses were quick in attempting to neutralize it. In 1802, when Henry Greville and others organized the Pic-Nic Society and engaged the old King's Concert Rooms in Tottenham Street for a "Dilletanti Theatre," Sheridan explained to this "old acquaintance" that by written sanction of the Crown any attempt to open another theatre, no matter how small the scale or how elaborate the pretence for taking money, "is directly contrary to the Pledge" of support given by the Monarch to the proprietors of the two patent theatres.[12]

Greville would not be intimidated, however, as he explained in a letter to the *Theatrical Repository* denying the proprietors' right to interfere.[13] His project, which was restricted to ten nights per season but not entirely suppressed,[14] is notable as the first of a long series of challenges in the early nineteenth century to the exclusive

9. Donaldson, pp. 120–21.

10. Letter to the Duke of Bedford [1789–90], in *Letters of Sheridan*, I, 215.

11. "Proposal respecting the disposition of Mr. Harris's dormant Patent in the present general arrangement of the three Theatres," October 1791, in *Letters of Sheridan*, I, 232; *Survey of London*, XXXV, 6.

12. Letter to Greville, 17 February 1802, in *Letters of Sheridan*, II, 170–71.

13. *Theatrical Repository; or Weekly Rosciad*, No. 26 (29 March 1802), pp. 402–5.

14. Edward Wedlake Brayley, *Historical and Descriptive Accounts of the Theatres of London* (London: J. Taylor, 1826 [for 1827]), p. 84.

dominance of the monopoly over London theatrical performance.

That challenge was, however, by no means the first ever mounted against the seemingly impregnable fortress of patent privilege. On 20 June 1787 the new Royalty Theatre, designed by John Wilmot to accommodate over sixty percent of its capacity of 2,594 in two roomy galleries, opened in Wellclose Square not far from the Tower of London.[15] The bill, featuring *As You Like It* and *Miss in her Teens,* was indistinguishable from patent house fare, but the contemporary historian W. C. Oulton's description of the type of audience it attracted—"The house was exceeding full, but far from brilliant, for no ladies of distinction ventured in; the contest for places was very violent"[16]—suggests both the character and size of the Royalty's potential clientele. The actor John Palmer, father of the project, was undeniably right in perceiving a need for a theatre in the City, but in founding his enterprise on no surer legal footing than the authority of the Lord Lieutenant Governor of the Tower to build within Tower jurisdiction and a license from the Tower Hamlets magistrates, he was naively courting disaster.[17] Last-minute threats of legal action from the patent theatre proprietors forced Palmer to skirt the restrictions on gainful performance by declaring the opening night a benefit for the London Hospital.[18] Palmer bitterly complained to his audience—"Tumblers and Dancing Dogs might appear unmolested before you; but the other performers and myself standing forward to exhibit a moral play, is deemed a crime"[19]—and claimed that Harris had even given the actor John Quick written permission to perform at the Royalty. But Harris's true attitude toward unlicensed competition appears in his letter to Quick dated 2 April 1787. Espousing the cause of the Royalty, Harris pointedly explains, will "degrade, vagabondize, and, as far as you are able, ruin all Theatrical Property, and in certain consequence, all its dependants [*sic*]!" "If Mr. Palmer can perform

15. The Royalty held 360 in the pit, 594 in front and side boxes, and 1,640 in first and second galleries; see *LS,* Part 5, II, 911.

16. W. C. Oulton, *A History of the Theatres of London,* 3 vols. (London: C. Chapple, 1818), I, 170.

17. Ibid., p. 173; Brayley, p. 78.

18. Brayley, p. 78.

19. Oulton, I, 176–77.

plays, &c. &c.," he added, "why not Mr. Hughes, Mr. Jones, Mr. Astley, and Sadler's Wells, and Freemasons Hall, &c."[20] Harris's reference is to the equestrian amphitheatres, the Royal Circus and Astley's, across the Thames in Surrey and to other places of miscellaneous entertainment in London. And his term "vagabondize" is a slur evidently derived from those statutes dating from Elizabeth's time which classify actors with "rogues, vagabonds and sturdy beggars."[21]

The point was clear. Palmer reopened the Royalty in July, but only for the performance of burlettas, pantomimes, and incidental pieces, or what a playbill for Tuesday, 16 October 1787 described as "musical and characteristic Entertainments." They included *Thomas and Susan, or the fortunate Tar,* a recitation of Gray's elegy by Palmer "with Descriptive Scenery and Musical Accompaniments," a new musical piece called *The Sailor's Resolve: Or, Love Yields to Loyalty,* a variety of catches and glees, Lee Lewes as "Hippesley's Drunken Man," a new song by Miss George, and, for the forty-third time, "a New, Grand, Tragi-Comic, Pantomime Entertainment" entitled *Don Juan, or The Libertine destroyed,* with Palmer in the title role.[22]

This bill, with its emphasis on musical and quasi-theatrical variety, nautical subjects, recitations and other solo entertainment, patriotism, and spectacle, comes close to epitomizing minor theatre fare in the late eighteenth century; only equestrian shows and feats of physical skill are lacking. The emphasis on music is even greater than what may be apparent in the bill, for *Thomas and Susan* is no "straight" play but a burletta, performed throughout in recitative and song, adapted from John O'Keeffe and William Shield's comic opera *The Poor Soldier* (Covent Garden, 1783).[23] That Palmer eventually sold his investment and that the Royalty led a precarious existence through the rest of the century[24] are not surprising facts in view of the tenacious grasp of the major theatres on their own

20. Ibid., p. 178.
21. The earliest is "An Act for punishment of rogues, vagabonds and sturdy beggars," 39 Eliz. c.4 (1597); see Ganzell, p. 386 and n.
22. Playbill, Folger Shakespeare Library.
23. Oulton, I, 183.
24. *LS,* Part 5, II, 998.

344

investments and prerogatives. No less tenacious, however, was the hold the minor theatres kept on the right to the quasi-theatrical implicitly granted them by the Act of 1752, reaffirmed in 1755 after a three-year trial period in the Act of 28 George II and kept in force through the end of the century and beyond.[25] Although the term *burletta* appeared nowhere in the Act of 1752 it came to be widely used by the end of the century as a portmanteau word describing a species of theatrical performance given entirely to musical accompaniment (anything from harpsichord continuo to full orchestral support), a form of entertainment that local magistrates were by and large willing to countenance. Originally the burletta form carefully eschewed any suggestion of the spoken word, the rights to which remained the jealously guarded possession of the patent theatres, as Palmer discovered to his cost. But in this distinction between the spoken and the nonspoken lay the very means of minor theatre survival. And not a few minor theatres survived through the eighteenth century and into the nineteenth—a century of unprecedented theatrical expansion—by means of at first careful then gradually only nominal adherence to the terms of a "burletta license," under whose wide umbrella they found it possible eventually to perform almost everything in evidence on the stages of the major theatres, finally usurping the privilege of the spoken word itself.[26]

Compared to our knowledge of late eighteenth-century patent theatre fare and practice, little is known about the minor theatres and certain other places of quasi-theatrical entertainment in London during this period, but not so little as has sometimes been supposed. The lack of interest in them by certain theatre historians (one thinks at once of the Reverend John Genest)[27] has been compensated for partly by extensive scholarship dealing with the pleasure gardens and other amusements of the London populace, and partly by recent interest in the history of the circus and other forms of popular entertainment. Although many of the materials for a full-scale study of the subject survive only as uncatalogued

25. Ganzell, p. 386.
26. See Joseph Donohue, "Burletta and the Early Nineteenth-Century English Theatre," *Nineteenth-Century Theatre Research*, 1 (1973), 29–51.
27. *Some Account of the English Stage*, 10 vols. (Bath: H. E. Carrington, 1832).

ephemera in disparate archives, it is possible to piece together the outlines of identity and activity of places in London where performances approached or even embraced the theatrical.

The English love of music and song, delight in show, and taste for tea explain to a considerable extent the character of entertainments available at the spas, pleasure gardens, taverns, circus rings, exhibition halls, and other pleasure resorts that dotted the map of London from north to south and east to west. Warwick Wroth, historian of London pleasure gardens, distinguishes three groups of establishments: resorts, such as Vauxhall, Ranelagh, and Marylebone Gardens, that offered evening concerts and in some cases fireworks, as well as facilities for eating and drinking; gardens or spas connected with a mineral spring, such as Bagnigge Wells, Sadler's Wells (the most famous and important), and the Dog and Duck in St. George's Fields; and tea gardens, found as far north as Highbury Barn and in almost every other district of London as well.[28] Colman's prologue to Garrick's comedy *Bon Ton* (Drury Lane, 1775) includes among the fashionable weekend delights of the Town "riding in a one-horse chair o' Sunday!" and "drinking tea on summer afternoons / At Bagnigge-Wells, with China and gilt spoons!"[29] Yet tea drinking was only the beginning of the pleasures to be found at these resorts, for much of their attractiveness depended on formal entertainment of a decidedly musical kind. The major gardens had permanent facilities for the performance of music and song. As early as 1742 Horace Walpole could describe the soon-famous Rotunda at the new Ranelagh Gardens in Chelsea as a "vast amphitheatre, finely gilt, painted and illuminated, into which everybody that loves eating, drinking, staring, or crowding, is admitted for twelvepence."[30] Love of music went without saying; it was the setting for its performance that required comment. "On entering the rotunda," Henry Angelo recalled, *"the coup-d'oeil* was magnificent."[31]

28. Warwick Wroth, *The London Pleasure Gardens of the Eighteenth Century* (London: Macmillan, 1896), pp. 4–7.

29. *Bon Ton; or, High Life above Stairs. A Comedy in Two Acts* (London: T. Becket, 1775).

30. Letter to Sir Horace Mann, 26 May 1742, in *Horace Walpole's Correspondence with Sir Horace Mann,* Yale Edition of Horace Walpole's Correspondence, Vol. XVII, ed. W. S. Lewis, Warren Hunting Smith, and George L. Lam (New Haven: Yale Univ. Press, 1954), p. 434. Wroth (p. 200) compares the size of the Rotunda to that of the British Library Reading Room.

31. *The Reminiscences of Henry Angelo,* 2 vols. (London: Kegan, Paul, Trench, Trübner, 1904), II, 3.

Concerts were the rule at many such places. At Vauxhall, for example, James Hook, music director for some forty-five years, played nightly on the organ and wrote over 2,000 songs.[32] By the 1780s such entertainment had become popular enough for whole clusters of establishments to have emerged, as in the case of the district just below Westminster Bridge where the Flora Tea Gardens, Temple of Flora, Apollo Gardens, and Dog and Duck flourished for a time along Westminster Bridge Road. The Temple of Flora, active from about 1788 into the 1790s, appeared to have been modeled partly on the fashionable Ranelagh, since it was advertised in 1789 as an exact copy of the Temple of Flora exhibited at the recent Grand Gala at that elite Chelsea resort.[33] The Dog and Duck, originally a seventeenth-century inn, became known in the 1770s for the medicinal effect of its mineral waters, and by 1785 the establishment included a bar, old and new tearooms, the latter with a music gallery, separate baths for ladies and gentlemen, each with a leaded dome, pleasure gardens, skittle grounds, and a bowling green.[34] Performances were not only of a musical kind, for as early as 1770 Sampson the equestrian set up a circus there. Even by the 1770s the place had become sufficiently attractive, and competitive to the major houses, to be satirized in a Drury Lane epilogue:

> St. George's Fields, with taste and fashion struck,
> Display Arcadia at the Dog and Duck,
> And Drury misses here in tawdry pride,
> Are there "Pastoras" by the fountain side;
> To frowsy bowers they reel through midnight damps,
> With Fauns half drunk, and Dryads breaking lamps.[35]

By 1787 the place had become a resort for dissolute persons, and the Surrey magistrates refused a license. The Temple of Flora endured a similar fate.[36] The Apollo Gardens, opened in 1788,

---

32. Roger Fiske, *English Theatre Music in the Eighteenth Century* (London: Oxford Univ. Press, 1973), p. 395.
33. Wroth, p. 266; Edward M. Borrajo, "Temple of Flora," *N&Q*, 7th ser., 11 (14 February 1891), 138.
34. *Survey of London,* Vol. XXV: *St. George's Fields,* by Ida Darlington (London: London County Council, 1955), pp. 52–53.
35. Quoted by Wroth, p. 273.
36. Borrajo, p. 138.

were somewhat more fortunate. The inaugural concert drew some 1,300 persons to hear a band of seventy instrumental and vocal performers, and by the 1790 season the management could boast of gardens with "elegant pavilions or alcoves" ornamented with paintings of Don Quixote and other subjects. Like other gardens, the Apollo was open from April or May through the summer, and, like many, its reputation rose and then declined. Known as a resort of cheats and pickpockets by 1792, it was suppressed by the magistrates soon after.[37]

The often uncertain existence, irregular tendencies, and miscellaneous fare of these places of public amusement may seem to make them tangential to the history of the late eighteenth-century theatre proper. That history, however, is in fact closely connected with the history of the circus and both are interwoven with the pleasure gardens in the overall character of public entertainment of the time. As the circus historian A. H. Coxe has explained, the pleasure gardens were the breeding grounds of the circus: "It was at places like The Three Hats, in Islington, the Star and Garter, between Chelsea and Pimlico, Penny's Folly in the Pentonville Road, Cromwell Gardens, Sadler's Wells, and the famous Dobney's or D'Aubigny's, that the character of this type of entertainment was formed by such men as Thomas Johnson, the Irish Tartar, Charles Hughes, later Astley's rival, Conyngham, Wildman and his bees, Zucher and his learned horse, Spinacuta and his monkey and ropedancers and acrobats galore."[38] The pleasure gardens could also reflect in a striking way the character of a more formal, more essentially theatrical, kind of amusement. The actor Edward Cape Everard tells the story of his being hired at the Apollo Gardens to take part in "a kind of fantoccini," or puppet show. Clagget the proprietor had prepared "a pretty stage in miniature, his scenes and all corresponding with his two-feet figures which were well made and properly dressed, with experienced persons to work them, and 'suit the action to the word.'" Everard's job was to speak and sing

---

37. Wroth, pp. 268–69; E. Beresford Chancellor, *The Pleasure Haunts of London during four centuries* (London: Constable, 1925), p. 366.

38. Antony Hippisley Coxe, "The Lesser-Known Circuses of London," *TN*, 13 (1959), 89.

the role of Mungo, the black servant in *The Padlock,* a comic opera by Isaac Bickerstaffe with music by Charles Dibdin (who also created the role of Mungo) first performed at Drury Lane in 1768. The piece was successful enough to be repeated "above seventy times."[39]

Puppet shows in fact enjoyed a pervasive popularity in eighteenth-century London, in private homes, public gardens, and even on the stages of major theatres. The history of the puppet show in London during this time may be said to begin with Samuel Foote, theatrical entrepreneur and accomplished mimic, who introduced a satirical sketch, *Tragedy a-la-Mode,* in which puppets were employed, in special seasons at Drury Lane in 1758 and the Haymarket in 1763. In 1773 he went on to offer at his Haymarket Theatre an ambitious production, "The Primitive Puppet Show," which included *The Handsome Housemaid, or Piety in Pattens,* a burlesque of sentimental comedy.[40] The association of puppet shows with satirical commentary on contemporary art and life appeared again in Charles Dibdin's puppet show in the Grand Saloon at Exeter Change, a large mercantile building on the north side of the Strand where Dibdin performed *The Comic Mirror,* in which, he explained, "puppets were made to personate well known characters . . . and every thing and person popular at that time."[41] Never one to neglect an opportunity, Dibdin later devised a show based on his *Comic Mirror* for performance in March 1780 at the Haymarket, where a small stage enclosed by canvas had been built near the proscenium.[42] Called "Pasquin's Budget, or, a Peep at the World," the production featured not only puppets but Chinese shadow figures "and other vehicles" and was full of "pointed and marking materials" that Dibdin later introduced again at the Royal Circus.[43] Meanwhile the Patagonian Theatre of puppets from Dublin had

39. *Memoirs of an Unfortunate Son of Thespis* (Edinburgh: James Ballantyne, 1818), pp. 144–45.
40. George Speaight, *The History of the English Puppet Theatre* (London: Harrap, 1955), pp. 111, 113. See *Samuel Foote's Primitive Puppet-Shew Featuring Piety in Pattens: A Critical Edition,* ed. Samuel N. Bogorad and Robert Gale Noyes, *TS,* 14, No. 1a (Fall 1973).
41. *The Professional Life of Mr. Dibdin, Written by Himself,* 4 vols. (London: Published by the Author, 1803), I, 154.
42. Brayley, p. 37n.
43. Dibdin, *Professional Life,* II, 65; *LS,* Part 5, I, 321.

opened at Exeter Change in October 1776 with a double bill including *Midas,* a burletta by the Irish wit Kane O'Hara. First produced in England at Covent Garden in February 1764, *Midas* quickly became a staple of the Covent Garden repertory and, well into the nineteenth century, remained the most-cited example of what a burletta really was.[44] Since the eighteenth-century history of *Midas* and of burletta in general reveals how flexible its form was and how easily it could be adapted to commentary on contemporary life, its performance by puppets, traditionally able agents of parody, burlesque, and satire, seems entirely appropriate. At the same time, it is notable that the repertory of the Patagonian Theatre in a series of remarkably successful seasons over five years included not only burletta but ballad opera, pantomime, perspective views, straight dramatic comedy, and even a masque, as well as more pointed fare rife with contemporary allusions.[45] Puppet shows of the time not only mocked the follies of human beings themselves but aped their favorite theatrical amusements.

Evidently, shows and entertainments with a close relationship to contemporary life were an important attraction for London audiences of the late eighteenth century. Prominent among them were shows by solo entertainers. Even before mid-century Samuel Foote had made a specialty out of razor-keen mimicry of contemporary celebrities, including Garrick, at the Haymarket. To this he soon added entertainments based on his own travels, setting a precedent followed by Charles Dibdin, Charles Mathews, and many other performers up through the nineteenth century.[46] For a decade beginning in 1764, George Alexander Stevens delighted audiences with his *Lecture upon Heads,* a series of satirical imitations of current character types featuring picturesque costumes, dramatic characterization and dialogue, and a "lively description of manners" in

44. See Donohue, "Burletta," pp. 31–32, and P. T. Dircks, "James Robinson Planché and the English Burletta Tradition," in *The British Theatre 1800–1900: Essays on the Nineteenth-Century Stage,* ed. Joseph Donohue and James Ellis, *Theatre Survey,* 17 (1976), 68–81.

45. Speaight, pp. 117–21.

46. I am indebted for some of the information in this paragraph to James Ellis's unpublished paper, "One Man in His Time: The Solo Entertainer on the London Stage," delivered at the University of Warwick Conference on Nineteenth-Century British Theatre, Coventry, June–July 1977.

narrative.[47] In the 1780s Charles Dibdin's experience with puppet shows soon led to the one-man entertainments he devised for performance in the grand saloon of the Lyceum and then at his own two theatres, called the Sans Souci, in the 1790s and up through 1805.[48] Over these years Dibdin presented numerous entertainments, with such titles as *Castles in the Air, The Sphinx,* and *A Tour to Land's End,* whose general form may have evolved from the loosely dramatic format of the puppet show. In *The Musical Tour of Mr. Dibdin* he described in detail an entertainment in which a series of songs, sung in character and accompanied by Dibdin himself at the harpsichord, are interwoven into the loose context of a recited narrative.[49] The narrative itself was likely to be based on a quasi-dramatic situation—an imaginary masquerade, for example, "made up of all those characters which generally distinguish it, . . . with a mixture of pertness, insipidity, folly, tinsel, glare, and dulness," Dibdin explained, and hence offering scope for satire on all persons "who break their constitutions, and run into expence, for no motive upon earth but to expose themselves" (p. 383).

The range and attractiveness of London entertainment, from solo performers, puppet shows, variety acts, and ubiquitous music and song to old-fashioned comedy and farce, tragedy in verse and prose, and Italian opera fostered incessant competition. In a prologue written for his Haymarket benefit on 7 March 1791 the actor Lee Lewes expressed his gratitude to a generous audience for choosing him over other attractions. The Lyceum alone, he pointed out, where "the great Fantoccini doors" invited spectators to the Italian puppet show, afforded a bewildering variety:

> Up stairs, waggs, oddities, the camp of pleasure;
> Boxing, rhinoceros, ostriches stupendous,
> A stentor at the door, with voice tremendous;
> . . . .
> Discord and harmony alternate follow,

47. Lee Lewes, "Essay on Satire," appended to Geo. Alex. Stevens, *A Lecture on Heads, as delivered by Charles Lee Lewes* (1799), p. 107, quoted by Ellis, p. 7.
48. See Robert Fahrner, "The First Sans Souci Theatre (1791–1796)," *TN,* 28 (1974), 59–64, and Fahrner, "The Second Sans Souci Theatre (1796–1835)," *TN,* 29 (1975), 69–73.
49. *The Musical Tour of Mr. Dibdin* (Sheffield: J. Gales, 1788), pp. 307ff.

First gladiators fight, now sings Apollo!
Musicians, bruisers, birds, beasts in a den,
Perdition! sure chaos is come again.[50]

Theoretically the choice between Haymarket or Lyceum—for example, Lewes's benefit bill of Mrs Centlivre's *The Busy Body* and a new farce, James Fennell's *The Advertisement; or, A New Way to Get a Husband,* on the one hand, and the "chaos" at the Lyceum, on the other—was an easy one. But such choices must often have been less clear-cut, despite the constant presence of the "legitimate" drama on the stages of Covent Garden, Drury Lane, and the Haymarket, and of opera at the King's. The performance of burletta again offers an illuminating example of how closely similar the fare could be at the major houses, minor houses, and pleasure gardens.

The Bermondsey Spa Gardens, for instance, located on the Surrey side near Southwark Park Road, developed from a mere tea garden to a spa, and by 1784 when its proprietor Thomas Keyse obtained a music license it had become something of a regular pleasure haunt featuring an orchestra, colored lamps, alcoves, and arbors—a sort of small-scale Vauxhall. Keyse would seem to have acquired a burletta license as well, for the songs of hunting, seafaring, and drinking that comprised much of the staple fare were augmented in the late 1780s by burlettas, along with duets and interludes, with such titles as *The Friars, The Quack Doctor, The Fop,* and *The Auctioneer.*[51] The words of the burlettas and songs were sometimes printed and sold for sixpence at the bar and in the exhibition room.[52]

By the time of its introduction at the Bermondsey, however, burletta at the pleasure gardens was no innovation. The first burletta ever given in such surroundings appeared as early as 1758 at Marylebone Gardens, situated on some eight acres on the east side

50. *Theatrical Guardian,* No. 2 (12 March 1791), p. 15.

51. J. T. Smith, *Book for a Rainy Day,* cited in Chancellor, p. 357; Wroth, p. 233. One wonders what connection the last title may have with the entertainment of the same name by T. J. Dibdin recorded in his *Reminiscences* as having been performed at an equestrian theatre in the Lyceum about 1796; see Allardyce Nicoll, *A History of English Drama 1660–1900,* rev. ed., 6 vols. (Cambridge: Cambridge Univ. Press, 1952–1959), III, 82, and citations there.

52. Wroth, p. 233.

of the High Street, Marylebone. The work was Pergolesi's *La Serva Padrona,* performed some seventy times that season in an English adaptation whose text, *The Servant Mistress, a burletta translated from the Italian,* could be purchased by patrons.[53] Intermittent but substantial popularity of burletta at Marylebone Gardens is reflected in entries in *The London Stage 1660–1800* calendar up to the closing of the gardens in 1776.[54] Roger Fiske, historian of English theatrical music, notes fourteen burlettas produced there in the 1770–1774 period, including fifty-five performances of *La Serva Padrona,* which by 1760 is described in the bills as "an English burletta."[55] Such performances may have included Thomas Chatterton's *The Revenge,* since a text of it published in 1770 explains that it was "a burletta acted at Marybone Gardens."[56] According to Henry Angelo, burletta was performed on the same stage on which fireworks, "a great inducement" of attendance, were exhibited. The clientele, Angelo later recalled, were "the gentry, rather than the *haut ton.*"[57] George Colman the younger remembered the Marylebone Gardens audience more comprehensively as "fashionable gentlemen, and would-be fashionable gentlemen; and ladies who were reputable, and ladies who would *not* be reputable; in short, it drew together a mélange of company, as at Vauxhall now."[58] Or as at Drury Lane, Covent Garden, or the Haymarket, one might add, the distinction being mainly that the various classes were more apt to mingle with one another in the relatively unrestricted spaces of the gardens, open through the summer, than in the boxes, pits, and galleries of the major houses.

What they saw performed there, Colman said, was "above all" burletta, which he defined as "a *drama in rhyme,* and which is *entirely musical*; a short comick piece, consisting of *recitative* and *singing,* wholly accompanied, more or less, by the orchestra" (I, 51). There is no doubt that the idea of a light piece entirely in recitative and song persisted through the century as the general notion of what

53. Fiske, p. 385; Donohue, "Burletta," pp. 36–38; Wroth, p. 97n.
54. See *LS,* Part 4, passim.
55. Fiske, p. 387; *LS,* Part 4, II, 799.
56. Wroth, p. 104n.
57. Angelo, II, 2–3.
58. *Random Records,* 2 vols. (London: H. Colburn and R. Bentley, 1830), I, 48.

burletta was, but no doubt also that this form was very close to the comic operas, operatic farces, and other related sub-genres frequently in evidence on the stages of the patent houses along with burletta itself. Colman cites the *Biographia Dramatica* as authority for asserting that more than a dozen different musical genres, from opera and ballad opera to musical farce and musical romance, existed distinct from burletta (I, 53). In fact, the substantial practical difference was simply that the house licensed only for burletta was forced to keep to recitative, venturing into spoken dialogue between songs only at considerable peril. Such restrictions would seem to have mattered rather little, for the taste for musical theatre was universal. In the last quarter of the century the nine most popular afterpieces at Covent Garden and Drury Lane were all operatic and almost all comic opera. *No Song, No Supper* (Drury Lane, 16 April 1790) with a score by Stephen Storace to a libretto by Prince Hoare achieved 151 performances over ten years to become the most successful afterpiece of the 1790s.[59] Frances Brooke and William Shield's *Rosina* exceeded two hundred performances over the rest of the century from its initial appearance at Covent Garden in December 1782, and O'Keeffe and Samuel Arnold's *The Agreeable Surprise* played for an even two hundred at the Haymarket beginning in 1781.[60] Meanwhile, toward the end of the period Thomas John Dibdin supplied at least ten burlettas to Sadler's Wells from 1794 to 1797, with such titles as *The Village Ghost* and *A Pennyworth of Wit*.[61] And during its uncertain existence through the end of the century the Royalty in Wellclose Square continued to offer a variety bill including "dances, burlettas, serious ballets, and pantomimes."[62]

Meanwhile, the sturdy talent of John Cartwright Cross supplied majors and minors alike during the 1790s and early 1800s with a variety of musical entertainments, ballet-pantomimes, interludes, and more serious, melodramatic pieces. Cross's major-theatre activity, documented in the pages of *The London Stage 1660–1800*

59. Fiske, pp. 412, 506.
60. Ibid., p. 412.
61. James Sandoe, "Some Notes on the Plays of T. J. Dibdin," *Univ. of Colorado Studies* (1940), pp. 205–20, cited in Nicoll, III, 382.
62. James Peller Malcolm, *Anecdotes of the Manners and Customs of London During the Eighteenth Century* (London: Longman, Hurst, Rees, and Orme, 1808), p. 422.

covering the last decade of the century, comprises nine works of a musical nature including a two-act musical interlude called simply *A Divertisement,* performed 22 times in the 1790–91 Covent Garden season and for a total of 55 times by the end of the century, and the popular *The Purse; or, Benevolent Tar,* which became a one-act melodramatic staple of the afterpiece repertory. No extensive data are available from Cross's minor-theatre work to compare with the total of 191 performances of eighteen pieces at the three major houses by 1800.[63] Some insight may nevertheless be gained from fragmentary information. The successful run of *A Divertisement* at Covent Garden, for example, for which Charles Dibdin wrote the overture and music, was preceded by its inclusion as part of an entertainment of Dibdin's called *The Oddities,* first performed by him at the Lyceum in December 1789.[64] And a cast list preserved by Cross for his *Genoese Pirate; or, Black Beard,* a ballet-pantomime that achieved only 3 performances at Covent Garden in 1798–99, indicates that the Covent Garden production postdates one of 9 April 1798 at the Royal Circus, the equestrian amphitheatre south of the Thames of which Cross himself became a proprietor that same year.[65] (Decastro attributes the failure of *Black Beard* at Covent Garden to the "Sons of the Drama being 'witlings' in acting spectacle."[66] *The Round Tower; or, The Chieftains of Ireland,* a brief ballet-pantomime given at Covent Garden for single performances in 1797–98 and 1798–99, was afterwards produced at the Royal Circus in 1803.[67] Earlier, Cross wrote a burletta for the Royal Circus called *The Village Doctor, or Killing no Cure,* apparently never performed at a major house.[68] This piece, which opened the season

63. Unless otherwise indicated, performance totals represent my count of performance entries in *The London Stage.*

64. *LS,* Part 5, II, 1305.

65. The cast list is printed in Cross's two-volume collection *Circusiana* (1809), I, cited in *LS,* Part 5, III, 2117; Brayley, p. 73.

66. *The Memoirs of J. Decastro, Comedian,* ed. R. Humphreys (London: Sherwood, Jones, 1824), p. 155.

67. Decastro, p. 152. The text of *The Round Tower* is printed in *Circusiana,* Vol. I. Several performers in the Covent Garden production were from the Royal Circus; see *LS,* Part 5, III, 2023–24.

68. The text is preserved in Cross's *Parnassian Bagatelles: Being A Miscellaneous Collection of Poetical Attempts. To which Are Added a Comic Sketch in One Act, Called The Way to Get Un-Married, As performing with universal Applause at the Theatre-Royal, Covent-Garden. And The Village Doctor, or Killing No Cure; a Favourite Burletta, Exhibited at Jones's Royal-Circus, St. George's Fields* (London, 1796), which includes a politic dedication to Thomas Harris.

at what was then called Jones's Royal Circus on Easter Monday, 25 March 1796, takes the familiar form of songs, some to be sung to familiar airs, interspersed with rhymed couplets intended for recitative—in short, the traditional form of English burletta dating back even beyond O'Hara's *Midas* to Henry Carey's burlesque of Italian opera, *The Dragon of Wantley*.[69] Clearly, as Cross's career illustrates, the burletta tradition was pervasive and thoroughly homogeneous, as well as long-lived, originating on the stages of the opera house and patent theatres but soon common to the repertory of major and minor theatres alike.

The provision of tea and the performance of music and song, even of burletta, required relatively limited facilities. Even the indulgence of the London audience's considerable taste for show did not necesssarily call for extensive resources. A handful of minor houses north and south of the Thames were able to cater extensively to these tastes, but it was the refurbished or rebuilt major theatres, which rose in lofty dominance during the early 1790s in Covent Garden and Drury Lane, that excelled in the production of spectacle, to the delight of most of their audiences. At the same time, the ever-increasing emphasis on the visual at the cost of the spoken word seemed to others a gross distortion of the traditional role played by the structures that housed legitimate drama.

When it comes to weary human beings' need for amusement, a late-century poet observed, "What then so fit as the theatric muse?"[70] In his view the "well-wrought science" of the stage was designed "to please the sense, and humanize the mind" (p. 20), but to many observers the trends of theatre building and theatrical production in the late eighteenth century called into question the traditional ends of "useful and instructive" entertainment.[71] Scott, a typical spokesman, deplored the enlargement of the patent theatres at the end of the eighteenth century for detracting from the art of the actor while failing to make spectacle other than ridiculous.[72] "Vacant folly," the satirist "Anthony Pasquin" called the major

69. Donohue, "Burletta," pp. 31ff.
70. [James Smith], *The Art of Living in London: A Poem in Two Cantos* (London: W. Griffin and J. Kearsly, 1768), p. 21.
71. The phrase occurs in the original patents of 1662 and 1663.
72. "Essay on the Drama," p. 390.

houses' habit of pouring money into spectacle, to the disadvantage of the actor:

> Money for dresses, money for new scenes,
> New music, decorations, and machines;
> The cost of these, including every freak,
> Would pay ten decent players four pounds a week.[73]

"The town has long been duped by nonsense, crammed upon their understandings, under the glitter of shew, spectres, sieges, &c.," complained the outraged author of a letter to the *Theatrical Guardian* in 1791, adding that "sense and sentiment have no longer any claim to a hearing on the stage."[74] The continued appearance of such playwrights as Elizabeth Inchbald and Richard Cumberland refutes his contention, but the fact remains that spectacle in both major and minor houses had markedly increased in popularity since the late Garrick years and gave no sign of abating.

An index to this love of show by the London audience may be found in the eighteenth-century delight in the masquerade. The "Grand Jubilee Masquerade in the Venetian taste," given at Ranelagh in 1749, is a good example.[75] Held at various times at pleasure gardens, in public rooms such as the Pantheon, and even on the stages of major theatres, masquerades afforded opportunity for considerable anonymous pleasure. A range of characters as great as the London audience itself sometimes appeared on display, from the Methodist parson, French peruquier, "soldier's wife with a natural pad, satirically intended," and running footman in evidence at Ranelagh in May 1793 to the two Harlequins, agile Columbine, Yorkshireman making shrewd remarks, *frizeur* twirling his comb, ballad singers, sailor, cobler, clowns, orange girls, Diogenes walking the Rotunda searching in vain for an honest man, and "Taylor riding on a Goose, hissing as he moved" in evidence at Ranelagh House in January 1802.[76] Night-to-dawn revelry was the custom,

73. [John Williams], "Innovation," in *The Devil* [1787], II, No. 2, 46, quoted in *LS*, Part 5, III, 2038.
74. *Theatrical Guardian*, No. 5 (2 April 1791), p. 39.
75. Wroth, p. 210.
76. *Thespian Magazine and Literary Repository*, 1 (May 1793), 270–71; *Theatrical Repertory; or, Weekly Rosciad*, 19 (25 January 1802), 306.

frequently enhanced by the sumptuous hot suppers, choice wines, and wit "chastened by decorum" that Henry Angelo fondly remembered at Pantheon masquerades, which for a while drew "people of the first fashion of both sexes."[77] So popular were these gatherings of fashion that the new opera house rising in the Haymarket in 1790 was equipped with boxes with removable partitions, so that roomy supper compartments could be formed on masquerade nights.[78]

The more permanent attractions at the Opera and throughout London, however, were those provided by professional performers. The singer and sometime manager of the King's Opera Michael Kelly could recall with pride Jean-Georges Noverre's magnificent ballet of 1793, *L'Iphegénie en Aulide,* with its spectacular scenery, rich decorations and costumes, triumphal horse-drawn cars, grand marches, and processions, all complementing the groupings of the corps de ballet with an effect of *"vrai* classicality."[79] Spectacle was available also, and in abundance, at the two equestrian amphitheatres across the Thames in Surrey. Although well into the 1780s the entertainment at Astley's Amphitheatre consisted largely of horsemanship and variety acts such as tumblers, ropedancers, trained dogs, learned pigs, and famous monkeys, along with music and dancing, pantomime with its appeal to the visual sense took an increasingly prominent place. Such appeal is evident enough in a bill for May 1784 featuring a pantomime called "The Vauxhall Jubilee, with the Temple and Temple walks superbly illuminated."[80] The advent of revolution in France later in the decade provided a sustained inspiration for spectacular production. On 5 August 1789 there were inserted into the Astley's pantomime "Two Extraordinary Scenes of the Bastille."[81] By the seventeenth of the month the bill featured "an entire new and splendid Spectacle" based on the revolution, called *Paris in an Uproar; Or, The Destruction of the Bastile* and boasting six scenes including the royal palace, exterior and interior views of the Bastille, and dungeons in

77. Angelo, I, 68.
78. *London Chronicle,* 7 October 1790, cited in *LS,* Part 5, II, 1277.
79. *Reminiscences,* ed. Roger Fiske (London: Oxford Univ. Press, 1975), p. 196.
80. Cited by Brayley, p. 61n.
81. Advertisement, Harvard Theatre Collection.

its depths, added to which was a model of the city of Paris so large as to cover the whole theatre and include streets, squares, public gardens, places of public amusement, and innumerable houses, all supposedly faithfully reproduced from the originals.[82] In early September Astley took further advantage of his public's eager response to topical subjects and introduced a three-act musical called *The Royal Naval Review at Plymouth; or, Devonshire and Cornwall Loyalty,* founded on the king's review of the naval squadron at Plymouth and touted as the most brilliant naval spectacle ever to appear on a stage.[83] Meanwhile *The Bastille* remained on the bill through the close of the season on 29 October.[84] To judge from subsequent productions in 1791 and 1792 of such pieces as *The Royal Fugitives; or, France in an Uproar, An East-India Military Divertisement,* and *Bagshot-Heath Camp; or, The Line of March,* equestrian and military spectacle, especially if dealing with topical subjects, had become a principal attraction at Astley's by the last decade of the century.[85]

Competing with Astley's and developing from its beginnings as a place for exhibitions of horsemanship that included children's performances of music, dancing, and oratory, the Royal Circus under Charles Hughes and his irritable partner Charles Dibdin was involved from 1782 in the performance of ballet, pantomime, and ultimately full-fledged spectacle as elaborate as Astley's.[86] Dibdin's plan was to heighten the artistic quality of equestrian exhibitions by building a stage adjacent to the ring for the performance of a series of "spectacles, each to terminate with a just [*sic*], or a tilting-match, or some other grand object, so managed as to form a novel, and striking *coup-de-theatre.*"[87] Although he severed his connection with Hughes a few years later, one may sense Dibdin's original intention of striking theatrical effect in the Royal Circus's response to the events of 1789 in France and, further, may perceive the competi-

---

82. Ibid. [17 August 1789].
83. Ibid. [5 September 1789].
84. Ibid., 29 October [1789].
85. Playbill, 9 August 1791, London Theatre Museum; playbill [31 August 1792], Hoblitzelle Theatre Collection, Univ. of Texas, Austin.
86. Chancellor, p. 111; Brayley, p. 68.
87. Dibdin, II, 105.

tion of major and minor houses in using those events as a basis for attracting audiences. Shortly after the fall of the Bastille Covent Garden put into rehearsal an entertainment entitled *The Bastille,* but it was denied a license by the Lord Chamberlain. Under no compulsion to submit a text for approval to that authority so long as they adhered to the terms of their burletta license, three minor theatres swiftly mounted spectacular versions of the event. Astley's tentative initial efforts, limited to scenes inserted in the pantomime, were extended by 17 August into a full-scale production. Meanwhile, as early as 5 August the Royal Circus mounted John Dent's *The Triumph of Liberty; or, The Destruction of the Bastille.* According to the *Times* review the piece employed over one hundred men onstage at once and included an assault of forty soldiers over a practicable drawbridge leading into the fortress, with much shooting going on. The production lasted for seventy-nine consecutive performances over the season.[88]

By 31 August Sadler's Wells had entered the competition with *Gallic Freedom; or, Vive La Liberte,* "an entire New, Grand, and Interesting Spectacle," the bill for 1 September proclaimed, in which particular emphasis is laid on "the Attack, Storming, and Demolition of the Bastile [*sic*]":

In the above piece will be correctly pourtrayed the Manners of the assembled Parisians at the Gate of St. Martin, previous to their Assault of the Bastile—The Massacre of those who first passed the Drawbridge—and the Sacrifice of the Governor and his Officers; with an authentic, minute, and affecting Representation of the

SUBTERRANEOUS DUNGEONS

Of that once terrific prison—the situation of the Prisoners in their state of confinement, and the Actual Descent of the Citizens and Soldiers to their release.[89]

88. *Times,* 8 August 1789, cited in A. H. Saxon, "Capon, The Royal Circus, and *The Destruction of the Bastille,"* TN, 28 (1974), 134. For a history of Astley's and the Royal Circus in this period see Saxon, *Enter Foot and Horse: A History of Hippodrama in England and France* (New Haven and London: Yale Univ. Press, 1968).

89. Playbill, 1 September 1789, Harvard Theatre Collection. See Dennis Arundell, *The Story of Sadler's Wells* (London: Hamish Hamilton, 1965), p. 44.

The bills credit Alexander Johnston, the ingenious Drury Lane machinist, with a beautifully executed "figure in the Iron Cage" for the subterranean dungeon scene.[90] A measure of the success of these various efforts and the implications they had for receipts at the major houses appears in the fact that John Palmer, engaged to play the central character of Henry du Bois in the Royal Circus production, through the influence of Sheridan, Harris, and Colman had an information lodged against him for "speaking Prose on the stage" in that character, and on 9 November he was imprisoned in Surrey jail as "a rogue and vagrant."[91]

Although contemporary taste for modern-day subjects was extensively catered to, much spectacle derived from history, folk tradition, nature, and fantasy. *Les Quatres Fils Aimond,* a "Superb Spectacle" at Sadler's Wells in 1788, was a romance set in the time of Charlemagne.[92] At Drury Lane in the late Garrick period and subsequently under Sheridan, Philip James De Loutherbourg devoted a certain attention to topical subjects such as the naval review at Portsmouth (produced in 1773 as finale to a revival of Thompson's masque *Alfred*), and in summer 1778 he made an excursion to the military camp at Coxheath in Kent to do sketches in preparation for Sheridan's patriotic musical entertainment *The Camp* (Drury Lane, 15 October 1778)—partly a response, it may be surmised, to Sadler's Wells' entertainment of the previous August called *A Trip to Coxheath,* which concluded with a distant view of the camp.[93] De Loutherbourg's essential interests, however, lay in rendering landscape perspectives, as evidenced in his extremely popular settings for *The Wonders of Derbyshire* (1779), the highly

90. Kalman Burnim and Philip Highfill, Jr, "Alexander Johnston, Machinist," *TN,* 23 (1969), 101.

91. Decastro, p. 125; Brayley, p. 71. Brayley (p. 72) refers to the repeated efforts of the major theatre proprietors during these years to prevent the Circus from "anything like histrionic success."

92. Playbill [1788], Hoblitzelle Theatre Collection, Univ. of Texas.

93. *BD,* IV, 300–314; *Public Advertiser,* 6 August 1778, cited in *The Dramatic Works of Richard Brinsley Sheridan,* ed. Cecil Price, 2 vols. (Oxford: Clarendon Press, 1973), II, 707. The Patagonian puppet theatre in Exeter Change seized its own opportunity with a new three-act comic opera, *A Tour to Coxheath; or, The Humours of a Modern Camp,* in January 1779, featuring "a Grand Perspective View of the Encampment, and an exact Representation of their Majesties passing the Line" (*Morning Post,* 22 January 1779); the bill for the tenth night, 29 January, is reproduced in Decastro, p. 229.

romantic, picturesque product of his 1778 tour of the Peak section of Derbyshire to make sketches for the scenes of this two-act pantomime.[94] De Loutherbourg's last work, for O'Keeffe and Shield's musical afterpiece *Omai, or A Trip Around the World,* produced at Covent Garden in December 1785, reveals the artist's familiar approach applied to a South Seas locale, with scenes based extensively on John Webber's paintings made on Captain Cook's third voyage, including transparencies of "moonshine, sunshine, fire, volcanoes, &c.," as O'Keeffe recalled.[95]

Singular as De Loutherbourg's achievements were, the tastes he catered to were utterly typical and of long standing. Not for nothing was John Rich, the early eighteenth-century manager of Covent Garden, described as "God of Pantomimes, Jubilees and Installations."[96] In any case, in the view of the self-styled censor Francis Gentleman, most members of the audience were more able to enjoy "sound and shew than solid sense."[97] What appears in the last decade of the century, then, is not a revolution in taste but an unprecedented cultivation of a taste that already prevailed, a taste now held by a rapidly increasing audience, many of them illiterate persons for whom the moderate-sized houses of the old Drury Lane, Covent Garden, and Haymarket offered plainly insufficient accommodation, as well as a dramatic repertory couched in a sophisticated style beyond their grasp.

Although Drury Lane and Covent Garden had undergone extensive enlargement by the end of the century, the Haymarket remained unchanged. The younger George Colman, who had taken over the reigns of Haymarket management from his father shortly before 1790, knew how inadequate his theatre was for the presentation of spectacle. "They are too magnificent for us," he makes the

94. Russell Thomas, "Contemporary Taste in the Stage Decorations of London Theatres, 1770–1800," *MP,* 42 (1944), 73 and n.; *BD,* IV, 307. See Ralph G. Allen, *"The Wonders of Derbyshire*: A Spectacular Eighteenth-Century Travelogue," *TS,* 2 (1961), 54–66.

95. *Recollections of the Life of John O'Keeffe* (London, 1826), quoted in *BD,* IV, 311; Thomas, p. 73; and Ralph G. Allen, "DeLoutherbourg and Captain Cook," *Theatre Research,* 4 (1962), 195–211.

96. Richard Warner, *A Letter to David Garrick, Esq.—on his conduct and talents as Manager and Performer* (1770), quoted in Paul Sawyer, "Processions and Coronations on the London Stage, 1727–1761," *TN,* 14 (1959), 7.

97. *The Dramatic Censor; or, Critical Companion,* 2 vols. (1770), I, 185, quoted by Sawyer, p. 9.

character of Waldron the prompter say of the new Drury Lane and refurbished Covent Garden in his *New Hay at the Old Market*.[98] Fustian, the aspiring dramatist in *New Hay*, gives up and goes home to "turn my play into a pageant, put a triumphal procession at the end on't, and bring it out at one of the Winter Theatres" (sc. i, p. 15). To judge from the amount of *processing* in view on the new stages of the winter houses, Colman's jibe was on target. One can easily visualize, for instance, the opulent symmetry of the hymeneal procession in James Byrn's ballet-pantomime *Hercules and Omphale* at Covent Garden in November 1794, with its four Amazons, four nymphs, four giants, "Two White Bulls," eight priestesses, twelve children, and sixteen priests.[99] Having begun dramatic performances in the new theatre with a spectacular *Macbeth* in April 1794,[100] the Drury Lane management went on in the next season to conceive a production "calculated to shew the extent and powers of the New Stage" by bringing out *Alexander the Great; or, The Conquest of Persia,* a full-length pantomime by the King's Opera ballet master James Harvey D'Egville, in February 1795. Powell, the Drury Lane prompter, wrote a properly appreciative note on 13 February, the second night: "Alexander's car was completed, and drawn by two elephants, and accompanied by Darius' car, drawn by three white horses, and another car laden with trophies, drawn by soldiers all of which [were] totally covered with burnished gold and silver."[101]

The expenses involved in mounting such lavish spectacles were as unprecedented as the stage effects themselves. The two hundred soldiers in *Alexander* were to have costumes that cost five pounds each, the *Morning Chronicle* announced—a considerable expense for a piece that never reappeared after the thirty-six performances of its first season.[102] The cost of Colman's *Blue Beard; or, Female Curiosity!* in January 1798 was estimated by the *London Chronicle* as

98. *New Hay at the Old Market; an Occasional Drama, in One Act* (London: W. Woodfall, 1795), sc. ii, p. 20.

99. Playbill, 17 November 1794, cited in *LS*, Part 5, III, 1705.

100. See Joseph Donohue, "Kemble's Production of *Macbeth* (1794): Some Notes on Scene Painters, Scenery, Special Effects, and Costumes," *TN*, 21 (1966–67), 63–74.

101. Quoted in *LS*, Part 5, III, 1728.

102. *Morning Chronicle*, 18 October 1794, cited in *LS*, Part 5, III, 1728.

"not less than £2,000."[103] The returns on such extravagant investment could sometimes be munificent, as in the case of Sheridan's *Pizarro* (Drury Lane, May 1799), which grossed £13,624 from its thirty-one nights the first season, a figure amounting to one-fourth of the season's total takings.[104] And yet, in the previous season, despite three such notable successes as *Blue Beard* (sixty-four performances), "Monk" Lewis's *The Castle Spectre* (forty-seven performances), and Kotzebue's *The Stranger* (twenty-six performances), Drury Lane ended with a deficit attributable to the high cost of spectacle.[105] For the six years from the opening of the new theatre up through 1799–1800 the Drury Lane account books show only three seasons—1794 (April–July), 1798–99 and 1799–1800—in which substantial net earnings accrued; the rest are marginal or uncertain.[106]

All the same, given the felt need by the patent house managers for production on this scale, the enlargement of the existing theatres became a foregone conclusion once the notion of a third

103. 18 January 1798, quoted in *LS*, Part 5, III, 2038.

104. *LS*, Part 5, III, 2097.

105. *LS*, Part 5, III, 1991. Taking postseason receipts and expenditures into account, the net deficit was about £300 (see n. 106 below).

106. Drury Lane journals, 1794–1800 (Folger Shakespeare Library). Figures for total Drury Lane receipts and expenditures provided by Hogan in his *London Stage* seasonal summaries are evidently drawn from these account books, but they do not reflect postseasonal entries attributable to the season in question. When these figures are taken into account, the results are as follows (asterisk indicates entries up through 3 June 1796 chargeable to the 1794–95 season; dagger indicates no running totals entered for expenditures; the total expenditures and net figure, estimated to the nearest whole pound, seem so much out of line as to suggest that the information is incomplete):

Season	Total Receipts	Total Expenditures	Net
1794 (65 nights)	£24,020/13/10	£22,079/11/0	£1,941/2/10
1794–95 (192 nights)	£51,854/12/3	£51,539/15/9*	£314/16/6
1795–96 (200 nights)	£45,107/4/4	£44,158/15/2	£948/9/2
1796–97 (200 nights)	[£44,853/11/7	£28,553 (est)	£16,300/-/-]†
1797–98 (200 nights)	£54,871/11/3	£55,177/15/7	-£306/4/4
1798–99 (213 nights)	£57,433/8/5	£49,997/5/9	£7,436/2/8
1799–1800 (200 nights)	£58,540/11/10	£55,368/-/-	£3,472/11/10

I class as "marginal" any net profit amounting to less than 3 percent of gross receipts.

theatre had been abandoned. The economics involved in running a theatre, then as now, are so relentless that attracting and accommodating an audience could easily end up taking precedence over other ostensibly more significant artistic concerns. For example, Garrick is often credited, and justly, with barring spectators from the Drury Lane stage in 1762, but doing so, he knew, meant enlarging the auditorium of the theatre to provide equivalent space for a paying audience.[107] The commercial motives that lay behind the phenomenal enlargement of the two patent theatres and the opera house within a few years of one another in the early 1790s cannot be neglected. At the same time, other factors of a sociological and artistic nature loom large.

To George Saunders, author of *A Treatise on Theatres,* the fundamental point in building a theatre was to rely on the force of the human voice. His idea of appropriate size follows as a consequence: "As it would be injudicious to build a theatre larger than the extension of the voice will allow, so on the other hand it would be wrong in a great and populous city to build one less."[108] Saunders's proposal for an ideal theatre, however, was based on a capacity of 2,420 persons, only slightly greater than the capacity of Drury Lane after the interior reconstruction in 1775 by Adam (nearly 2,300) or that of Covent Garden following the enlargement within existing walls in 1782 by Richards (2,170).[109] Within four years after Saunders's treatise appeared, however, Michael Novosielski's huge opera house and Henry Holland's enlarged Covent Garden and new Drury Lane had been completed, dwarfing Saunders's notions of ideal size. In addition to its estimable capacity of almost 2,500 the new King's Opera was constructed on a lavish scale intended, James Boaden pointed out, "for the display of beauty in higher life"; La Scala in Milan aside, the King's was overall the largest theatre in Europe.[110] The 1792 Covent Garden, extensively reconstructed to

107. Thomas Davies, *Memoirs of the Life of David Garrick, Esq.,* new ed., 2 vols. (1808), I, 377–78, cited in Richard Leacroft, *The Development of the English Playhouse* (Ithaca: Cornell Univ. Press, 1973), p. 119.

108. *A Treatise on Theatres* (London: Printed for the Author, 1790), p. 43.

109. Saunders, p. 87; *LS,* Part 5, I, xliii.

110. John Feltham, *The Picture of London in 1806* (1806), quoted in *Survey of London,* Vol. XXIX: *The Parish of St. James Westminster,* Part 1 (London: Athlone Press, 1960), p. 240; James Boaden, *Memoirs of Mrs. Siddons,* 2 vols. (London: Henry Colburn, 1827), II, 309; *LS,* Part 5, II, 1277.

designs by Holland, boasted an even greater capacity estimated by the architect at 2,797 but actually reaching 3,013.[111] Holland's Drury Lane outdid even that, not only in the original estimate of 3,919 persons but even in the lesser actual figure of 3,611.[112]

Capacity figures by themselves, however, only begin to signify what these enlarged auditoriums (and increased stage areas) meant for contemporary audiences. James Boaden, biographer of several major theatrical figures of the late eighteenth century, saw an indicative symptom of change in the fact that, in Garrick's theatre, "the gallery formed more of his plan, than it does of ours."[113] Calculating the percentages of capacity of box, pit, and gallery relative to the total for each theatre reveals a marked trend toward expansion of the boxes and a correlative decrease in gallery space, while the pit shows only a modest increase in size. Richards's 1782 Covent Garden gives 33 percent of its space to boxes, whereas the actual figures (as distinct from Holland's estimates) for the 1792 theatre show an increase in boxes to 40 percent. Similarly, the 1794 Drury Lane shows the box capacity already high at 39 percent in Holland's preliminary estimates and reaching an astounding 50 percent in the finished structure. At the same time, gallery figures fall off from a substantial 50 percent in the 1784 Covent Garden to 40 percent in the 1792 building, and Holland's estimate of 36 percent gallery space for the 1794 Drury Lane falls to a mere 24 percent in the completed auditorium. The contrast of these figures to those for Palmer's Royalty, which allowed for 63 percent of capacity in the galleries and only 23 percent in the boxes, is notable, and ironic. In such a context Saunders's ideal of 25 percent of capacity in boxes and no less than 60 percent in the galleries appears totally at variance with the facts of life that obtained in 1790, when his book appeared.

Those facts suggest a striking paradox: just at the time that a new, lower-class audience is emerging in London and clamoring for entertainment suited to its interest, capacities, and pocketbooks,

111. Ian Donaldson, "New Papers of Henry Holland and R. B. Sheridan: (I) Holland's Drury Lane, 1794," *TN*, 16 (1962), 92; Brayley, p. 15n.

112. Donaldson, "New Papers (I)," p. 92; Brayley, p. 7n.

113. *Memoirs of the Life of John Philip Kemble, Esq.*, 2 vols. (London: Longman, Hurst, Rees, Orme, Brown, and Green, 1825), II, 41.

the major theatre proprietors reconstruct their theatres so as to exclude as much of that audience as possible, and then commence charging higher prices to the rest. It is hardly surprising that a riot took place on the occasion of the opening of the reconstructed Covent Garden on 17 September 1792 to "as brilliant an audience, as ever graced a British Theatre" when it was discovered not only that the prices had been generally raised but that the second, or one-shilling, gallery had been deliberately done away with—on instructions from Thomas Harris himself, as it turned out.[114] Harris compromised by restoring the one-shilling gallery but explained that higher prices were an inevitable result of higher costs. The audience had no choice but to capitulate. In fact, Harris and Sheridan had evidently been pursuing a policy of exclusivity from the start, and even before their time a gradual identification and separation of the various classes frequenting the theatre had occurred. In an earlier age Wren's Drury Lane appears to have had a single entrance door, but subsequent designs and reconstructions of London theatres multiplied and separated the places of entrance for box, pit, and gallery.[115] Surely the most extreme instance in the period of such social stratification appears in a description of 1784 and 1785, probably by Harris, of the proposed third theatre. Harris explains that it would be built on a smaller scale "without Pit or Galleries" and with admission "at a superior Price."[116]

Yet even the boxes themselves presented their own peculiar problem. "In a corrupted metropolis like London," Sir Walter Scott acknowledged, it is impossible to exclude "a certain description of females from public places."[117] Evidently, the proposed third theatre was to be designed to alter a situation in which the front boxes were "absolutely rejected" by "Ladies who are dress'd."[118] People of rank and private parties, Saunders explained, must resort to the side boxes "to avoid being incommoded by the much complained of admission of all characters into the front boxes."[119]

114. *Thespian Magazine and Literary Repository*, 1 (Oct. 1792), 103; LS, Part 5, III, 1487.
115. Leacroft, p. 124.
116. Quoted in Donaldson, "New Papers (II)," p. 120.
117. "Essay on the Drama," p. 392.
118. Quoted in Donaldson, "New Papers (II)," p. 120.
119. Saunders, p. 82.

Undoubtedly such characters included the "Drury misses" in their "tawdry pride" who sometimes became "Pastoras" by the fountain at the Dog and Duck. Evidently, the managements of the major theatres had their own paradoxes to face. The author of the *Theatrical Guardian* in 1791 explained what he believed were the cynical premises and unfortunate consequences of the situation:

It is well known . . . that the divisions of the front and green boxes [at Covent Garden] were removed for the purpose of opening a convenient market for debauchery. The argument of the Manager on that occasion was this: the women of the town are the best support of my theatre; if, therefore, I can adapt it to their accommodation, they will make it their constant place of evening resort, and where they are, the bucks and bloods will consequently attend, so that I shall secure by no means a small part of the public. . . . Thus has a Theatre Royal, in the metropolis of Great Britain, been made little less than a public brothel.[120]

The presence of prostitutes remained a source of perennial complaint, and attraction, as the eighteenth-century London theatre gave way to the nineteenth. Undeniably, it drove certain elements of the audience out of the theatre even as it brought others in, but the root of the difficulty lay elsewhere than in the mere influx of "undesirable" persons. To John Adolphus, looking back over a half century and more to the palmy days of Garrick, it was the moderate size of the theatre itself that held the various elements of London's playgoing population in coherent relationship:

No man who knows the world, or considers the state of a luxurious and overgrown metropolis, will expect that, in a play-house, the prevention of a mixture of improper company with those who are pure and virtuous, should be enforced with a too rigid caution; but still some guard could be interposed while houses were of moderate size, which it would, at this time [1839], be useless to attempt, and vain to expect. The dress-boxes in the old theatre were exclusively occupied by those who could sustain the appearance required at an evening party of the first character. The front-

120. *Theatrical Guardian*, No. 5 (2 April 1791), pp. 27–28.

boxes, and the tier above the dress-boxes, called the green-boxes, were filled, for the most part, with families and individuals of respectable station in life; and, if persons of character not quite so unequivocal found places in them, they were bound to the utmost propriety of demeanour. The upper boxes, or slips, were left to the females who frequent play-houses as a mart for their charms, and the tavern-haunting youths who went with the intention of becoming their customers. Such was the general arrangement; and, if it was not at all times enforced in its utmost strictness, still the benefits derived from it were perceived and acknowledged. A parent retiring either at the close of the entertainment, or at an earlier hour, had not then to conduct his wife and daughters through a lane of immodest females and licentious coxcombs. He had not, while waiting for his carriage, to witness their gambols and hear their ribaldry. The lobbies, the stairs, and all the other avenues and adjuncts to the boxes, were kept in a state of unexceptionable propriety.[121]

Adolphus's retrospective view may be colored by passing time, but his sense of the healthy balance of social classes in a carefully planned architectural space is essentially accurate. At the same time his premise, revealed in his pointing out that this stratification within limits of moderate size was "of extreme importance to the interests of private life, in the high, the wealthy, and all other respectable classes" (I, 258) is also clear. It seems likely, then, that the enlargement of theatre auditoriums, the concerted managerial efforts to attract an upper-class audience at the expense of a lower-class one, and the emergence in London of an unprecedentedly large population in search of entertainment, combined to destroy the dynamic balance Adolphus described.

In any case, decades before Bulwer's Select Committee of 1832 looked into the chronic ills besetting the theatre of that day with a view toward abolishing patent privilege and endorsing a policy of laissez faire, the London theatre of the late eighteenth century was entering a period of profound, disturbing change. Only in the long perspective of history might it be viewed as a period of renewal in

121. John Adolphus, *Memoirs of John Bannister, Comedian,* 2 vols. (London: R. Bentley, 1839), I, 258–59.

which signs of fresh vitality were beginning to emerge.[122] To Sheridan, the *"great* and *important feature"* of his theatrical property was "that the monopoly is, morally speaking, established for ever, at least as well as the Monarchy, Constitution, Public Funds, &c."[123] Sheridan of course spoke for one set of interests. The rioters at Covent Garden in 1792, the full house at the Royalty in 1787, and the audiences taught contemporary history at Astley's, the Royal Circus, and Sadler's Wells, spoke eloquently enough for quite another.

122. See the discussion of tradition and innovation in the theatre and drama of the 1790s in Joseph Donohue, *Theatre in the Age of Kean* (Oxford: Basil Blackwell, 1975); see also Donohue, *Dramatic Character in the English Romantic Age* (Princeton: Princeton Univ. Press, 1970).

123. Thomas Moore, *Memoirs of Richard Brinsley Sheridan,* 2nd ed. (1825), pp. 593–94, quoted in Donaldson, "New Papers (II)," p. 123.

Bibliography for "The Theatres" Index

Bibliography for "The Theatres"

EDWARD A. LANGHANS

Asterisks indicate works that are sources for figures in the charts.

Adam, Robert, and James Adam. *The Works in Architecture of Robert and James Adam.* Ed. Robert Oresko. London: Academy Editions, 1975.

Adams, Joseph Quincy. *Shakespearean Playhouses.* 1917; rpt. Gloucester, Mass.: Peter Smith, 1960.

Algarotti, Count. *An Essay on the Opera.* London: L. Davis and C. Reymers, 1767.

Angelo, Henry. *Reminiscences.* Notes and memoir by H. Lavers Smith. 2 vols. Philadelphia: J. B. Lippincott, 1904.

Arundell, Denis. *The Story of Sadler's Wells, 1683–1964.* London: H. Hamilton, 1965.

Athenaeum, 2 September 1848, pp. 883–84 (on the sale of the Lincoln's Inn Fields Theatre building).

*Avery, Emmett L. "The Capacity of the Queens Theater in the Haymarket." *Philological Quarterly,* 31 (1952), 85–87.

———. *Congreve's Plays on the Eighteenth-Century Stage.* New York: Modern Language Association, 1951.

*Barlow, Graham. "Sir James Thornhill and the Theatre Royal, Drury Lane, 1705." In *The Eighteenth-Century English Stage.* Ed. Kenneth Richards and Peter Thomson. London: Methuen, 1972.

Baur-Heinhold, Margarete. *Baroque Theatre.* London: Thames and Hudson, 1967.

373

Bell, Hamilton. "Contributions to the History of the English Playhouse: II—On Three Plans by Sir Christopher Wren." *The Architectural Record,* 33 (1913), 359–68.

Bentley, Gerald Eades. *The Jacobean and Caroline Stage.* Vol. VI: *Theatres.* Oxford: Clarendon Press, 1968.

*Boswell, Eleanore. *The Restoration Court Stage.* Cambridge, Mass.: Harvard Univ. Press, 1932.

Britton, John, and Augustus Pugin. *Illustrations of the Public Buildings of London.* 2 vols. London: J. Taylor, 1825–28.

Brown, Thomas (of Shifnal). *Works.* 4 vols. London: Edward Midwinter, 1730.

Brownsmith, John. *Dramatic Time-Piece.* London: For J. Almon, T. Davies, and J. Hingeston, 1767.

Brunet, Françoise. *Voyage en Angleterre.* British Library Add. MS 35,177.

Burnim, Kalman A. *David Garrick, Director.* Pittsburgh: Univ. of Pittsburgh Press, 1961.

Campbell, Lily B. *Scenes and Machines on the English Stage During the Renaissance.* Cambridge: Cambridge Univ. Press, 1923.

Carter, Rand. "The Drury Lane Theatres of Henry Holland and Benjamin Dean Wyatt." *Journal of the Society of Architectural Historians,* 26 (1967), 200–216.

Chancellor, E. Beresford. *The Annals of Covent Garden and Its Neighborhood.* London: Hutchinson, 1930.

———. *The Romance of Lincoln's Inn Fields and Its Neighborhood.* London: Richards, 1932.

Chappuzeau, Samuel. *L'Europe vivante.* Geneva: For the Author, 1667.

Cibber, Colley. *An Apology for the Life of Mr. Colley Cibber.* Ed. Robert W. Lowe. 2 vols. London: John C. Nimmo, 1889.

A Comparison Between the Two Stages. 1702. Ed. Staring B. Wells. Princeton: Princeton Univ. Press, 1942.

Contant, Clement, and Joseph de Filippi. *Parallèle des principaux théâtres modernes de l'Europe et des machines théâtrales Francaises, Allemandes et Anglaises.* 1860; rpt. New York: Benjamin Blom, 1968.

Cumberland, Richard. *Memoirs.* 2 vols. London: Lackington, Allen, 1807.

*De Marly, Diana. "The Architect of Dorset Garden Theatre." *Theatre Notebook,* 29 (1975), 119–24.

The Description of the Great Machines, of the Descent of Orpheus Into Hell. Presented by the French Commedians at the Cock-pit in Drury-lane. London: Robert Crofts, 1661.

Dibdin, Charles, Jr. *History and Illustrations of the London Theatres.* London: For the Proprietors of the "Illustrations of London Buildings," 1826.

The Diverting Post, 28 October and 25 November–2 December 1704, 7–14 April 1705.

Dobbs, Brian. *Drury Lane.* London: Cassell, 1972.

*Donaldson, I. "New Papers of Henry Holland and R. B. Sheridan. (1) Holland's Drury Lane, 1794." *Theatre Notebook,* 16 (1962), 91–96.

The Dramatic Censor, February 1811. London: G. Brimmer, 1811.

"The Duke's Theatre, Portugal-Street, Lincoln's Inn Fields." *Illustrated London News,* 2 September 1848, p. 132.

Dumont, C. P. M. *Parallèle de plans de plus belles salles de spectacles d'Italie et de France.* 1774; rpt. New York: Benjamin Blom, 1968.

D'Urfey, Thomas. *Collin's Walk Through London and Westminster, a Poem in Burlesque.* London: For Richard Parker and Abel Roper, 1690.

*Eddison, Robert. "Capon and Goodman's Fields." *Theatre Notebook,* 14 (1960), 127–32.

———. "Capon, Holland and Covent Garden Theatre." *Theatre Notebook,* 14 (1959), 17–20.

Elkin, Robert. *The Old Concert Rooms of London.* London: Edward Arnold, 1955.

Fahrner, Robert. "The First Sans Souci Theatre (1791–1796)." *Theatre Notebook,* 28 (1974), 59–64.

———. "The Second Sans Souci Theatre (1796–1835)." *Theatre Notebook,* 29 (1975), 69–73.

Fitzgerald, Percy. *A New History of the English Stage.* 2 vols. London: Tinsley Brothers, 1882.

Forsyth, Gerald. "The Sans Souci Theatre." *Theatre Notebook,* 4 (1950), 36.

Genest, John. *Some Account of the English Stage from the Restoration in 1660 to 1830.* 10 vols. Bath: For H. E. Carrington, 1832.

The Georgian Playhouse. Ed. Iain Mackintosh and Geoffrey Ashton. London: For the Arts Council, 1975.

Godfrey, Walter. "The Apron Stage of the Eighteenth Century as Illustrated at Drury Lane." *Architectural Review,* 37 (1915), 31–35.

Gray, Philip H., Jr. "Lenten Casts and the Nursery." *PMLA,* 53 (1938), 781–94.

*Guildhall MS 11,936D, item 52. Sun Fire Office Papers.

Haslewood, Joseph. *Of Plays, Players, and Playhouses.* British Library 11791 dd 18: 9 MS vols, c. 1820.

———. *Roxburghe Revels.* Edinburgh: For Private Circulation, 1837.

Heckethorn, Charles. *Lincoln's Inn Fields.* London: E. Stock, 1896.

Highfill, Philip H., Jr., Kalman A. Burnim, and Edward A. Langhans. *A Biographical Dictionary of Actors, Actresses, Musicians, Dancers, Managers, and Other Stage Personnel in London, 1660–1800.* Carbondale and Edwardsville: Southern Illinois Univ. Press, 1973–.

Hogan, Charles Beecher. "The China Hall Theatre Rotherhithe." *Theatre Notebook,* 8 (1953–54), 76–80.

*———. "The New Wells, Goodman's Fields, 1739–1752." *Theatre Notebook,* 3 (1949), 67–72.

Hogarth, William. *Hogarth's Graphic Works.* Comp. Ronald Paulson. 2 vols. New Haven: Yale Univ. Press, 1970.

Holmes, Martin. "The Two Stages at Sadler's Wells." *Theatre Notebook,* 8 (1953–54), 62–63.

*Hotson, Leslie. *The Commonwealth and Restoration Stage.* Cambridge, Mass.: Harvard Univ. Press, 1928.

*Hughes, Leo. *The Drama's Patrons.* Austin: Univ. of Texas Press, 1971.

*Hume, Robert D. "The Dorset Garden Theatre: A Review of Facts and Problems." *Theatre Notebook,* 33 (1979), 4–17.

Illustrated London News, 2 September 1848, p. 132.

Jackson, Allan. "The Frontispiece to Eccles's *Theater Musick* 1699." *Theatre Notebook,* 19 (1964–65), 47–49.

*Jenkins, David Clay. "The James Street Theatre at the Old Tennis-Court." *Theatre Notebook,* 23 (1969), 143–50.

Jusserand, J. J. *English Essays from a French Pen.* 1895; rpt. New York: AMS Press, 1970.

———. "A French Ambassador's Impressions of England in the Year 1666." *Nineteenth Century and After,* 19–20 (April 1914), 786–96.

BIBLIOGRAPHY FOR "THE THEATRES"

Keith, William Grant. "The Designs for the First Movable Scenery on the English Public Stage." *Burlington Magazine,* 25 (1914), 29–33 and 85–98.

————. "John Webb and the Court Theatre of Charles II." *Architectural Review,* 57 (1925), 44–55.

*Kennedy-Skipton, Laetitia. "Notes on a Copy of William Capon's Plan of Goodman's Fields Theatre." *Theatre Notebook,* 17 (1963), 86–89.

*Langhans, Edward A. "A Conjectural Reconstruction of the Dorset Garden Theatre." *Theatre Survey,* 13 (November 1972), 74–93.

————. "The Dorset Garden Theatre in Pictures." *Theatre Survey,* 6 (November 1965), 134–46.

*————. "Notes on the Reconstruction of the Lincoln's Inn Fields Theatre." *Theatre Notebook,* 10 (1956), 112–14.

————. "Pictorial Material on the Bridges Street and Drury Lane Theatres." *Theatre Survey,* 7 (November 1966), 80–100.

————. "A Picture of the Salisbury Court Theatre." *Theatre Notebook,* 19 (1965), 100–101.

————. "Players and Playhouses, 1695–1710 and Their Effect on English Comedy." *Theatre Annual,* 29 (1973), 28–38.

————. "Staging Practices in the Restoration Theatres, 1660–1682." Diss. Yale 1955.

————. "The Vere Street and Lincoln's Inn Fields Theatres in Pictures." *Educational Theatre Journal,* 20 (1968), 171–85.

*————. "Wren's Restoration Playhouse." *Theatre Notebook,* 18 (1964), 91–100.

Lawrence, William J. *The Elizabethan Playhouse and other Studies.* 2 vols. 1913; rpt. New York: Russell and Russell, 1963.

————. "A Forgotten Restoration Playhouse." *Englische Studien,* 35 (1905), 279–89.

————. *Old Theatre Days and Ways.* London: George G. Harrap, 1935.

Lawrenson, T. E. *The French Stage in the XVIIth Century.* Manchester: Manchester Univ. Press, 1957.

Leacroft, Helen, and Richard Leacroft. *The Theatre.* London: Methuen, 1958.

*Leacroft, Richard. *The Development of the English Playhouse.* London: Eyre Methuen, 1973.

————. "Wren's Drury Lane." *Architectural Review*, 110 (July 1951), 43–46.

Leclerc, Helene. *Les Origines Italiennes de l'architecture théatrale moderne.* Paris: E. Droz, 1946.

Loftis, John, Richard Southern, Marion Jones, and A. H. Scouten. *The Revels History of Drama in English.* Vol. V: *1660–1750.* London: Methuen, 1976.

The London Stage. 5 parts in 11 vols. (1960–68).

Lynch, James J. *Box Pit and Gallery.* Berkeley: Univ. of California Press, 1953.

Lysons, Daniel. *Collectanea.* Scrapbooks at the British Library and the Folger Shakespeare Library.

*Mackintosh, Iain. "Inigo Jones—Theatre Architect." *Tabs,* 31 (September 1973), 99–105.

*Macomber, Philip A. "The Iconography of London Theatre Auditorium Architecture, 1660–1900." Diss. Ohio State 1959.

Magalotti, Lorenzo. *Travels of Cosmo the Third Grand Duke of Tuscany, through England during the Reign of King Charles the Second.* 1669; rpt. London: J. Mawman, 1821.

*Mander, Raymond, and Joe Mitchenson. *The Lost Theatres of London.* London: Rupert Hart-Davis, 1968.

————. *The Theatres of London.* New York: Hill and Wang, 1961.

Maude, Cyril. *The Haymarket.* London: Grant Richards, 1903.

Milizia, Francesco. *Del teatro.* Venice: Giambatista Pasquali, 1773.

Misson, Henri. *M. Misson's Memoirs and Observations in his Travels Over England.* Trans. John Ozell. London: D. Browne, 1719.

Monconys, Balthasar de. *Journale des voyages de Monsieur de Monconys.* 3 vols. Lyon: Horace Boissat and George Remeus, 1666.

Mullin, Donald C. *The Development of the Playhouse.* Berkeley: Univ. of California Press, 1970.

*————. "The Queen's Theatre, Haymarket Vanbrugh's Opera House." *Theatre Survey,* 8 (November 1967), 84–105.

*————. "The Theatre Royal, Bridges Street: A Conjectural Restoration." *Educational Theatre Journal,* 19 (1967), 17–29.

————. "The Theatre Royal, Bridges Street An Architectural Puzzle." *Theatre Notebook,* 25 (1970), 14–19.

BIBLIOGRAPHY FOR "THE THEATRES"

*Mullin, Donald C., and Bruce Koenig. "Christopher Wren's Theatre Royal." *Theatre Notebook,* 21 (1967), 180–87.

Nagler, Alois M. *Shakespeare's Stage.* New Haven: Yale Univ. Press, 1958.

———. *Sources of Theatrical History.* New York: Theatre Annual, 1952.

*Nalbach, Daniel. *The King's Theatre 1704–1867.* London: Society for Theatre Research, 1972.

Nicoll Allardyce. *The Development of the Theatre.* 5th ed. New York: Harcourt, Brace and World, 1966.

Odell, George C. *Shakespeare from Betterton to Irving.* 2 vols. New York: Charles Scribner's Sons, 1920.

Oliver, H. J. "The Building of the Theatre Royal in Bridges St.: Some Details of Finance." *Notes and Queries,* 217 (1972), 464–66.

Ordish, T. F. *Early London Theatres,* 1894; rpt. London: White Lion, 1971.

*Orrell, John. "Inigo Jones at the Cockpit." *Shakespeare Survey,* 30 (1977), 157–68.

Oulton, Walley C. *The History of the Theatres of London.* 2 vols. London: Martin and Bain, 1796.

———. *A History of the Theatres of London.* 3 vols. London: C. Chapple, 1818.

*Pedicord, Harry William. *The Theatrical Public in the Time of Garrick.* New York: King's Crown Press, 1954.

Pepys, Samuel. *The Diary of Samuel Pepys,* ed. Robert Latham and William Matthews. 11 vols. Berkeley: Univ. of California Press, 1970–.

Perrin, Pierre. *Ariane.* London: Thomas Nieucomb, 1674.

Phillips, Hugh. *Mid-Georgian London.* London: Collins, 1964.

Pozzo, Andrea. *Rules and Examples of Perspective.* Trans. John James. London: Benjamin Motte, 1707.

Price, Cecil. *Theatre in the Age of Garrick.* Totowa, N.J.: Rowman and Littlefield, 1973.

Public Advertiser, 30 September 1775, 19 February 1781.

Richards, Kenneth, and Peter Thomson, eds. *The Eighteenth-Century English Stage.* London: Methuen, 1972.

Rosenfeld, Sybil. "Shepherd's Market Theatre and May Fair Wells." *Theatre Notebook,* 5 (1951), 89–92.

———. *The Theatre of the London Fairs in the 18th Century.* Cambridge: Cambridge Univ. Press, 1960.

*————. "Theatres in Goodman's Fields." *Theatre Notebook,* 1 (1946), 48–50.

————. "Unpublished Stage Documents." *Theatre Notebook,* 11 (1957), 92–96.

*Rowan, D. F. "The Cockpit-in-Court." In *The Elizabethan Theatre.* Ed. David Galloway. London: Macmillan, 1969.

*————. "A Neglected Jones/Webb Theatre Project, Part II: A Theatrical Missing Link." In *The Elizabethan Theatre II.* Ed. David Galloway. Toronto: Macmillan, 1970.

*Saunders, George. *A Treatise on Theatres.* London: Printed for the Author, 1790.

*Sawyer, Paul. "The Seating Capacity and Maximum Receipts of Lincoln's Inn Fields Theatre." *Notes and Queries,* 199 (1954), 290.

*————. *The New Theatre in Lincoln's Inn Fields.* London: Society for Theatre Research, 1979.

*Scanlan, Elizabeth. "Reconstruction of the Duke's Playhouse in Lincoln's Inn Fields, 1661–1671." *Theatre Notebook,* 10 (1956), 48–50.

*————. "Tennis-Court Theatres and the Duke's Playhouse, 1661–1671." Diss. Columbia 1952.

————. "Tennis Court Theatres in England and Scotland." *Theatre Notebook,* 10 (1955), 10–15.

Settle, Elkanah. *The Empress of Morocco.* London: For William Cademan, 1673.

Shattuck, Charles. *The Shakespeare Promptbooks.* Urbana: Univ. of Illinois Press, 1965.

Sherson, Erroll. *London's Lost Theatres of the Nineteenth Century.* London: John Lane, 1925.

Smith, Irwin. *Shakespeare's Blackfriars Playhouse.* New York: New York University Press, 1964.

Sorbière, Samuel de. *A Voyage to England.* London: J. Woodward, 1709.

Southern, Richard. *Changeable Scenery.* London: Faber and Faber, 1952.

————. "Concerning a Georgian Proscenium Ceiling." *Theatre Notebook,* 3 (1948), 6–12.

————. *The Georgian Playhouse.* London: Pleiades Books, 1948.

Speaight, George. *The History of the English Puppet Theatre.* London: G. G. Harrap, 1955.

*Spring, John R. "Platforms and Picture Frames: A Conjectural Reconstruction of the Duke of York's Theatre, Dorset Garden, 1669–1709." *Theatre Notebook,* 31 (1977), 6–19.

Stroud, D. *Henry Holland.* South Brunswick, N.J.: A. S. Barnes, 1967.

Summers, Montague. *The Playhouse of Pepys.* London: Kegan Paul, Trench, Trubner, 1935.

————. *The Restoration Theatre.* London: Kegan Paul, Trench, Trubner, 1934.

Survey of London. Esp. Vols. XIII, XIV, XX, XXV, XXIX, XXX, XXXI, and XXXV. London: For the London County Council, various dates.

*Thaler, Alwin. *Shakespere to Sheridan.* Cambridge, Mass.: Harvard Univ. Press, 1922.

Theatre, No. 65; 1775. Clippings in Folger Shakespeare Library.

Theatre Architecture and Stage Machines: Engravings from the Encyclopedia . . . Edited by Denis Diderot and Jean le Rond d'Alembert. C. 1780; rpt. New York: Benjamin Blom, 1969.

Theatrical Monitor, 19 March 1768.

The Torrington Diaries. Ed. C. Bruyn Andrews. Vol. IV. London: Eyre and Spottiswoode, 1938.

Van Lennep, William. "The Death of the Red Bull." *Theatre Notebook,* 16 (1962), 126–34.

Victor, Benjamin. *The History of the Theatres of London & Dublin from the Year 1730 to the Present Time.* 2 vols., 1761, 1771; rpt. 2 vols. in 1; New York: Benjamin Blom, 1969.

Vincent, Howard P. "John Rich and the First Covent Garden Theatre." *Journal of English Literary History,* 17 (1950), 296–306.

[Vincent, Samuel.] *The Young Gallant's Academy.* London: J. C. for R. Mills, 1674.

Visser, Colin. "The Anatomy of the Early Restoration Stage: 'The Adventures of Five Hours' and John Dryden's 'Spanish' Comedies." *Theatre Notebook,* 29 (1975), 56–67 and 114–19.

Ward, Ned. *The London Spy.* Ed. Arthur L. Hayward. London: Cassell, 1927.

Whistler, Laurence. *Sir John Vanbrugh, Architect and Dramatist.* New York: Macmillan, 1939.

Wickham, Glynne. "The Cockpit Reconstructed." *New Theatre Magazine,* 7 (Spring 1967), 26–36.

*———. *Early English Stages 1300 to 1660.* Vol. II, Part 2. London: Routledge and Kegan Paul, 1972.

*Wilkinson, Robert. *Londina Illustrata.* 2 vols. London: R. Wilkinson, 1819–25.

Wilson, Albert E. *The Lyceum.* London: Dennis Yates, 1952.

Wilson, John Harold. "A Theatre in York House." *Theatre Notebook,* 16 (1962), 75–78.

Wright, James. *Historia Histrionica.* London: G. Croom, 1699.

Wroth, Warwick. *The London Pleasure Gardens of the Eighteenth Century.* London: Macmillan, 1896.

Index

383

INDEX

Hamlet, 205; on William Mountfort, 234; on audience, 243–44; on Master of the Revels, 299, 300; on new modesty of stage, 300; mentioned, 4, 4*n,* 9, 27, 29, 31, 153, 157, 167, 194, 195, 202, 204, 267, 292, 313, 316
—*Apology for the Life of Colley Cibber,* 305
—*Careless Husband, The,* 197, 320
—*Lady's Last Stake,* 233
—*Love Makes a Man,* 197
—*Love's Last Shift,* 197
—*Non-Juror, The:* profits from, 310, 311
—*Papal Tyrrany:* set scene in, 86; publication of, 325
—*Perolla and Izadora,* 310
—*Provok'd Husband, The,* 201, 203, 318
—*Rival Fools, The:* publication of, 312
—*Tender Husband, The:* publication of, 314; mentioned, 320
—*Woman's Wit:* publication of, 314; mentioned, 31
Cibber, Susanna Maria Arne: feud with Kitty Clive, 176
Cibber, Theophilus: on Barton Booth's acting style, 168; mentioned, 26, 153, 161
Circus entertainments, 348
Clinch, Lawrence: brogue, 172, 173
Clive, Catherine Raftor: feud with Susanna Cibber, 177; mentioned, 145, 150, 178, 200
Clouds: as properties, 33–34
Cockpit (earlier Phoenix) Theatre: in Drury Lane, 35; early use, 35; modified by Inigo Jones, 36; statistics, 61; mentioned, 69, 237
Coffee, Charles: *The Devil to Pay,* 201
Collier, Jeremy, 293, 298, 300
—*Short View of the Immorality and Profaneness of the English Stage, A:* on actors, 299
Colman family, 149, 178, 185
Colman the elder, George: *The English Merchant,* 278; mentioned, 26, 194, 251
Colman the younger, George: on model figures, 103; on audience at Marylebone Gardens, 353; mentioned, 282, 346, 354
—*Blue Beard; or, Female Curiosity:* set scene in, 87; cost of production, 363–64
—*Iron Chest, The:* political comment in, 281
—*New Hay at the Old Market,* 103, 115, 362–63
Company management: legal authority, 2–6; ownership and administration, 6–12; finances, 12–23; daily operations, 23–33
Conger: defined, 329
Congreve, William, 8, 211, 212, 213, 240
—*Double-Dealer, The,* 241, 321
—*Love for Love,* 49, 66, 197, 241
—*Mourning Bride:* Congreve's revision of, 322; mentioned, 232

—*Old Batchelour, The:* Purcell's music for, 211–13; mentioned, 197, 241, 321
—*Way of the World, The,* 49
Copyright Act of 1710, 311, 312
Coronation, The, 113
Covent Garden Theatre: built by John Rich, 6, 11, 46; expanded by Thomas Harris, 15; admission prices, 17–18; salaries of actors at, 20–23; fine schedule, 28; house charges, 31–32; sea effects at, 36, 106; capacity, 48–49, 365–66; Richard Cumberland on, 54; comparison of past to present, 54; statistics, 62; sceneshifting machines at, 78, 79; use of borders at, 84; inventory of "pieces" at, 85; act curtain, 90; traverse curtain, 91; traps, 94, 98; machines for descent, 101; model figures, 103; costs and income, 185, 186; mentioned, 120, 131, 135, 137, 147, 155, 157. 172, 174, 175, 176, 192, 200, 201, 242, 245, 246, 251, 277, 318, 337, 339, 340, 341, 344, 350, 352, 353, 354, 355, 356, 360, 362, 363, 367, 370
Cross, John Cartwright: theatrical activity, 354–56
—*Divertisement, A,* 355
—*Genoese Pirate, The; or, Black Beard,* 355
—*Purse, The; or, Benevolent Tar,* 355
—*Round Tower, The; or, The Chieftains of Ireland,* 355
—*Village Doctor, The, or Killing no Cure,* 355
Cross, Richard, 28, 123, 124, 127, 128, 137
—*Diary:* on disturbance at performance of *The Founding,* 190–91; on riots at performance of *The Chinese Festival,* 249–50; on riot at *A Word to the Wise,* 250
Crowne, John: *Sir Courtly Nice,* 197, 234; *City Politiques,* 297; mentioned, 215, 217, 267
Cumberland, Richard: on enlargement of Drury Lane and Covent Garden, 54; mentioned, 251, 278, 328, 357
Cupid and Psyche: use of trap in, 96–97
Curtains: act drop, 90; as drops between scenes, 90; traverse, 90–91; in discovery area, 91–92; in drop scenes, 92; mechanism, 92; mentioned, 123
Curwen, Samuel, 252
Cutter of Colman Street (Abraham Cowley): political satire in, 257

Davenant, Sir William: playhouse options in 1660, 2, 6, 7, 8, 35, 338–39; builds Lincoln's Inn Fields, 38, 67; alters proscenium doors at Lincoln's Inn Fields, 69; mentioned, 2*n,* 54, 68, 71, 120, 236, 289, 290
—*Siege of Rhodes, The:* use of doors in, 69; designs for, 72, 73; use of shutters in, 73;

INDEX

—*Tyrranick Love:* use of traverse curtain in, 91; mentioned, 66

Dublin; pirated editions of plays, 333, 334, 335

Duke's Company: actors' stock in, 7; mentioned, 38, 42, 218

Durfey (D'Urfey), Thomas, 229, 233, 235, 267

—*Cinthia and Endimion:* bird sounds in, 108

—*Don Quixote:* plot, 228–31; Purcell's music for, 229–31; John Eccles's music for, 229, 231; mentioned, 212

—*Massaniello, The Famous History of the Rise and Fall of:* plot, 225–28; music, 226–28; mentioned, 211

—*Old Mode and the New, The,* 316

—*Wit and Mirth, or Pills to Purge Melancholy,* 225

Eccles, John: music for *Don Quixote,* 229, 231; mentioned, 235

Egyptian Festival, The (Andrew Franklin): use of trap in, 99

Emery, John: comic accent, 173; mentioned, 152

English Opera House (formerly Lyceum), 338

Estcourt, Richard, 149, 244

Etherege, Sir George, 69, 240, 255

—*Comical Revenge, The:* social satire in, 257

—*Man of Mode, The; or, Sir Fopling Flutter:* contemporary criticism of, 255; mentioned, 240

—*She wou'd if she cou'd:* use of doors in, 69; social satire in, 257–58; mentioned, 240

Evelyn, John: on William Pate, 228

Everard, Edward Cape: on hardships of actor's career, 176; at Apollo Gardens, 348–49

Examiner of Plays, 274, 275, 276, 280, 305, 306, 307

Exclusion Crisis, 262, 268, 288, 297, 298

Fabris, Jacopo: and sceneshifting machines, 25, 79

Fane, Sir Francis: *Love in the Dark,* 43

Fanshawe, Lady Anne, 256

Farquhar, George: contemporary collected editions of, 330; publication of plays, 332; mentioned, 188, 201, 232, 233, 267, 314, 321, 332

—*Beaux Stratagem, The:* publication of, 311, 313, 315, 327; mentioned, 196, 197, 201, 208, 233, 330, 331

—*Constant Couple, The:* revised for publication, 321–22; mentioned, 171, 301, 330, 331

—*Inconstant, The,* 330, 331, 320

—*Love and a Bottle,* 330

—*Recruiting Officer, The:* publication of, 311, 313, 315; mentioned, 195, 196, 242, 330, 331

—*Sir Harry Wildair,* 330, 331

—*Stage-Coach, The:* publication of, 327; mentioned, 197

—*Twin-Rivals, The:* publication of, 312–15; variations from playhouse version in publication of, 318; mentioned, 331, 330

Farren, Elizabeth: liaison with Earl of Derby, 146–47

Fate of Villainy, The, 273

Fawcett, John: number of roles, 177

Fearon, James: number of roles, 177

Fennell, James: first performance, 145

The Advertisement; or, A New Way to Get a Husband, 352

Fenton, Lavinia: liaison with Duke of Bolton, 146

Fielding, Henry: on Christiana Horton's voice, 169; on his acting company, 178; political views in his plays, 270–72; attitude toward Walpole, 303n; mentioned, 200, 293, 302, 322

—*Author's Farce, The:* political satire in, 270; publication of, 314; mentioned, 322

—*Don Quixote in England:* political satire in, 271

—*Eurydice Hissed,* 271, 304

—*Grub-Street Opera, The,* 270, 271

—*Historical Register, The,* 271, 304

—*Lottery, The,* 200–201

—*Modern Husband, The:* social criticism in, 271; dedicatory epistle to Walpole, 271

—*Pasquin:* use of trap in, 97; mentioned, 271, 303

—*Shamela,* 282n

—*Wedding Day, The,* 307

Filmer, Edward: preface to *The Unnatural Brother,* 319

Fleetwood, Charles, 18, 248

Fletcher, John, 94, 124, 197, 265

—*Maid's Tragedy, The:* traps in, 94

—*Pilgrim, The,* 124, 134, 197

—*Prophetess, The:* use of curtain in, 92, 92n; use of scene trap in, 100; mentioned, 265, 266

—*Royal Merchant, The,* 197

—*Rule a Wife and Have a Wife,* 197

Foote, Samuel: learning, 148; on travel, 159; political satire in his plays, 277–78; and puppet shows, 349; mentioned, 5, 175, 178, 245, 248, 350

—*Author, The:* suppressed, 306

—*Englishman in Paris, The,* 202

—*Maid of Bath, The,* 279

—*Mayor of Garrat, The,* 201

—*Minor, The,* 148, 306–7

—*Tragedy a-la-Mode,* 349

387

INDEX

Harris, Thomas: as Covent Garden manager, 12, 15, 16, 18, 22, 24, 25, 26; builds new Drury Lane with Sheridan, 340–42; mentioned, 176, 343, 361, 367
Hartley, Elizabeth: voice and appearance, 170; mentioned, 156
Harvey (scene painter), 125
Haughton, Hannah: voice, 169
Havard, William, 148n, 153
Hawkesworth, John, 116, 139
—*Edgar and Emmeline:* stage lighting in, 116–17
Haym, Nicolino Francesco: *Camilla,* 197; *Pyrrhus and Demetrius,* 314
Haymarket Theatre: statistics, 63; "long" scenes at, 83; scene drops used at, 90; model figures at, 103; water effects at, 105; lighting, 112; transparencies, 116; mentioned, 5, 14, 56, 169, 175, 192, 196, 197, 200, 201, 232, 242, 268, 271, 303, 304, 340, 349–53 passim, 358, 362. *See also* King's Theatre
Herbert, Sir Henry (Master of the Revels): administration, 289–90; censorship of *The Cheats,* 294–96; mentioned, 2, 303
Hercules and Omphale (James Byrn): described, 363
Hervey, Lord: on Fielding's *The Lottery,* 200–201; mentioned, 294, 303n
Higgons, Beville: *The Gernerous Conquerer,* 268
Hill, Aaron: on oblique wings, 75n; *Merope,* 75; *The Walking Statue,* 197
Hill, John: on James Quin, 164; on Benjamin Johnson, 170–71
Hills, Henry, Jr.: as pirater of plays, 333
History of Dioclesian, 210, 220
Hoare, Prince: *No Song, No Supper,* 354
Hogarth, William: and "country conditions," 157
—*Strolling Actresses Dressing in a Barn:* stage machinery in, 107, 109
Holbrook, Ann Catherine: on theatrical agencies, 154
Holcroft, Thomas: on acting companies' division of profits, 158
—*Rival Queens, The:* wind effects discussed in, 110; mentioned, 202, 203
Holland, Charles: number of roles, 177
Holland, Henry: design for Prince of Wales Theatre, 341; mentioned, 46, 365, 366
Home, John: *Agis,* 193; *The Fatal Discovery,* 193; *The Siege of Aquileia,* 306
Hopkins, William: *Diary,* 190; mentioned, 123, 140, 172n
House charges at theatres, 30–33, 184
Howard, Sir Robert, 81, 211, 220, 221, 222, 238, 240
—*Committee, The:* attack on Parliamentarians in, 256–57; mentioned, 172, 197
—*Country Gentleman, The,* 296
Hughes, Charles, 344, 348, 359
Hughes, John: *Apollo and Daphne,* 197
Hulett, Charles: voice, 169
Hull, Thomas: number of roles, 177; founds Covent Garden retirement fund, 178; mentioned, 179
Hunter, Maria Susanna Cooper: Mistress of John Hayes St. Leger, 146; mentioned, 158

Inchbald, Elizabeth: on Garrick as Don Juan in *The Chances,* 142; mentioned, 150, 328, 357
—*Lover's Vows:* social comment in, 282–83; political comment in, 283–84
—*Such Things Are:* political comment in, 282
Incledon, Charles Benjamin, 149, 161

Jackson, John: voice, 169; mentioned, 150
Jacob's Wells Theatre: smallness of stage, 160
James I, 259, 288
James II: and Battle of the Boyne, 265, 266; mentioned, 241, 261, 268
James Street Tennis Court (theatre): statistics, 63
Johnson, Benjamin, 170–71
Johnson, Charles, 134
—*Force of Friendship, The:* promptbook, 133
Johnson, Nannette, 171
Johnson, Samuel: on Shakespeare, 120; on Garrick, 141–42; opinions of actors, 145–46, 148n; *Irene,* 145, 192; mentioned, 152, 208, 304
Johnson, Thomas: as invader of copyright, 332–33; mentioned, 328, 348
Jones, Inigo, 36, 58, 68
Jonson, Ben: *Volpone,* 232; *Every Man in His Humor,* 251; mentioned, 53, 148, 181, 182
Jordan, Dorothy: liaison with Duke of Clarence, 147
Juvarra, Filippo (scene designer), 85

Kelly, Hugh, 200, 250, 251n, 278
—*False Delicacy, The:* publication of, 325; mentioned, 279
—*Word to the Wise, A:* riot at performance (1770), 250
Kemble, John Philip: *Lodoiska,* 87–88; production of *Macbeth,* 93; promptbook for *The Merry Wives of Windsor,* 126–27, 127n; mentioned, 11, 32, 119, 120, 129, 135, 136, 163, 166, 338
Killigrew, Charles: as Master of the Revels, 297, 298; mentioned, 3, 290

389

INDEX

Killigrew, Thomas: playhouse options in 1660, 2, 35, 338–39; management of King's Company, 3, 7, 8; at Venice, 37; builds Vere Street Theatre, 37–38; use of trap in *Bellamira,* 99; as Master of the Revels, 297; mentioned, 36, 54, 70, 99, 182, 236, 289, 294, 296, 342

King, Thomas: on The Grand Order of the Bucks, 246–47; mentioned, 159, 178

King's Company: managerial difficulties, 3; house charges, 30; mentioned, 6, 37, 42, 70, 91, 295, 296

King's Opera House, 192, 199, 200, 201, 242, 339, 352, 358, 363, 365

King's (formerly Queen's) Theatre: described by the *Diverting-Post,* 10, 11; capacity, 11; fine schedule, 28; burned and rebuilt, 47; Michael Novosielski's plan of, 47; statistics, 64; purchased by Sheridan and Harris, 341; mentioned, 12, 242. *See also* Haymarket Theatre

Kirkman, Francis: as pirater of plays, 333

—*Wits, The:* frontispiece showing stage lighting, 112–13

Kotzebue, August Friedrich Ferdinand von: social themes in plays of, 282–84; *Die Spanier in Peru,* 284; *The Stranger,* 364; mentioned, 166. 285

Lacy, John, 14, 172, 249

Larpent, John (Examiner of Plays), 276, 280, 281

Lediard, Thomas: uses transparencies in *Brittania,* 116

Lee, Nathaniel, 84, 91, 107, 213, 214

—*Lucius Junius Brutus:* banned, 262, 297; mentioned, 255

—*Theodosius:* use of painted figures in, 84

L'Estrange, Roger, 295, 296

Leveridge, Richard, 219, 228, 232, 233

Lewes, Lee: on the Lyceum, 351–52

Lewis, Matthew Gregory: *The Castle Spectre,* 364

Licensing Act of 1737: purpose, 304–5; mentioned, 6, 252, 254, 270, 271, 275, 276, 287, 288, 292, 293, 300, 303, 339

Lichtenberg, Georg Christoph: on stage machinery, 109–10; mentioned, 110*n*, 192*n*

Lighting, theatre: early, 43; types of, 111–13; simulation of darkness, 113; sidelights, 114; conflagrations, 115–16; transparencies, 116; changes in from "Baroque" to "Romantic," 116–17; directions for, in promptbooks, 128–30; mentioned, 67

Lillo, George, 243, 255, 334

—*Christian Hero, The,* 334

—*London Merchant, The (George Barnwell):* pirated editions, 334; mentioned, 208, 243

Lincoln's Inn Fields Theatre: licensed, i; Sharer's Agreement, 14; managerial difficulties, 26; size compared to Vere Street Theatre, 39; altered by John Rich, 45; statistics, 64; described, 67; under Davenant, 68; perspective scenes at, 73; act drop at, 90; traps at, 94–96; mentioned, 40, 69, 71, 91, 125, 196, 197, 237, 240–43 passim, 302, 303, 318

Locke, Matthew: music for *The Empress of Morocco,* 217–19; mentioned, 220

Lord Chamberlain: power of licensing, 2; silencing Christopher Rich, 4; mentioned, 8, 9, 183, 233, 254, 264, 265, 269, 270, 276, 277, 288, 296, 298, 301, 302, 304–8 passim, 339, 341, 360

Lowndes, Thomas, 327, 330, 331

Luttrell, Narcissus: on prohibition of *Cleomenes,* 265–66

Lyceum, the (theatre), 338, 351–52, 355

Machinery, stage: to shift scenes, 75–80; to raise traps, 94, 100; for descents, 101–3; model figures in, 103; for water effects, 104–5; for sea and ship effects, 104, 105–6; mentioned, 66

Mackintosh, Matthew: *Stage Reminiscences,* 154; on hiring actors, 154–55

Macklin, Charles: as drama instructor, 155; versatility of, 159; acting style, 164–65; length of acting career, 176; as Shylock, 187; mentioned, 151, 163, 170, 206, 248

—*King Henry VII; or, The Popish Imposter,* 275

—*Man of the World, The (True-born Scotchman):* political comment in, 275; mentioned, 276

Macky, John: on audience of 1714, 244

Majesty Misled; or, The Overthrow of Evil Ministers, 273

Malone, Edmond, 320, 320*n*

Marylebone Gardens: burletta at, 352–53; mentioned, 346

Master of the Revels: decline of power, 291; mentioned, 288, 289, 290, 294, 295, 296, 298, 299, 200, 201, 204

Mercurians, 243

Mickle, William: *Siege of Marsailles,* 193

Mills, William, 153, 243

Mohocks, 242

Montagu, Lady Mary Wortley, 146

Motteux, Peter: *The Island Princess,* 197

Mountfort, William: *The Fall of Mortimer,* 273; mentioned, 234

Muralt, Beat Louis de: on "Oedipus Tower," 86

Murphy, Arthur: *The Citizen,* 201; mentioned, 144, 148, 251, 278

Music: importance in London stage, 210–11, 212, 213; in *The Old Batchelour,* 211–13;

390

INDEX

in *The Duke of Guise,* 213–14; in *The Empress of Morocco,* 214–19; in *The Indian Queen,* 219–24

Newcastle, T. Pelham-Holles, Duke of, 274–75, 301
Necromancer, The, 197
North, Roger, 219, 235
Noverre, Jean-Georges, 358
Novosielski, Michael: plan of King's Theatre (1782), 47–48; mentioned, 365

Oedipus (Penzance), 125
O'Hara, Kane: *Tom Thumb,* 208, 270; and censorship of *The Golden Pippin,* 307, 308; *Midas,* 350, 356
O'Keeffe, John: *The Poor Soldier,* 344; *The Agreeable Surprise,* 354; on set designs for *Omai, or A Trip Around the World,* 362
Olympic Theatre, 338
Opera, English dramatic: decline of, 231–32; mentioned, 219–20
Opera, Italian: in England, 232–34; as reforming influence in English theatre, 232–33; mentioned, 234–35, 351
Oroonoko (Thomas Southerne): stage scenery in, 127–28; revival (1751), 138; performances of, 197
Orrery, Robert Boyle, Earl of: use of trap in *Guzman,* 96; *History of Henry the Fifth,* 240
Orpheus and Eurydice, 202
Otway, Thomas, 120, 261, 262, 263
—*Caius Marius:* bird sounds in, 108; mentioned, 186
—*Friendship in Fashion,* 248
—*Orphan, The,* 29, 202, 203
—*Venice Preserv'd:* satirical portrait of Shaftesbury in, 261–63; publication history, 324; mentioned, 49
—*Works,* 329
Oxford, Earl of, 267, 306

Palmer, John: on fire in Liverpool Theatre, 160; founds Royalty Theatre, 343, 344; mentioned, 153, 172, 361
Palmer, Robert, 148–49
Pantheon, 56
Paris in an Uproar; Or, The Destruction of the Bastile: described, 358–59
Patagonian Theatre, 349
Pate, William: career, 228; mentioned, 232
Patents and Licenses: 1660 to the present (diagram), 10
Payne, Henry Nevil: satirizes Shaftesbury in *Siege of Constantinople,* 260–61
Pennyworth of Wit, A, 354
Pepys, Samuel: at Cockpit, 35; on Vere Street theatre, 38; complaints at poor seating at theatres, 42–43; on audience at

Duke's Theatre, 238–39; mentioned, 228, 240
Pergolesi, Giovanbattista: *La Serva Padrona,* 201, 353
Philips, Edward: *Harlequin Skeleton,* 202
Phoenix Theatre. *See* Cockpit Theatre
Pinkethman, William: in prologue to *Massaniello,* 225
Play texts, piracy of, 327, 332–35
Pleasure gardens, 346–48
Pope, Alexander (actor), 149, 176
Porter, Thomas: *The Villain,* 240
Powel, John: *Tit for Tat,* 29
Powell, George: on revivals of old plays, 182; *The Treacherous Brothers,* 182
Powell, William: description of *Alexander the Great,* 363; mentioned, 11, 26, 163
Princess, The: use of tiring-house wall in, 70
Printing Act of 1662, 311, 312
Pritchard, Hannah, Mrs. William, 67, 192, 203
Pritchard, William: *The Fall of Phaeton,* 102; mentioned, 152, 179
Prodigal Son, The, or The Libertine Reclaimed: censored, 293
Promptbooks: scene designations in, 122–25; scene painters mentioned in, 125–26; stage machinery in, 126–28; lighting in, 128–30; cue signals in, 130–32; actor's directions in, 132–34; stage business in, 134–36; revisions of plays in, 136–39; publication of plays from, 315–16; mentioned, 120, 121
Prompter: powers of, in theatre, 28; duties, 122
Proscenium: use of, 67–72; mentioned, 85, 89, 90
Proscenium walls: doors and balconies in, 68–69; scenic function, 70; use in mid-eighteenth century, 71–72; mentioned, 66, 67
Publication of plays: author's profit through, 310–13; time lapse from production to print in, 313–15, 319; censorship in, 316–18; variations from playhouse version in, 318; revision by playwright in, 318–23; bookseller's profits from, 323; collected editions, 328; piracy in, 332–35
Puppet shows, 348–50, 351
Purcell, Henry: music for *The Old Batchelour,* 211–13; music for *The Indian Queen,* 220–24; *Dido and Aeneas,* 224; music for *Don Quixote,* 229–31; mentioned, 233, 234, 235

Queen's Theatre. *See* King's Theatre
Quin, James: acting style, 164; onstage with Garrick, 165; as Tancred, 187; mentioned, 67, 153, 163, 170, 203, 206

391

INDEX

Ralph, James: on strolling actors, 157; *The Fall of the Earl of Essex,* 274
Ranelagh: masquerade at, 357–58; mentioned, 56, 341, 346
Ravenscroft, Edward, 98, 201
—*Anatomist, The; or, The Sham Doctor,* 201, 212
—*London Cuckolds, The:* use of trap in, 98–99; lighting in, 129; failure of revival of, 137
Red Bull Theatre: associated with Killigrew and King's Company, 35; early use of, 35; described, 35, 36; mentioned, 237
Rees, A. (*The Cyclopedia; or, Universal Dictionary of Arts, Sciences, and Literature):* on wing and shutter machinery, 78–80; on "pieces" (used in set scenes), 85; on traps, 94, 100; on machines for descent, 101; on sea effects, 105–6; on ship effects, 106; on stage lighting, 113, 114, 115
Repertory: revivals of old plays in, 181–82, 202–3; effect of house charges on, 183–87; adaptations of old plays in, 186–87; effect of public taste on, 188, 194–209; effect of management on, 192–94; genres in, 194
Revels Office, 290, 301
Rich, Christopher: and Actors' Rebellion, 8; silenced by Lord Chamberlain, 9; statement of house charges, 31; management of Drury Lane, 44; alteration of Drury Lane forestage, 44, 68; mentioned, 3, 4, 13, 14, 32*n*, 33, 91, 314, 314*n*
Rich, John: and new Lincoln's Inn Fields, 45; and Covent Garden, 46; mentioned, 4, 6, 14, 17, 32, 69*n*, 78, 125, 185, 186, 192, 194, 362
Richard Coeur de Lion (John Burgoyne): set scene in, 87
Richardson, Thomas: dramatic schools of, 155
Robinson, Mary ("Perdita"): liaison with Prince of Wales, 147
Rowe, Nicholas: *Tamerlane,* 197, 232, 243, 263, 267, 268, 269; *The Fair Penitent,* 202, 203; *Jane Shore,* 202, 203, 300
Royal Circus: entertainment at, 359, 360; mentioned, 56, 344, 349, 355, 356, 361, 370
Royalty Theatre, 343, 354, 370
Rutland House, 69, 72, 73
Ryder, Dudley: on tragic acting, 164
Ryves, Elizabeth: *Adelaide,* 193

Sabbatini: sea effects illustrated in *Practica di fabricar scene e machine ne' teatri,* 105; mentioned, 107
Sadler's Wells: entertainment at, 360–61; mentioned, 56, 340, 344, 346, 348, 354, 370

Salisbury Court Theatre: associated with Davenant and Duke's Company, 35; described, 35, 36; mentioned, 237
Saunders, George: on legroom in theatres, 48–49; on forestage, 72; *A Treatise on Theatres,* 365; on ideal theatre, 365; mentioned, 367
"Scald Miserables," 243
Scott, Sir Walter: on decline of theatre, 337; mentioned, 98, 338, 367
Scena per angolo, 85
Scenes: "long," 83; "pieces" in, 85; set, 86; behind drop or shutters, 86; and stage picture, 88–89
Sea effects, illustrated. *See* Rees, A.; Sabbatini
Settle, Elkanah, 74, 104, 211, 214, 217, 220, 267
—*Cambyses:* use of trap in, 96
—*Empress of Morocco, The:* Crowne, Shadwell, and Dryden's criticism of, 214–15; plot, 216–17; music in, 217–19; casting for, 219; mentioned, 224
—*Fairy Queen, The:* water effects in, 104–5; mentioned, 220
—*Female Prelate, The:* use of shutters in, 73–74
—*World in the Moon, The,* 74*n*
Shadwell, Thomas: political sympathies, 264, 267; mentioned, 113, 124, 197, 215, 217, 240, 316
—*Amorous Bigot, The,* 264
—*Bury Fair:* political comment in, 264
—*Lancashire Witches, The:* censored in publication, 316; mentioned, 264
—*Squire of Alsatia, The,* 124, 197, 264
—*Virtuoso, The,* 240
Shaftesbury, Anthony Ashley Cooper, Earl of: dramatic attacks on, 260–63; mentioned, 259
Shakespeare, William: eighteenth-century audience reception of, 251; mentioned, 119, 120, 148, 171, 181, 201, 253, 300
—*All's Well That Ends Well,* 119
—*As You Like It,* 190, 343
—*Coriolanus,* 187
—*Hamlet,* 98, 135, 187, 195, 197, 201, 208, 252
—*Henry the Eighth:* use of "long" scene in, 83; mentioned, 197
—*Henry the Fourth,* Part I, 197, 203
—*Julius Caesar:* Genest on, 120; stage cloth in, 135; mentioned, 126, 197
—*King Lear:* Genest on, 120; mentioned, 186, 197, 203, 208
—*Macbeth:* use of drop scene in, 93; use of trap in, 98; lighting in, 130; cue signals in, 132; stage cloth in, 135; stage business in, 135–36; mentioned, 29, 197, 363
—*Measure for Measure,* 135, 224, 321

392

393

394